Rare and Unusual Artifacts Of The First Americans

By

Ray Parman, Jr.

Published by Fred Pruett
2928 Pearl St.
Boulder, CO 80301

Cover Photos

Top row:

Left. This is a combination scraper (No. 34) and a steatite pan (No. 78) made with the scraper, found at the same site at different times.

Center. These are animal bones, shaped to represent a large bear and cub. (No. 114)

Right. An artifact made from an antler, thought to have been used to kill sheep caught in a trap. (No. 53)

Bottom row:

Left. While these specific artifacts are not described in the text, they are lithic tools recovered from the two caves described in numbers 113 through 116.

Center. This shows a point embedded in the right femur of a buffalo. (No. 117)

Right. This hand held weapon was fashioned from a teardrop shaped piece of lava. (No. 80)

Rare and Unusual Artifacts

P.O. Box 1665 Riverton WY 82501

1SBN 0-9623868-0-4

TABLE OF CONTENTS

61. BEAUTIFUL CLOVIS POINT
62. CODY KNIFE, UNKNOWN POINT
63. THROWING STONE
64. HOE OR HEAVY DUTY SCRAPER
65. SPLENDID EAGLE EFFIGY
66. FANTASTIC CEREMONIAL PIECE
67. UNIDENTIFIED ARTIFACT
68. OLD KNIFE BLANK
69. INCOMPLETE BURIAL PIECE
70. BEAUTIFUL, OLD KNIFES
71. UNUSUAL & RARE EFFIGIES
72. REMARKABLE, HAFTED HAMMER STONE
73. TREASURED FINDS
74. BEAUTIFUL, OLD POINTS
75. EPPS & ANGOSTURA POINTS
76. RIO GRANDE POINTS
77. McKEAN POINTS
78. STEATITE PAN (shards)
79. BEAUTIFUL, UNUSUAL ARTIFACTS
80. HAND WEAPON, KILLING STONE
81. FORERUNNERS OF KNIFE BLADES
82. MESERVE & MALLORY/SAN RAPHAEL
83. TANNING STONE
84. A RARE FIND
85. AN OLD, BEAUTIFUL KNIFE
86. DIGGING STONE
87. UNIQUE SCRAPER
88. SANDIA I & II (fragments)
89. A RARE, GREEN RIVER POINT
90. KNIFE, SLITTER, LANCE TIP
91. UNUSUAL STONE POUNDER
92. A CLASSIC TOMAHAWK
93. SIX KNIFE FRAGMENTS
94. RARE ANTLER ARTIFACT
95. PEMMICAN, A FANTASTIC FIND
96. CEREMONIAL MANO
97. RARE, BEAUTIFUL POINTS
98. BESANT, POSSIBLE HANNA
99. REED POINT ? OLD CLUB HEAD
100. UNUSUAL SCRAPER, LANCE TIP
101. SKINNING KNIFE, ELKO EARED
102. THROWING STONES
103. ASSEMBLAGE OF OLD POINTS
104. CRUDE CHOPPER
105. DALLAS POINTS
106. LOOKINGBILL POINTS
107. DECATUR-HANNA & PRYOR POINTS
108. TWO HIDE STONES
109. TWO OLD KNIVES
110. UNUSUAL POINTS
111. A COUNT OF COUP IN STONE
112. WATERDOG EFFIGY
113. AN ASSEMBLAGE OF BONE TOOLS
114. BIG BEAR, LITTLE BEAR
115. THUMB SCRAPER
116. A THONG CUTTER
117. A POINT IN BONE

INTRODUCTION

This book describes, with sketches, photos and text, rare and unusual artifacts held in numerous private collections across Wyoming and the West. The opportunity of viewing these collections resulted from a weekly column by the author in the *Sunday Star Tribune* of Casper, Wyoming from March, 1984 through August, 1986.

There are numerous private collections of Native American artifacts throughout the North American continent and together they comprise a substantial source of archaeological information. The author suggests that others interested in this subject make an effort to examine these various collcctions, photograph or sketch the rare & unusual artifacts, and accumulate information about each. This information, if published, would give us a wider view of how the earliest Americans lived.

Identification of the function of the artifacts is the author's best estimate of each item. Holding the artifact in one's hand gives a sense of how it might have been used, but it remains, after the passage of centuries, only an estimate.

Photos by: *Reynolds Photographer*

SPECIAL ACKNOWLEDGEMENTS

To Miss Judith Ann Strausberger, who, with truly remarkable command of the English language, edited the entire manuscript of this book. Without previous experience in matters of archaeological nature, she never failed to grasp what was intended, moved various sentence structures about, repeatedly removed superflous words, and corrected innumerable misspelled and mistyped words... all resulting in a text infinitely more readable.

To Carolyn B. Tyler, Richard High, Jane Alexander, and Brenda Cadwallader, who contributed greatly to the success of the Wyoming Amateur Collector column.

The author expresses a great volume of heartfelt appreciation to the private collectors who submitted these artifacts for publication. Neither their collections nor their hospitality shall be forgotten.

This book is for Tracy Renee Rector, a dear and delightful granddaughter and Kristen, her mother, of whom I am most proud.

Sundowner STATION

1616 North Federal Blvd.
Riverton, Wyoming 82501
(307) 856-6503

March, 1989

Re: A Special Invitation, By
Arrangement Of The Author

Dear Private Collectors,

The Sundowner Station in Riverton, Wyoming invites you to spend your next vacation in the wonderful state of Wyoming.

Riverton is situated near the eastern slope of the beautiful Wind River Mountains. Good Fishing, fantastic vistas, and abundant vacation facilities are readily available. There are several, interesting Native American sites within fifty miles of Riverton as well.

If you have truly rare, unusual artifacts in your collection (one or more you have shared with your friends), then as you call for reservations, let the reservations clerk know you are bringing artifacts. You will receive a special discount on daily room charges and arrangements will be made for you to discuss your artifacts with Mr. Parman. If future publication is indicated, drawings of the artifact/s will be completed at this time.

Mr. Parman will be available to act as your guide, by appointment, on Fridays and Saturdays.

For stays between May and September, reservations should be made early, by the end of March if possible. Reservations are available by Toll Free number: 1-800-874-1116.

Sincerely,

SUNDOWNER STATION
Riverton, Wyoming 82501

Judy Craigie

Judy Craigie,
Manager

JC/bc

FOREWORD

Many of us share a common curiosity about the past. We want to know how people survived before our modern technology was available. We are also fascinated with the artifacts of the prehistoric past -- how they were made, how they were used, and what they mean. The science of archaeology provides answers to these questions. Archaeology, however, can also provide insights into problems we face today, such as how have other populations adapted to changing environments or how did they adjust to the loss of important resources or the addition of new resources. By understanding the past we can better prepare for the future.

Raymond Parman's book is a very informative and useful publication. There are excellent illustrations and descriptions of interesting artifacts. But, he goes beyond the descriptions and encourages avocational archaeologists to become more than collectors, to become participants in the archaeological enterprise. He provides the initial step to bridge the gap between the avocational archaeologist and the professional archaeologist by encouraging the avocational archaeologist to communicate with others about collections.

Archaeological resources are a fragile, nonrenewable resource. As a science, archaeology depends upon the interpretation of relationships -- relationships between artifacts and other modifications of the natural environment by human contact. Once a site is disturbed, the relationships are lost and the potential understandings will never be found. Even unintentional disturbance of a site may destroy significant relationships.

What does this mean for the avocational archaeologist? He must develop a professional orientation and attitude toward these archaeological resources. This includes maintaining accurate written records and descriptions of artifacts, such as provided by Parman in this book, as well as their source. He must also work cooperatively with state archaeologists and historic preservation offices. Once this has occurred, the avocational archaeologist will become a valuable asset to the field of archaeology. He will enrich the field and be enriched as he gains new and deeper understandings of the prehistoric past and appreciation of the artifacts of the past.

Donald N. Brown
Professor
Oklahoma State University

HARPOON ? No. 1
From the collection of:
Raymond B. Parman, Sr.
Elk City, Oklahoma

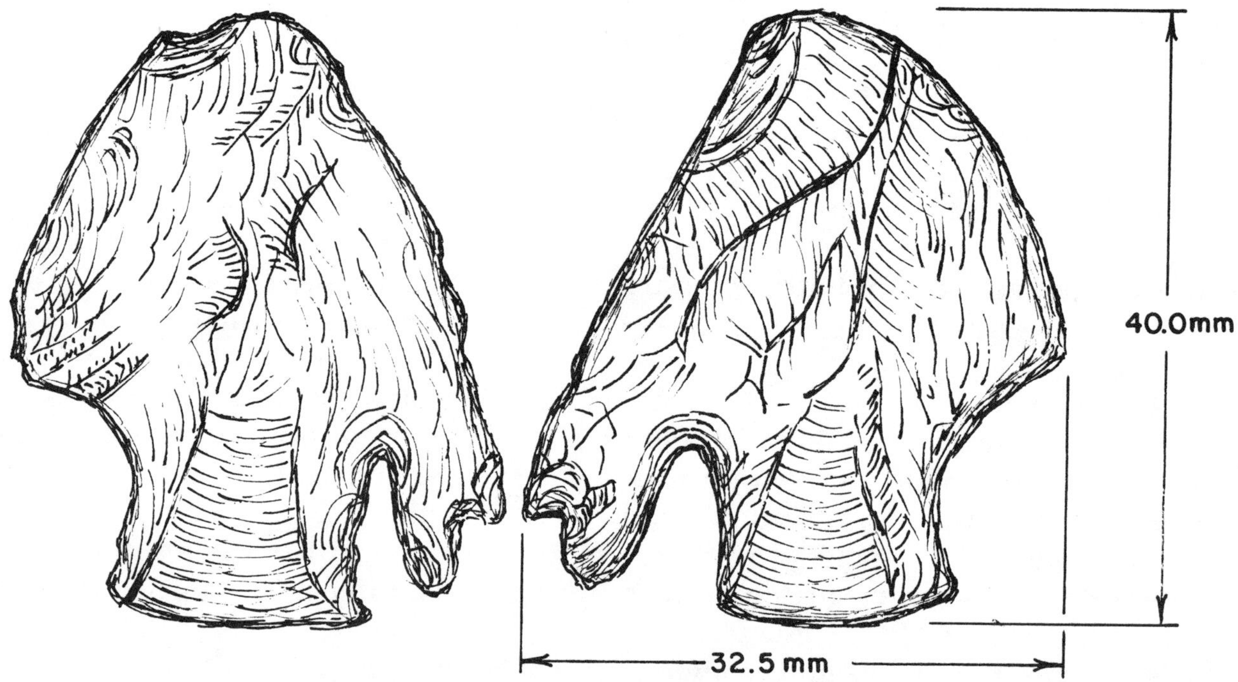

Drawn from photo by: RAY PARMAN, JR.

Fishing Point

HARPOON ?

Color & Material: Probably grey to dark grey, argillaceous quartzite.

Location: Assumed to be western Oklahoma.

This point was selected from the collection of the author's father, the late Raymond B. Parman of Elk City, Oklahoma. There was only a single, black & white photograph of the point. However, it was selected as the logo for a weekly newspaper column. The logo appears as the artwork for this first artifact.

The actual point was not available for further study and it is possible that Mr. Parman had simply photographed the point. A letter to Mr. Parman from Dr. Robert Bell, University of Oklahoma, indicated probable identification as a Calf Creek point.

The overall contour of the artifact coupled with the end notch of the tang, suggest possible use as a harpoon. Further basis for identification as a harpoon tip requires that the distribution of the Calf Creek point be considered.

In general, Calf Creek points have been found near larger, slowly moving rivers with shallows suitable for harpooning catfish and carp. It would be difficult to affix a point to the end of a shaft in such a manner that a struggling, 20 pound catfish could be lifted from the water. If a line were attached to the tang, then the point could be driven home by the shaft. The line could then be used to guide the fish for recovery in shallow water.

The Calf Creek point is considered to be Early Archaic and is expected to date from 7,500 B.C. to 6,500 B.C.

AXE HEAD No. 2
From the collection of:
Raymond B. Parman, Jr.
Riverton, Wyoming

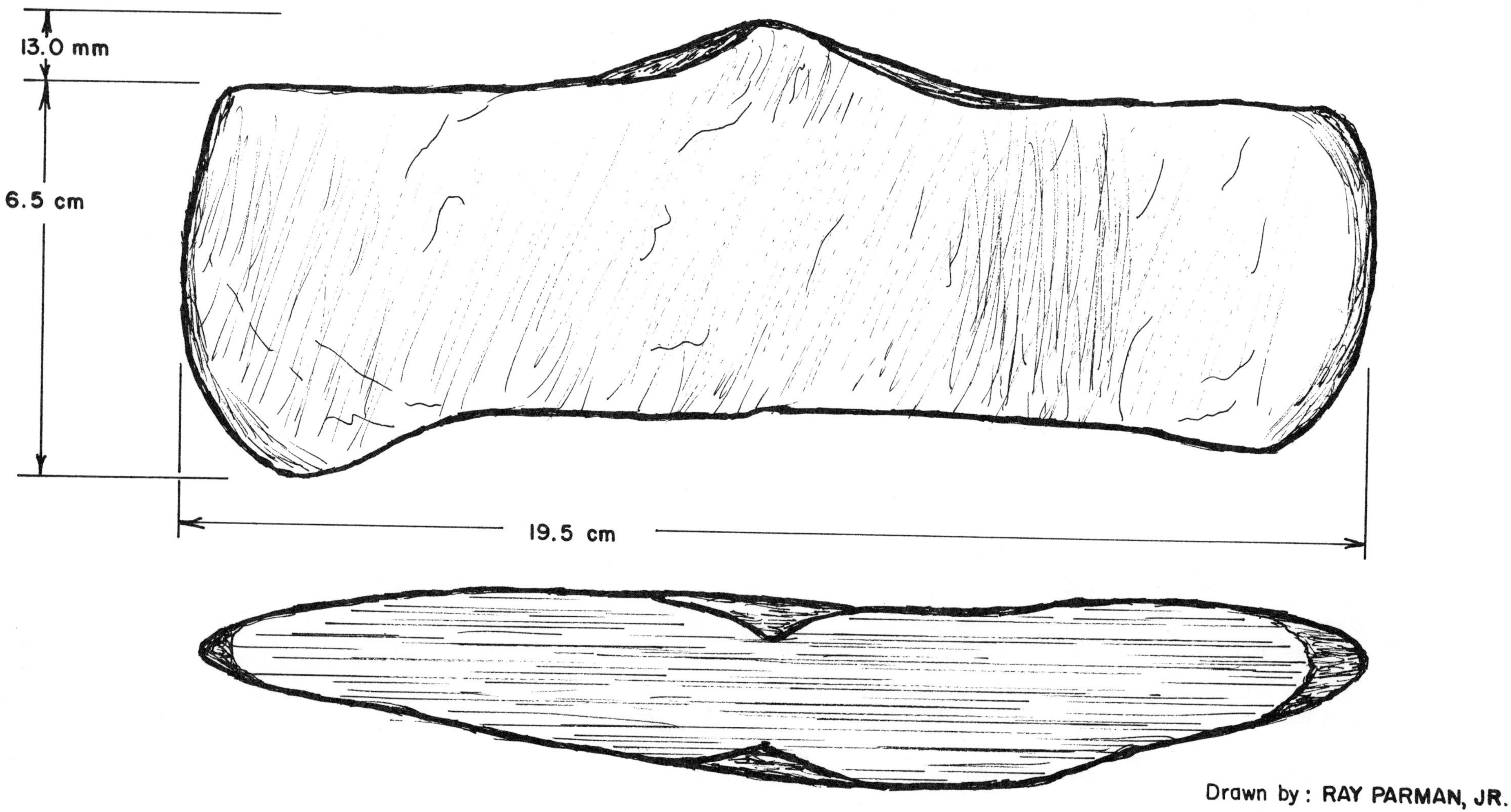

AXE HEAD

AXE HEAD (double blade)

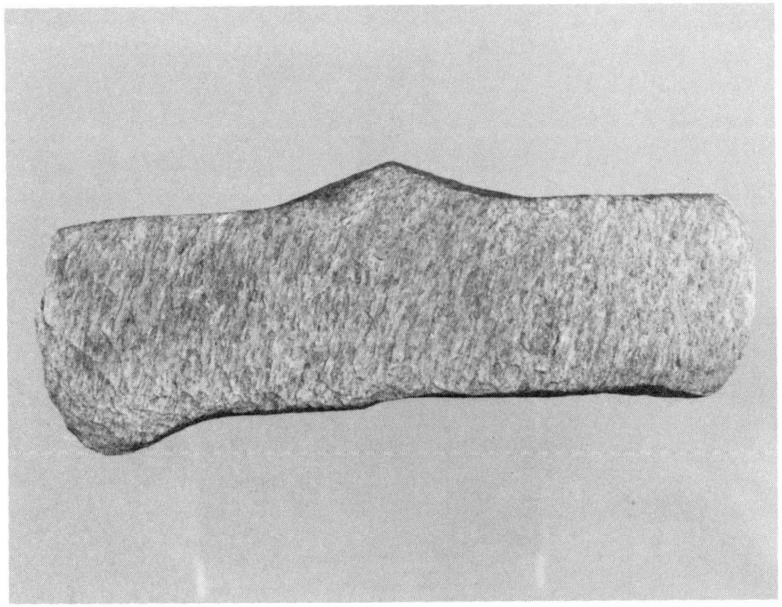

Color & Material: Pale grey green, matamorphic quartzite with distorted micro-lamina in planes parallel to artifact's widest two dimensions.

Location: North of Riverton, Fremont County, Wyoming.

This artifact appears to have been shaped by grinding. There is no evidence of chipping or flaking. However, it's surface displays marked, mechanical weathering (exfoliation by freezing) and therefore, this evidence could have been destroyed.

The artifact lay with one side imbedded in soil deposited in a shallow depression that trapped surface run-off. This lower side was thus subjected to alternate freezing and thawing which removed a layer from the artifact from one millimeter to thirteen millimeters thick. This weathered side had also been encrusted by minerals from evaporating water.

In view of the remarkable weathering that has affected this artifact, it is thought, by this writer, to be quite old.

Was it held in the hand ? Or, was it shaped for a handle ?

SAW No. 3
From the collection of:
Ray Parman, Jr.
Riverton, Wyoming

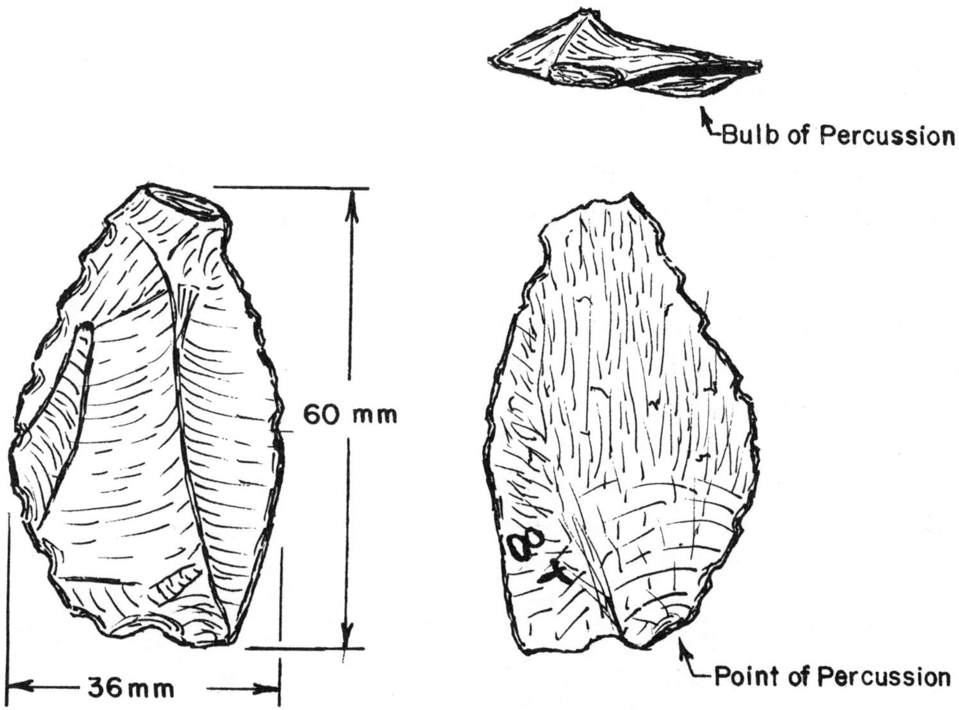

Drawn by: RAY PARMAN, JR.

Unifaced, Ribbed, Flake

SAW

SAW (ribbed flake)

Color & Material: Light tan, fine to medium grained quartzite.

Location: Northeastern Fremont County, Wyoming.

Early in man's art of crafting stone tools he discovered that a greater amount of cutting edges, and a greater amount of useable tools could be crafted from a single cobble of good material if the cobble stone was first prepared into now what has come to be called a core. By removing a large flake from the cobble, thus making one surface relatively flat (other smaller flakes might have been removed as well to make the surface more even), many blades could be struck from the stone by utilizing this flattened surface as a striking platform. By striking progressively around the edge of the core many blades, of even length and quality, could be taken from the stone.

This artifact was fashioned from a flake struck from a core. The rib is evidence that a previous flake had been struck from the same core. The bulb of percussion is very evident on the unworked side.

Three pressure flakes were removed from the ribbed side and subsequently nine notches were formed along one edge with the larger notch near the bulb of percussion.

The teeth, formed by these notches, were almost worn away before the tool was discarded. The larger notch might have been utilized as a shaft scraper for arrow shafts, and the saw for the nock of the arrow.

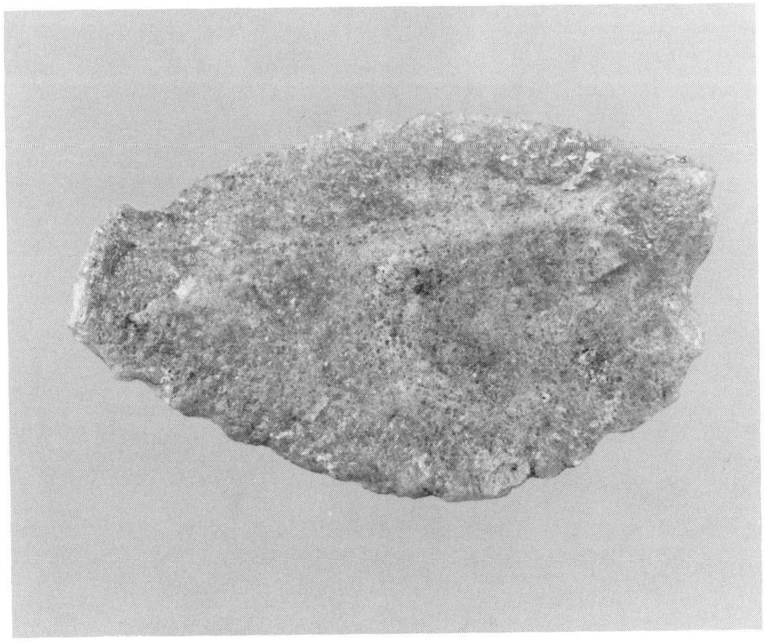

RARE SURFACE FINDS No. 4
From the collection of:
E. Dwayne Scott
Walsh, Colorado

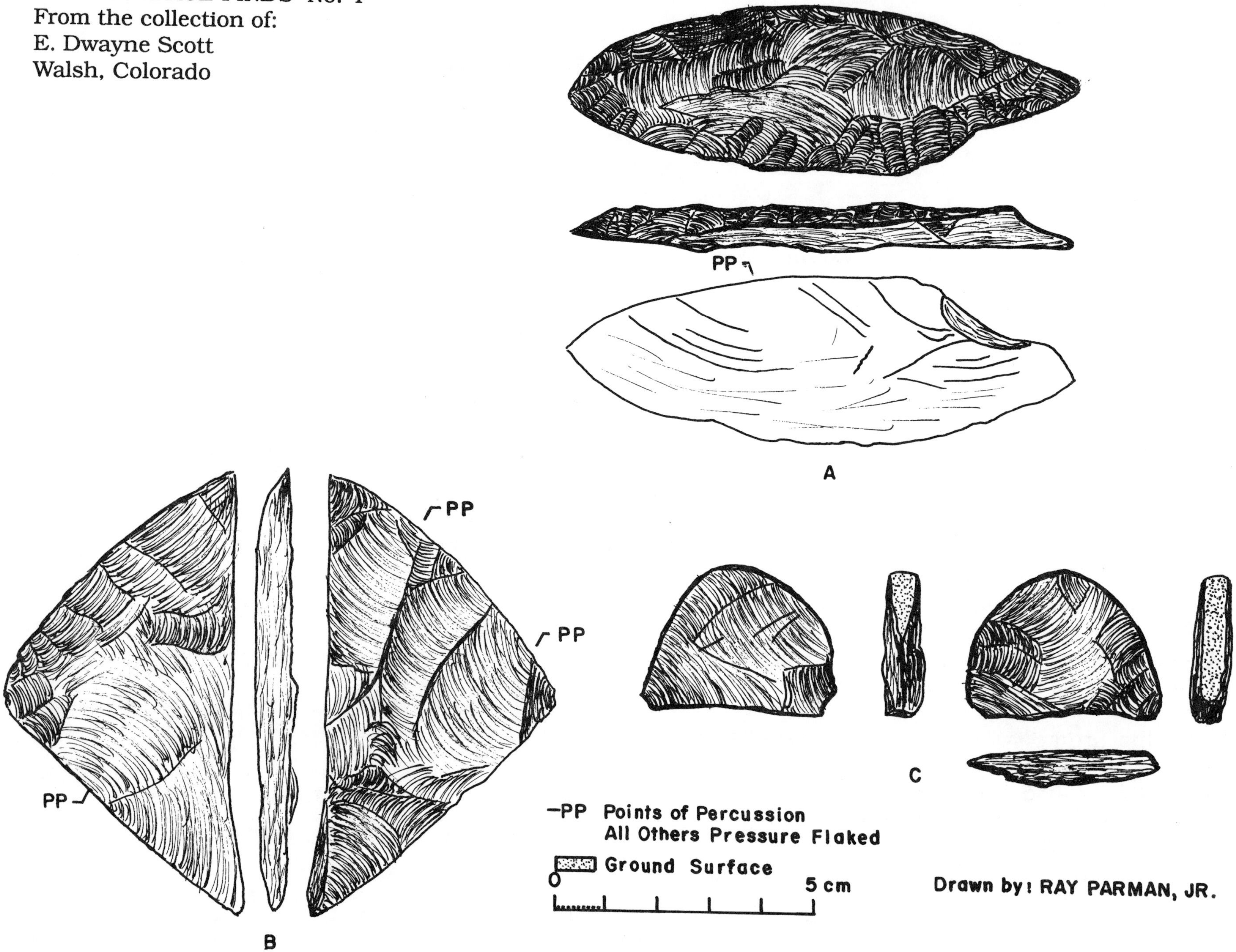

RARE SURFACE FINDS

A. KNIFE

Color & Material: Light greyish purple. Chalcedony with abundant Oolites.

Location: Southeastern Colorado.

This knife was fashioned from a percussion flake of almost glasslike chalcedony containing abundant Oolites and some microscopic, Oolicastic porosity. It was worked on one side only and shows no evidence of rework (resharpening after previous use).

B. KNIFE (fragment)

Color & Material: Light grey with slight orange cast. Quartzite.

Location: Southeastern Colorado.

This knife, when whole, was quite thin for its width. Three flakes were removed from this fragment by percussion. The balance of the flaking was caused by pressure or by hammer and point.

C. UNKNOWN (fragment ?)

Color & Material: Brown fine to meduim grained quartzite.

Location: Southeastern Colorado.

This artifact was crudely fashioned and appears to be only a fragment. The rounded edge is a ground, flat surface. The author does not know if it is part of a finished product or part of a tool used for grinding.

Anyone knowing of the location of the quarry for the oolitic chalcedony is asked to write to the author.

STEMMED KNIFE? No. 5
From the collection of:
Norman E. Boese
Thermopolis, Wyoming

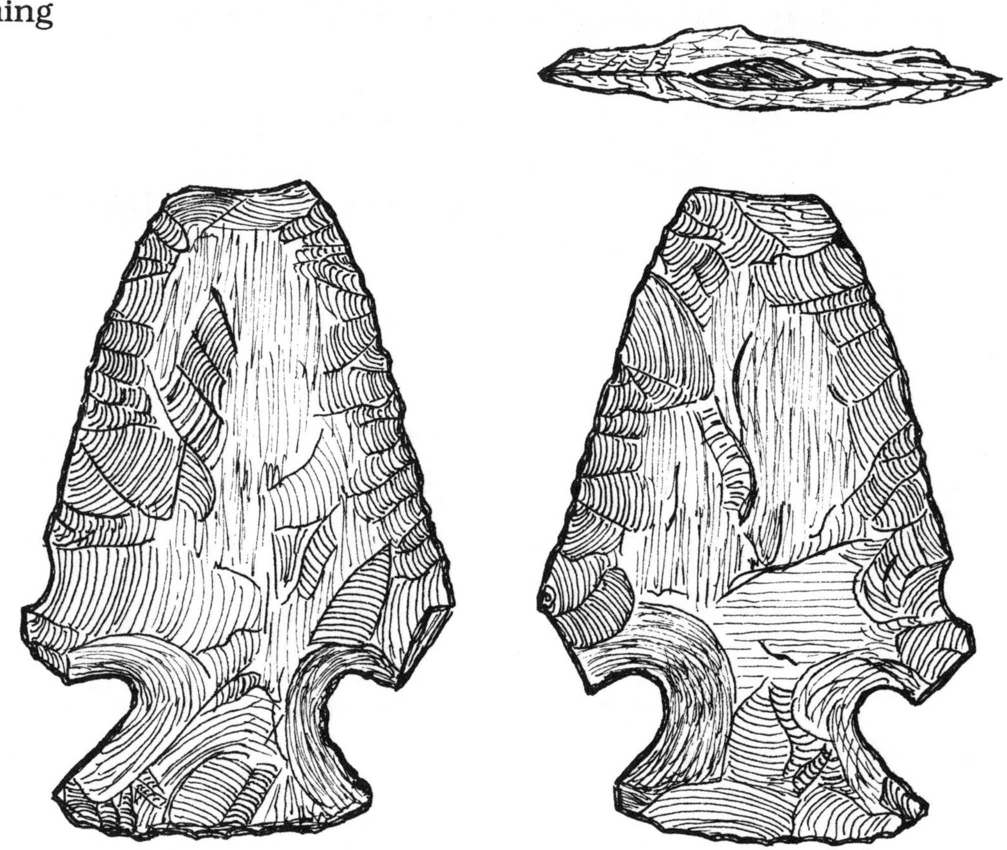

0 1 5 cm

Drawn by: R. Parman, Jr.

STEMMED KNIFE ?

Color & Material: A dark tan jasper having large veins of translucent, milk-white chalcedony (Montana agate).

Location: Northeastern Montana. A cave find by the late John J. Boese.

Dimensions: Length-9.1cm, Width-5.7cm, Thickness-1.1cm.

This artifact resembles both the Brewerton and Jack's Reef corner notched points. The author is not certain but calls this a stemmed knife. It is so wide that it would not pass between the ribs of a buffalo unless it were turned parallel to the ribs.

The quarry site of this agate is known. Many have called this a "spear point". Binding of this corner notched artifact to a shaft would firmly affix it to the shaft. With barbs the intent would have been for it to remain in the animal. Thus, the shaft of the spear would be lost.

This might have been a dart point intended for use with the throwing stick called the atlatl. Here it would have been affixed to a foreshaft intended to fall away from the throwing shaft.

COBBLE AXE No. 6
From the collection of:
Ray Parman, Jr.
Riverton, Wyoming

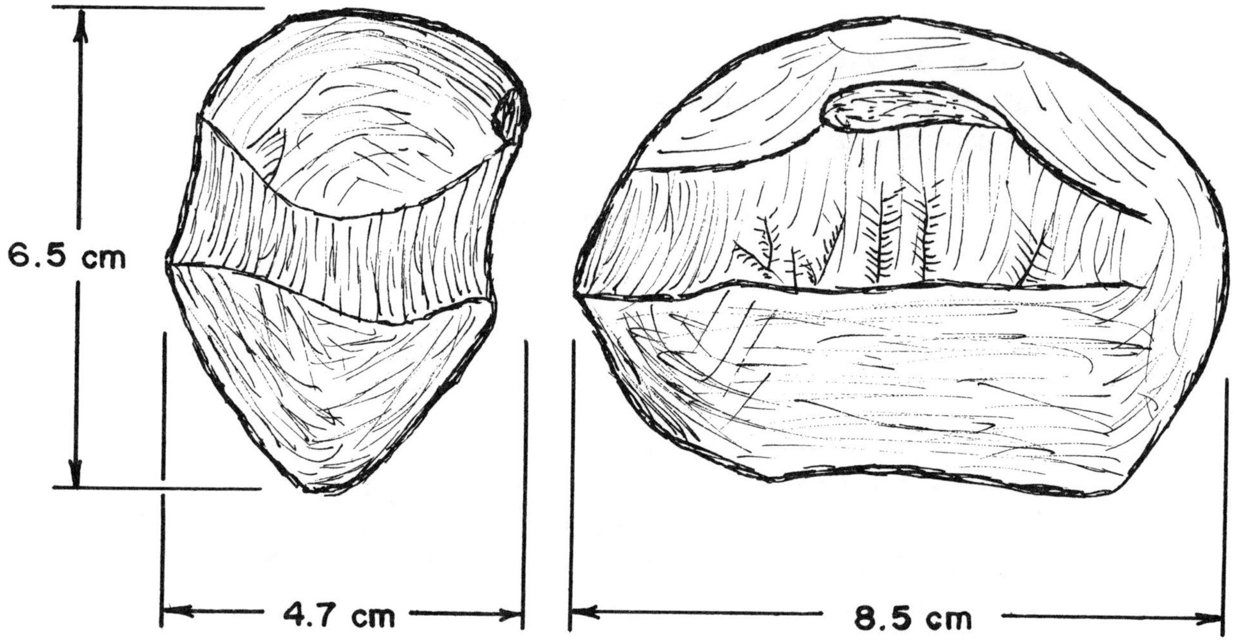

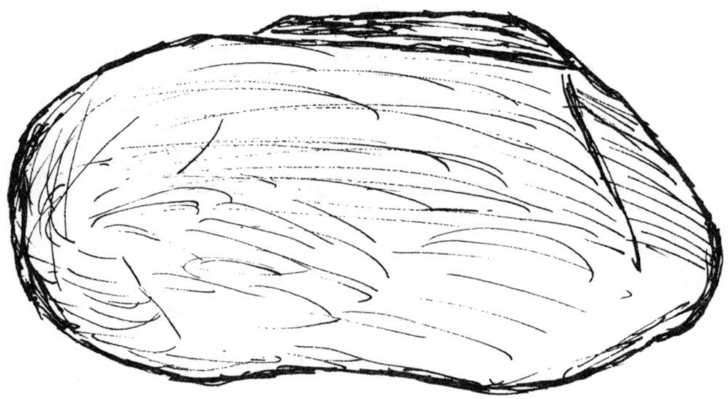

Drawn by : RAY PARMAN, JR.

6th EDITION
COBBLE AXE

COBBLE AXE (Three-quater grooved)

Color & Material: Light tan quartzite river cobble having pale yellow cast.

Location: A surface find from northern Fremont County, Wyoming. It is in the author's collection as a gift from Michael James Harris of San Diego, California, who said "I laid my bike down and when I came to, this was right in front of my nose."

A significant attribute of this cobble axe is the amount of wind polish that has occurred since it was made. The groove on one side appears to have been made by repeatedly striking it with a pointed hammer stone perpendicular to the surface. The groove on the other side has faint evidence of the removal of flakes lateral to the groove by pressure flaking or by using a hammer stone and chisel. The groove has been smoothed by wind blown sand to the point where the flaking just barely shows.

The mass of this axe was not sufficient for it to have been used for breaking up fire wood. With a rawhide handle affixed about the groove, it might well have been used as a "war club".

Thanks to Mike Harris for this fine gift. It remains the only grooved axe in the author's collection.

Author's note: Please notice the cobble was selected for having both a rounded, and a cutting, edge.

TANG KNIFE No. 7
From the collection of:
Pete Todd
Riverton, Wyoming

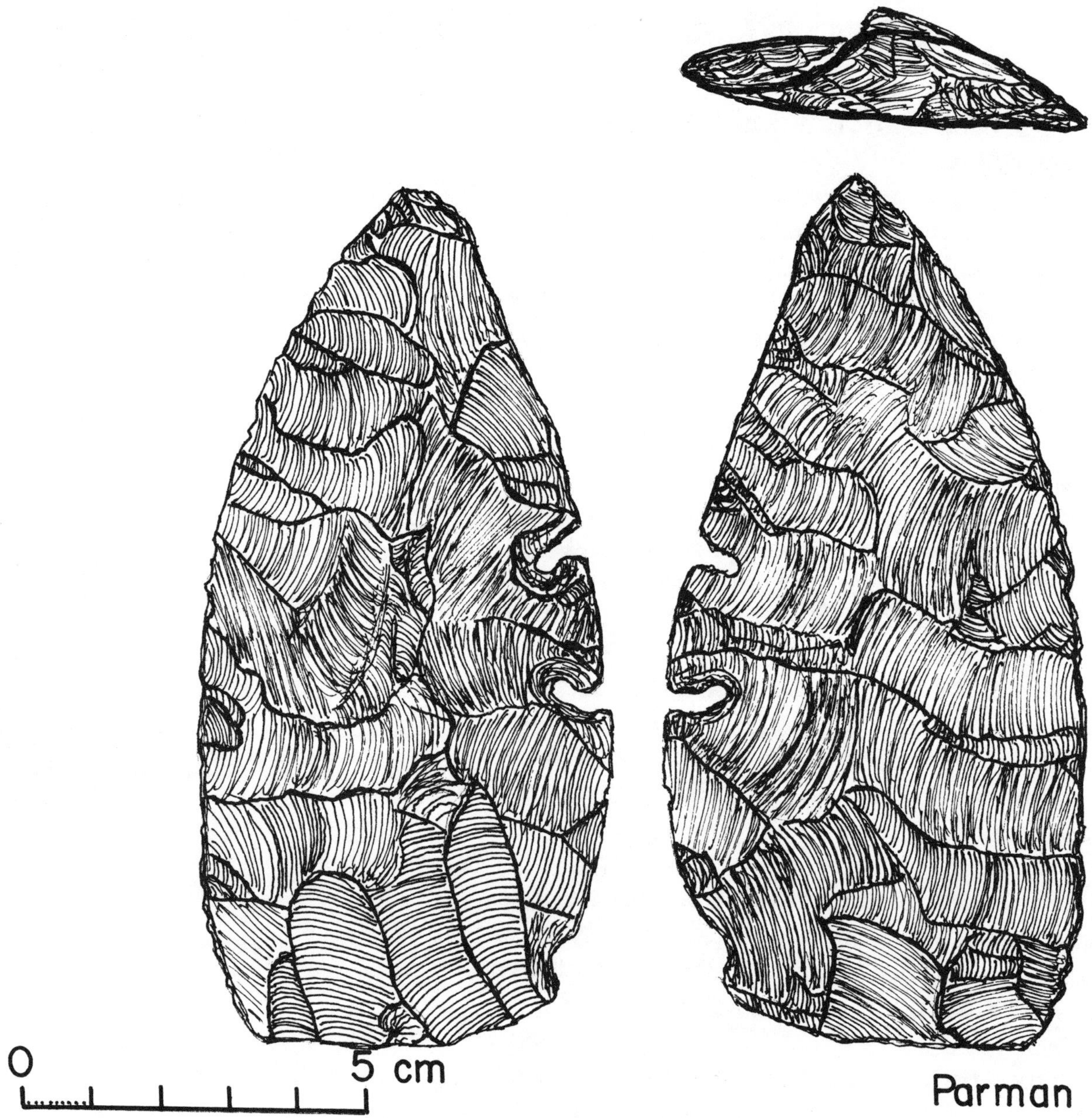

TANG KNIFE

TANG KNIFE (side tang)

Color & Material: A pale pastel green, extremely fine quartzite.

Location: Found south of Wamsutter, Sweetwater County, Wyoming, by Pete Todd.

This beautiful, large tang knife is the first having a side tang this writer has seen. It was crafted from an extremely fine-grained quartzite having no depth of color (very much like jasper). Possibly the material should have been called orthoquartzite.

The blade of the knife curves about five millimeters thru its longest dimension and is slightly twisted. This is evidence that it was crafted from a large percussion flake.

Mr. Todd was very proud of this find. It was one of his first, and he thought it very old.

The author returned to Mr. Todd's home in September of 1986 to re-examine this knife after a new notching technique was discovered (109). It was then determined that the notch nearest the point (on the side in view to the left) had been pre-drilled on that one side only.

Pete Todd was most knowledgable in mineralogy and assisted the Smithsonian Institute on digs in Northern Fremont County of Wyoming in his earlier years. He and his wife, Flaudie, were most gracious as hosts and helped the author identify materials that had been used to craft artifacts many times. Pete died in 1987 and Flaudie the following year. They are missed but not forgotten.

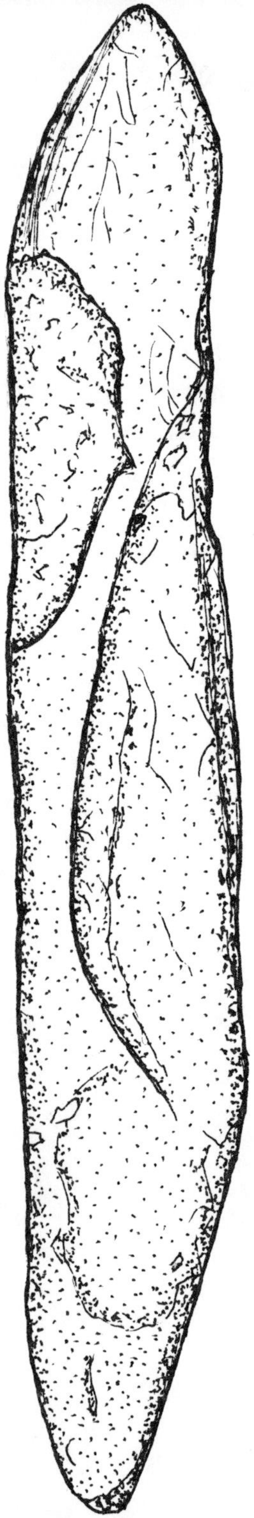
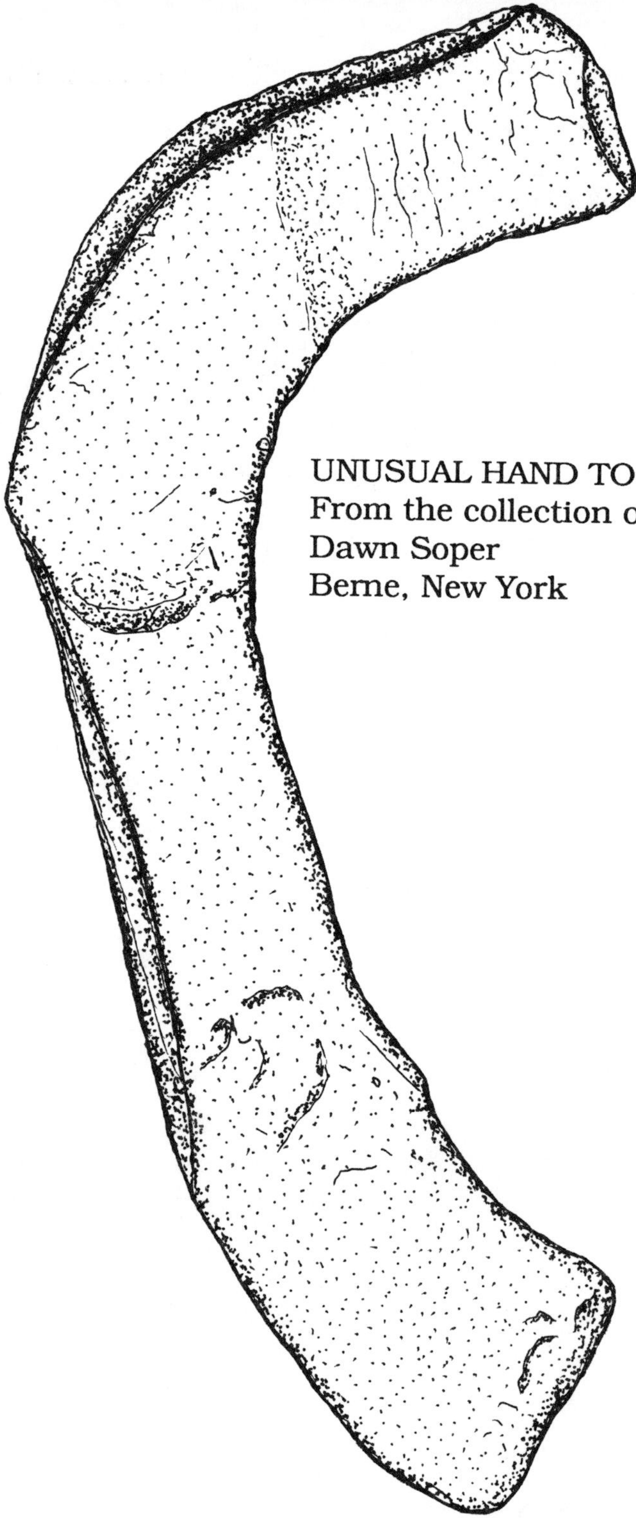

UNUSUAL HAND TOOL No. 8
From the collection of:
Dawn Soper
Berne, New York

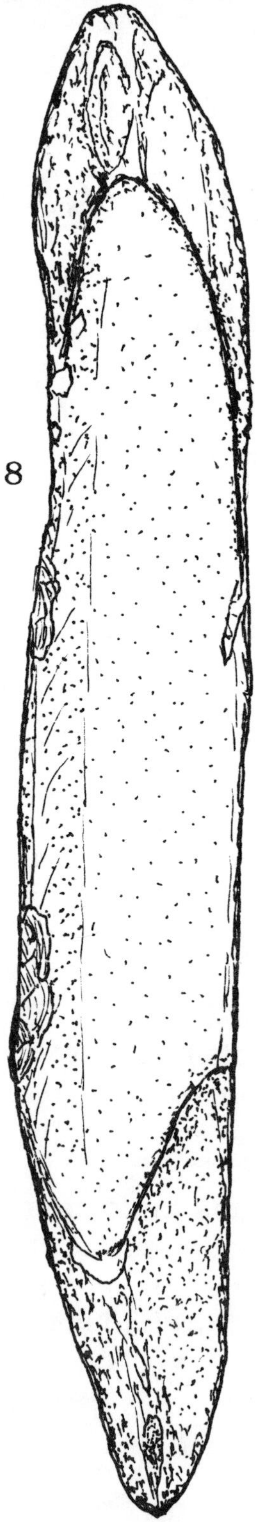
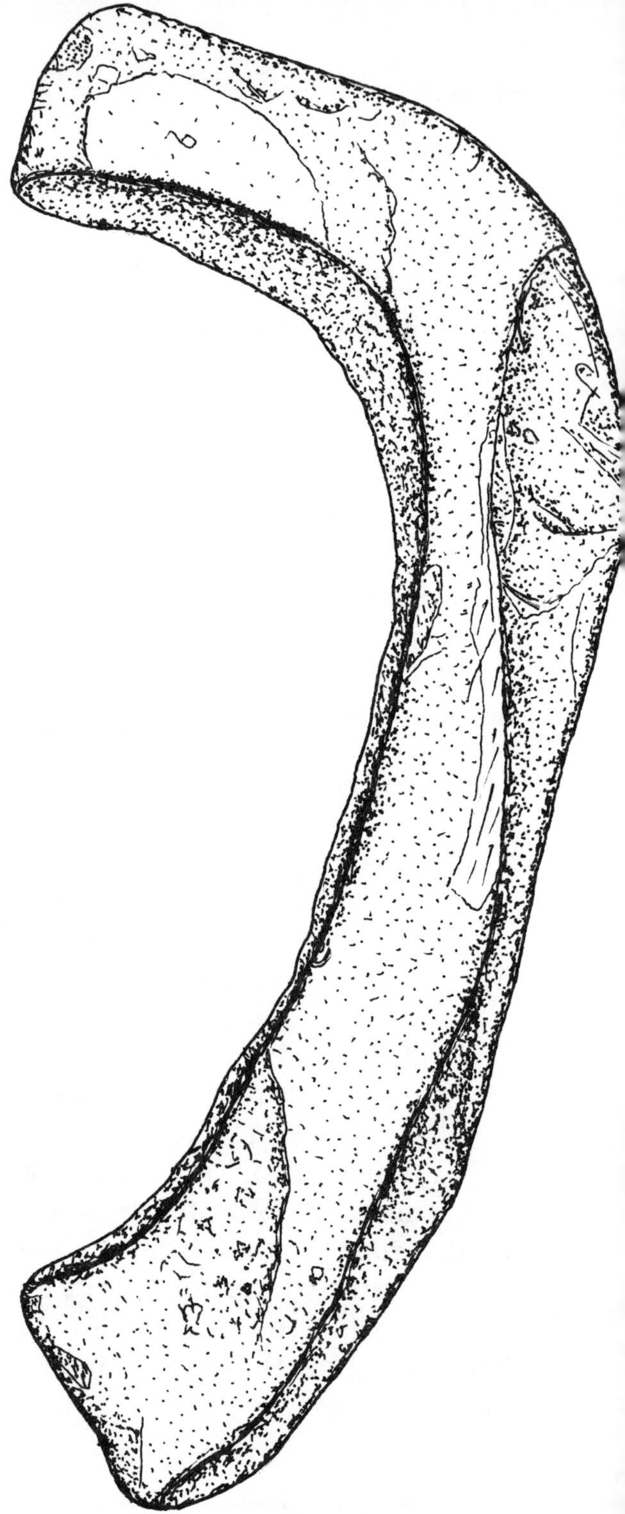

UNUSUAL HAND TOOL

Color: Light greyish brown with a patina that darkens the surface. The patina has been abraded away along the center of the right edge of the side (view to the left).

Material: Slightly argillaceous, silicious siltstone.

Location: Helderberg Mountains near Berne, SW Albany County, N.Y.

When the Sopers were visiting their son in Riverton the author happened to meet them in a local restaurant. Shared interest in artifacts was discussed briefly. Later Mrs. Soper sent sketches and description of this item and questioned what it might be. From the sketches it seemed likely that the piece was naturally formed. It was then mailed to the author and examination confirmed that although it was most likely formed by nature, it was indeed an artifact and had been used as a hand tool.

At one time the artifact was the cap of a pedestal that was exposed to water and/or wind erosion. Born of a sedimentary formation, this particular piece parted from the softer formation below. Thus, we have this beautifully sculptured, hard, most useful looking stone. A native American thought it looked useful as well.

A few flakes were removed from the raised edge of the interior curve best viewed as the right edge of the second view from the left.

The arrangement of the flakes percussed from the edges of the ends indicate it was used as a hammer against something hard. Very likely it was a flaking stone used to remove flakes from a core.

The lighter area at the lower end of the left view shows evidence of being polished at one time. The patina hides it almost completely. It is thought, by this writer, to have been used to rub seams (in leather) flat as they dried.

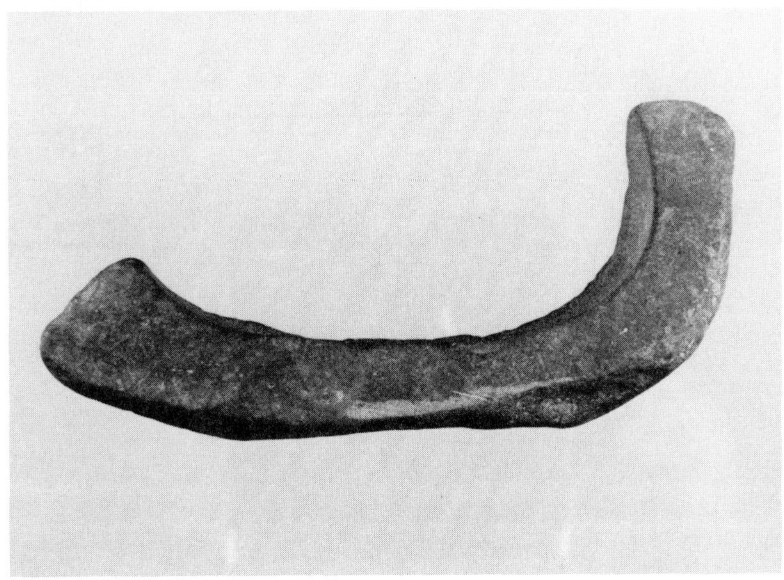

GRAVER No. 9
From the collection of:
Forest & Mickey Baskett
Shoshoni, Wyoming

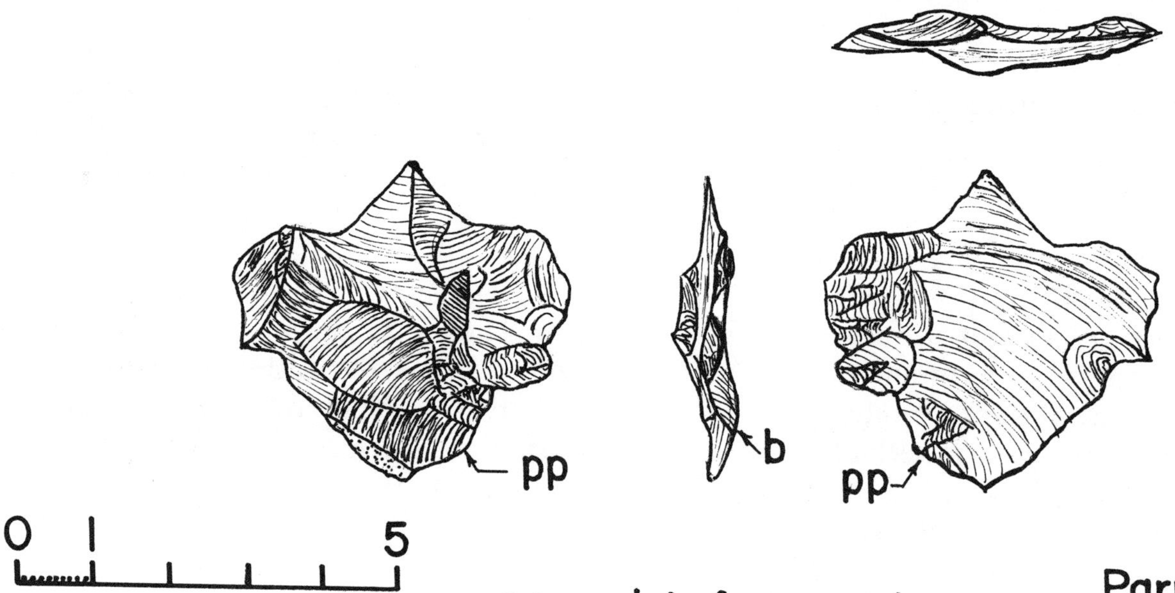

Parman

pp: point of percussion
b : bulb of percussion
: ground surface

GRAVER

GRAVER

Color & Material: Light bluish grey with tan cast. Light tan translucent edges. Chert.

Location: Northeastern Fremont County, Wyoming

This graver was crafted from a percussion flake of chert and exhibits two engraving points that are ribbed yet very thin and delicate. It also exhibits one ground surface which sharpens one edge.

Three-fourths of the edge on which the percussion point occurs is dull. All remaining edges are knife sharp. The largest of the two engraving points evidences a small amount of wear.

A similar engraver (No. 34) was determined to have been used to craft, or shape steatite (soapstone). However, the worn surface of the larger graving point does not evidence the polish that occurs when steatite is worked.

Considering how thin and delicately this graver was crafted, it is very likely that it was used to engrave pottery. The Basketts report that clay is present near where this artifact was found.

Each year when the Basketts till their garden, one, or more, artifacts is recovered. To date, approximately thirty-five stone tools have been recovered in this manner.

Under the guidance of Mr.Craig Bromley, Bureau of Land Management archaeologist, the Fremont County Archaeological Society has begun a test dig at this garden site. To date no living floor has been encountered. Artifacts from the Archaic to Historic periods have been recovered from alluvium to a depth of twenty two inches.

BOLA No. 10
From the collection of:
William H. Crymble
Riverton, Wyoming

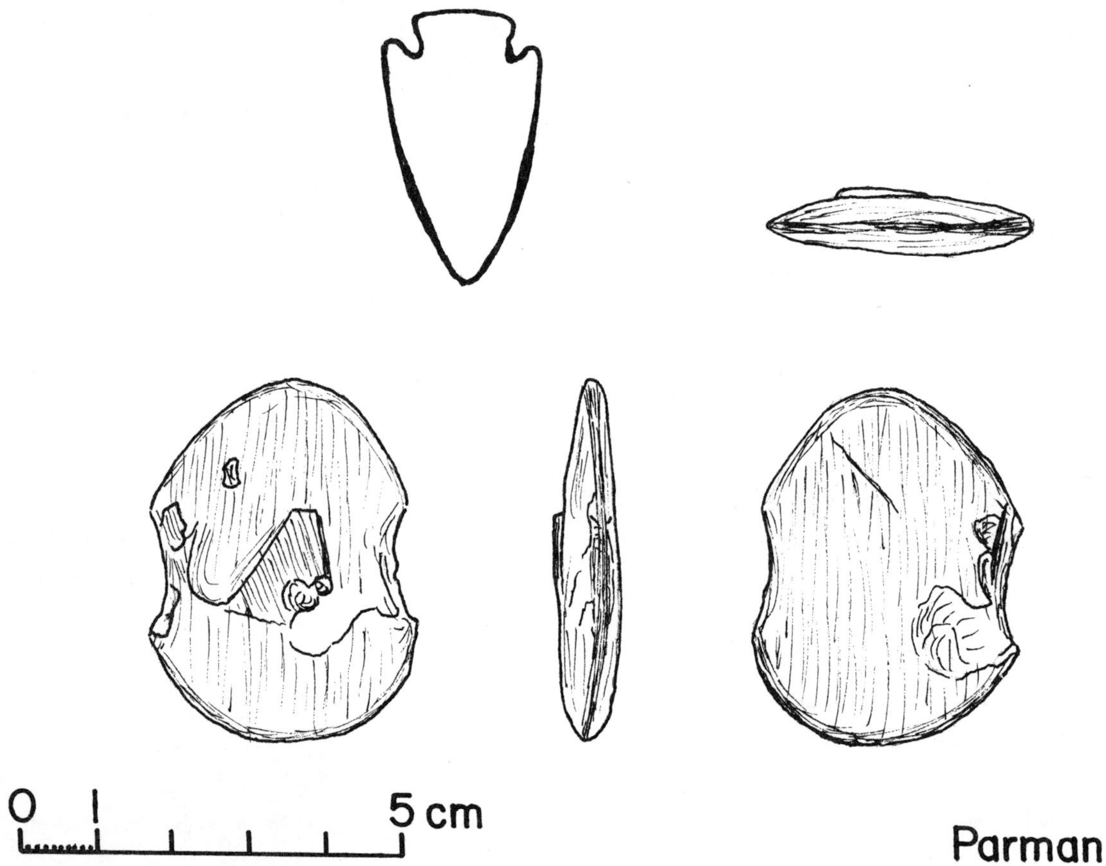

BOLA
(net-sinker)

BOLA (net sinker)

Color & Material: Dark brownish grey, extremely fine grain, shaly quartzite.

Location: Central Fremont County, Wyoming.

This artifact was taken with seven others of similar form, as a surface find from a single campsite. It was crafted from a flat, waterworn, oval shaped stone by simple notching on opposing edges so that it could be attached to the edge of a net for the capture of birds or fish.

The reason flat stones were used for this purpose is that only two notches are necessary for a line encircling the stone to remain fast.

A picture of bolas, essentially identical to this, being used to capture birds in this manner may be found on page 13 of INDIAN & ESKIMO ARTIFACTS OF NORTH AMERICA, by Charles Miles.

The point, drawn in outline above the bola, was taken from the same campsite.

The author can picture stones, notched in this manner, being used as fasteners (as a button would be used) for the closure of openings of the teepee or of parfleches.

TWO UNUSUAL SURFACE FINDS No. 11
From the collection of:
Henry & Clara Jensen
Lysite, Wyoming

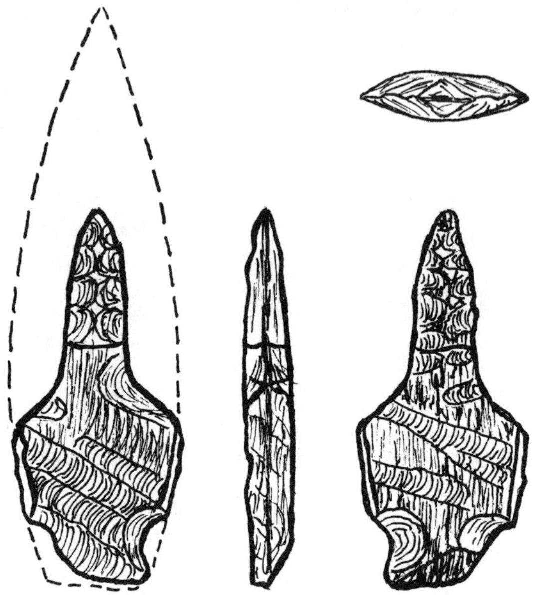

AWL
(bi-faced, made from
broken point, very old)

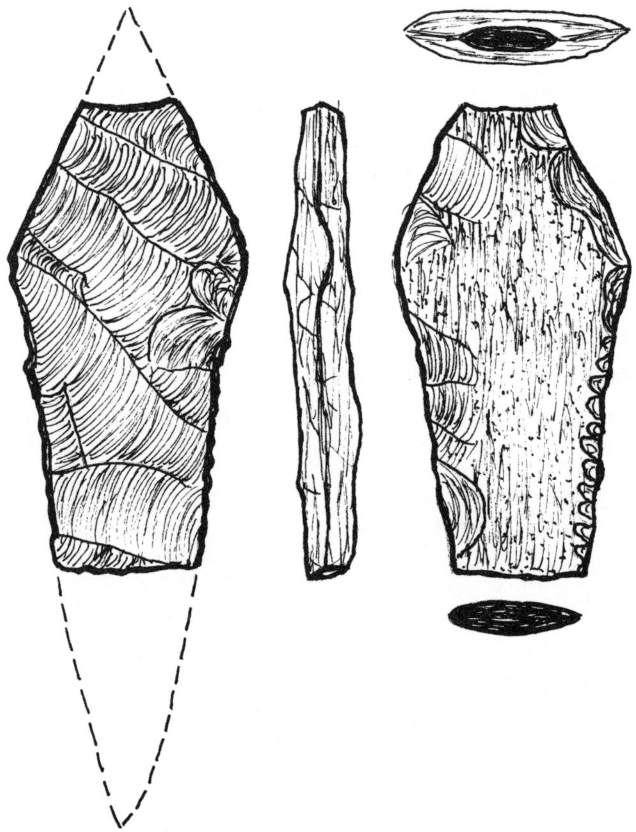

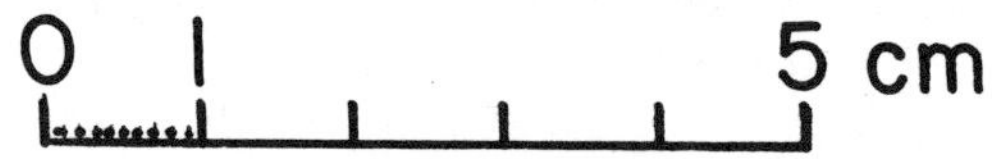

TWO UNUSUAL SURFACE FINDS

Color & Material: Knife (frag.), tan and light reddish brown, medium grain quartzite. Awl, brown with light cream oxidation of the surface. Agatized wood.

Location: Both taken from northeastern Fremont County, Wyoming. The fragments of the awl are from near the junction of Bridger and Badwater Creeks.

The base of the awl was found first. One year later the tip was found approximately one hundred feet from where the base was found.

This agate hydrates to form a light cream colored oxide on its surface. This artifact displays evidence of having been worked first as an Eden type projectile point (dotted lines) long ago. Oxidation turned the thin edges of the point light cream colored. These edges are still present as the edges of the awl's base. A great period of time later the base of the broken point was found and was then crafted into an awl. These new edges (of the awl) show some degree of oxidation and, as yet, the notches show none. The notches were crafted into the base of the awl still later.

Some day, techniques similar to obsidian hydration may disclose more about this artifact.

The knife fragment, which at first was thought to be a projectile point fragment, is distinctive, and the dotted lines indicate what is thought to be the configuration of the complete knife.

AN OLD, OLD, CHOPPER No. 12
From the collection of:
Henry & Clara Jensen
Lysite, Wyoming

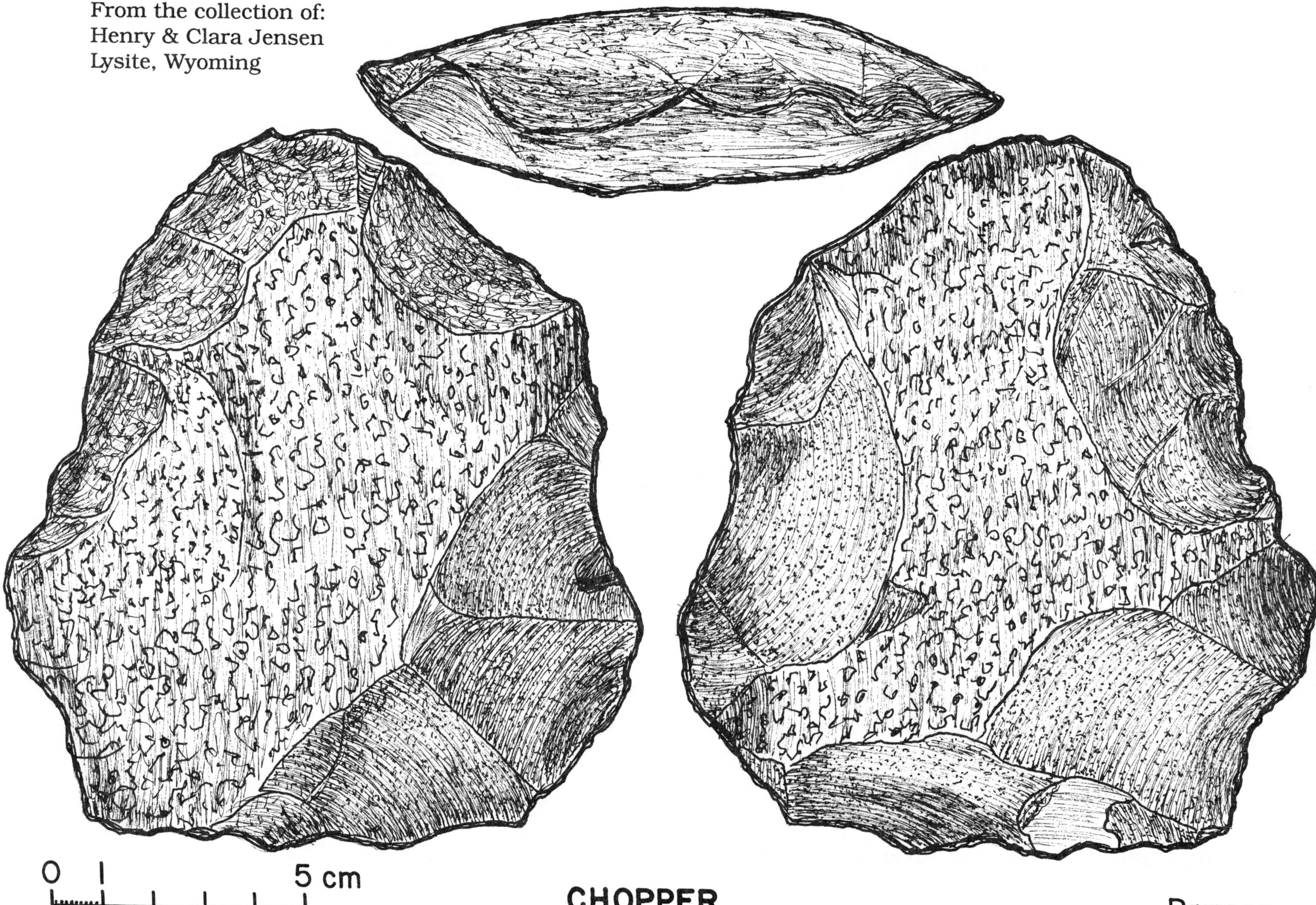

CHOPPER
(bi-faced)

Parman

AN OLD, OLD CHOPPER

Color & Material: Light greyish tan with slight blackening of the edges on both sides. Coarse grain quartzite.

Location: Northeastern Fremont County, Wyoming

This chopper was crafted from a stone spalled from the surface of a large quartzite boulder. It is thought to be extremely old, for the surfaces exposed when the flakes were removed, now appear almost as weathered as the surface of the originial boulder. The edges of the flaking are not as sharp and clearly defined as they appear in the drawing. The slight blackening of the edges might be the result of fire. A small flake has been removed (lower edge of the right side view) fairly recently and displays a much lighter, unweathered texture.

The first tool known to have been crafted by man was the simple hand axe, or chopper. Flakes were struck from one edge of a stone, making it more sharp and therefore more effective as an axe.

The author believes man has been present on this continent no less than 40,000 years, and that artifacts such as this represent evidence of the level of stone technology that long ago. Granted functional tools such as this chopper were crafted in Historic times as they are yet today in some African tribes. This belief is simply born of the fact that weathering of flaked surfaces (on stone tools of primitive types, such as this chopper) frequently exceeds that found on artifacts known to be of Paleo origin.

HOE? No. 13
From the collection of:
Patt Brown
Riverton, Wyoming

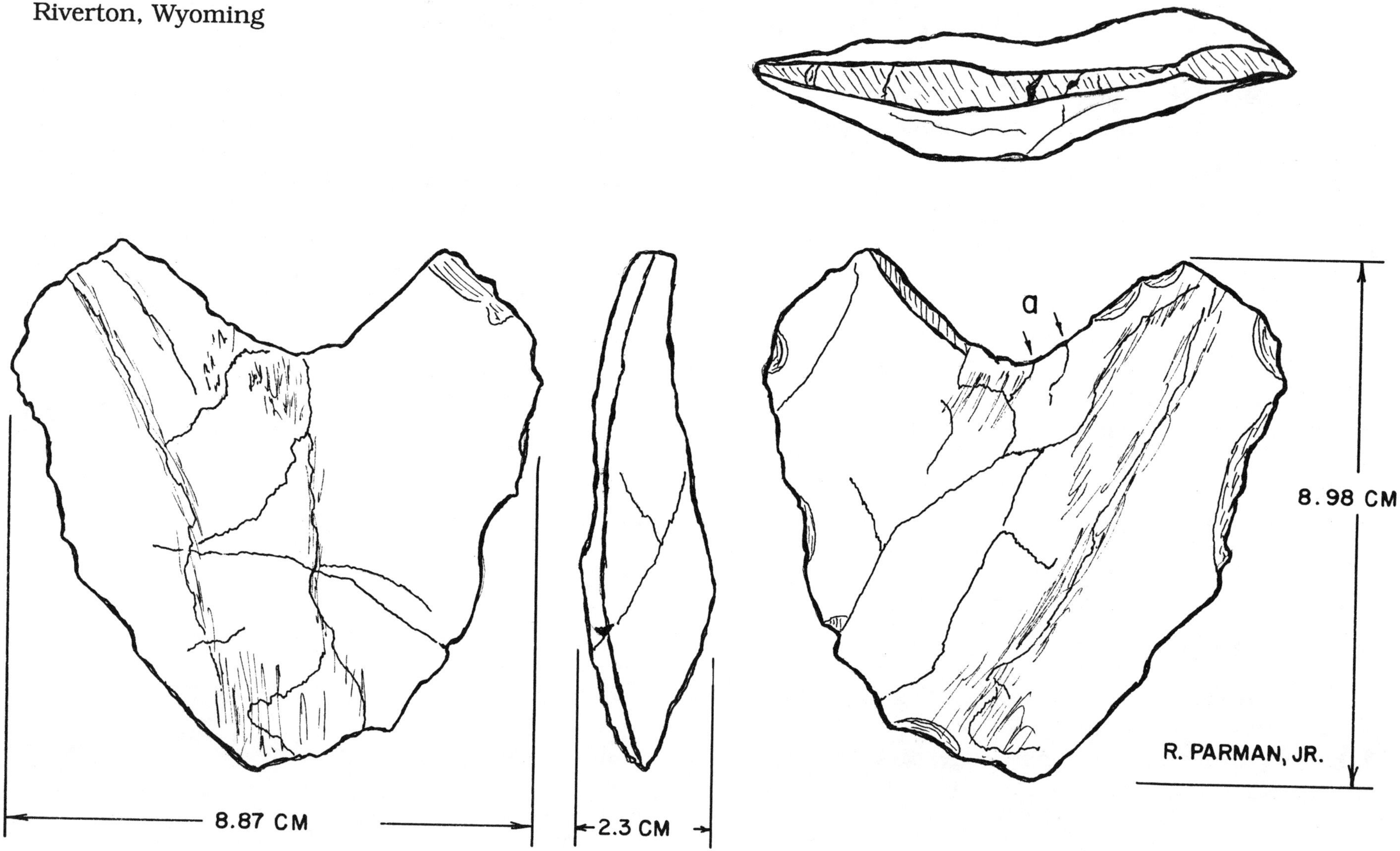

HOE ?

Color & Material: Clear to white to light grey, opaque, with light grey to black staining along fractures with some infusion of the stain into the material adjoining the fractures. This is most likely what is called "dead oil stain". Fractured quartz, re-cememted.

Location: Southern Fremont County, Wyoming.

This is a puzzling artifact. It was found protruding from an eroding bank approximately three quarters of a meter below the surface. This would support a very early age, and with no history of crop cultivation by pre-historic inhabitants of this region, it is difficult to consider this artifact a hoe. Holding it, however, one becomes more convinced it was shaped to be hafted to a handle having a crook near its end. A cultivation hoe gets the author's vote.

The letter "a" indicates two fractures having porosity. A light brown seed was found to be trapped within one of these two pore spaces. Though it shattered when removal was attempted, the fragments have been saved and the portion remaining in the pore has been protected. It is possible that a paleobotanist might still be able to identify the plant species of the seed. If the species were found to be extinct, or not present in this region at this time, it could be useful in dating this artifact.

Author's note: Possible dating of cultivation in this region, see number 106.

POCKET KNIFE & TANG KNIFE No. 14
From the collection of:
Don Davis
Thermopolis, Wyoming

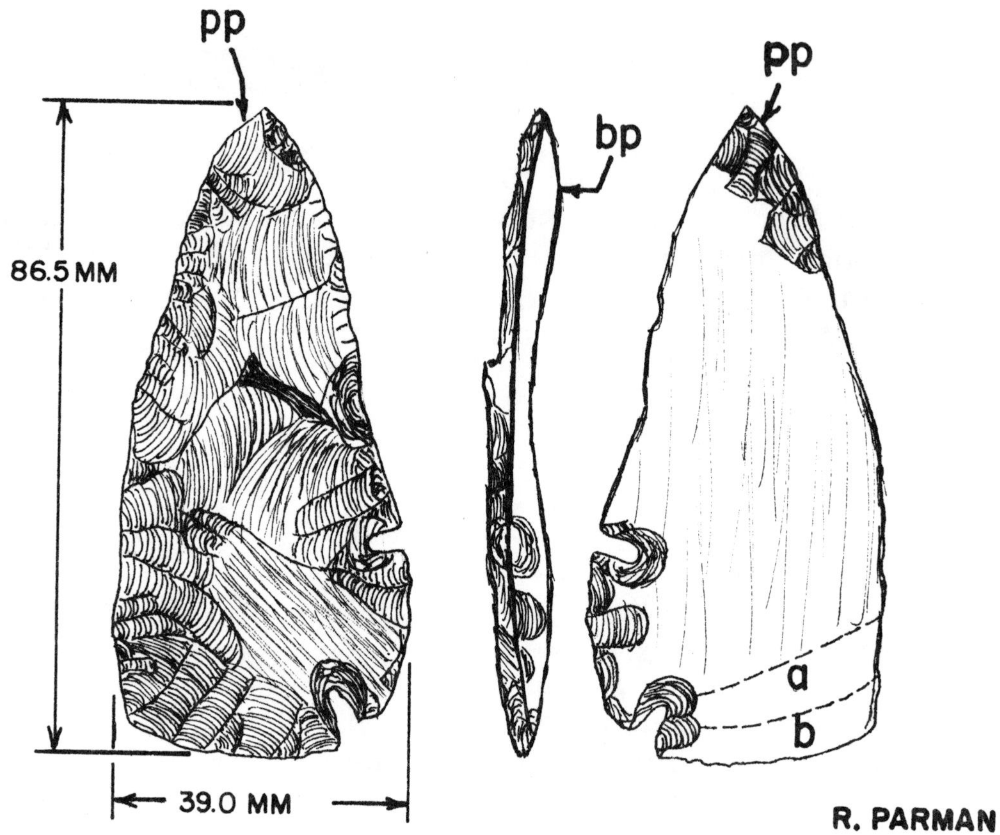

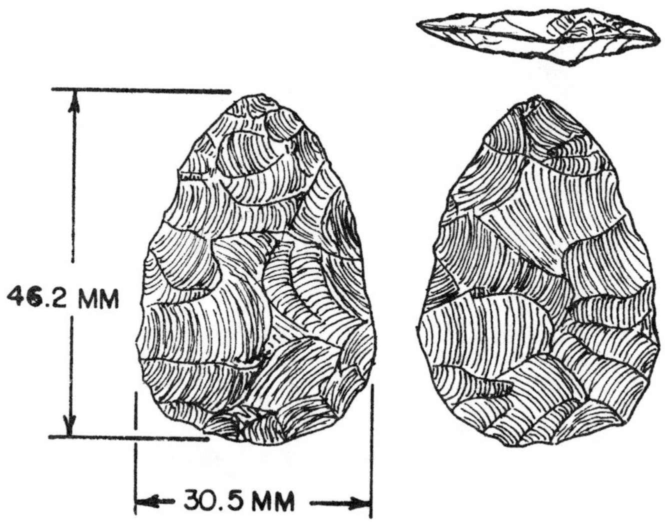

TANG KNIFE

brown agate w/trace of oolites (possibly Youngite)

a – surface ground & polished
b – surface ground & polished
pp – point of percussion for initial flake
bp – bulb of percussion

KNIFE

dark brown, translucent agate

POCKET KNIFE & TANG KNIFE

Color & Material: Pocket knife, dark brown, translucent agate. Tang knife, brown agate w/ trace of oolites. (possibly Youngite)

Location: Gas Hills region, Fremont County, Wyoming.

Tang knives are relatively rare and this one, (from the collection of Don Davis of Thermopolis, Wyoming) has unusual features that should be mentioned.

It was fashioned from a large, percussion flake and only a small amount of flaking was necessary on one side. All observed by this writer to date have been bi-facial and essentially straight. The remarkable feature is the two ground surfaces at its base. This is really open to speculation. There are two planes of grinding that both occurred before the notches were crafted. Whether the grinding was to thin the base, or simply the result of work having been done on something else is not known.

The small knife is very simple. It could be used later to craft a projectile point and probably at one time was part of a chopper.

As a knife it was probably carried in a pouch as we might carry a pocket knife today.

Native Americans used what might be called a "reduction technology". Even the tiniest flakes of a good material were utilized.

WEDGE FOR DRESSING GAME No. 15
From the collection of:
Patt Brown
Riverton, Wyoming

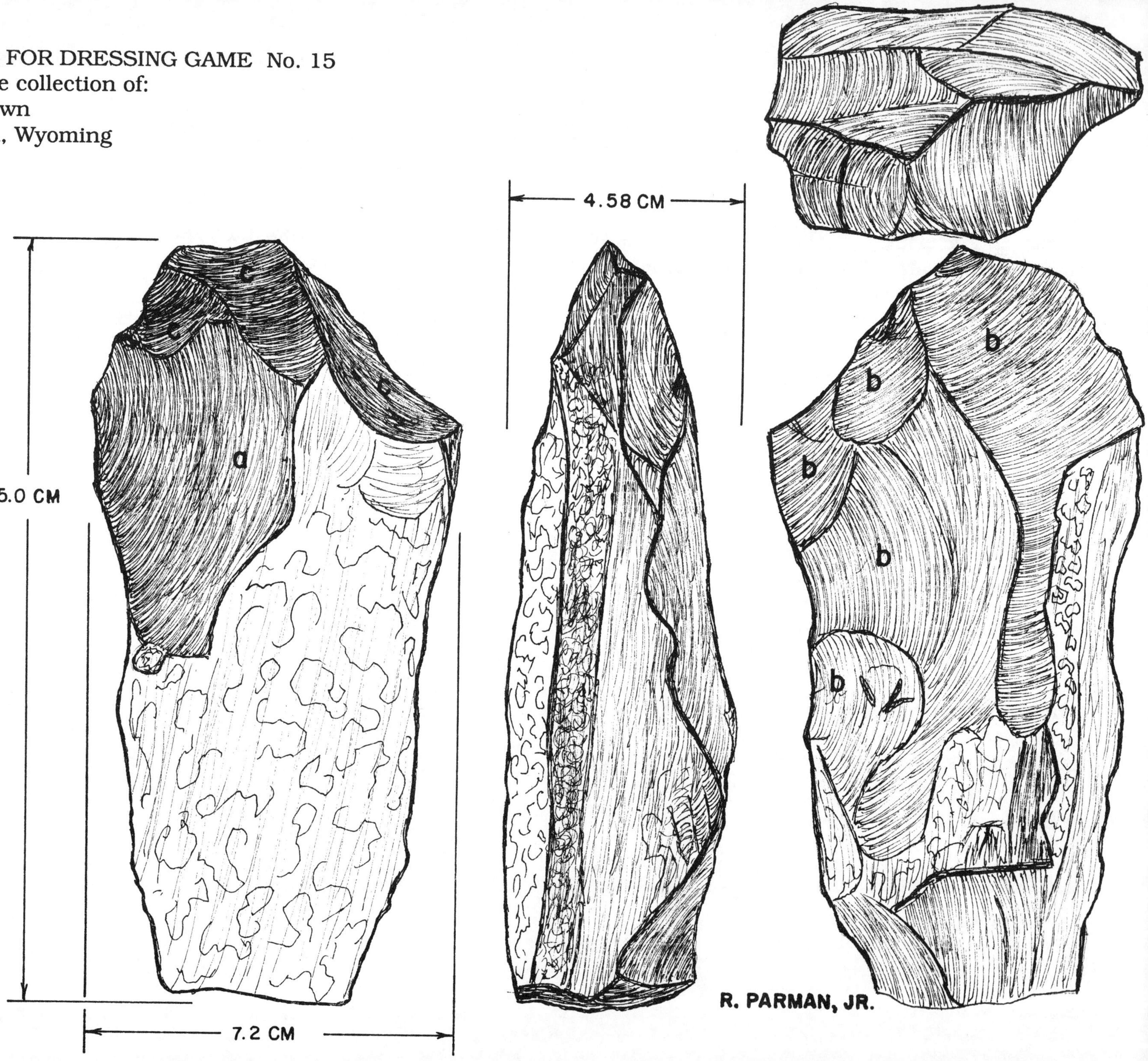

WEDGE FOR DRESSING GAME

Color & Material: Dark reddish brown rind, yellowish brown interior with slight green cast. A metamorphic stone from a sediment containing abundant algae and quartz grains with trace of oolites and oolitic porosity. Thought to be from a quarry near Oregon Butte, Southern Fremont County, Wyoming.

Location: Northern Sweetwater County, Wyoming.

This artifact is thought to be very old, for the flaking that shaped it displays varied amounts of rind formed on the flake surfaces.

The surface labeled "a" has a distinctly heavy rind. Surfaces "b" appear to have rinds essentially equal, and they appear to be considerably younger than that of "a", but not as young as those flaked surfaces labeled "c".

Since surfaces "b" & "c" are on opposing sides, it is possible that the amount of exposure to weathering could account for the slight difference in rinds, but other methods of examination would be necessary to make this determination.

The flat surface of the smaller end of this tool has been struck, for there are several irregular pieces missing. This indicates possible use as a wedge, or that it was hammered into the ligaments of a bone joint to assist in reducing killed game into portable segments. It could also have been used as a hand held chopper.

A GROOVED AXE No. 16
From the collection of:
Patt Brown
Riverton, Wyoming

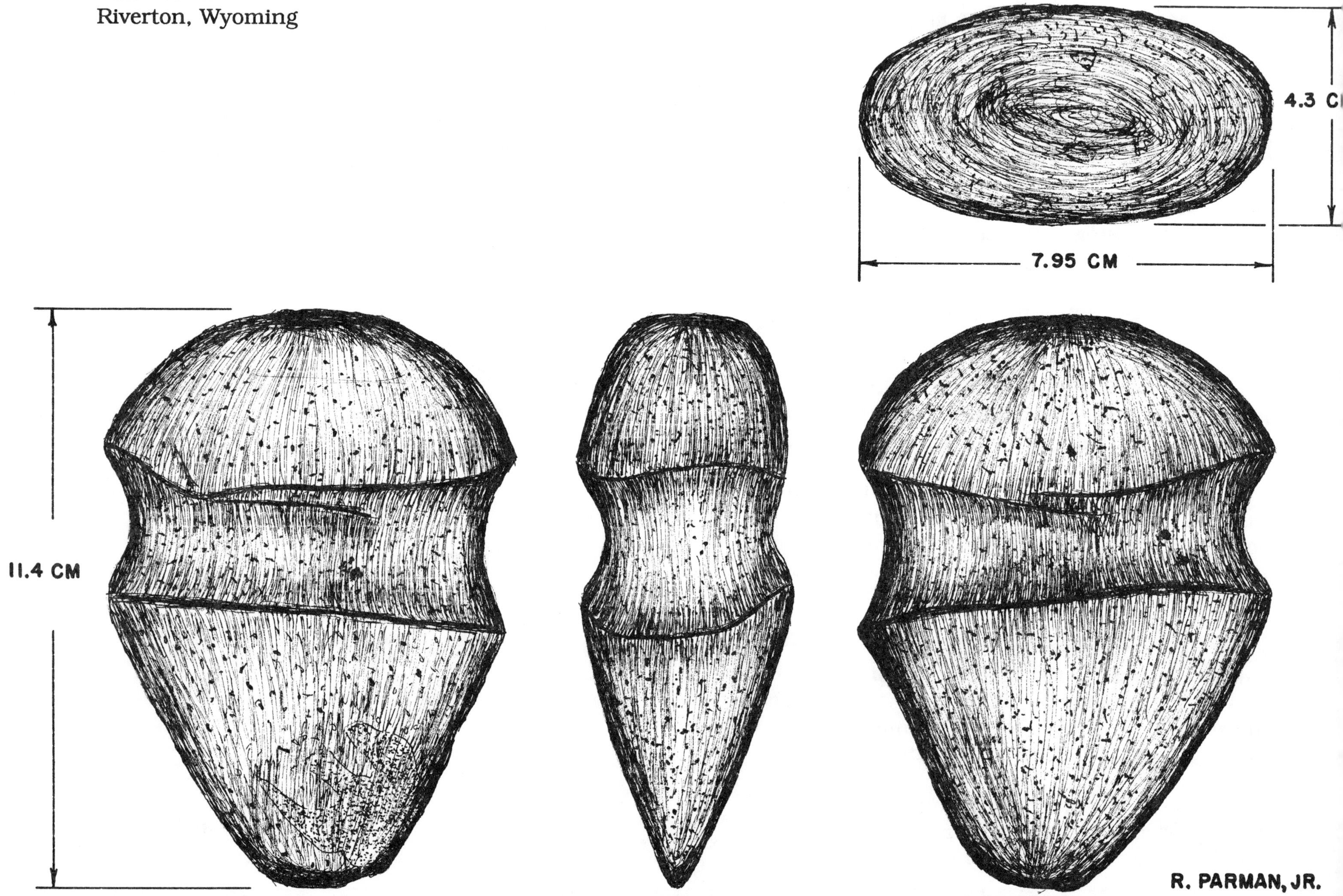

A GROOVED AXE

Color & Material: Brownish grey quartzite.

Location: West central Arkansas near Gamden.

This axe is unusual, for great care was taken to patiently shape its entire surface. It is a utility tool rather than ceremonial.

Light blows, perpendiclar to the surface, have removed a considerable amount of material as evidenced by the depth of the groove and the reduced size of the more pointed end.

The groove made it possible for a rawhide handle to be attached and then this very fine grained, hard, quartzite axe would have been useful as a war club for a large individual, and for opening skulls and breaking long bones for marrow.

The author's personal vote is for the war club. Mainly because it would have been a very treasured item warranting the time and patience needed to have crafted it.

THUNDERBIRD No. 17
From the collection of:
Alfred & Virginia Lindell
Lander, Wyoming

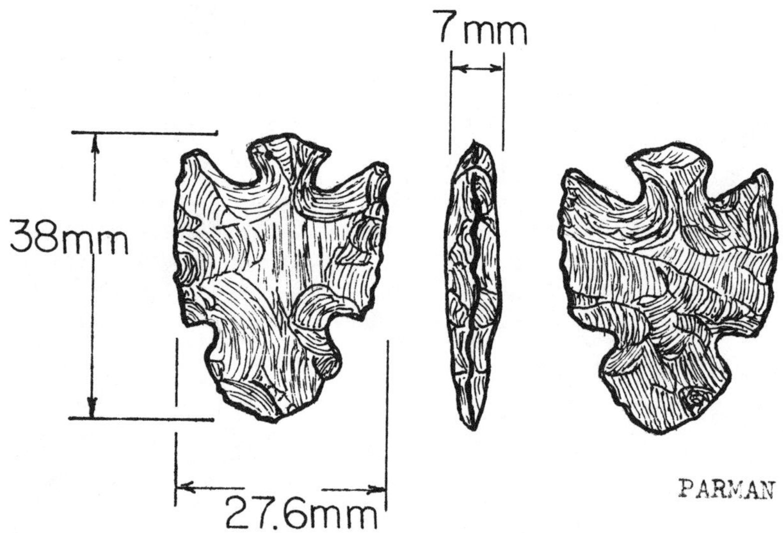

THUNDERBIRD

THUNDERBIRD

Color & Material: Bone white to light grey with orange and maroon washes. Agate.

Location: Oregon Buttes in north central Sweetwater County, Wyoming.

Certain North American tribal mythology embraced a large bird which was thought to have caused lightning, thunder, and rain. It has come to be called "Thunderbird".

It is believed this artifact was carved in effigy to Thunderbird and was used by the tribal shaman, or medicine man, in rituals for rain.

Thunderbirds are most rare. Other than photographs and drawings, this writer has not had the opportunity of seeing one before. The author expresses sincere appreciation to Mr. and Mrs. Alfred E. Lindell for making this rare artifact available for publication.

NATURAL OR MAN MADE? No. 18
From the collection of:
Mr. & Mrs. Wayne Steinberg
Glenrock, Wyoming

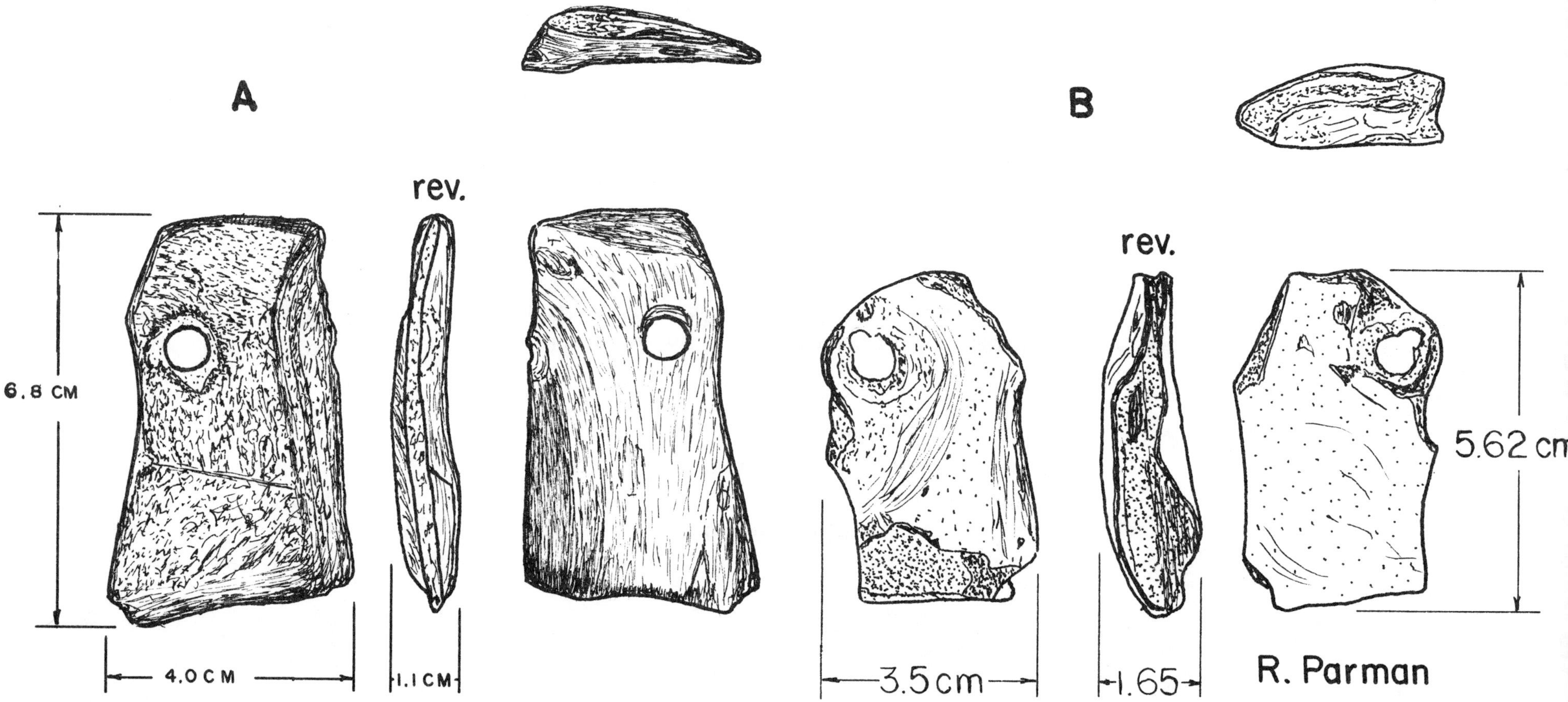

NATURAL OR MAN MADE ?

Color & Material: Artifact A, Mottled greyish tan with slightly darker patina. Sandstone, laminated light grey and light tan through largest plane.

Location: Badwater drainage area of Southern Big Horn Mountains, Natrona County, Wyoming.

Mr. & Mrs. Steinberg have long questioned whether this find should be considered an artifact. From all appearances it was brought to its present contours by natural forces. The exceptions are areas where the uniformity of the patina is interrupted, and where there are possible wear faces bordering the circumference of the hole and along the edges. Whether the straight line indentation, appearing on one face, was formed naturally is also questioned.

This find was of great interest to me because an artifact of mine, taken from the Bad Water drainage near Lysite, Wyoming (artifact B), is very similar. Its hole evidenced wear from a line having been passed through it.

It is probable the holes were formed naturally and that they (the two artifacts) were used as net weights.

Authors note: See No. 10

SCALPING KNIFE? No. 19
From the collection of:
Girl Scout National Center, West
Ten Sleep, Wyoming

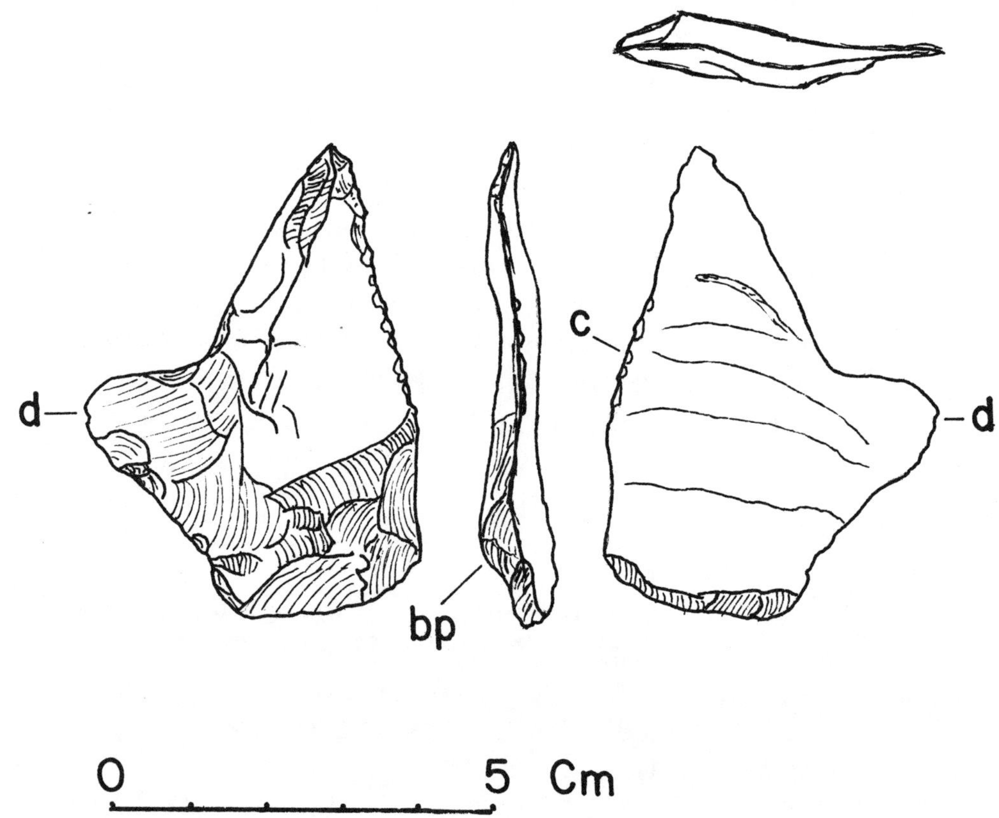

Parman

SCALPING KNIFE ?

Color & Material: Dull reddish maroon. Chert.

Location: Pow-Wow site on the grounds of the center.

This artifact was fashioned from a percussion flake of very dense chert. The bulb of percussion (bp) was used to provide the thick, strong base. Essentially the artifact is unifaced, however a small number of chips were removed from the unworked side (c) to sharpen the edge.

Overall the artifact resembles a utility knife-scraper and it has characteristics most suitable for a slitter. With a handle mounted on the larger projection (bottom of drawing), the bulb of percussion would permit the binding to lock the blade to the handle.

The long point could be used to pierce the scalp and would then slide along the skull while the sharp edge of the side arm (d) would separate the scalp.

It is a beautiful artifact and was delicately worked. It could just as well have been a grandmother's sewing scissors or her skinning knife for the small animal skins needed for the children's moccasins.

UNUSUAL AXE & POINT No. 20
From the collection of:
Mr. & Mrs. Lee Jamerman
Sweetwater, Wyoming

A

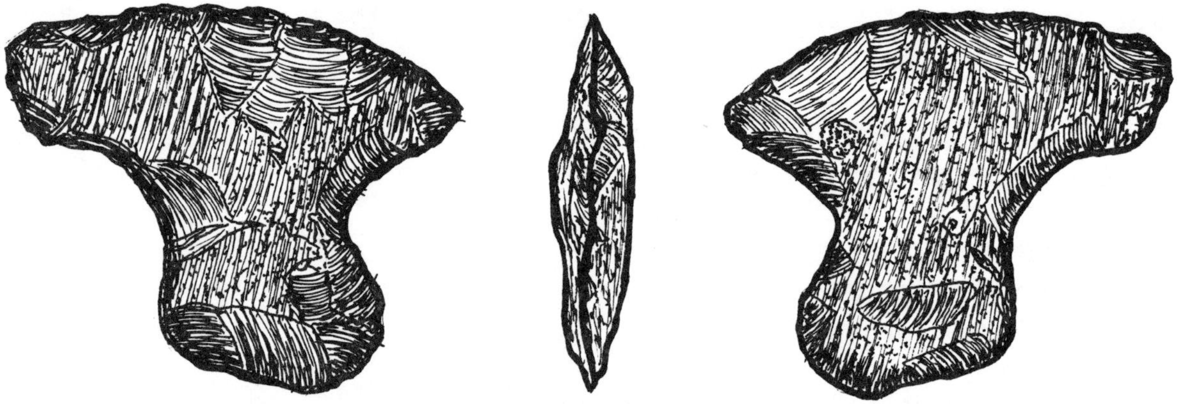

THROWING AXE ?
WAR CLUB ?

B

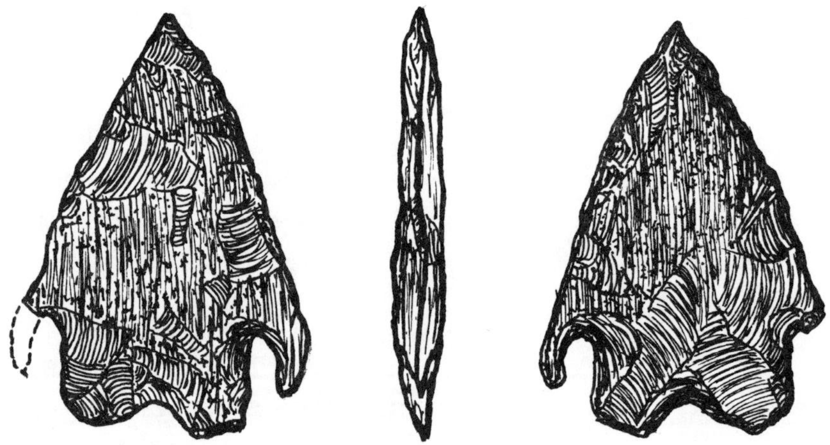

R. Parman

UNUSUAL AXE & POINT

Color & Material: Artifact A, light grey with slight brown cast. White wash and inclusions. Fine-grain quartzite with trace of microfossils present.

Artifact B, light grey, very slight green cast. A smooth, hard flint. Possibly chert.

Location: Artifact A, southeastern corner of Fremont County, Wyoming.

Artifact B, north central Sweetwater County, Wyoming

The artifact that is possible a throwing axe, or war club, was crudely fasioned, and did not require delicate flaking to have sharp working edges. Its overall appearance (both sharply rounded and pointed ends as well as a gently curving, knife-sharp edge perpendicular to the stem for hafting) suggests that it had many uses. Fitted with a short handle, it would have been an effective throwing axe.

This projectile point, artifact B, now has been determined to be an Elko Eared point as defined by Robert Heizer and M.A. Baumhoff (1961:128). Except for the base notch, it is quite similar to a Calf Creek point.

THUMB PRESS & KNIFE No. 21
From the collection of:
Mike Henry
Douglas, Wyoming

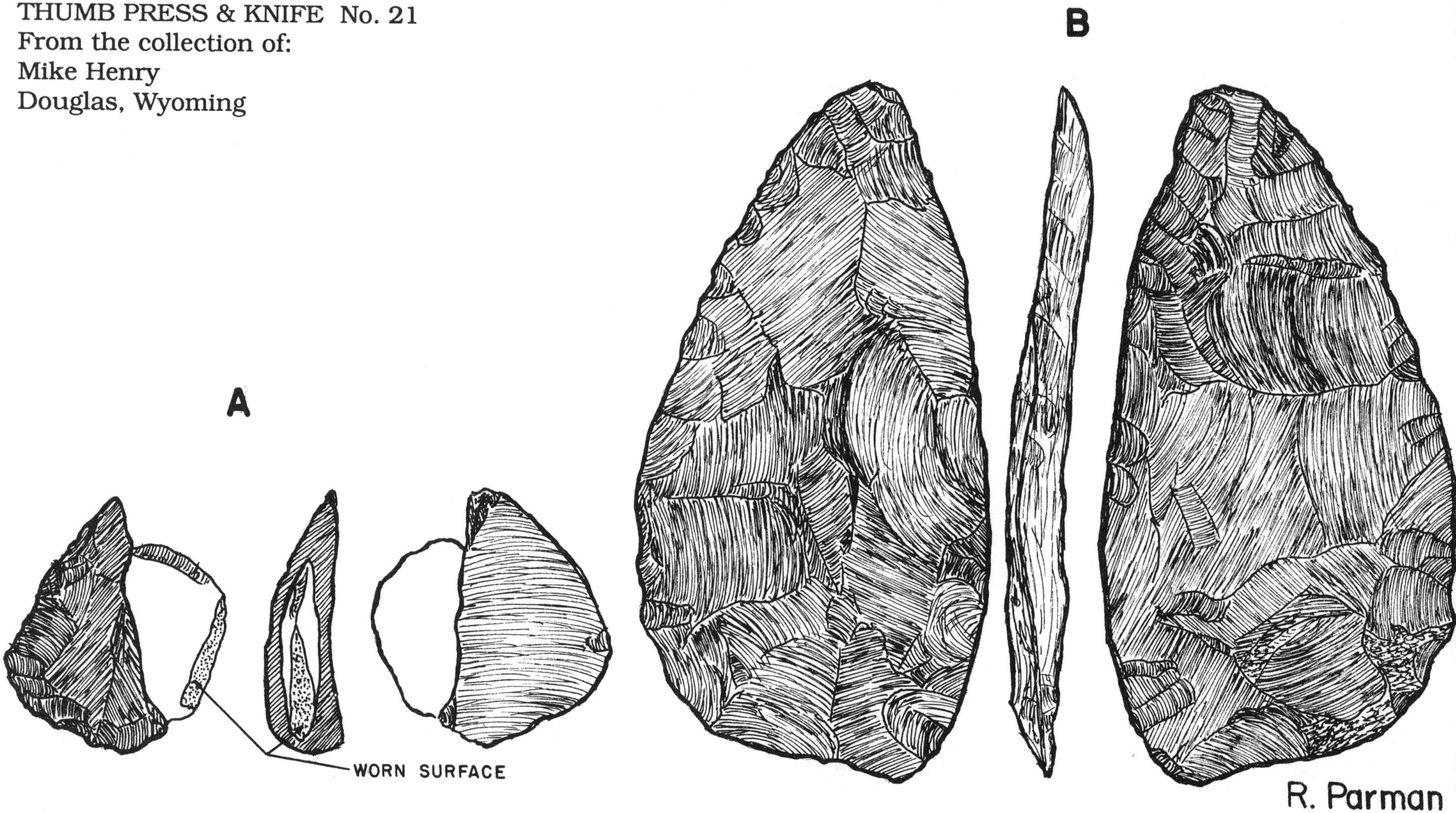

THUMB PRESS (fragment)
with
Scrapper Inside

KNIFE

0 1 2 3 4 5
cm

THUMB PRESS & KNIFE

Color & Material: Artifact A, calf-liver brown with with very slight maroon cast. Pale green and light tan washed inclusions with abundant dark, pin point inclusions also. Chert.

Artifact B, pale maroon with pale tan cast to one half and having evidence of a darker strata and a worm hole like, bone white inclusion. There are abundant, dark, pin point inclusions also. Chert.

Location: Artifact A & B, north central Converse County, Wyoming.

This fragment, A, of a thumb press (scraper) parted along an old fracture plane to expose a nodule of hard sandstone within. It appears possible that one edge of the inner nodule may have been worn sharp through use as a scraper. Mr. Henry said that he spent some time looking for the other fragment, but was not successful.

This large knife, B, was crafted from chert taken from the same quarry as the thumb press (above). The chert is of such good quality and remarkable in color that over a year later this writer was examining a large, beautiful scraper and recognized the material as being from the same quarry. See No. 87.

This knife is beautiful to hold and evidences fine craftsmanship. The slight curve of the longest dimension indicates it was made from a large flake taken by striking the flat surface of a core near the edge. The curve of the convex surface of the knife is the bulb of percussion of the flake removed from the core just before.

The striking similarity of this knife with the side tang knife submitted by Pete Todd of Riverton, Wyoming (No. 7) makes one feel both could have been crafted by the same person.

The contour of the larger end of this knife, and that of Mr. Todd's might identify which complex, or cultural affiliation these knives could be assigned to. Anyone having information about this please write to the author.

CHOPPER-COMB No. 22
From the collection of:
Fred Underwood
Dublin, Texas

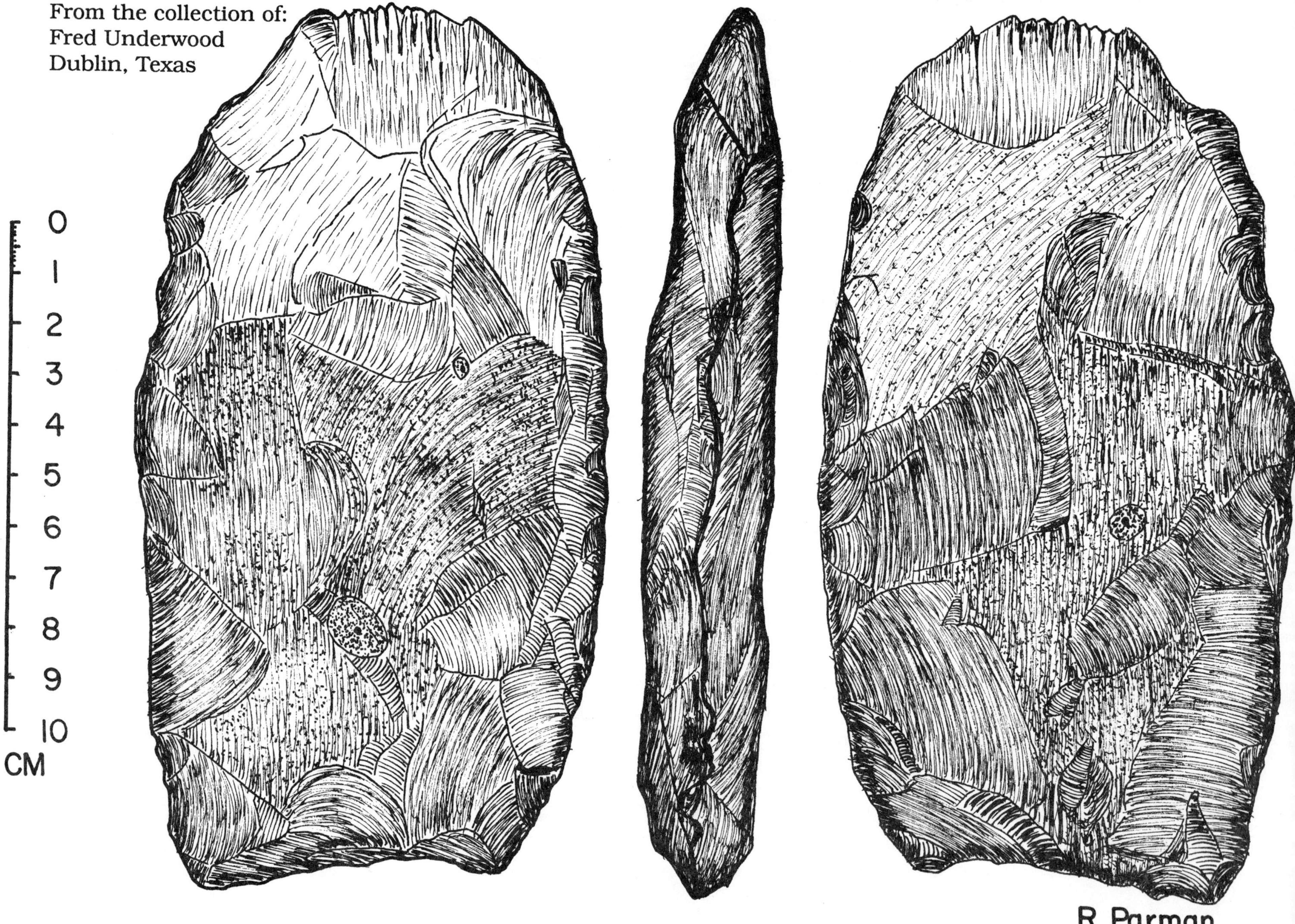

CHOPPER-COMB

Color & Material: Light tan with very thin, uneven, dark brown patina on the larger end. Very slight green cast and having two small, ferrous inclusions, one on each side. Medium grade chert.

Location: Southwest corner of Erath County, Texas.

This is an ususual artifact in that it was crafted as a chopper but had ten teeth carved into one end. It evidences considerable wear and polish on the end having the teeth.

This tool was probably used to both scrape the hides and to clean the fur. The polished surfaces of the teeth and the end of the chopper would have occurred from pulling it through the fur as a comb.

It was found by Mrs. Bowlsby's father on their family farm near Dublin, Texas. This was Comanche territory and it is likely that it is of that origin.

The author is most proud of a framed drawing by Mrs. Bowlsby that hangs on the den wall. It depicts a wolf with such a look of resignation upon its face, each rib clearly defined, such a lean belly and bedraggled tail and having the caption: "IT'S BEEN A GREAT YEAR". He has lifted the spirit in time of need, just as an old friend might.

AN UNUSUALLY STEMMED POINT No. 23
From the collection of:
Wilford & Dorothy Vaughn
Maybell, Colorado

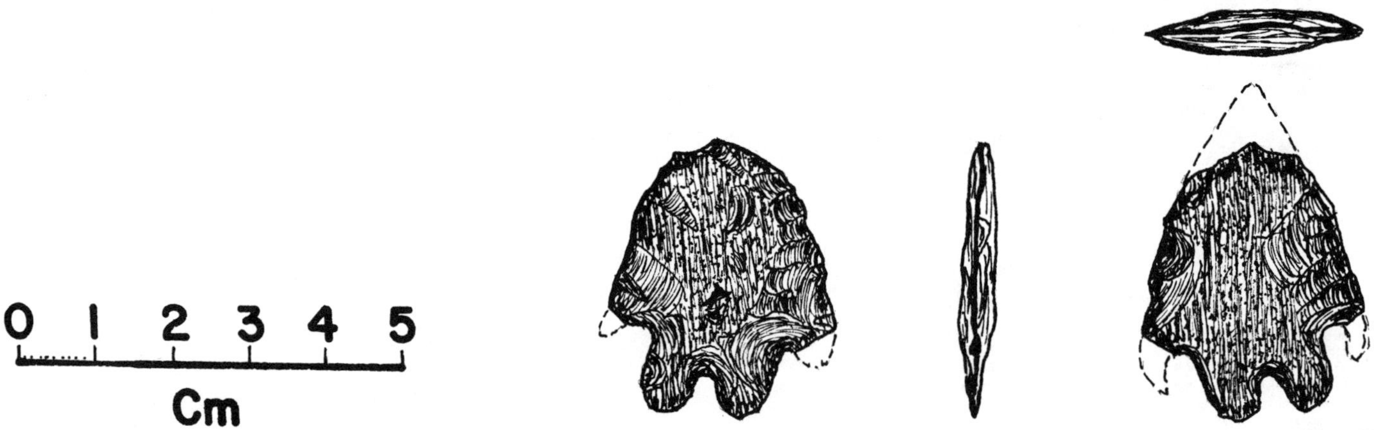

R. Parman, Jr.

CALF CREEK ?
(reworked)

AN UNUSUALLY STEMMED POINT

Color & Material: Light to dark grey banded quartzite with a slight maroon cast along the left edge of the left side view. Quartzite.

Location: Northwest corner of Moffat county, Colorado.

This uniquely stemmed point displays rather crude craftsmanship and the flaking evidences marked weathering. Both characteristics lead one to believe it is quite old.

The author looked through four volumes containing two hundred known types of dart points and projectile points and could not find a single type resembling this point.

The unusual point submitted by the Jamermans (No. 20) and the point described in No. 1 were both thought to be Calf Creek points dating from 3,000 to 5,000 years B.C. They also resembled Calf Creek points, but it has now been determined that this point is an Elko Eared point as defined by Robert Hiezer and M.A. Baumhoff (1961:128)

The dotted lines illustrate two possible configurations of the original point. It is possible that the original tip was broken and the point was reworked to its present shape.

AXE OR WAR CLUB? No. 24
From the collection of:
Louis Cabrera, Sr.
Rawlins, Wyoming

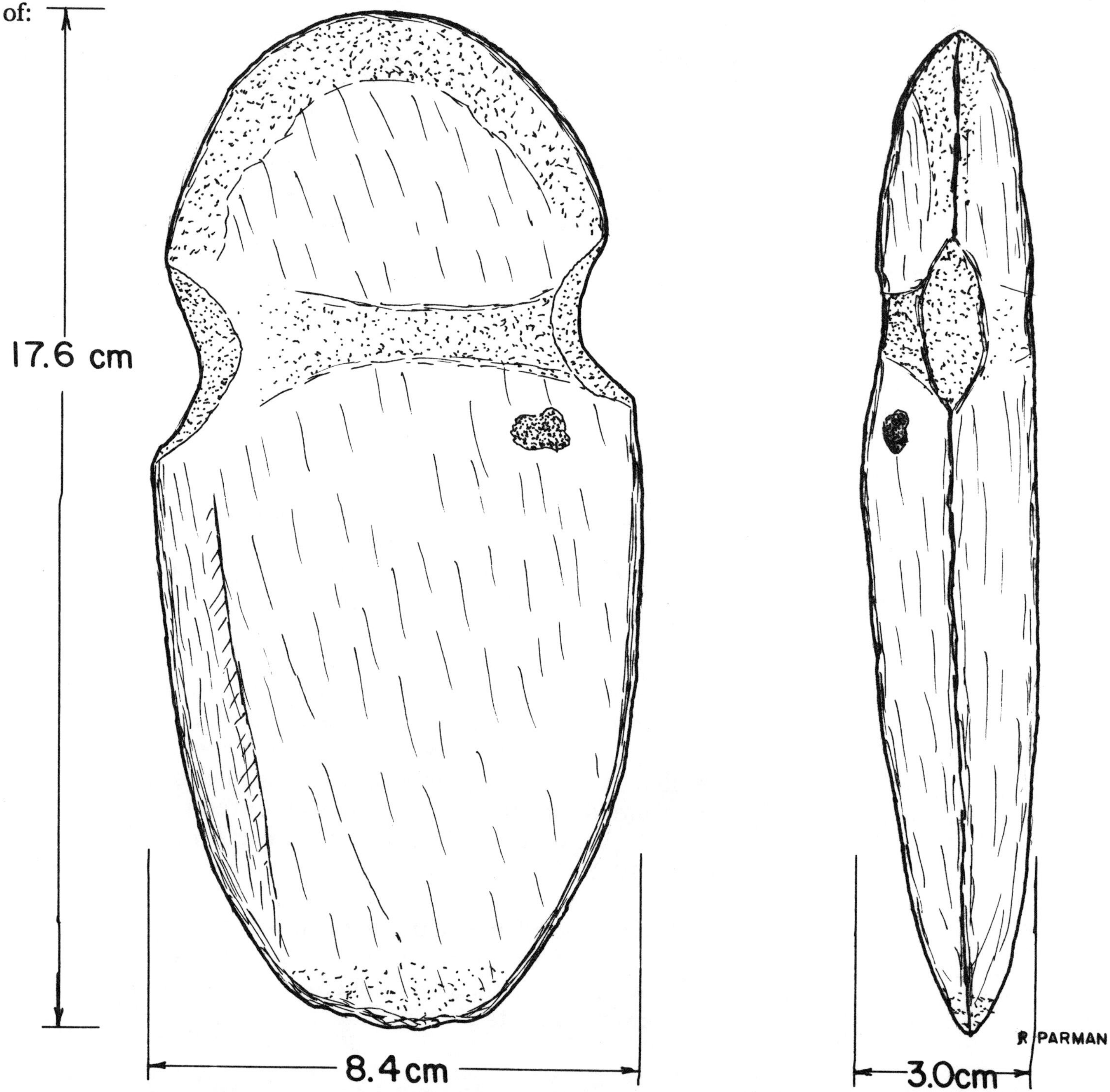

AXE OR WAR CLUB ?

Color & Material: Light green to green with faint, thin, white lamina and several white feld-spar inclusions. Quartzite.

Location: Southwest corner of Carbon County, Wyoming.

This axe was found partially buried on a flat, narrow ridge by sight from the mesa above. There were fire pots nearby but no teepee rings were found.

As a description "axe" seams to fit rather than "pounder", for it is too light to have been effective for breaking up firewood.

The blunt end evidences shaping by both percussion and grinding. The thin lamina of the sharp end appears to have been crushed by use.

The notches were formed by percussion and one side has a faint lateral groove that shows individual percussion points.

In view of a sharp line along one side, sepa-rating the curve of the side from the curve of the edge, it is possible the original, flat, polished, river cobble stone was used as a mano for grind-ing seeds and nuts before it was notched as an axe.

Is it light enough to have been a war club? It would have been effective for opening skulls of buffalo.

A BEAUTIFUL KNIFE No. 25
From the collection of:
Mrs. Walter Scott
Powell, Wyoming

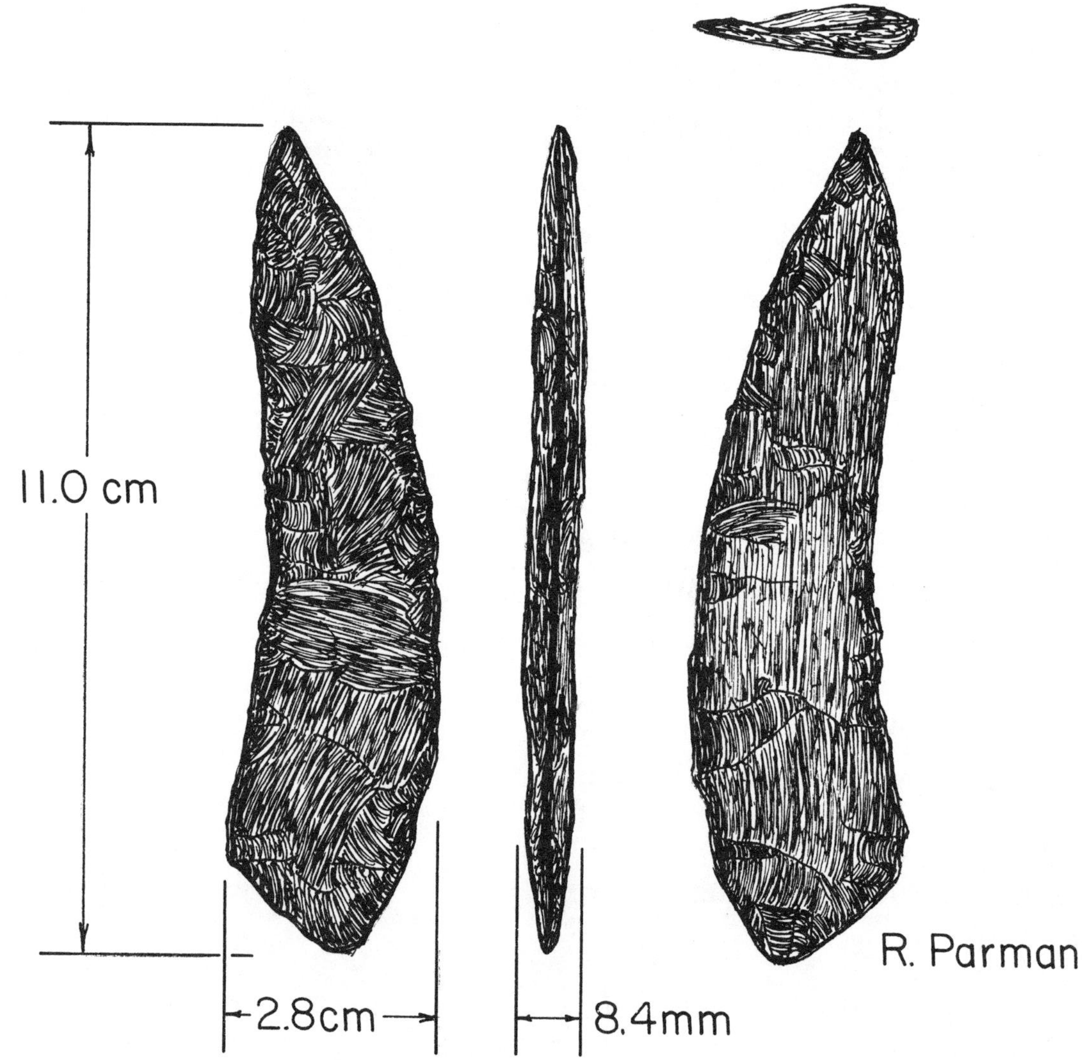

KNIFE

A BEAUTIFUL KNIFE

Color & Material: Very pale tan with slight grey cast.

Location: A sandbar in Clarks Fork River at the mouth of Clarks Fork Canyon, Northern Park County, Wyoming.

This unusual knife was quite beautiful to hold and look upon. The flaking evidences no lateral or bi-lateral pattern but does show good craftsmanship for such symmety through the smallest dimension.

It is easy to visualize this knife being used to slice meat into jerky strips: the long, gently curved edge being used to make the long cuts down the sides of the strips and the slight, re-curved tip of the concave edge being used for the more difficult cuts.

RARE FINDS No. 26
From the collection of:
Joe & Arlene Tyrrell
Lovell, Wyoming

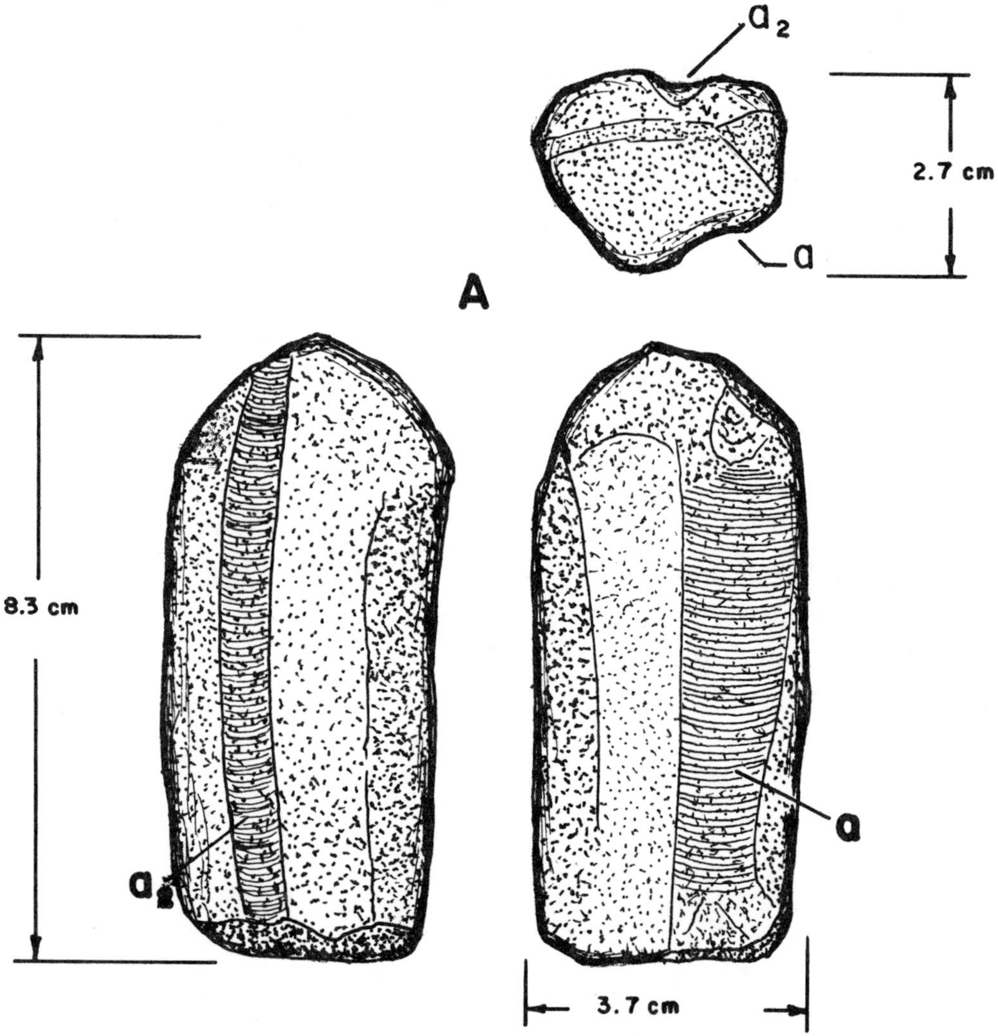

SHAFT SCRAPER

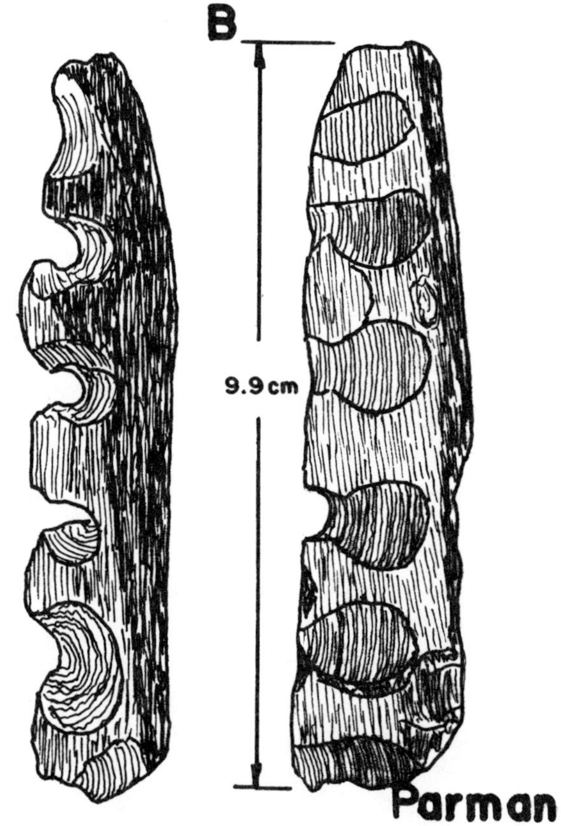

FIRE STARTER STICK

RARE FINDS

Color & Material: Artifact A, dirty light brown with yellow cast. Coarse sandstone.

Artifact B, light to dark brown with varnish like patina, partly blackened by fire. A light, almost porous, brittle wood.

Location: Artifacts A & B, Big Horn County, Wyoming.

This shaft scraper evidences no shaping by man other than an even rounding, straightening and smoothing of the natural groove in the right side view (a).

Course sandstone made this tool as effective as modern sandpaper and it was used (a pair of similar stones held in the palm of the hand, one on either side of the shaft) to smooth and shape arrow shafts. The natural, slightly curved, groove in the left view (a-2) was not used as a scaper even though it was available.

The fire starter stick was taken from a campsite having a fire pit nearby. It was found under a small overhang of sandstone buried by eloian sand deposited in a crack.

Originally it was longer, but one of the fire holes weakened it sufficiently for this end of the stick to beak off and be discarded.

The fire starter stick was placed on the ground in front of the seated native, who would then bring the soles of his feet nearly together with the sides of the feet lying across the stick. The end of a slender, straight spinning stick was then placed upon it and spun by the rubbing action of the palms of the hands.

Heat generated by the friction of the end of the spinning stick against the starter stick would be sufficient to ignite fibers of the starter stick. Tiny bits of fuel (crushed, dried leaves, grass etc.) would be placed into the hole and the native would then faintly blow into the hole to ignite a larger flame. The burning bits of fuel would then be tipped into the starting tinder of the intended fire pit. The soles of the feet would be protecting this activity much like the palms of the hands cupped around a match.

Several of the holes have been worn completely through the stick, and one has a shiny black, carbonized bottom. The darkened areas of the stick's surface also are carbonized from burning. The surfaces not burned have a sheen much

RARE FINDS No. 26
From the collection of:
Joe & Arlene Tyrrell
Lovell, Wyoming

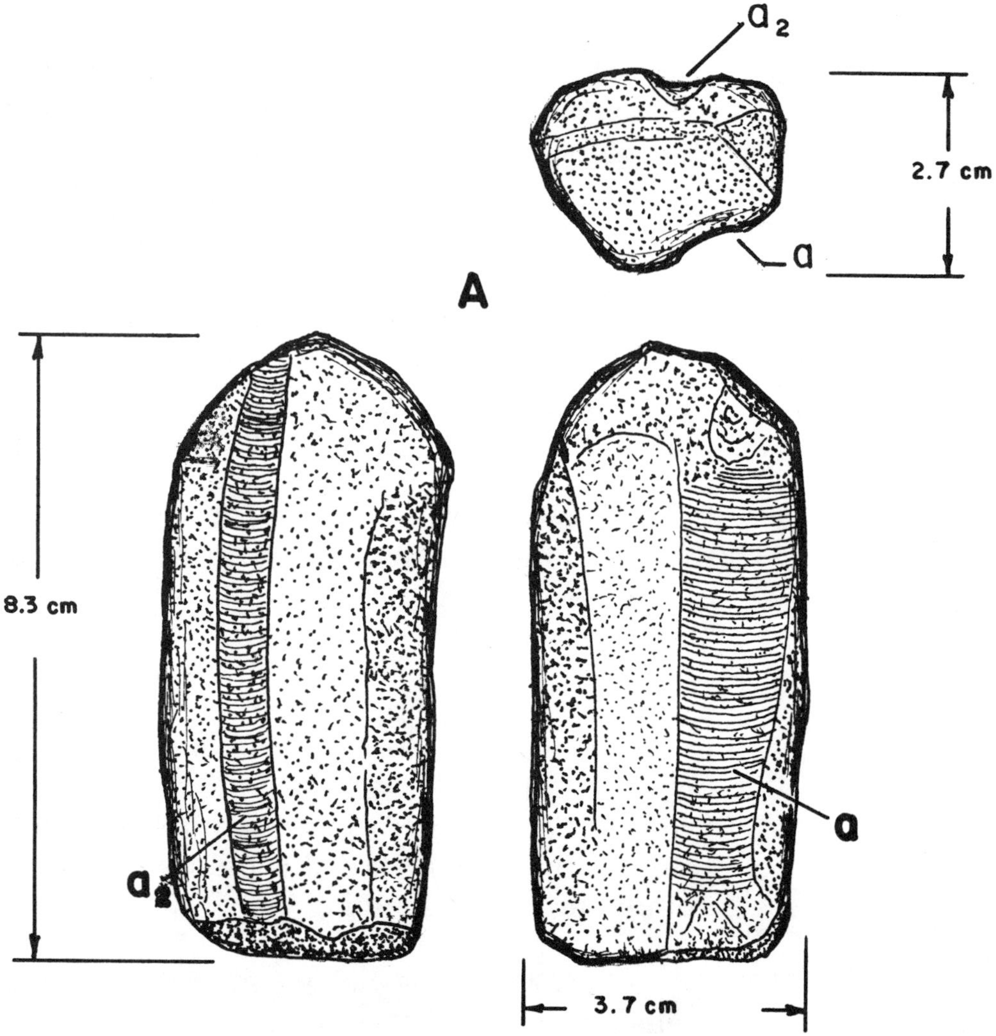

SHAFT SCRAPER

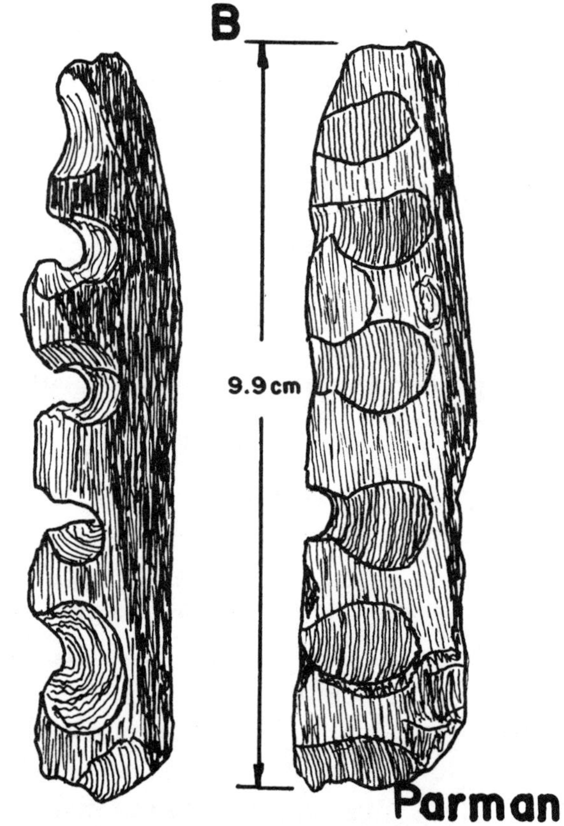

FIRE STARTER STICK

like old varnish. Oil from the hand or the cambium of the wood might account for this sheen

Barbara Swenson, of Hanna, Wyoming, wrote to the Tyrrells letting them know that mountain mahogany was the wood most likely used for the fire starter stick. Research has indicated there is a species of this bush-tree (?), that has its range primarily in Arizona and does extend into the southwest of Wyoming.

SPANISH SPEAR TIP? No. 27
From the collection of:
Mr. & Mrs. Lee Jamerman
Sweetwater, Wyoming

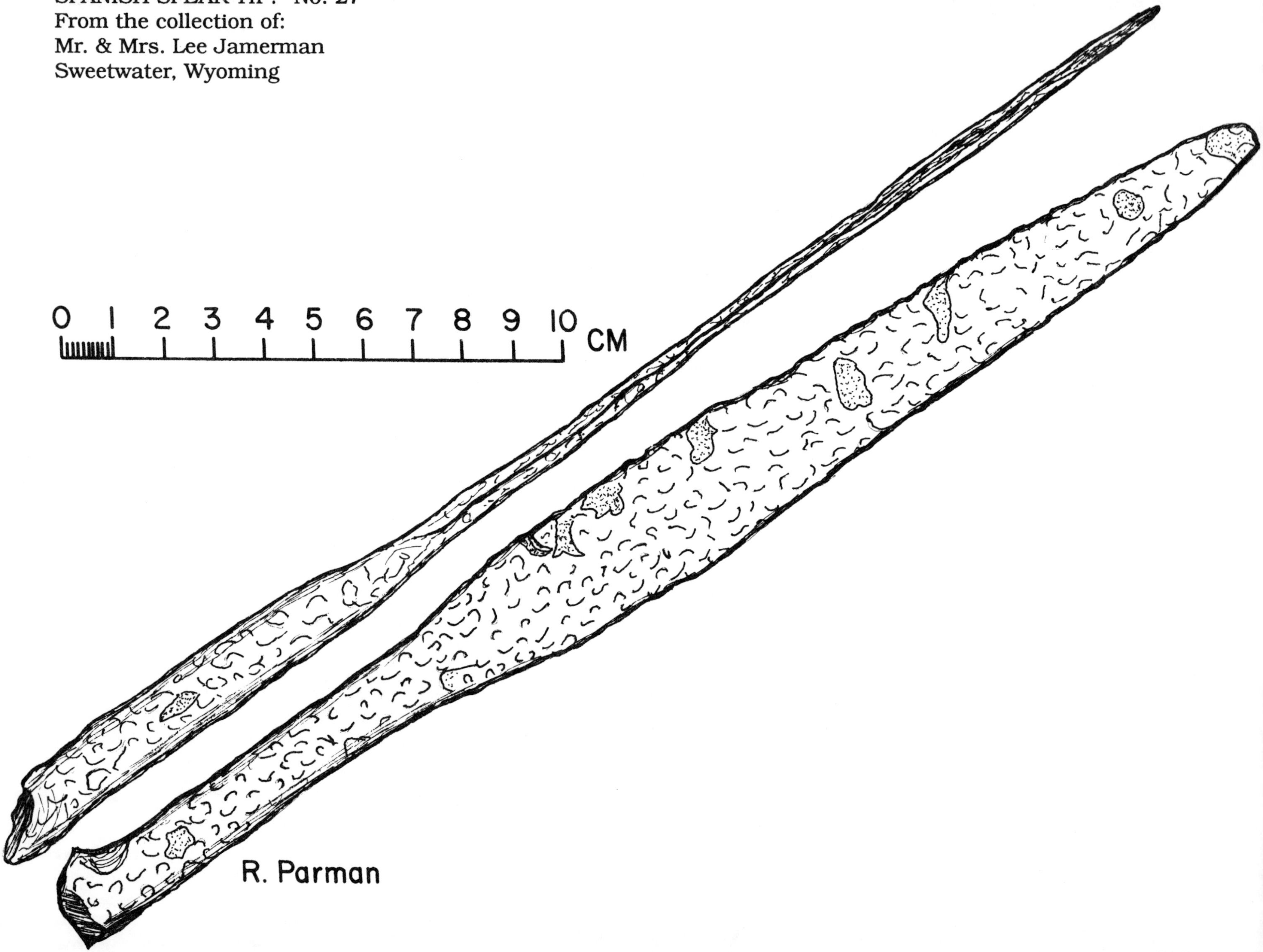

SPANISH SPEAR TIP ?

Color & Material: Very dark brown to black, having a brown cast to the oxide patina. Thought to be cast iron or very low carbon steel.

Location: South central Fremont County, Wyoming.

The author returned to Sweetwater Station just to bring this metal spear tip to the attention of private and professional collectors who might be interested.

Whether or not Spanish explorers came this far north, the appearance of this artifact leads one to believe it is of Spanish origin. Its surface displays the even, dark brown cast of rusted iron. If it had been forged of steel, ground down to a sharp edge and then polished, its surface would have been more susceptible to oxidation (rust) and it probably could not have remained intact.

Overall configuration, lack of forge markings, and the uneven, dimpled surface convince this writer that it was cast in a sand mold. It is most doubtful that Native Americans were capable of casting metals. Were the Spaniards needful of arming their troops and therefore made casts of existing spear tips? Were the casts made by a trading company as trade items? Or, did an early-day village smithy cut a length of steel rod, begin forging a knife and then leave it incomplete to have oxidation bring the artifact to its present configuration?

This artifact should be brought to the attention of someone trained in metallurgy and Spanish weaponry.

KNIFE OF RARE MATERIAL No. 28
From the collection of:
Betty & Hubert Johnson
Powell, Wyoming

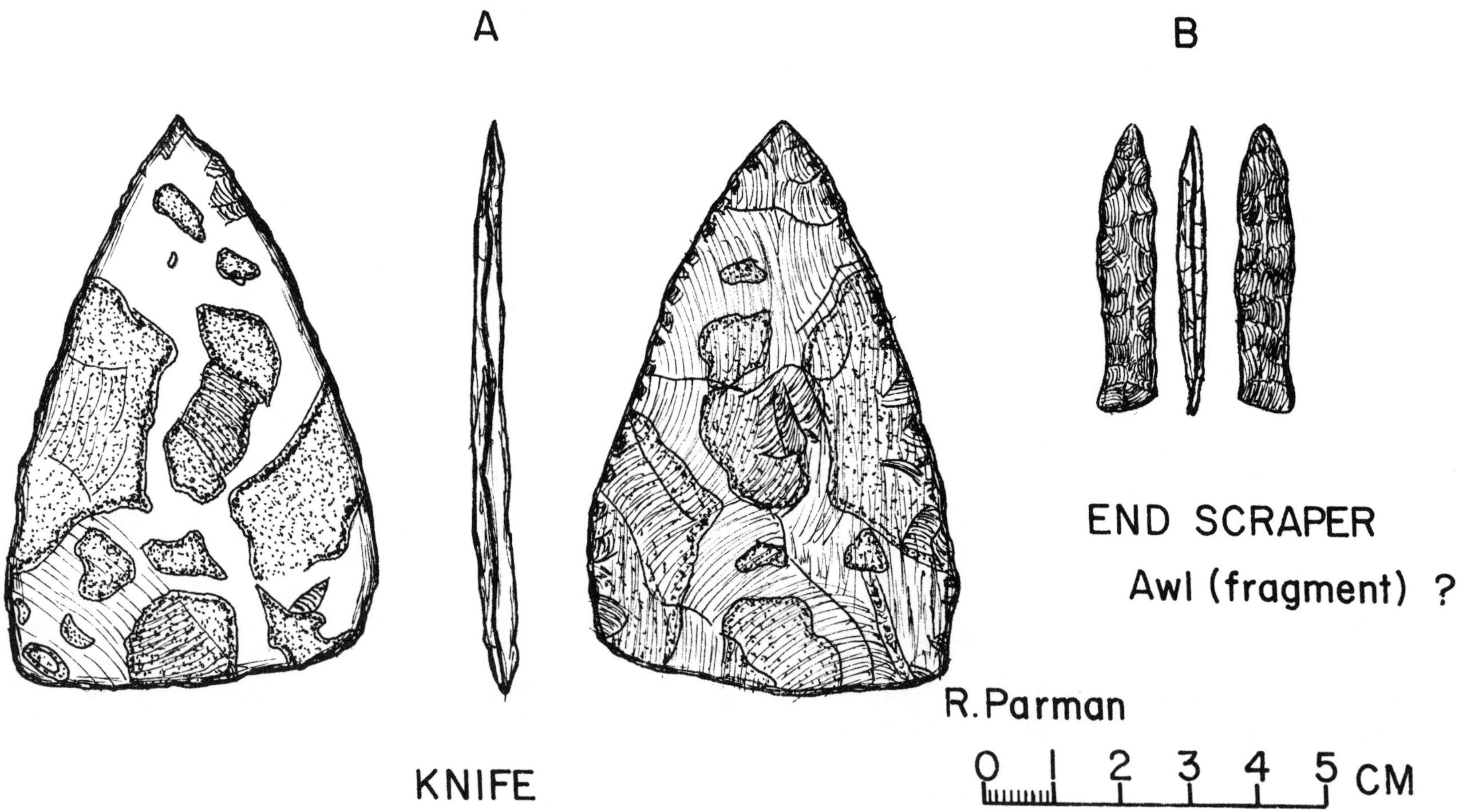

KNIFE OF RARE MATERIAL

Color & Material: Knife, A, white to very light grey, having stain like light brown spotting of irregular shapes. The edges of the spots are dark brown as though fluid moved through porous areas and deposited the brown material at the edges. This would be much like a chromatographic effect. The material is almost glass-like and does not have depth of color. It is probably a form of porcelanite.

Artifact B, pale brown with slight reddish cast and very slight pale yellow washing through one edge and base. Agate.

Location: A, northeast of Rock Springs, Wyoming. B, Big Horn Mountain east of Lovell, Wyoming.

This knife is distinct in both shape and the material used. The craftsmanship is remarkable with more flaking than was possible to depict.

If anyone should recognize this stone and know its source, please write to the Johnsons. Their address is 456 North Douglas, Powell, Wyoming 82435.

Artifact B, is an awl fragment that has been reworked to form a delicate end scraper where the handle of the awl begins to flare out.

UNUSUAL SCRAPER No. 29
From the collection of:
Robert Tresler
Casper, Wyoming

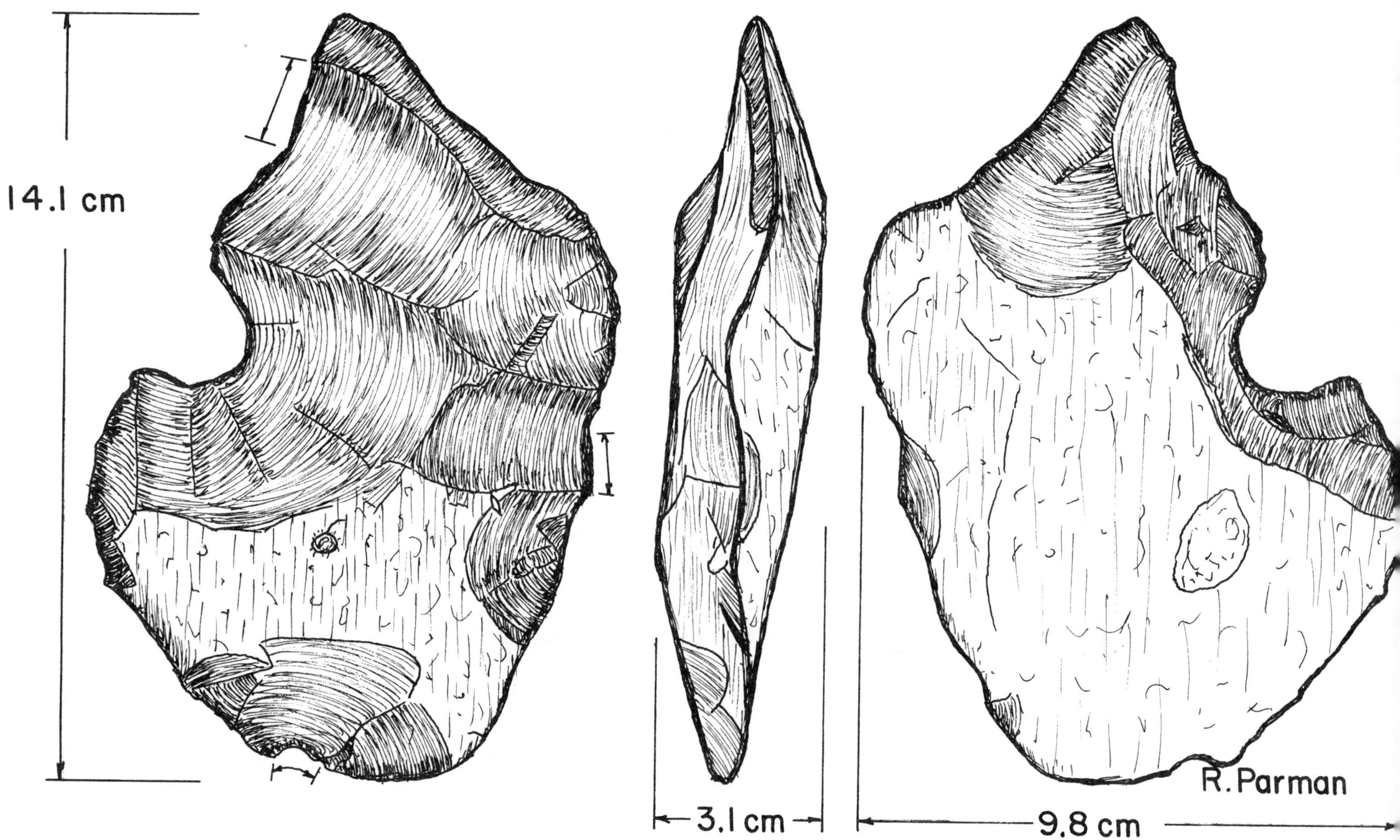

UNUSUAL SCRAPER

Color & Material: Pale tan with very light yellowish grey cast and slightly darker yellowish tan rind. Very fine grain quartzite.

Location: Central Fremont County, Wyoming, on northwest slope of Lost Well Butte.

This scraper could be considered a heavy duty production tool. The deep notch evidences marked wear and has probably been reflaked for sharpening. Three other edges have been used (marked) for scraping also.

This scraper was fashioned from a polished, and slightly bruised, river cobblestone with a great portion of the original surface remaining intact on the side depicted to the right.

Its size leads one to feel this tool was used in a base camp, most likely winter, when inclement weather made long hours available for the production of lance shafts and arrows.

A FAKE ARTIFACT No. 30
From the collection of:
Robert C. Parker family
Casper, Wyoming

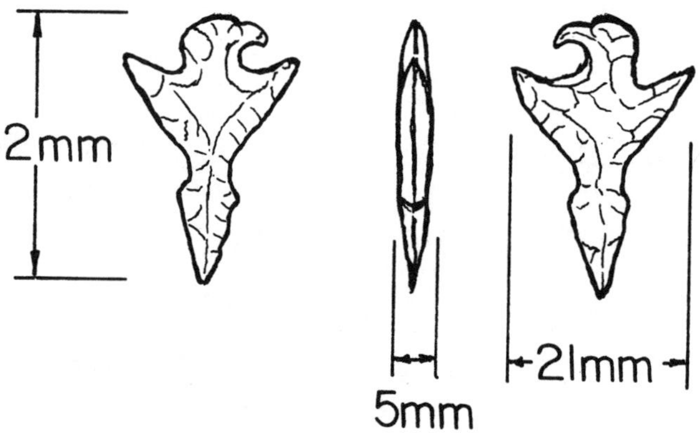

EAGLE EFFIGY
(ceremonial)

A FAKE ARTIFACT

Color & Material: Ruby red, clear flawless glass.

Location: Originally in the collection of the late Horace Evans, who operated the tourist center at Hell's Half Acre west of Casper, Wyoming from the 1930's.

When the author first viewed this "artifact", he accepted it as an authentic eagle effigy, beautifully done, and he speculated that the material, apparently obsidian, could have come from Oregon or Central or South America. We are showing this to remind the collector of the possibility of the counterfeit artifact.

After publishing an article describing this item, the author heard from Robert E. Bergstrom of Lebanon, Oregon, who suggested the effigy was fake. When traveling through the Columbia River region, the author interviewed serveral private collectors and determined the following origin of the piece: (See No. 72)

Shortly after World War ll, a man thought to be a veteran of the war, drifted into Lower Wishram, Washington, on the Columbia River, across from The Dalles, Oregon. He had lost an arm below the elbow, and was permitted to build a shed of scrap lumber against the back wall of the railroad round table in Lower Wishram. He came to have the nickname, "Wing".

For several years, Wing crafted eagles, turtles, and other effigies and artifacts. Some of these were made from the red glass used in railroad lanterns, some from black obsidian and other materials. He sold these to tourists to make his living.

Wing aged his artifacts by placing them in the sand of the floor of his shack. Just by walking on them the sharper edges of the flakes were worn away and the articles were given an authentic looking patina. Three points of his making were sent to the Smithsonian. They were returned with tribal affiliation and age for each of them.

Citizens of Lower Wishram were successful in obtaining veteran's benefits for Wing for the loss of his arm. When these funds arrived Wing departed, leaving no forwarding address.

VERY OLD ARTIFACT No. 31
From the collection of:
Bryce Harmelink
Casper, Wyoming

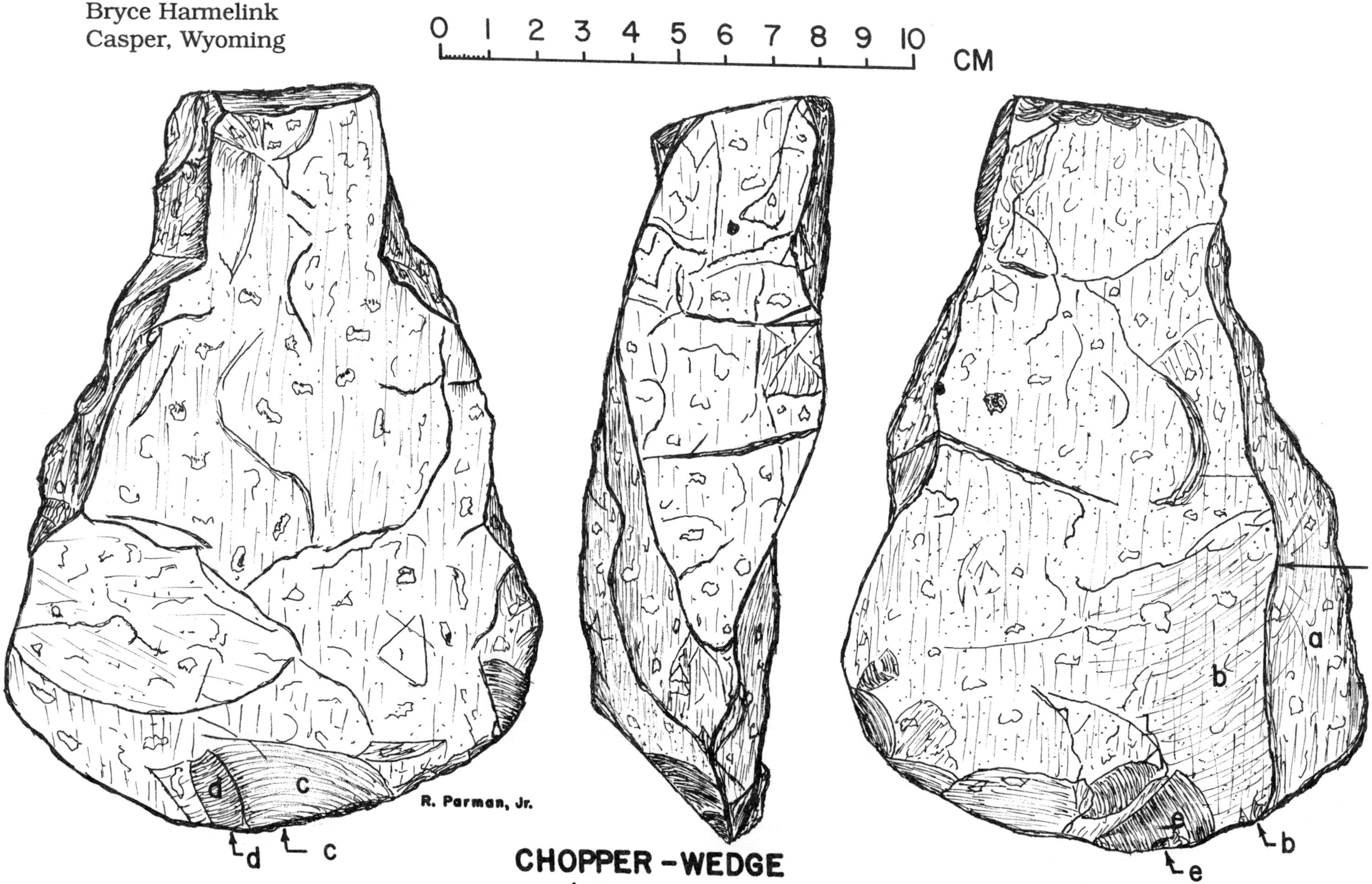

CHOPPER - WEDGE
(VERY OLD)

VERY OLD ARTIFACT

Color & Material: Medium grey with slight blue cast and pale rust orange patina on all surfaces but the left side view. Darker orange staining at three spots: one on the edge view and two on the right side view. Medium to coarse grain, silicious quartzite that is slightly fossil bearing. It has a fracture that has re-cemented (center, left edge of right side view).

Location: Northwest of Douglas, Converse County, Wyoming.

This crude chopper, or wedge, is thought to be very old. Anthropologists and archaeologists have not yet determined how long man has occupied the American continents. The most accepted theory is that he crossed the Bering land bridge from Asia during an ice age. The question now is which ice age?. The time of his crossing is moving back. More evidence is needed.

One author, Jeffrey Goodman, American Genesis, 1981, has put forth the theory that modern man had his origin in Southern California, and that migration across the Bering land bridge did, in fact, take place but with the movement going the other way.

This chopper-wedge, submitted to the author by Bryce Harmelink of Casper, Wyoming, is thought to be one of the oldest appearing tools the author has ever held. It was fashioned from a stone spalled from a large boulder. It appears naturally formed with exception of five flakes (marked a through e) that were removed leaving points of percussion (arrows marked a through e) visible. The pale orange patina has formed on flake surfaces c & d but is not as pronounced on the right side or edges. The convex surface of the left side view is the original surface exposed when the stone was spalled. It has a patina that is only slightly darker than all of the flaked surfaces.

It would have been used as a chopper. It has the form of what is thought to be the first type of tool used by man.

Ronald Dorn, a geographer at Texas Tech University, is doing work on dating artifacts through analysis of the varnish (patina) that forms on the surface of stone. If successful, it might become possible to accurately date this type of artifact.

Its shape indicates possible use as a wedge to cut ligaments binding a joint together. Could this tool have been used to butcher a mammoth?

SCRAPER-FLESHER No. 32
From the collection of:
Forest & Mickey Baskett
Shoshoni, Wyoming

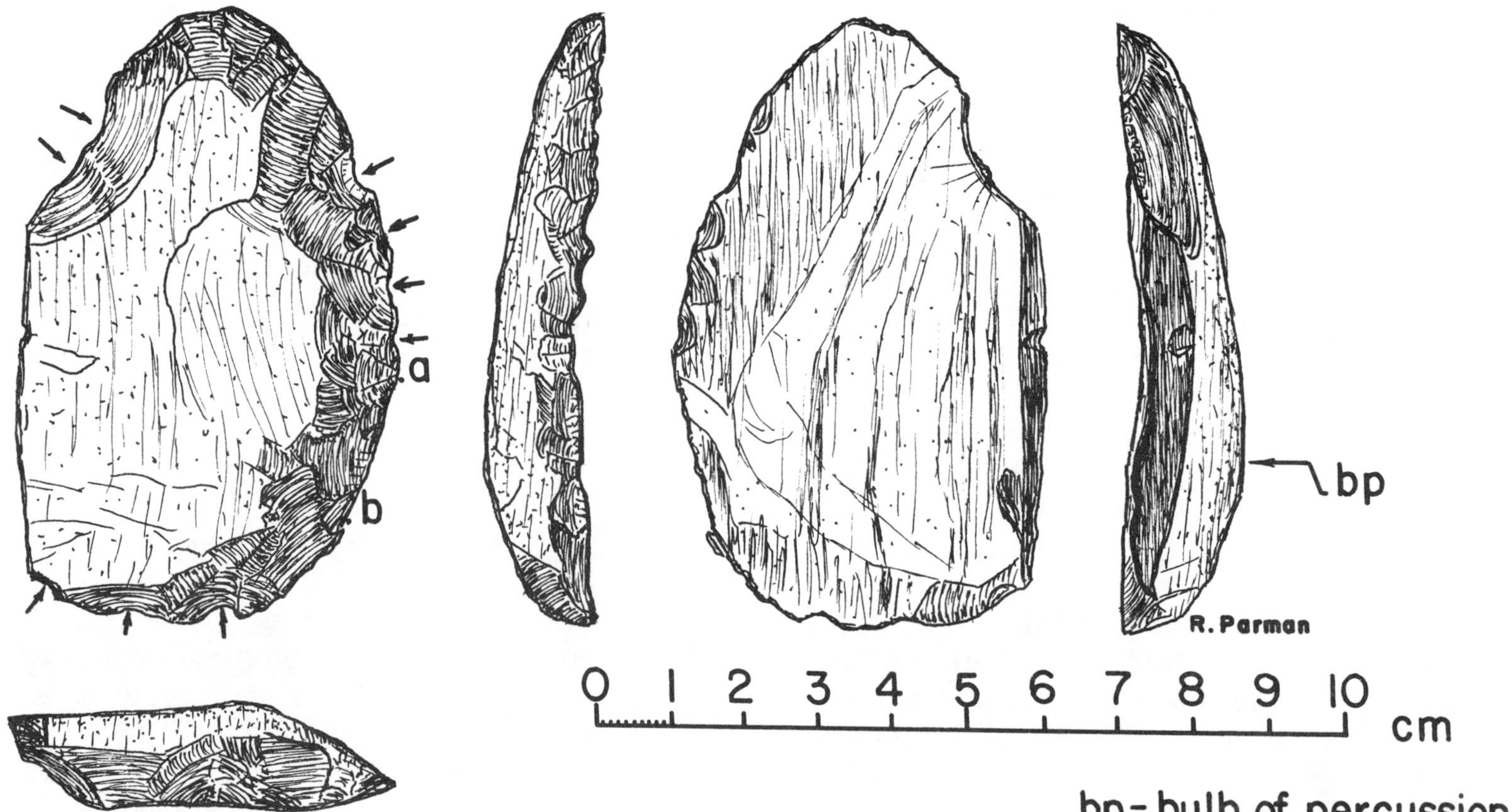

SCRAPER - FLESHER
(multi - use)

SCRAPER-FLESHER

Color & Material: Overall a dull maroon having as many as twenty-seven thin laminae (.5 mm to 2.5 mm thick) visible on the convex surface (left side view), alternating dark maroon and maroon in its lower half, then dark maroon and buff in color for the upper half of the convex surface. An extremely fine grain quartzite, very hard, with the variation in color caused by varied amounts of dark maroon argillaceous (shaley) material in the laminae.

Location: Northeastern Fremont County, Wyoming.

Each time the Basketts till their garden, they bring in new artifacts. This unusual tool seems to fit a pattern of those found in a sheltered, winter camp, where long hours would have been spent preparing hides for clothing and other articles. It is believed this type of campsite occured in the area.

This artifact has been crafted from a flake struck from a core. The bulb of percussion has been indicated (bp). There are six larger notches and three smaller with all evidencing wear. The edge of the smaller, rounded end, and two centimeters of edge (ab) show wear as a scraper.

Preparation of hides might have caused this wear and the notches of varied sizes could have scraped leather thongs for sewing.

Three other artifacts have been submitted by the Basketts and they appear later in this volume.

POSSIBLE SANDIA I POINT No. 33
From the collection of:
John W. Larsen
Rawlins, Wyoming

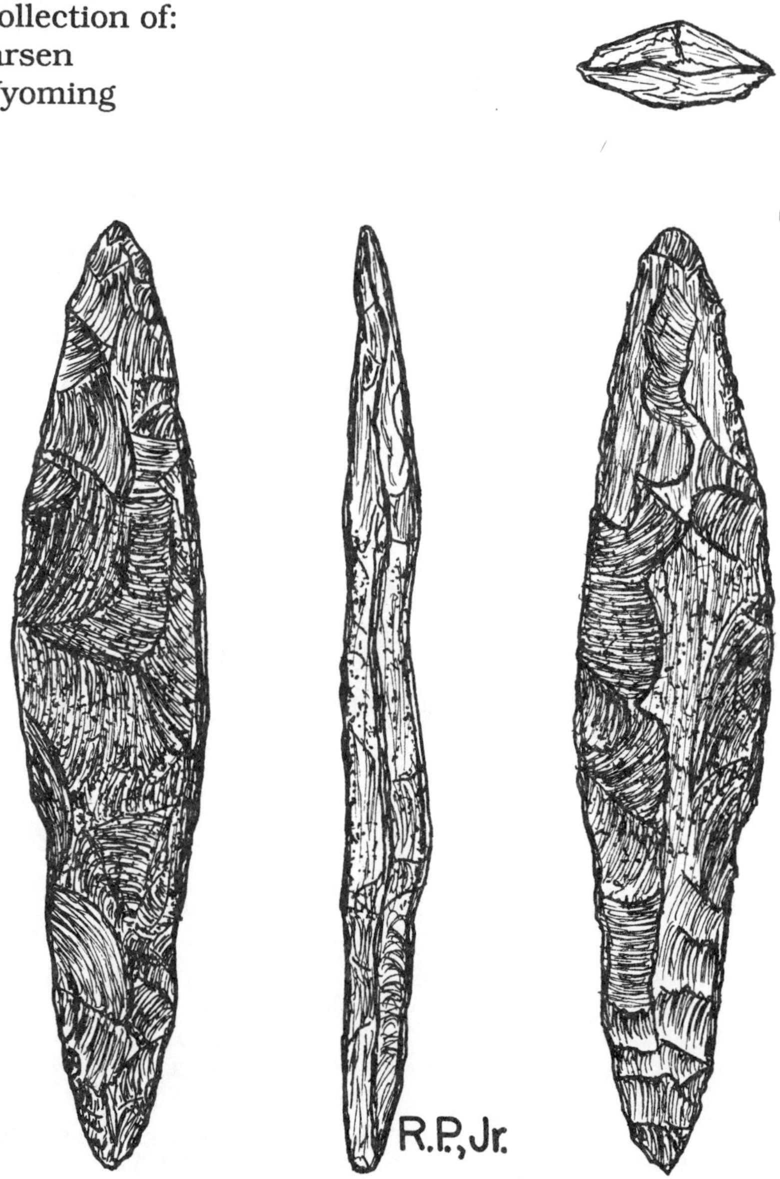

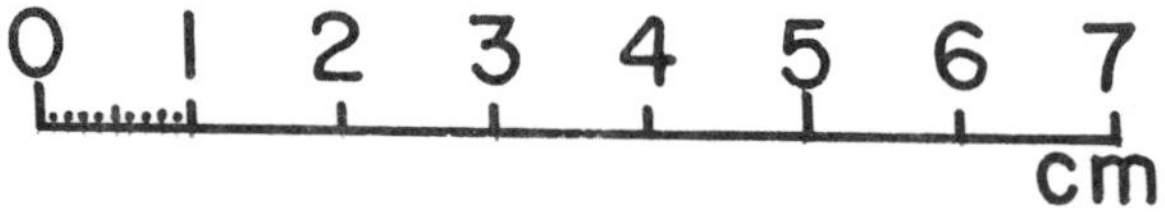

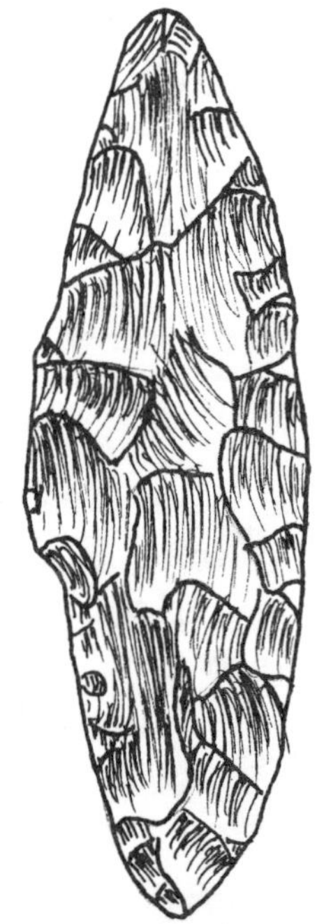

TYPE EXAMPLE
(Hibben, 1946-pl. 11e)

POSSIBLE SANDIA I POINT

Color & Material: Flat, bone white with dull light greyish tan patina. Chalcedony or chertlike material.

Location: Southwest corner of Carbon County, Wyoming.

Mr. & Mrs. Larsen have been collecting artifacts for sixty-one years, and they have assembled a most extensive collection. One is aware of a feeling of wonder as eyes travel along row after row of neatly arranged Native American artifacts of all types.

The distinct, asymetrical shape of the Sandia I point drew my attention to this artifact instantly. Its display of Sandia characteristics (crude, large flaking with minor amount of secondary chipping, no basal thinning, flat oval cross section), readily convinces one holding it that it is indeed a Sandia I point.

Another feature reinforces this identification. The material used to craft this point had a band of minute inclusions through its middle half. In the time that has passed since this point was crafted, these inclusions have eroded leaving pinpoint porosity where they were exposed to the surface. The depth of this porosity is equal on all surfaces of both sides whether flaked or not. This would indicate that the entire surface of the point was brought to its present configuration at essentially the same time. Recently, a tiny flake was accidentally chipped from the edge, exposing a near white material immediately beneath the surface.

The Sandia I projectile point has been named from discoveries at the Sandia Cave, 25 miles northeast of Albuquerque, New Mexico, during excavations over a period from 1936 to 1940 (Hibben, 1941). The point was associated in the same deposits with bones of extinct species of horse, bison, camel, mastodon, and mammoth. Radiocarbon dating suggested an age of 20,000 years ago. Positive identification of Sandia I points will almost necessitate discovery in association with extinct animal remains.

The author wishes to thank Mr. Larsen for permitting publication of this rare point. A large portion of this fine collection is displayed in the family hardware store in downtown Rawlins, Wyoming. If you are by that way, make it a point to stop in and see it.

COMBINATION BURIN-SCRAPER No. 34
From the collection of:
Ray Parman, Jr.
Riverton, Wyoming

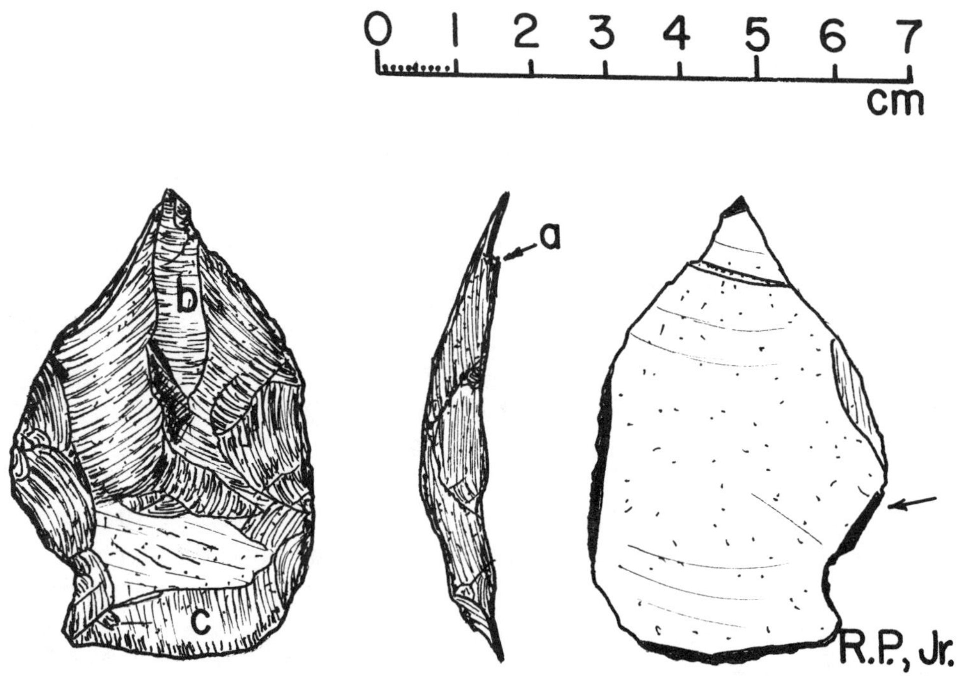

COMBINATION BURIN-SCRAPER

Color & Material: Light blue-grey with faint, light tan washed inclusions and very light yellow cast patina. Black pin-point inclusions throughout. Chert.

Location: South of Rawlins, Carbon County, Wyoming.

This tool was fashioned from a percussion flake of chert where a fracture plane had caused the marked thinning of one end (a). Subsequently a pressure flake (b) was removed, reducing the burin point to needle sharpness. Another flake (c) was removed from the larger, rounded end bringing it to a thin, translucent edge not more than one millimeter thick, five millimeters back from the edge.

All flaking of the tool occured on the convex side only. The concave surface has not been altered other than well defined wear surfaces (darkened areas of the right side view) along the edges. It was these wear surfaces that caused this simple tool to be selected for publication.

All of the edges showing wear from use, including the burin point, have three things in common: 1. The wear surfaces are polished. 2. There are tiny nicks along the edges, some new and others almost polished away. 3. All of the wear surfaces have well defined lines of separation between the natural surfaces and the worn, polished areas of wear.

The surface worked by this tool had to be sufficiently ridged to form the line of separation mentioned, yet soft enough to polish chert. Leather and wood would polish chert but would not form the line. Hard stone would form the line and cause the nicks, but would scratch rather than polish chert. It was at this point that steatite (soapstone) came to mind. A call to Mr. Osbourne determined that shards of a steatite bowl had been found in the area. The talc in soapstone would polish chert and the impurities contained in it would cause the nicks.

The fine point of the burin displays a single plane of wear, indicating that the tool was held in the right hand with its long axis parallel to the thumb, which was held against the concave surface. The burin point would extend about 1.5 centimeters beyond the end of the thumb. The point was then drawn along the surface being worked in a direction toward the thumb. In the case of a steatite pot, the point was drawn along the inside surface of the pot from the bottom upward. The point of the tool would be used to

COMBINATION BURIN-SCRAPER No. 34
From the collection of:
Ray Parman, Jr.
Riverton, Wyoming

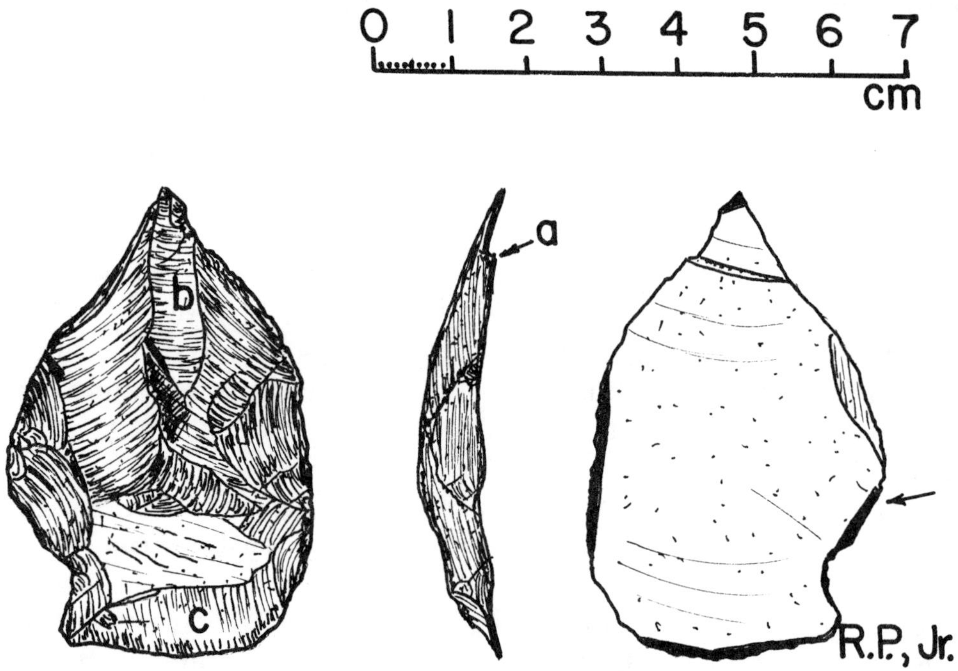

cut numerous parallel grooves, weakening the surface of the steatite. The tool would then be rotated so that the wide, gently curved edge could be used to scrape away the weakened area of the surface. All of the working edges of this tool could have been used to shape either the inside or outside contours of a steatite bowl, cup, or pot.

Months later, the author discovered that this tool was used to create the steatite pan described in No. 78. These two artifacts were then given to the author by Jim Osbourne, with the words, "Ray, you discovered these went together; you deserve to have them".

SCRAPER No. 35
From the collection of:
Forest & Mickey Baskett
Shoshoni, Wyoming

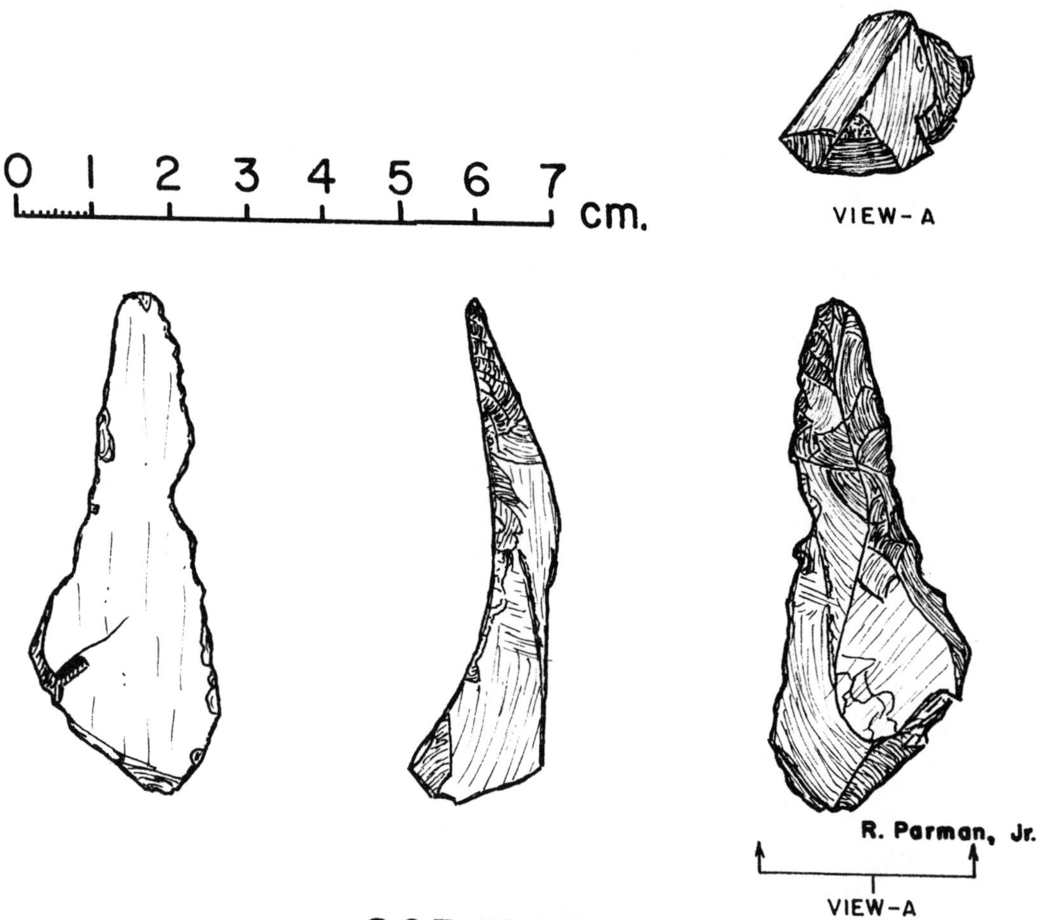

SCRAPER
(multi - use)

SCRAPER

Color & Material: Chocolate brown with pale off-white wash through the larger end. Several small, bone-white inclusions. Agate.

Location: Fremont County, Wyoming. Northeast of Bonneville.

This is another tool from the Baskett's garden. It has been crafted from a percussion flake taken from a core. Fracture planes within the agate have caused many flat surfaces that are apparent in View-A (upper right). Nearly all of the circumference of the left side view shows marked wear and chipping from use as a scraper. The small, narrow end is blunted, nicked and slightly polished from use.

It would be interesting to know just how this scraper was used. If someone has a suggestion, please write to the author.

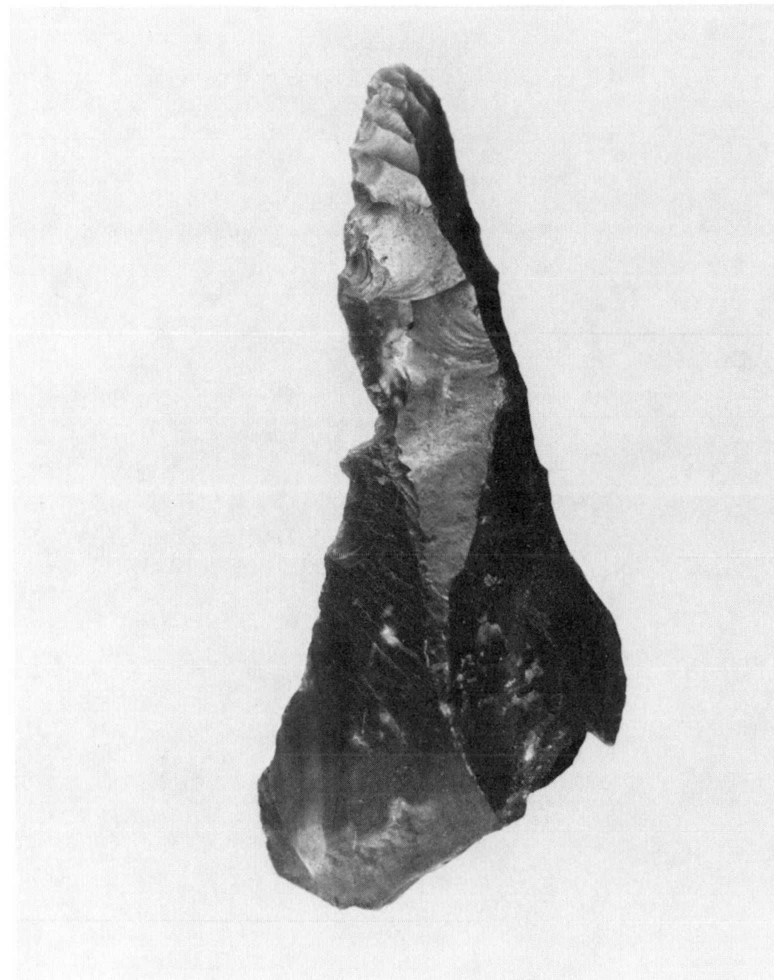

SMALL UNUSUAL FINDS No. 36
From the collection of:
John W. Larsen
Rawlins, Wyoming

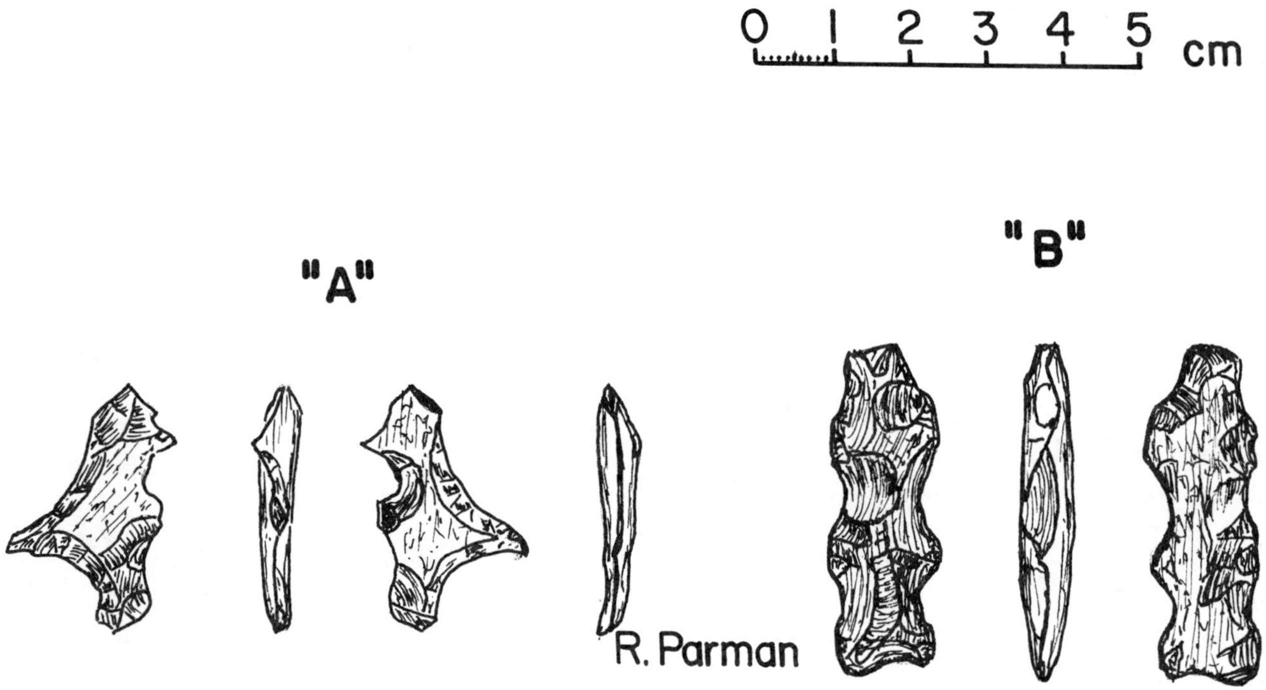

BURIN - AWL

SCRAPER

SMALL UNUSUAL FINDS

Color & Material: Artifact A, light tan with very slight, pale orange cast. Fine-grain quartzite.

Artifact B, dark, calf-liver brown with a very slight yellow-green cast to a thin patina covering the entire piece. A jasperlike agate.

Location: Artifacts A & B, southwest corner of Carbon County, Wyoming. South of Wamsutter.

The small, delicate burin, or awl, has five curved scraping surfaces evidencing wear. The small burin point and the larger one, that could have been used as an awl (or drill), both show some wear though the tip of the awl has been broken. Its small size makes one wonder what it was used for.

The artifact labeled as a scraper (under the drawing) could have been used in that manner; however, it has been discovered that the configuration is that of a centipede effigy.

The bulges are opposite each other. If they had been offset in a zigzag pattern from one side to the other with one end enlarged, it would have been a lightning effigy. The enlarged end would represent the thunder cloud.

It was first thought that the wear, evident in the bottoms, was from use as a scraper. It is now thought to be the product of the manner in which the artifact was crafted.

A RARE, BEAUTIFUL, CEREMONIAL CRESCENT No. 37
From the collection of:
Patt Brown
Riverton Wyoming

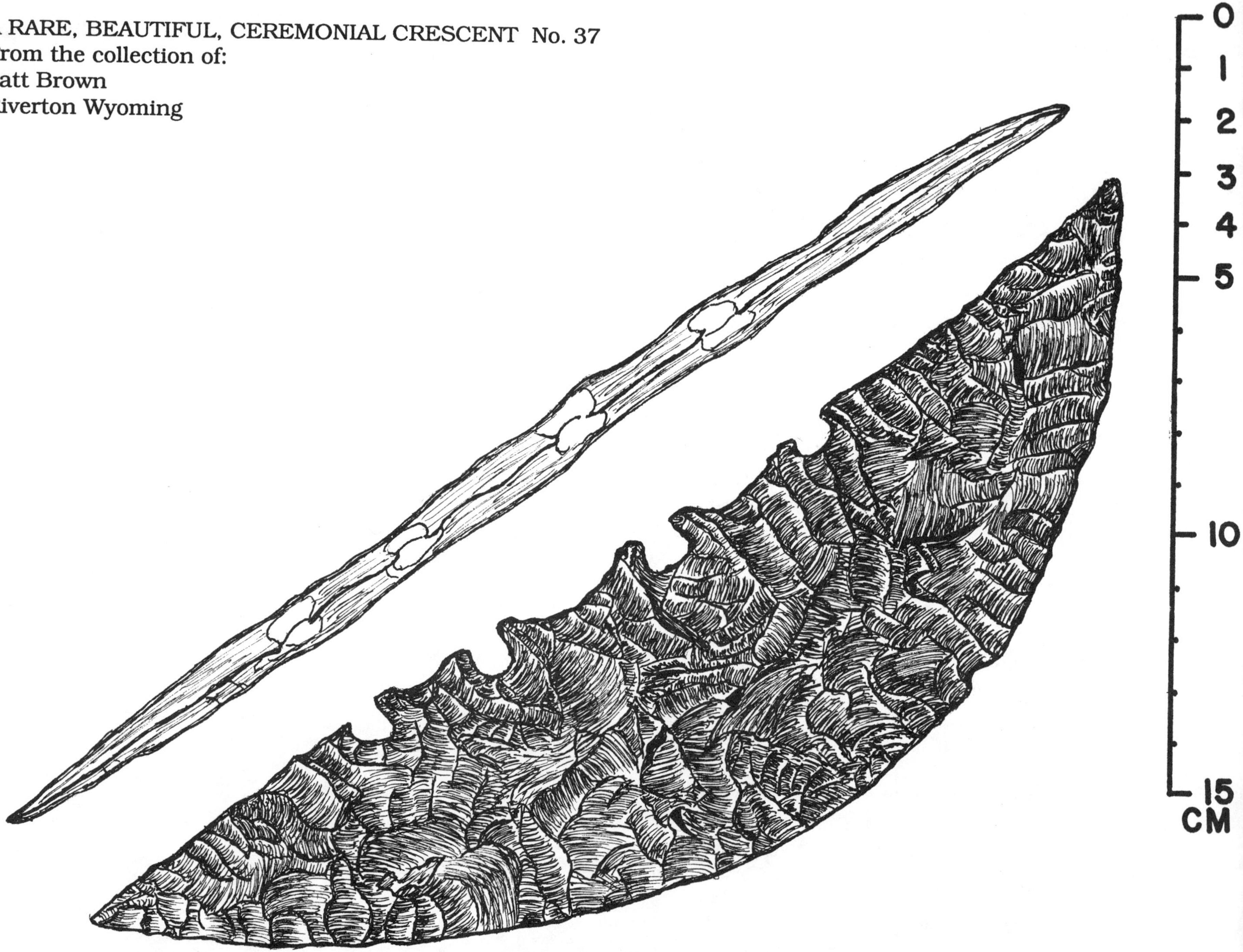

CEREMONIAL CRESCENT
(Probably Comanche)

A RARE, BEAUTIFUL, CEREMONIAL CRESCENT

Color & Material: Light greyish tan with slender, slightly darker tan wash. Quartzite or orthoquartzite.

Location: Northwest of Punkin Center, Colorado. East of Colorado Springs.

This beautiful artifact was a surface find by an acquaintance of Patt Brown of Riverton, Wyoming, who subsequently sold it to her, saying "It isn't a very pretty rock." Patt had assisted this person in sending photos and data to the Smithsonian Institute and they had received a reply before the sale price was agreed upon. Quoting Patt..."When a price was asked, I drove there very quickly."

The Smithsonian has indicated this crescent shaped artifact is probably "ceremonial", "Comanche", and dates from "early to mid 1800".

The size, beautiful craftsmanship, and symmetry all blend to make this a truly rare artifact. Thankfully, an acrylic cast was available for the art work, Even then I envisioned this beautiful object sliding from the work table and shattering on the floor.

Artifacts of this nature, and the eagle effigy described in No. 65, are often the work of shops devoted to the manufacture of fakes, solely for monetary gain. Though it is possible these are of that source, in view of the Smithsonian (from photographs) having indicated this one as probably of Comanche origin and it having been taken as a surface find in open flats, five miles from anywhere, onc must lean toward this being a true artifact. Therefore, the effigy described in No. 65 would be authentic as well.

The trading posts of the late 1700's and early 1800's supplied native Americans of all tribes with many items. Western fiction has devoted many pages to "whiskey and guns" trade, but there were also pots, pans, tobacco, blankets, cloth, teepee covers of heavy duck, and many more items. Could it have been possible that the Comanche set up their own shop to turn out these objects solely for trade? It is highly possible.

A RARE, OLD SANDIA I POINT No. 38
From the collection of:
Helen Lookingbill
Riverton, Wyoming

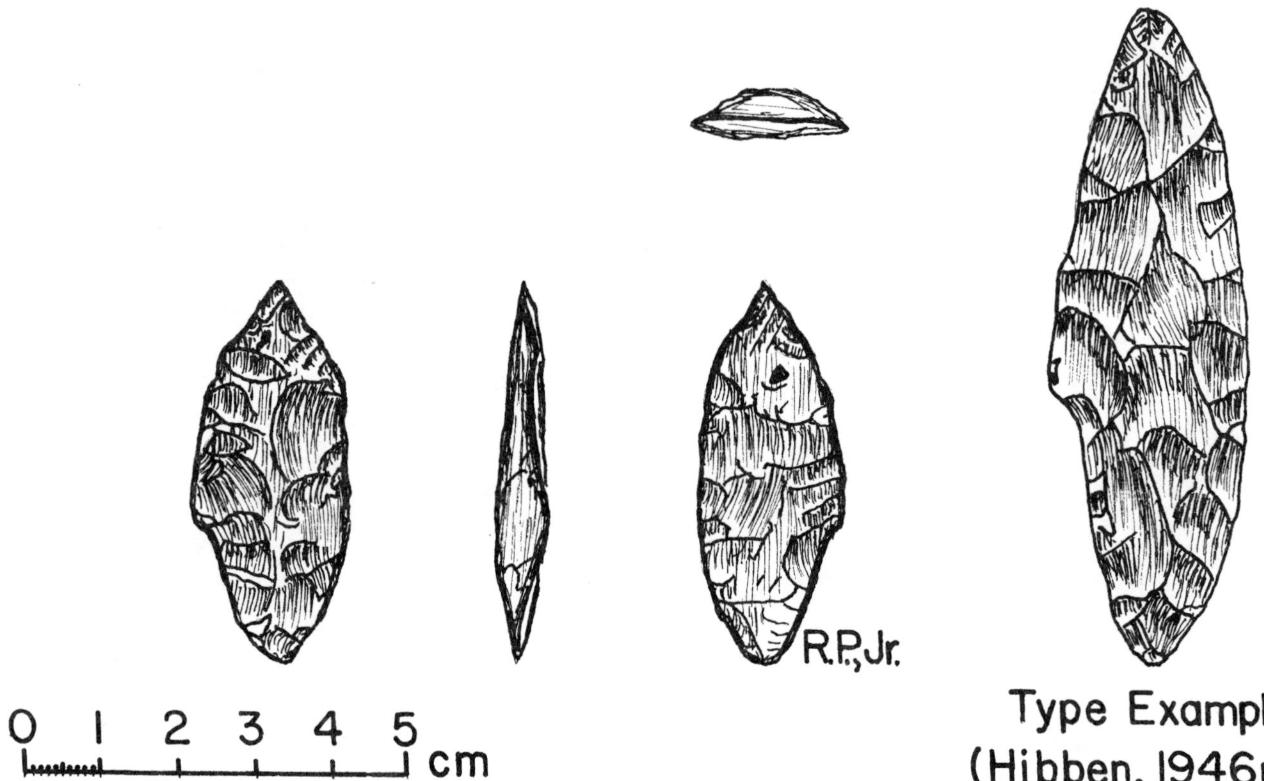

Type Example
(Hibben, 1946 pl. II,b)

SANDIA I POINT
(possible 20,000 years old)

A RARE, OLD SANDIA I POINT

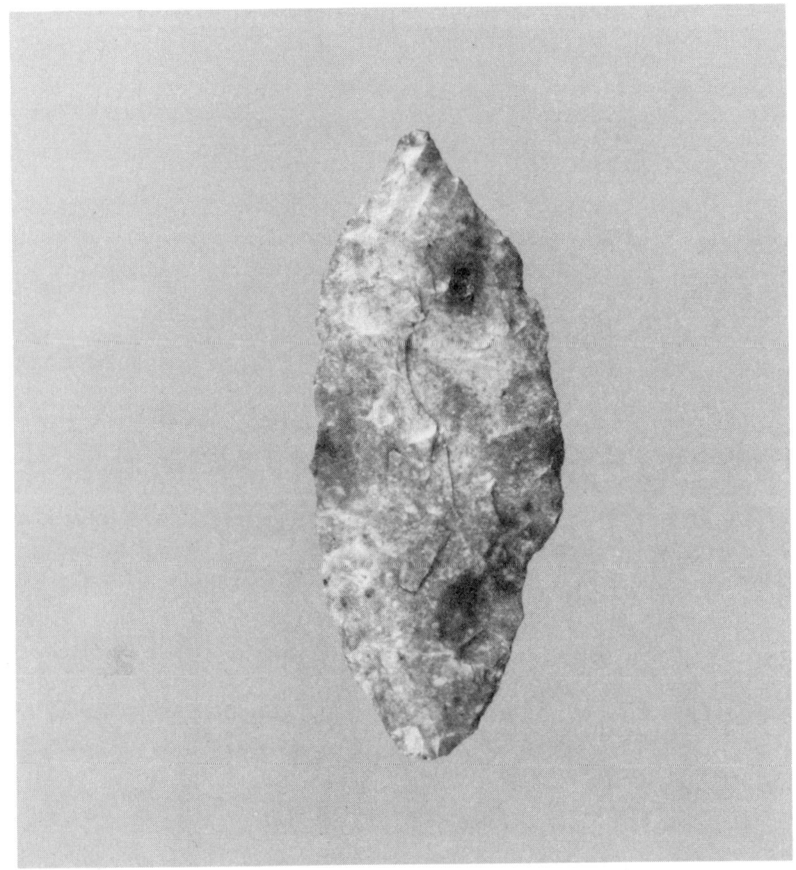

Color & Material: Light blue grey with pale, bone-white intrusions. Two tiny rust stained pore spaces. Orthoquartzite with chalcedony intrusion.

Location: This point was a surface find by Helen Lookingbill's son, Bud Lookingbill, while he was working in southwestern Arizona in 1980.

Though it is smaller than the example to the right, the average quality, gross flaking, the distinctive asymmetrical profile, and a patina evenly covering all surfaces of the point lead one to feel this is truly a Sandia I point.

The Sandia I point was named from specimens taken from the Sandia Cave excavations (Hibben, 1941), 25 miles northeast of Albuquerque, New Mexico. Points of this type were found associated in the same deposit with remains of extinct horse, bison, camel, mastodon, and mammoth. Positive identification must be reserved for specimens taken in the above manner.

Radiocarbon dates based upon an analysis of antler from the Sandia Cave deposit suggest an age of about 20,000 years. Therefore, the Sandia I point represents one of the oldest artifacts of man in the New World (*Guide to the Identification of Certain American Indian Projectile Points*, Robert E. Bell, 1958).

DETAILING TECHNIQUES No. 39
From the collection of:
Ray Parman, Jr.
Riverton, Wyoming

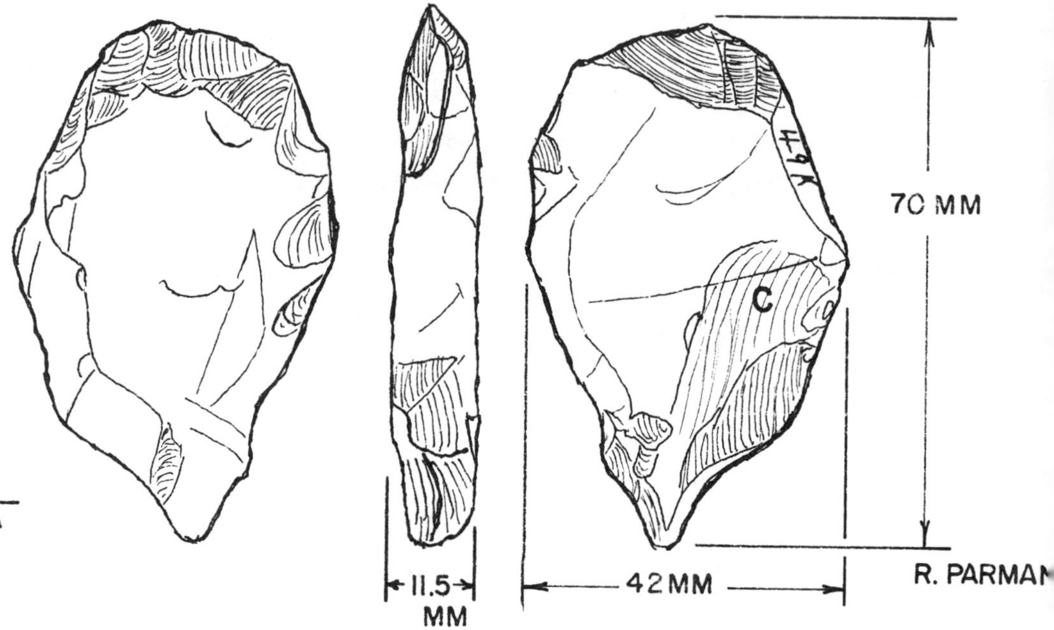

FLESHER OR UNFINISHED KNIFE

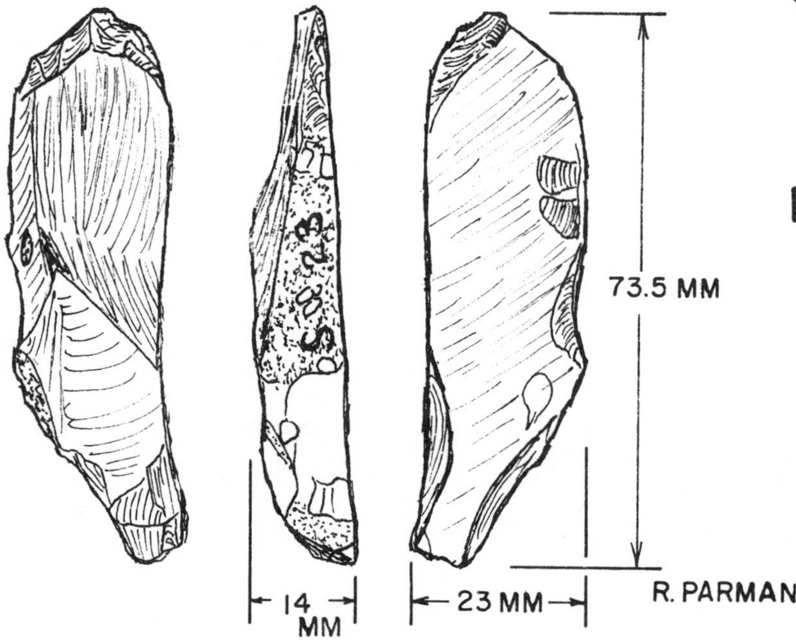

END SCRAPER

DETAILING TECHNIQUES

Color & Material: End scraper, dull brown with slight maroon cast and pale yellow-green patina (very near a rind) thinly covering all surfaces. Jasper.

Flesher, pale grey with very slight green cast. Tan to light brown rind on unflaked surfaces and very light tan patina on flaked areas. Jasper.

Location: Both, west of Lysite; Fremont County, Wyoming.

These artifacts were selected from the author's collection, not only for possible interest in them, but also for their special features that illustrate terms used in this book.

In describing the color and material of these tools the words rind and patina have been used. Patina may be so thin as to be difficult to see. Usually the patina is lighter in color than the material on which it is formed, e.g., "dull brown with slight maroon cast and pale yellow-green patina...". Patina may also be called "rock varnish". Rind is thicker and usually it is opaque and totally hides the color of the material on which it has formed. It is the product of an actual chemical alteration of the material (or the hydration and oxidation of the surface of the material). The word "cast" has been used to describe, as accurately as possible, the color of the material beneath the patina.

The material of both of these tools has been called jasper. Some might view these and say "chert". Others, "flint". I cannot strike a collector's treasured point against steel to see if sparks occur. That is the only way I know of determining whether a stone is flint, or not. I must go by what might be called "depth of color". Chert, agate, and chalcedony usually (certainly not always) display color that seems to come from below the surface. To me, both jasper and flint have color coming from only the surface (or very near so).

Soon after they were crafted, both of these artifacts were exposed for a long time to wind blown sand. This action rounded the ridges between flakes, and polished all surfaces. This is why they are in my collection. They are thought to be very old.

The author has given the numbers, S23 and 49K, as his own catalog numbers. Anyone collecting artifacts should always prepare an index card which should record: 1, symbol and number (placed on the artifact in ink); 2, color

DETAILING TECHNIQUES No. 39
From the collection of:
Ray Parman, Jr.
Riverton, Wyoming

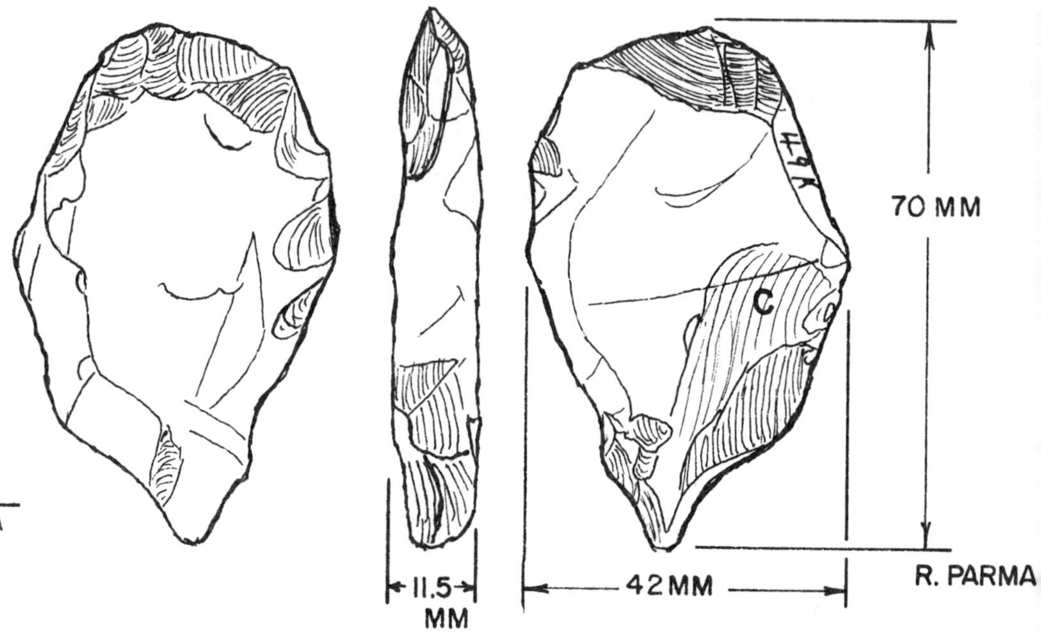

FLESHER OR UNFINISHED KNIFE

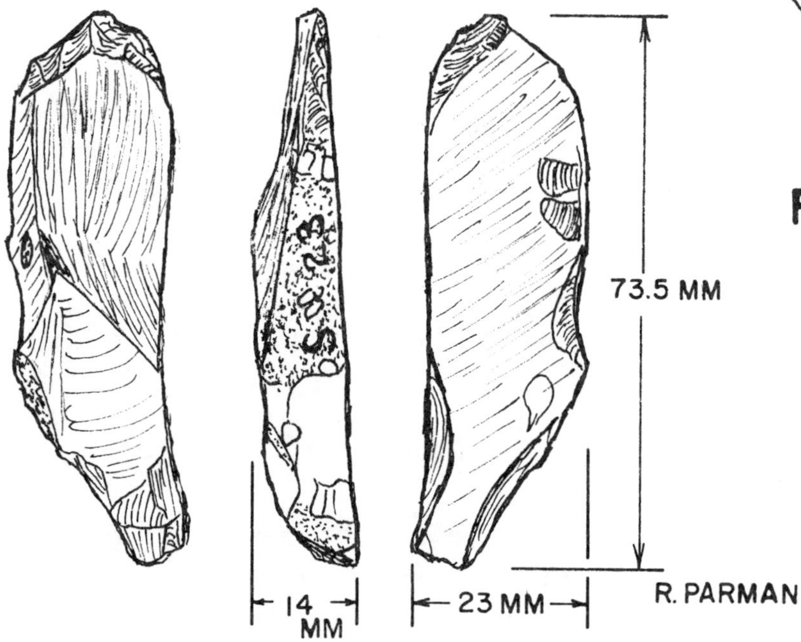

END SCRAPER

and material; 3. location; 4, dimensions; and 5, remarks. One may not realize how important it is to do this. In the future, there will be dating techniques beyond imagination, and surface finds will play an important, and vital role in recording our past.

Back to the tools. More recently, both must have lain either buried or well protected from wind-blown sand for the patina to have begun forming. These tools also display many surfaces that have not been flaked by man. Only the ends of the scraper (left side view) and the larger end of the flesher, evidence the flaking. Natural surfaces rarely occur on artifacts that are crafted from flakes struck from a core, or from stone taken from a quarry. In the case of the end scraper, the edge view in the center and a small area in the left side view display natural surfaces.

The balance of the unflaked surface of the scraper is relatively smooth, and I have used rapidly drawn, sweeping lines to illustrate this. While the right side view has relatively straight lines to designate a flat surface, the left side view uses slightly curved lines to show contour.

In contrast, the flesher has been crafted from a stone found lying on the ground. At one time, hundreds of thousands of years ago (or even hundreds of millions), the mineral formation containing the material of this stone was under great pressure from the formations above it. With the uplifting of mountains, this dense, brittle material shattered. The formations that were above it eroded away, exposing this shattered formation. Since then, fragments have been moved by flooding waters, drifting sand, sliding glaciers, and by Native Americans.

This particular stone had a hard time of it. We can tell it has been nicked at different times through a very long past, because each nick has a different amount of rind formed over it. The entire unflaked surface of the flesher is covered by a tan to light brown rind. What caught the author's attention was the number of flakes, seemingly removed by man, that have varied amounts of rind; and the fact that the last flakes removed by man bear the patina of time. The artifact last mentioned has also been called an "unfinished knife". The author's conjecture yields the following narration:

Note the almost straight line across the middle of the right side view of the unfinished knife. It depicts a fine, hairline fracture that does not extend to the edges. At first the author thought it had been drawn there, and tried to erase it.

It is the author's belief that a native began crafting a knife from the stone he had found. He

DETAILING TECHNIQUES No. 39
From the collection of:
Ray Parman, Jr.
Riverton, Wyoming

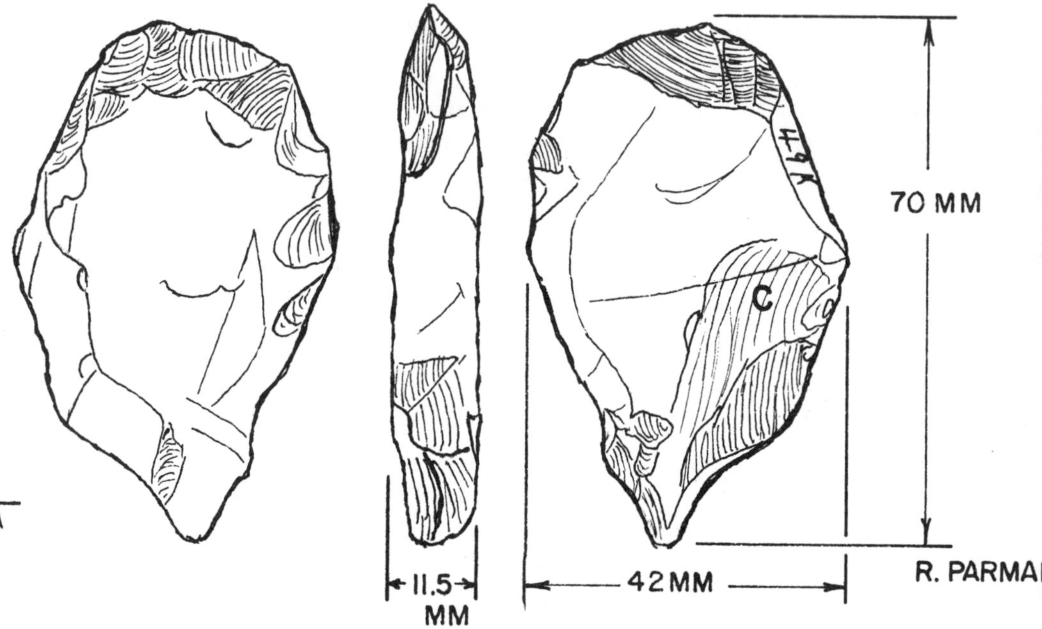

FLESHER OR UNFINISHED KNIFE

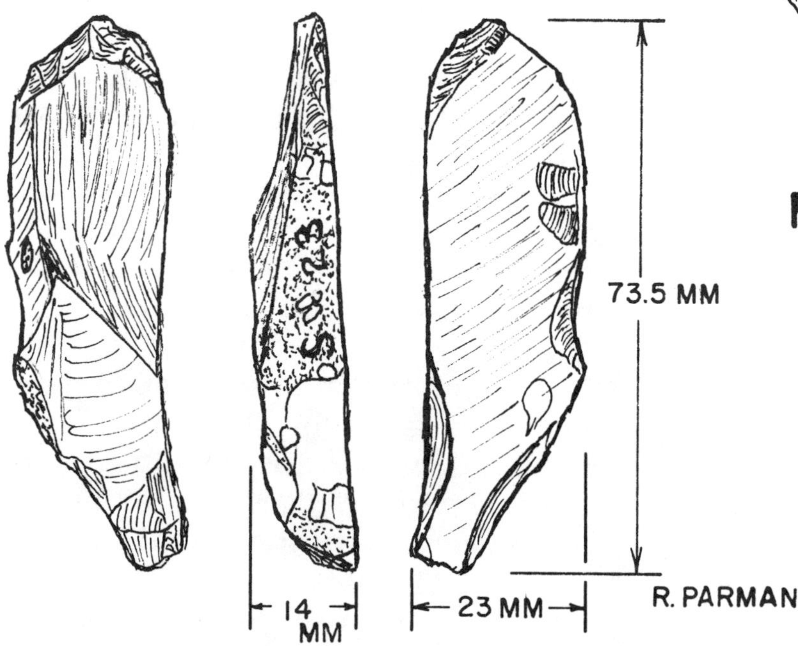

END SCRAPER

removed all the flakes illustrated and when flake "C" was struck off, he discovered the fracture extended quite deeply into the stone and realized that if he continued flaking the knife, the stone would break. He discarded it possibly twenty thousand years ago. Just to know that he too had held it in his hand, and that his eyes studied the characteristics of the stone as closely as the author has now, is most rewarding. To have become aware of his sense of dismay as he discovered that a minute fracture made the stone worthless, was really astonishing.

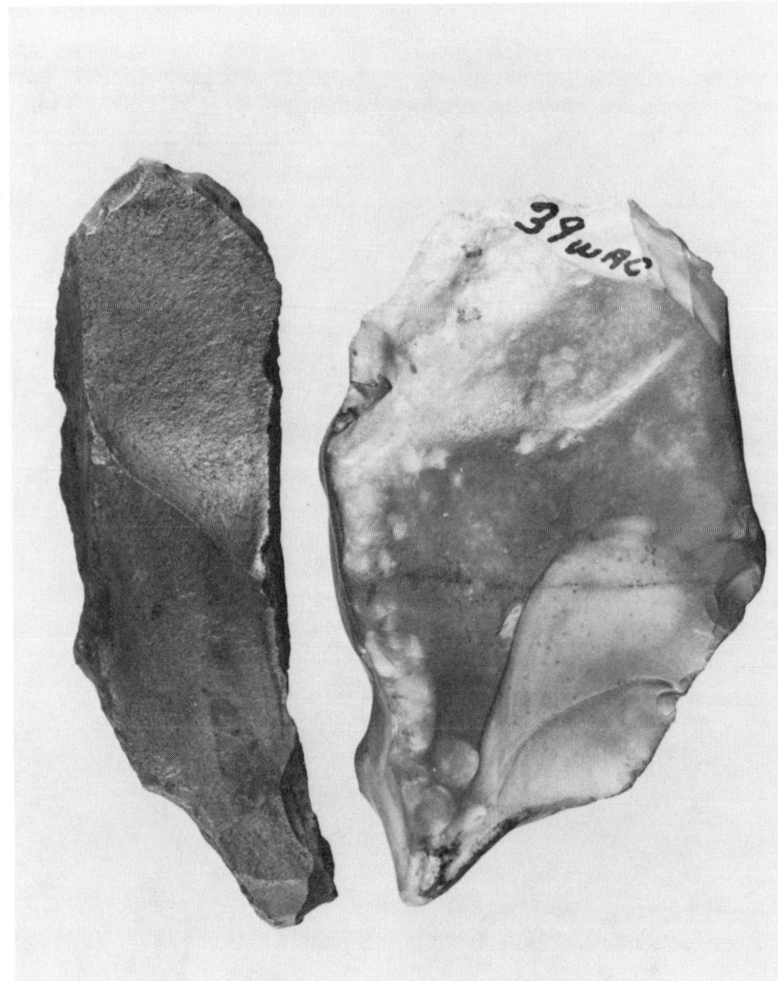

AN ASTONISHING DISCOVERY No. 40
From the collection of:
Dave & Teri Klippert
Casper, Wyoming

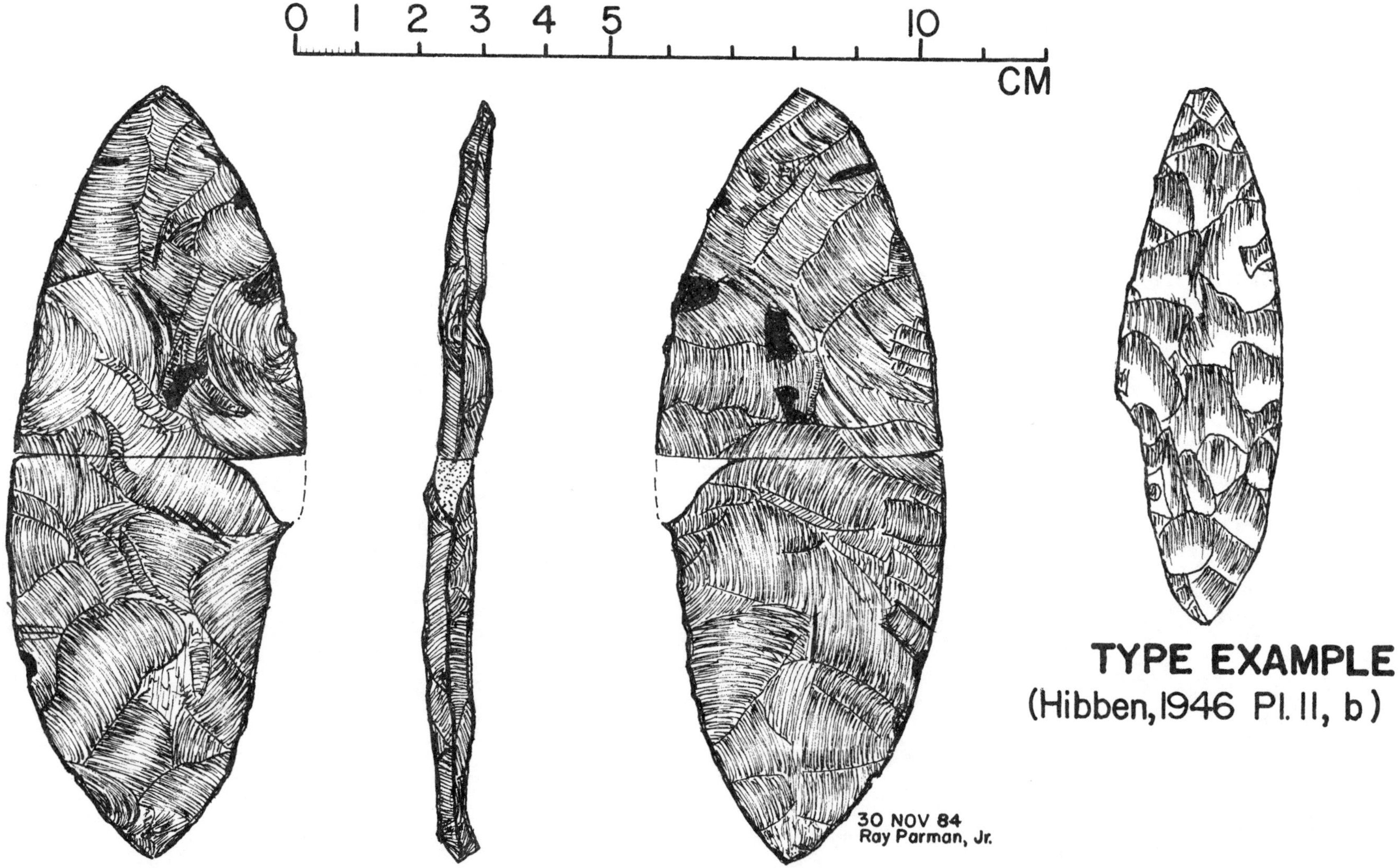

TYPE EXAMPLE
(Hibben, 1946 Pl. II, b)

SANDIA I ? PROBABLE

AN ASTONISHING DISCOVERY

Color & Material: Translucent tan to light brown with very slight maroon and light yellow cast. Indistinct, bonewhite washes and inclusions. Lower three-fourths of lower fragment has thin, light greyish white rind or heavy patina over all surfaces. Upper fourth and upper fragment do not have this rind and colors bright. Orthoquartzite with numerous chalcedony inclusions of varied size and shape. The lower (thought to have been buried) fragment, with rind, displays several dark, pinpoint inclusions just under the surface that are probably due to prolonged wetting that would occur just under the surface.

Location: West central Natrona County, Wyoming.

On October 21, 1984, Dave and Teri Klippert of Casper, Wyoming, submitted to the author excellent photos and descriptive sketches of what appeared to be two beautiful, broken knives. On November 27th the author stopped by their home to do the preliminary sketches and determine the color and material of the two knife fragments. The two were displayed as separate artifacts and the rind on one effectively masked it's true colors. While holding the first fragment in sunlight, the author wrote down its color and material. While holding the second fragment, the author ignored the rind and realized that the material was from the same quarry. It was at that moment, that the two fragments were brought together, and it was found that there was a single artifact involved. The asymmetrical profile of a Sandia I point leaped out and pushed the adrenaline button hard.

These two beginning collectors, with only a small collection, were thrilled to find that they now have one of the oldest known artifacts of man in the New World. Photographs and drawings by the author, along with a description of the knife, were sent to the Smithsonian. Their response indicated that it could not be confirmed as a Sandia artifact, because it had not been found associated with the remains of extinct animals.

The following are the features of the Sandia I point as listed in "Guide to the Identification of Certain American Indian Projectile Points", by Robert E. Bell, 1958:

1. Lanceolate or elliptical shape having a shoulder on one side of the stem.

2. Asymmetrical or lopsided in outline.

AN ASTONISHING DISCOVERY No. 40
From the collection of:
Dave & Teri Klippert
Casper, Wyoming

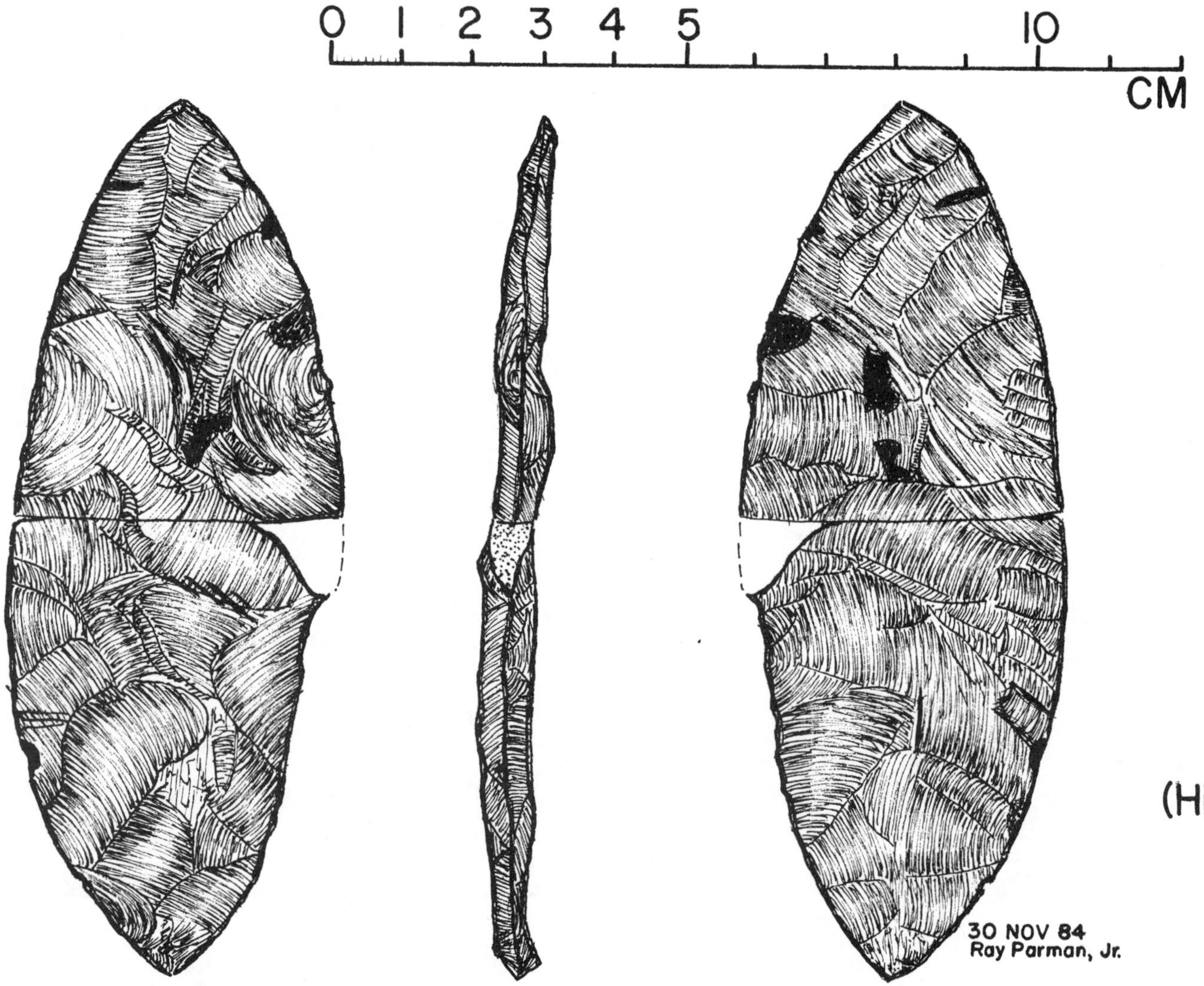

TYPE EXAMPLE
(Hibben, 1946 Pl. II, b)

SANDIA I ? PROBABLE

3. Stem tapering from shoulder, gently rounded with no effort at basal thinning.

4. Stem exhibits grinding along sides and base. Cross section lenticular or flattened oval in shape.

5. Average chipping but not fine. Large flaking with minor amount of chipping.

It is easy to see that this artifact displays all of these features.(The author failed to determine whether there was basal grinding or not.)

The Sandia I point was named from specimens taken from the Sandia Cave excavations near Albuquerque, New Mexico (Hibben, 1941).

DUNCAN POINT No. 41
From the collection of:
Timothy A. Mikita
Riverton, Wyoming

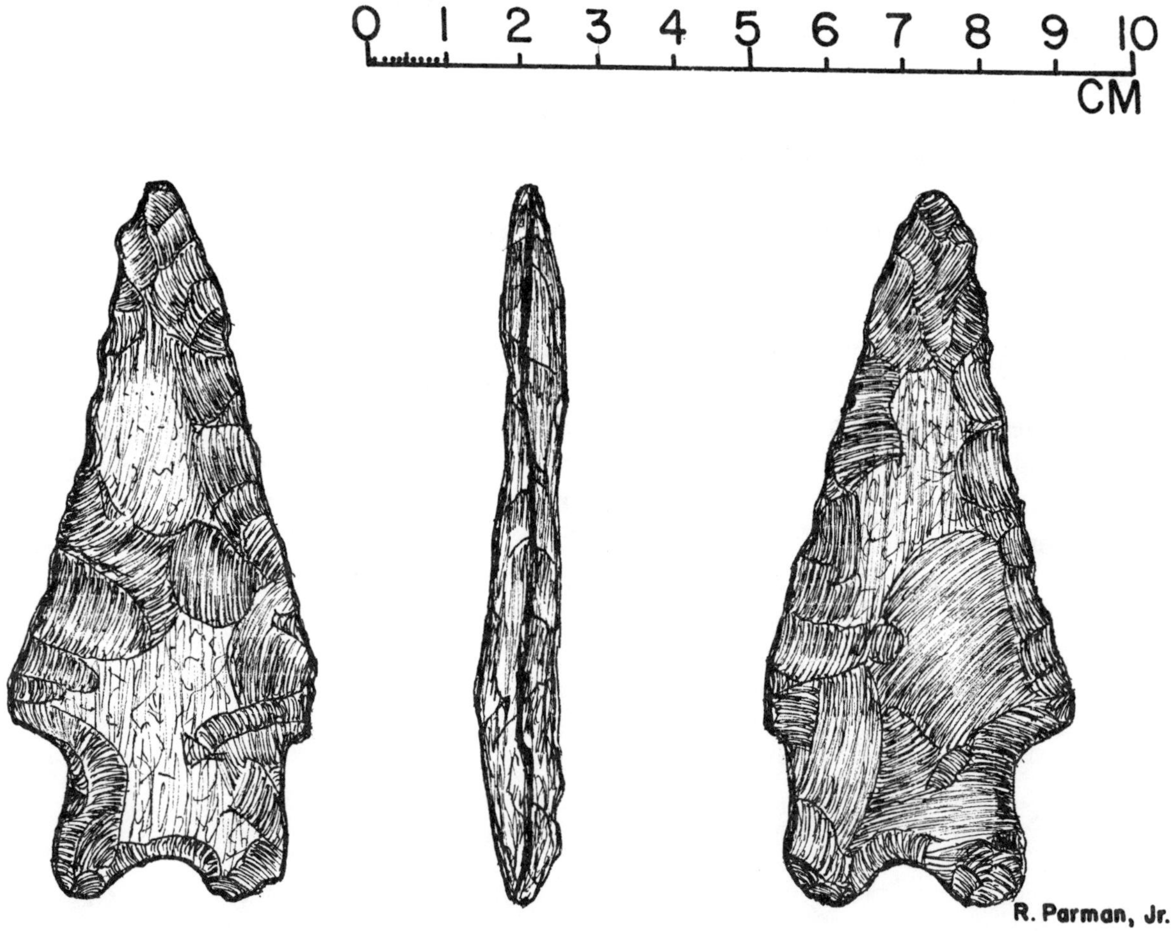

A DUNCAN POINT
(Dates to 2500 B.C.)

D

G
Type Examples
(R. E. Bell, 1958, Pl 13)

DUNCAN POINT

Color & Material: Light grey with brown cast and numerous inclusions. Very slight, light yellow to tan patina. Medium grain quartzite.

Location: North of Gillette, Campbell County, Wyoming.

Timothy (Tim) Mikita submitted this point for publication, wanting to know if it could be identified. It appeared rather old for there is little secondary chipping and it has not been worked very thin.

Type examples are at right. The quality of flaking and chipping are about the same. Tim's specimen seems to have characteristics of both examples, the straight edges of "D" and the shallower base, notch and size of "G".

The Duncan point has been named and described by Wheeler (1954:7) for a type found in Wyoming. Distribution: Saskatchawan, Alberta, Montana, The Dakotas, Wyoming, Colorado, Kansas, Nebraska, and Oklahoma.

Duncan points date back from 850 B.C. to 2500 B.C.. They have been found in association with Hanna and McKean points.

A BEAUTIFUL BUTTERFLY DRILL (AWL) No. 42
From the collection of:
Joe & Arlene Tyrrell
Lovell, Wyoming

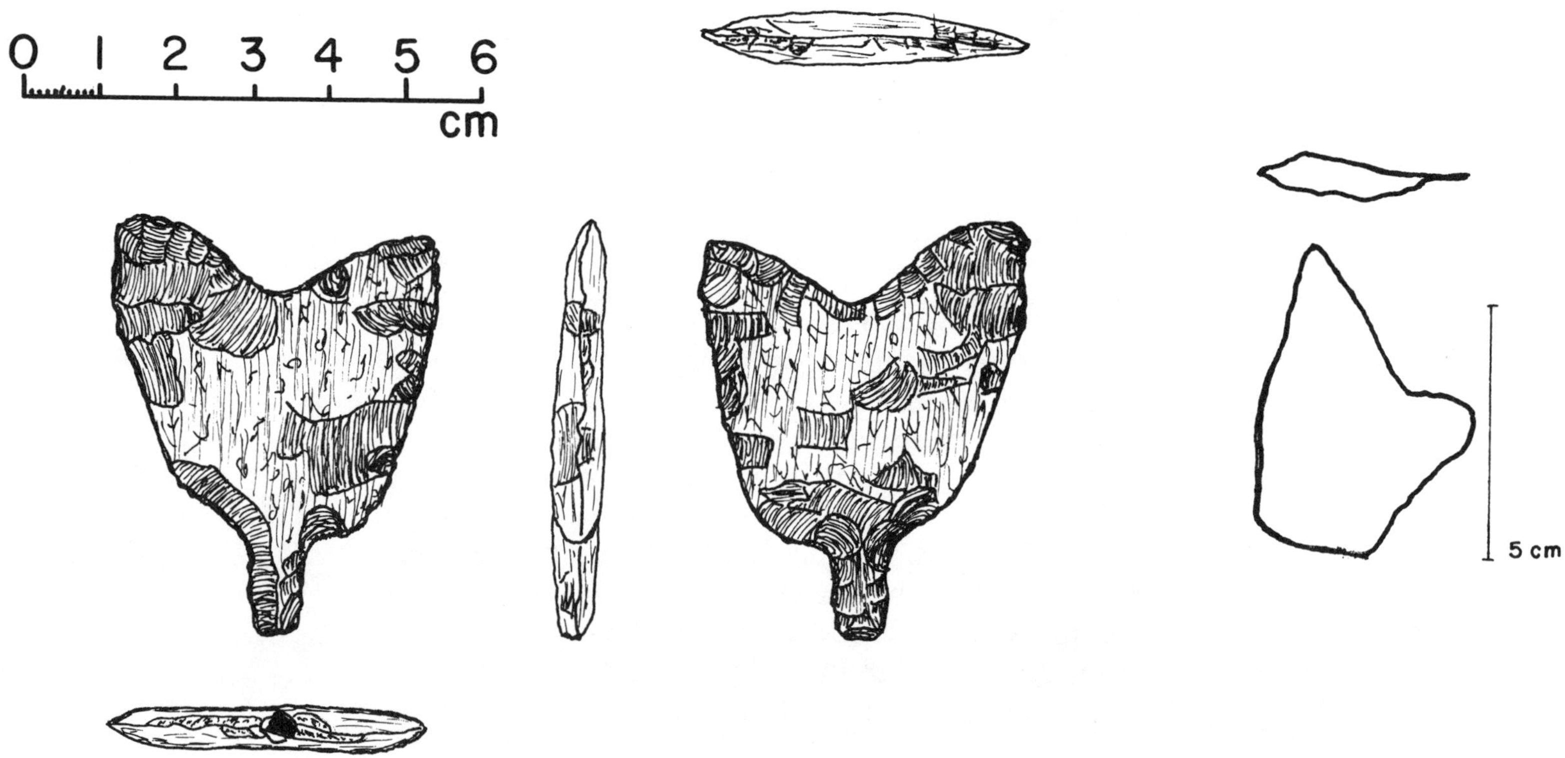

DRILL
(or awl)

A BEAUTIFUL BUTTERFLY DRILL (AWL)

Color & Material: Dull light grey to grey, mottled with trace of bone-white washing and inclusions. Orthoquartzite with inclusions of chalcedony.

Location: Eastern Washakie County, Wyoming; near Ten Sleep.

This uniquely shaped drill (or awl) is quite pretty. Unfortunately, the tip is missing. It was found in the general area of the Girl Scout National Center West, near Ten Sleep. A possible scalping knife, of similar workmanship, also was submitted to the author by the National Center (No. 19). Outlines of two views of the knife appear to the right. A scale line of five centimeters has been drawn beside them which shows the two artifacts are about the same size.

The natives living in this area at the time these two artifacts were fashioned apparently appreciated aesthetic values as evidenced in the workmanship of their tools.

Joe and Arlene's collection would put some museums to shame. Sincere appreciation is expressed for their submitting this unusual drill for publication.

UNUSUAL FLAKING HAMMER No. 43
From the collection of:
Darryl & Brenda Cadwallader
Riverton, Wyoming

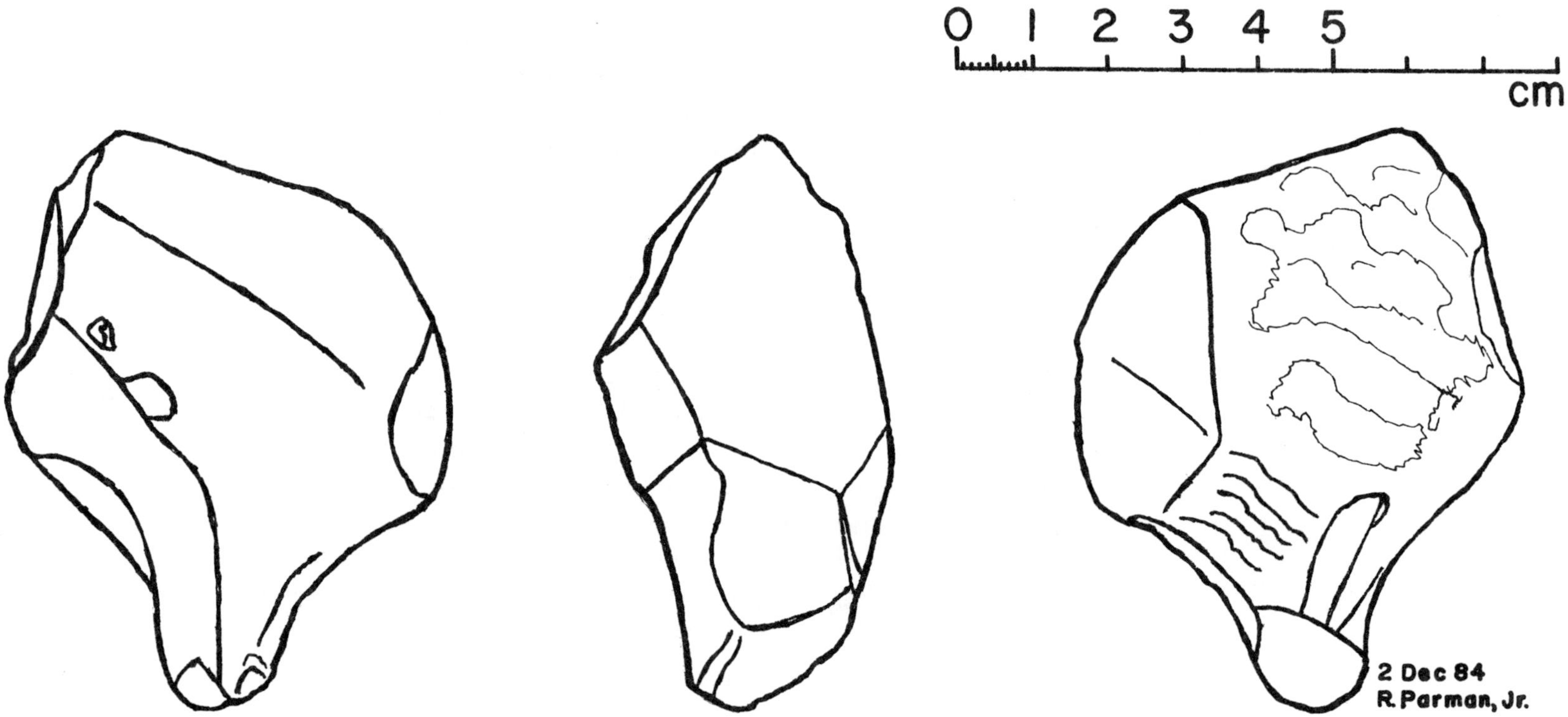

FLAKING-HAMMER STONE
(Chert nodule - naturally formed)
(Extensively used)

UNUSUAL FLAKING HAMMER

Color & Material: Dark chocolate brown, with an even darker brown rind covering all accept the numerous edges. The rind appears just as the scum that forms on hot chocolate. The convex surface, displayed in the right side view, has a thick white crust of calcium carbonate adhering to about 40% of that surface. A clean, hard, dense chert.

Location: East of Lysite, northeastern Fremont County, Wyoming.

Much of this material was written "on the road" while touring Wyoming and the west. Once, while logging an oil well south of Lovell, Wyoming, a rental typewriter was needed, so the author stopped in the Lovell city office to inquire. There the author met Senator Cal S. Taggart, and it is his portable typewriter that has whipped out this and the three prior segments. Thank you, Senator.

This flaking hammer, or hammer stone, was selected because it is an excellent example of a tool that is totally formed by nature, yet displays most extensive use as a flaking hammer. Even though the chert making up this hammer is an extremely hard material, nicks from blows struck while flaking tools are evident on the multitude of edges and the blunted end of the slender protrusion.

The author was told that Senator Taggart purchased an ad in the local newspaper thanking everyone for their support in the past election. His wife purchased one too, thanking those who did not. Suppose she is happy to have him home?

SANDIA I VARIANTS? No. 44
From the collection of:
Tom L. McCall
Casper, Wyoming

No. 11

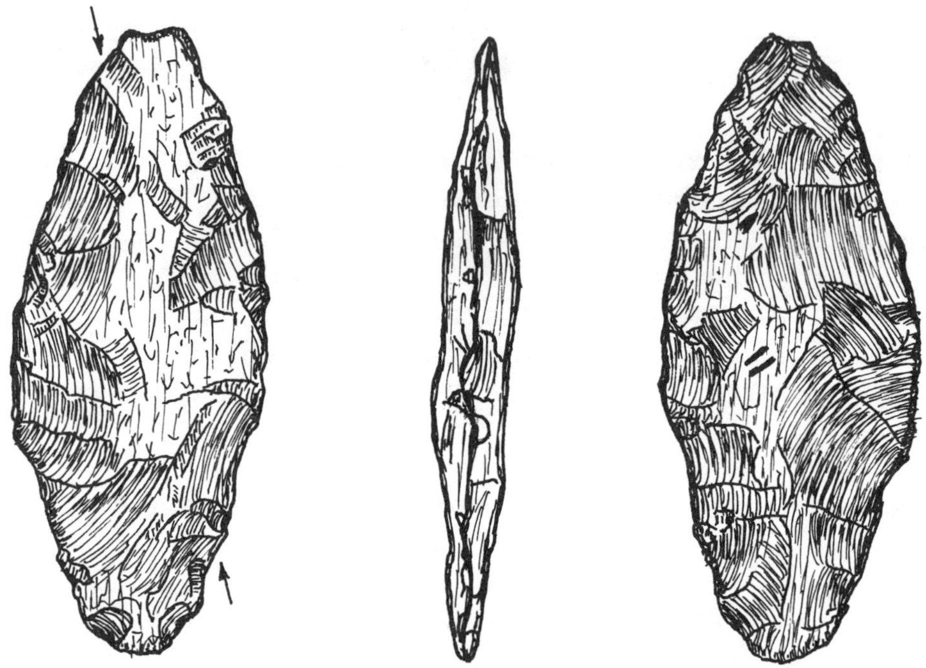

One shoulder more pronounced.

These points are from the collection of Tom's Father - the late John D. McCall of Powell, Wyoming
They were collected in 1950's

No. 3

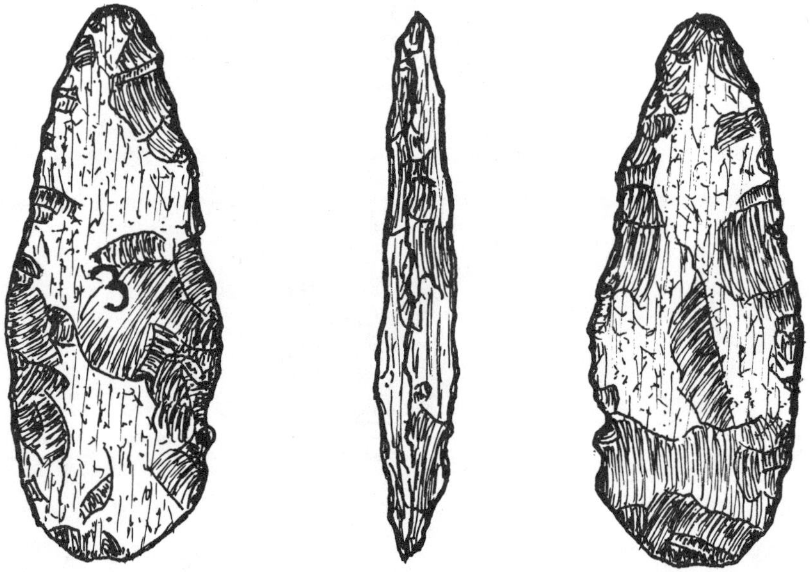

No basal thinning.

SANDIA I VARIANTS?

Color & Material: Artifact A, dull, medium light grey with one faint, light tan wash. Slight brown staining to the surface (left of the two arrows on the view to the left). Fine grain quartzite.

Artifact B, bone white with irregular, chromatographic, diagonal bands of light grey, light blue grey, and dark grey in evidence and two irregular bands of dull, light tan chalcedonous inclusions approximately parallel to the grey bands. Fine grain quartzite.

Location: Both of these artifacts are from the collection of the late John McCall of Powell, Wyoming.

These two artifacts have been selected for publication because both display such similar overall configuration, technique and craftsmanship that it is possible they were crafted by the same individual. Both display many Sandia-like characteristics. Those common to both are: 1. Crude flaking; 2. Little secondary flaking; 3. Lanceolate shape; 4. Cross section is lenticular (flattened oval); 5. Size. Artifact A displays the pronounced shoulder of the Sandia I but the edge view discloses basal thinning which is acharacteristic. Artifact B does not have the shoulder; but has not been basally thinned, which is characteristic of the Sandia I. The slight brown staining of A is believed to have been caused by microscopic porosity exposed to the surface of the artifact through this area, making it possible for the staining to occur.

If these two artifacts are variants of Sandia I points, their age is most likely in excess of 15,000 years. The frequency at which points (as old as Sandia I, and points as similar as these two) are turning up in private collections, is an indication of the volume of archaeological history that stands ready to be recorded by studying the thousands upon thousands of artifacts making up these private collections.

One feature of these thousands of artifacts is considered most important by this writer: the material from which they have been crafted.

If a sufficient number of Sandia I points can be recorded, then several crafted from the same material (stone taken from the same quarry, or struck from the same core) might be found. Recording a similar number of artifacts, from successively younger cultures, would disclose those crafted of this same material at each cultural level. Then there would be an extablished base, with adequate parameters, to develop a

SANDIA I VARIANTS? No. 44
From the collection of:
Tom L. McCall
Casper, Wyoming

No. 11

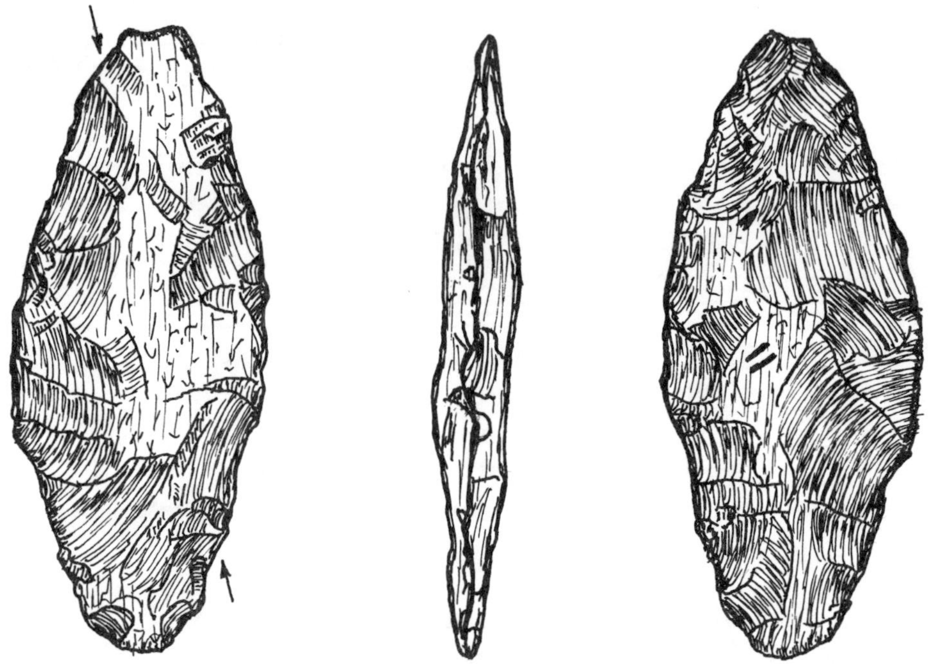

One shoulder more pronounced.

These points are from the collection of Tom's Father - the late John D. McCall of Powell, Wyoming They were collected in 1950's

No. 3

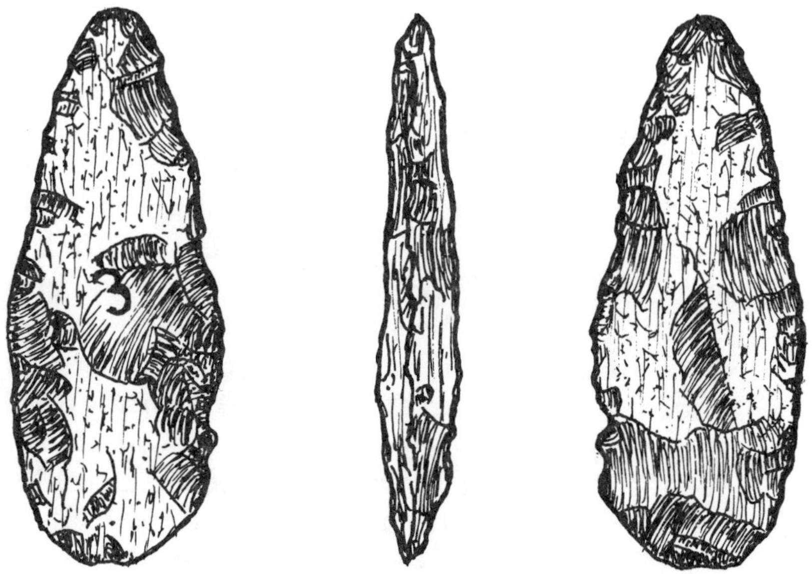

No basal thinning.

method of dating from studying the material of a surface find alone.

Author's note: The numbers 3 & 11 appearing on these artifacts are Mr. McCall's index numbers.

A MOST UNUSUAL ARTIFACT No. 45
From the collection of:
Amoss H. Welty
Dubois, Wyoming

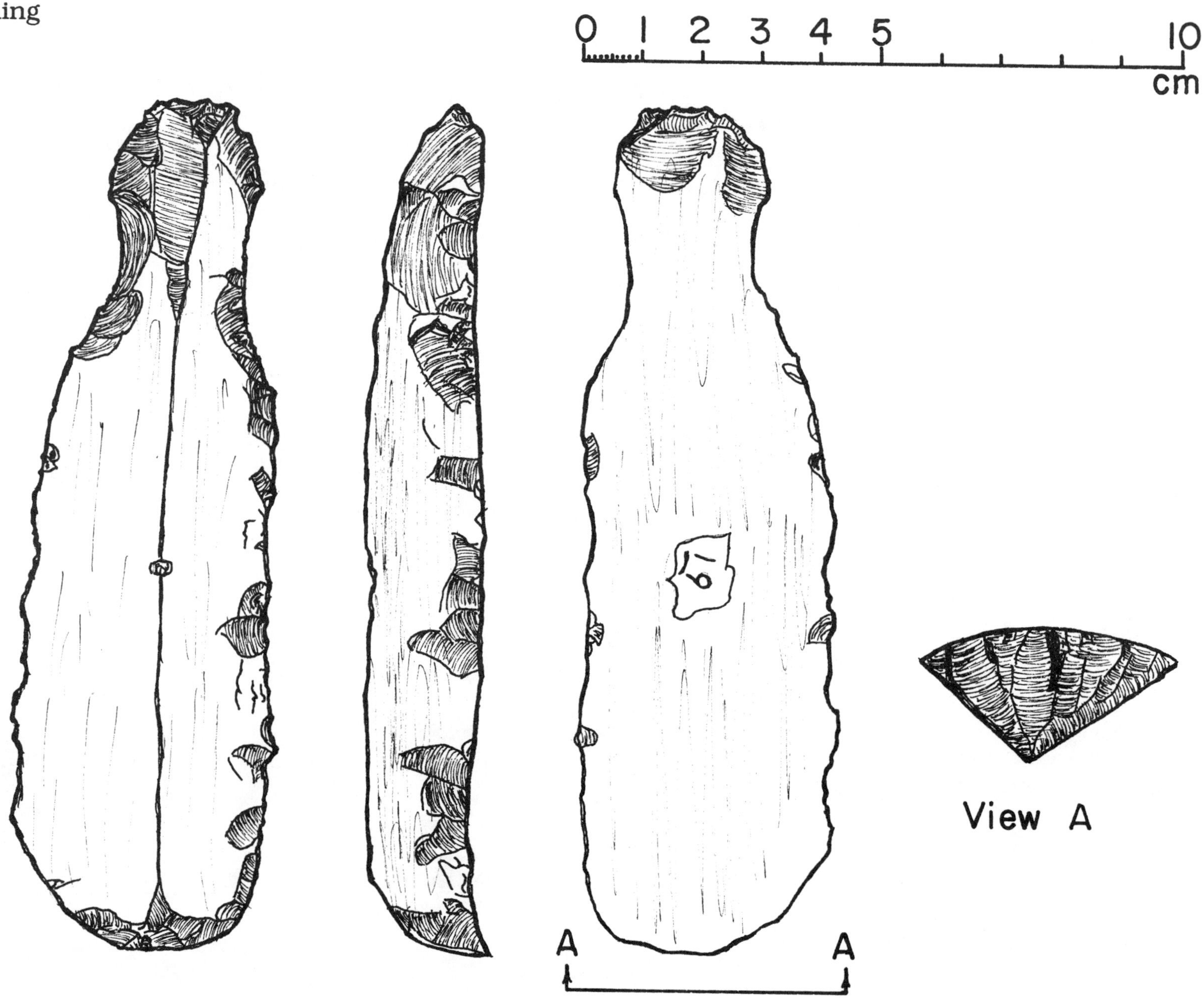

A MOST UNUSUAL ARTIFACT

Color and Material: Light grey, light blue-grey, tan and brown banded diagonally thru the longest dimension. Heavy brown cast overall. Agate with tan bands of chalcedony. There are several irregular inclusions of tan chalcedony with some vugular porosity in alignment with the bands.

Location: Found by Mr. Welty's daughter, Patricia Maxon, on Torrey Creek in northwestern Fremont County, Wyoming.

This artifact is a puzzle. It doesn't fit in the hand no matter which way it is turned. If a handle were attached, would it have been parallel to its long axis or perpendicular to it ? If perpendicular, would it have been placed in the same plane as the large, flat face (on which the catalog number appears), or perpendicular to that plane? If the handle were attached parallel to the tool's long axis, how long would the handle have been?

The blunt end has been worked into an end scraper having a very strong shoulder nearly perpendicular to the working edge. Oddly there is no evidence of wear on the edge of this scraper, or any damage to its flaked face. Of the three edges of the triangular body, only one (right edge of the left side view) evidences alteration from the natural edge; it is believed this flaking has been caused from use.

The two large notches that reduce the circumference of the smaller end appear to have been necessary for the hafting of a handle, or for simply the attachment of a leather thong. This thong could have been wrapped around the palm of the hand to assist in holding the tool by the smaller end.

While holding the smaller end in the right hand, it was possible for the author to easily chop away about a quarter of an inch, and round the corner of a yellow pine two by four. It was difficult to hold the tool; but with a thong or handle, it would have made an excellent, light axe.

If a handle were hafted to this tool, perpendicular to its long axis and in the same plane as the wide, flat face (numbered face), it would have been a highly useful tool The end would be a hatchet (sharpened just before it was lost); the straight, chipped and damaged edge would be a chisel if held in position by the handle and struck by a mallet on the face opposite the working edge.

If anyone has a tool similar to this, please write to Amoss and Janet Welty, Box 575, Dubois, Wyoming 82513

UNIDENTIFIED POINT No. 46
From the collection of:
Ken & Karma Ball
Casper, Wyoming

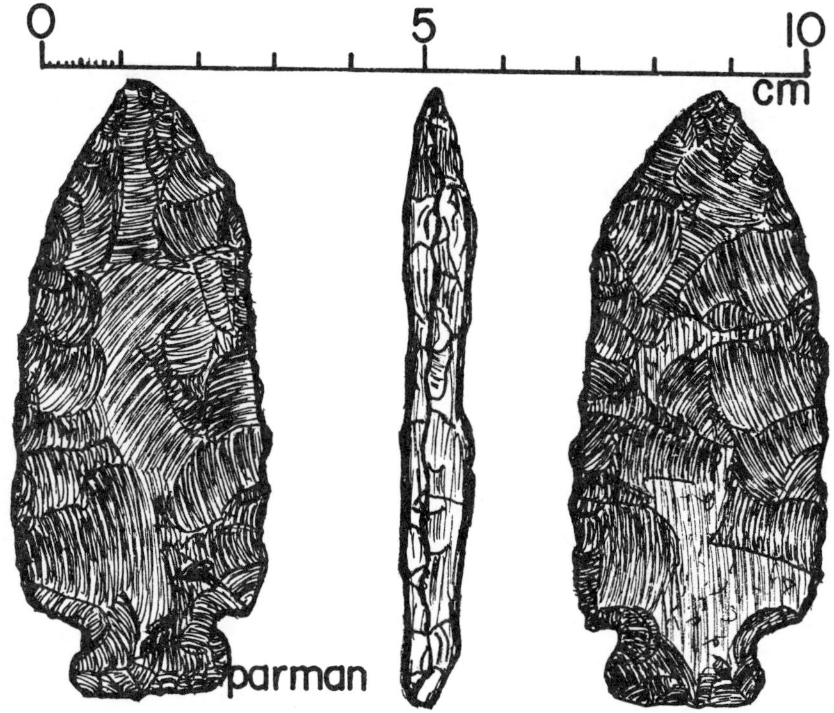

UNIDENTIFIED POINT

Color & Material: Dark brown with two very light tan rind spots; in center at shoulder of point and near the stem on the opposite side. The surface displayed in the right side view has a very faint, light tan patina, or extremely thin rind, covering all of it evenly. Chert.

Location: Eastern slope of Big Horn mountains, Northwest Natrona county, Wyoming.

This point was not found in any of my guides to identification, but it was selected for publication because its overall characteristics are those of older types.

In view of the asymmetrical shape, it is possible it was crafted as a knife, with a handle to be attached.

The crude flaking, the reduced amount of secondary flaking, and the lack of tip and basal thinning, leaving it rather thick for its size (particularly when crafted from chert) causes one to suspect a stone-knapping technology that was not too advanced.

The two rind spots mentioned were formed before the point was crafted, indicating it was crafted from a stone picked from the surface, rather than being struck from a core.

A BEAUTIFUL, UNUSUAL SCRAPER No. 47
From the collection of:
Amoss H. Welty
Dubois, Wyoming

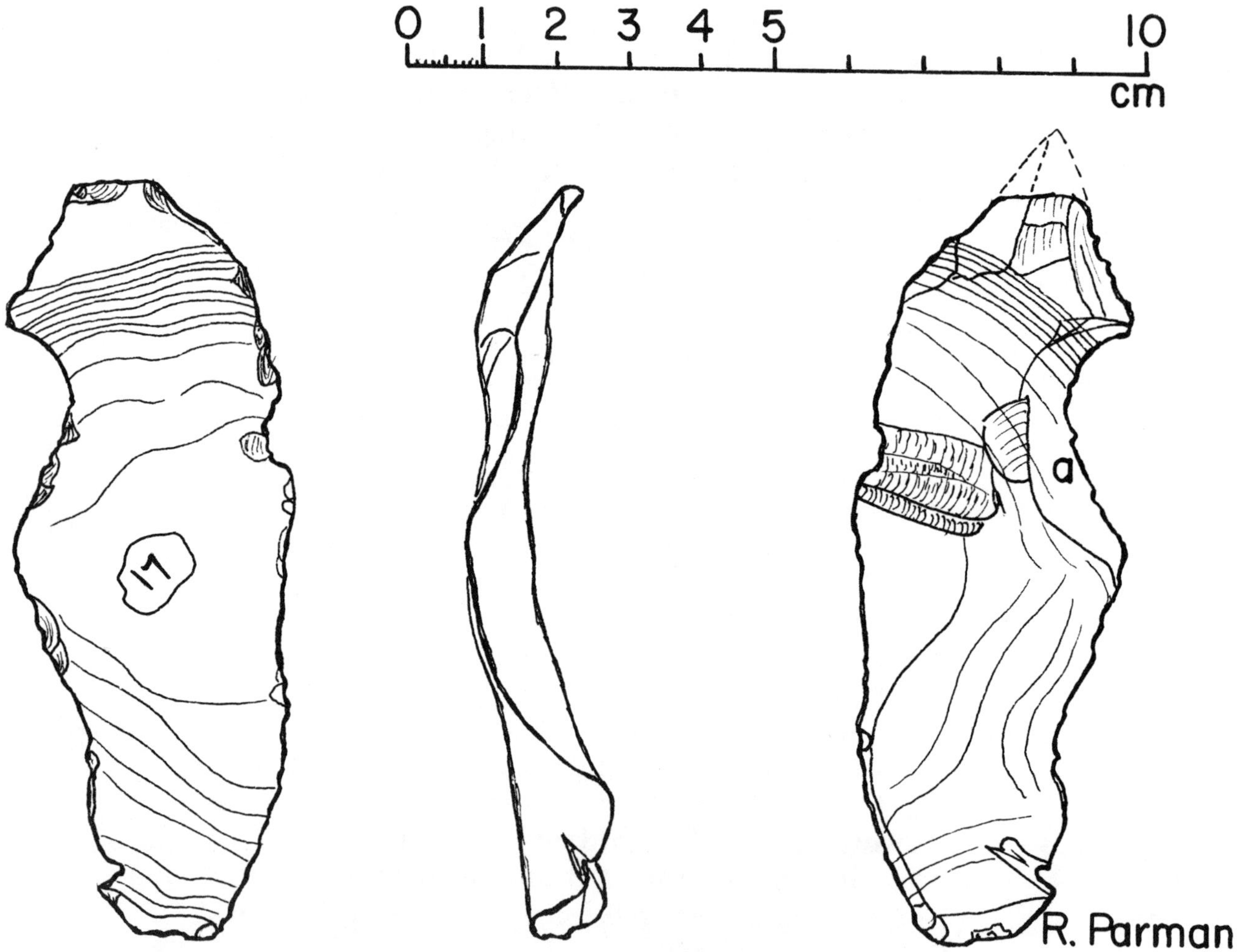

THOUGHT TO BE VERY OLD

A BEAUTIFUL, UNUSUAL SCRAPER

Color & Material: Light tan, dark brown, banded as growth rings with the ends of the tool such a dark brown as to appear black. It is thought that the winter growth and the bark have become the dark brown growth rings and the brown-black ends. Agatized wood with reduced depth of color, very much like jasper.

(Author's note: It was later discovered this material is known to be called "tiger chert" from a quarry in central Uinta County, Wyoming. The rings were fromed by layers of algae.)

Location: Found by Janet Welty on East Fork of the Wind River, northwest corner of Fremont County, Wyoming.

This beautiful scraper was selected for publication because it displays what strongly resembles intentional flaking by man (particularly the upper end of the right side view) and yet has been totally polished in some manner other than tumbling. The ridges between flake surfaces are all gently rounded, even the long lateral flakes that appear to have been removed from the left edge of the right side-view. There are numerous tiny flakes along the edges that are polished, and others appear newly formed as from recent use.

The edge having the large, gently curved notch and the small, deep notch at the other end appears to have been used, through its entire length, as a scraper. Crushing, nicking, and some erosion from wear is believed to have occured both before and after the overall polishing.

Thus one might come to the conclusion that thousands of years ago, this beautiful stone was crafted into a tool by flaking one end into a point (dashed lines); removal of one large percussion flake (A); and the crafting of the small, deep notch. This notch is rounded from use.

It was then lost and lay where wind blown sand could polish all its surfaces. The point was broken off before this time of polish, but it was again picked up and used as a scraper to account for the fresh nicks that are not polished.

It has been suggested that the crushing and nicking of the edges might be from scraping flesh away from bones and/or from harvesting of reeds (cattail or yucca) and the processing of these for basket making.

AN IMAGE OF THE PAST No. 48
From the collection of:
Teddy Wright
Kemmerer, Wyoming

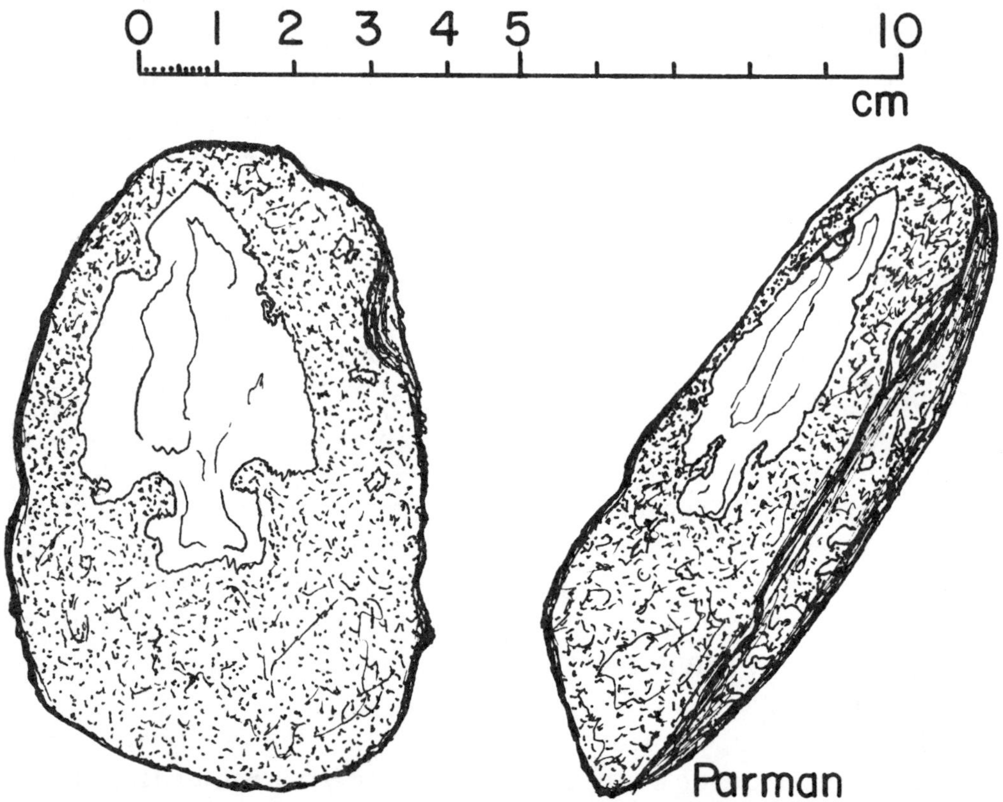

MINERAL IMPRINT OF GLENDO POINT

AN IMAGE OF THE PAST

Color & Material: Bone white mineral (most likely calcium carbonate) deposit on tan, coarse-grained, sandstone cobble fragment.

Location: Found by Teddy Wright near the Big Muddy in north central Uinta County, Wyoming.

Though the artifact was not present when Mr. Wright picked up this cobblestone fragment, there was certainly a record of a Pelican Lake (formerly Glendo) point having lain upon it, undisturbed, for some length of time.

In some way, this cobble fragment, with the point lying upon it, was wetted by mineral laden water repeatedly. Each time this water was trapped beneath the point, it evaporated slowly, leaving behind a small quantity of the dissolved minerals.

The thickness of the mineral deposit is greater just to the left of the center-line of the image, indicating that the flat surface of the cobble was not quite horizontal. There is no imprint of the point on the surface of this mineral deposit, which would indicate the point was removed long enough before for erosion to erase this evidence.

Mr. Wright found this unusual stone around 1970. Private collectors, having taken finds (specifically this type of point, 5.67 cm long and 3.52 cm wide) from this area during the 1960s, are asked to check and see if they have a point of this type bearing a white mineral deposit on one side.

AN OLD, OLD POINT No. 49
From the collection of:
Mitch and Connie Frayser
Frontier, Wyoming

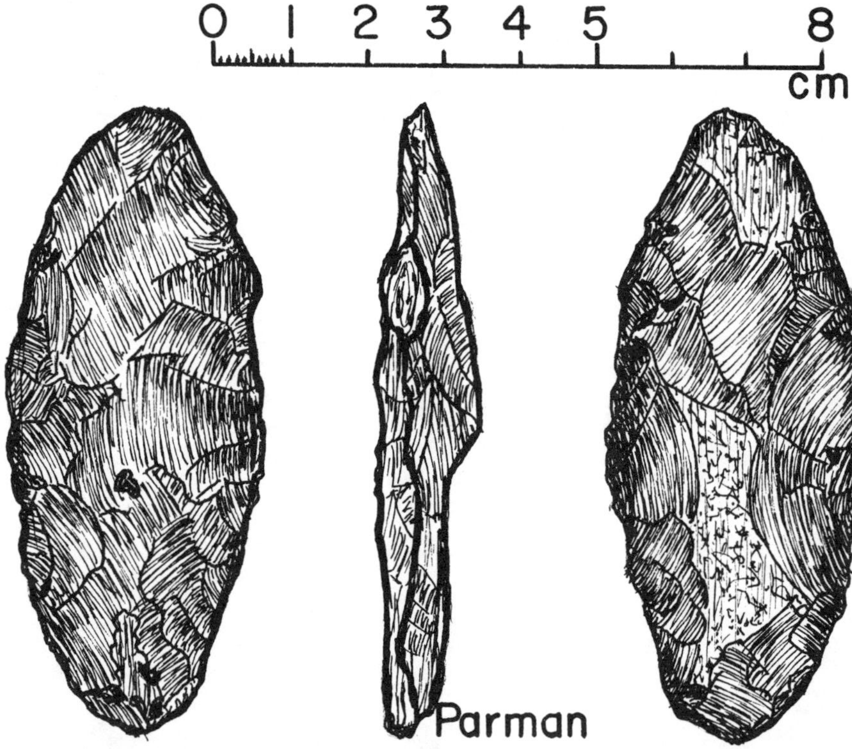

Type Example
Secrist's Guide, p 34
(3rd edition)

AN OLD, OLD POINT

Color & Material: A cocoa brown with abundant light tan inclusions of irregular size and shape. Several dark brown inclusions shown on the left side view. A faint, light tan patina over the surface in the left side view and a heavy, light tan patina, or faint rind over the surface in the right view. Chert.

Location: North central Uinta County, Wyoming.

By the time I got around to writing this (the art work had already been done), I was convinced there was slim chance that this point was an example of the Blanco point described in Secrist's Simplified Identification Guide (Third Edition,p.34). According to Secrist, the Blanco point is found in South and Central America, and in Texas and New Mexico. It is possible the natives could have recovered points of this type and transported them into Wyoming at a much later period of time. The location of this find does not discredit it as a possible Blanco as much as the lack of a more pointed end, such as displayed by the example shown to the right. Secrist listed the size range as 1.5" to 3". This specimen exceeds the largest by .25" In Secrist's words... "Positive identification depends mainly on the discovery site and on the other things found in association with them." Though the source was not given, Secrist dated the Blanco at 30,000 B.C., if not earlier.

SMALL SCRAPER & RARE DUCK EFFIGY No. 50
From the collection of:
Mitch & Connie Frayser
Frontier, Wyoming

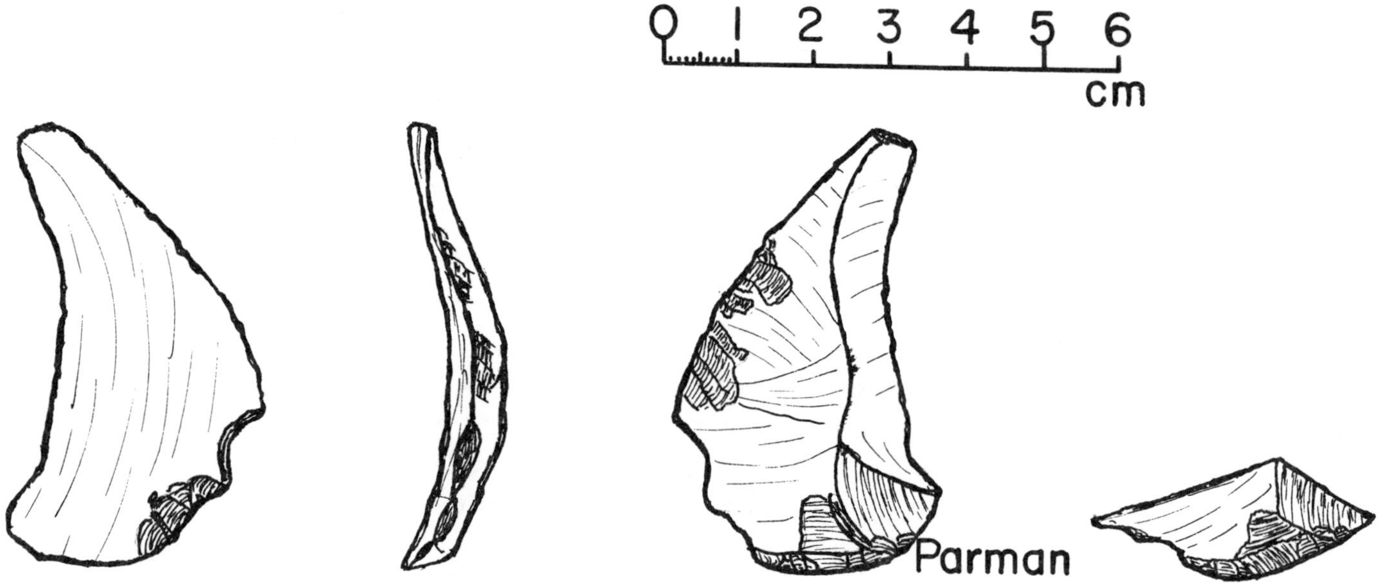

SCRAPER FOR SMALL SKINS ? OR WHAT ?

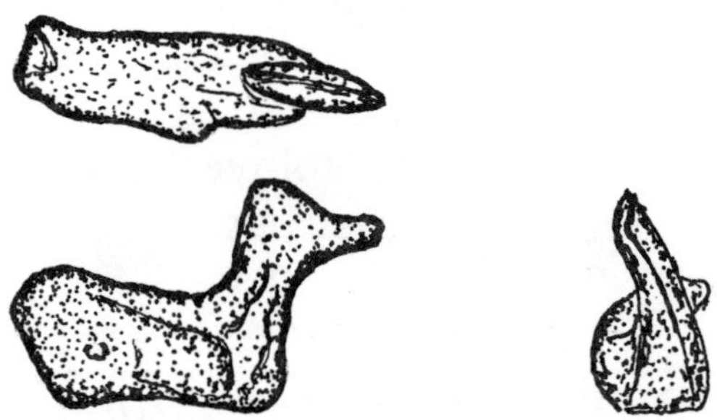

UNUSUAL EFFIGY TAKEN FROM CLIFF FACE

SMALL SCRAPER & RARE DUCK EFFIGY

Color & Material: Small scraper, dark brown with two, dull tan, most irregular, bubbly, swirly bands approximately 1/3 cm. wide across the tool, one quarter the length from each end. Chert.

Duck effigy, tan, medium-grain sandstone.

Location: Small scraper, north central Uinta County, Wyoming.

Duck effigy, sandstone cliff at the edge of the lava beds (Malpais) approximately fifteen miles south of Grants, Cibola County, New Mexico.

This small scraper was likely used when working with the small skins of otter, mink, and ferret. The entire edge of the left side view seems to be dulled, but there are no nicks. No line of wear could be found. One might wonder if the skin could have been drawn tight over a finger, and the notched edge then used.

While Mitch and Connie were hunting nearby, their son, Robert, rappelled one hundred feet down a cliff face to a small cave that was about two hundred feet from the base. There he found this small duck effigy on a ledge in the cave wall. It is very likely that the tribe of natives associated with this effigy utilized migratory waterfowl as part of their food source.

Was this effigy part of a warrior's "vision quest"? Or, was it used in a shaman's ritual?

This is the first duck effigy the author has seen. Are there many in other areas?

AN OLD & UNUSUAL ARTIFACT No. 51
From the collection of:
Leo & Karma Osborn
Evanston, Wyoming

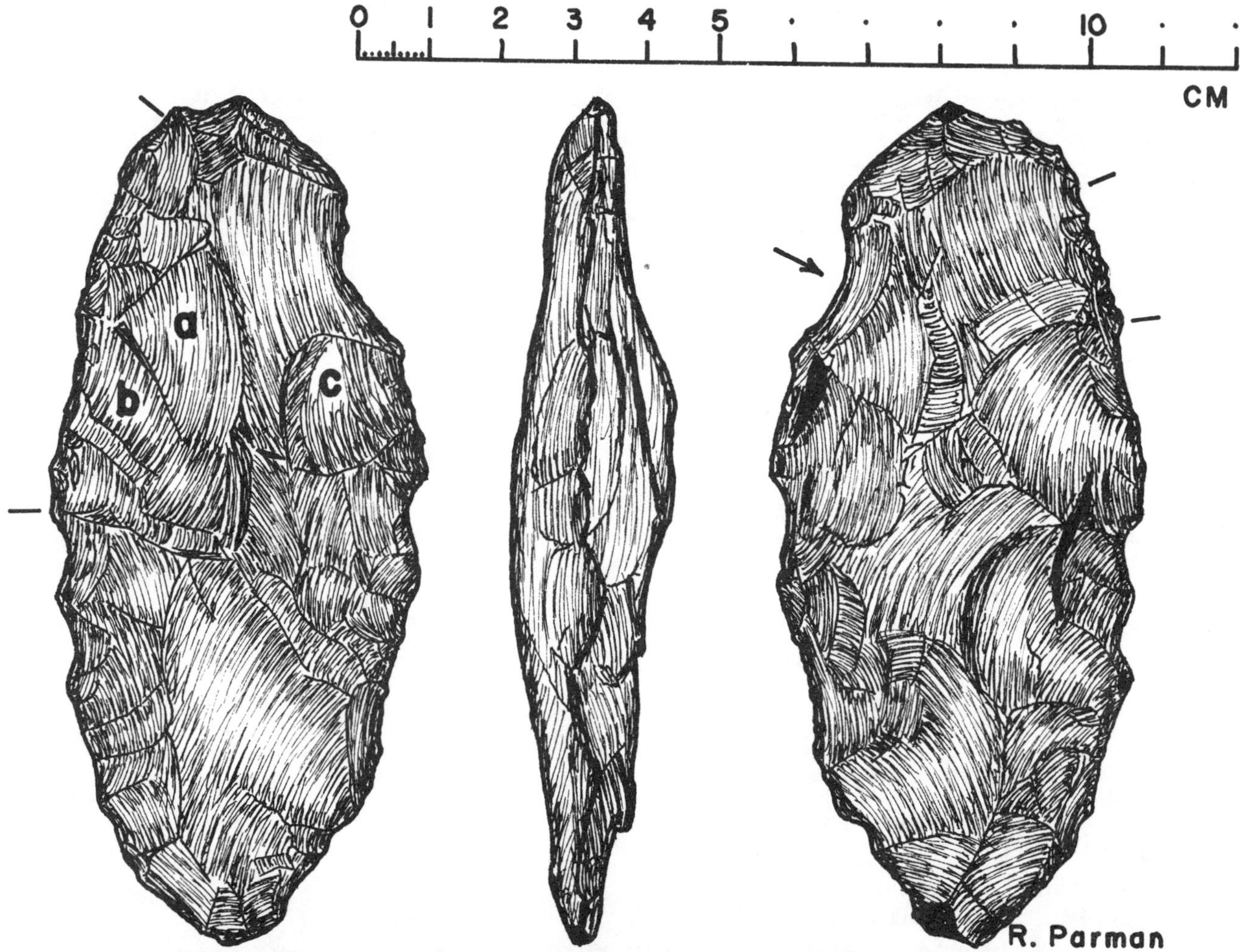

TRADE BLANK SPEAR TIP OR KNIFE ?
(Later Re-worked and used as scraper)

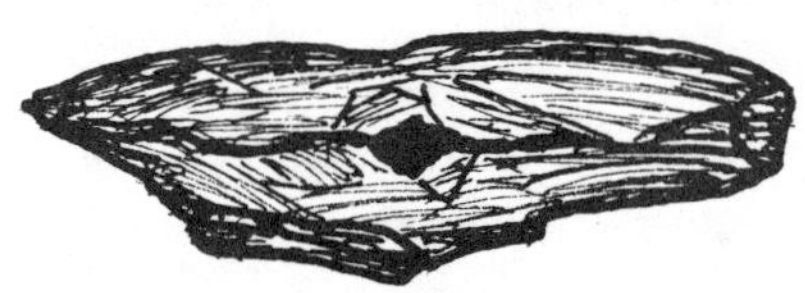

AN OLD & UNUSUAL ARTIFACT

Color & Material: Laminated light tan to light brown for the half displayed in the left side view. Dark brown through a thin middle plane. Light brown to dark brown for the half displayed in the right side view. Light tan, irregular sized and shaped inclusions throughout. A very thin patina having a slight green cast covering the surface displayed in the right side view. A poor grade chert with chalcedonous inclusions.

Location: Southern Sweetwater County, Wyoming.

This tool displays characteristics that lead one to believe it is very old. The ridges between flakes are well rounded, particularly on the side displayed in the left view. It is likely this side was up, and exposed to wind blown sand until the time it was reworked.

Those edges outlining flakes a, b, and c are sharp, and indicate the passage of a relatively short period of time from when the tool was found and reworked, to the present.

Flakes a, b, and c were percussion flakes, and as the tool was reworked, nine pressure flakes were removed between the lines of the left view, and four were removed from the reverse side (between lines of the right view).

The edge between these lines is essentially straight and indicates some use as a scraper. The notch (arrow) evidences considerable wear and polish on the surface in the right view. Other than these two points, no wear is indicated.

It is thought this artifact was first crafted thousands of years ago, as a trade blank for a lance point or knife. Its thickness, crude flaking and lack of use before being reworked, coupled with the marked weathering of the original flaking, lead to this conclusion.

Two small surfaces (note the blackened areas at each end of the drawing on the right) appear to be intentionally left in place. The next artifact (No. 52), crafted of chert from the same quarry, displays this same feature and it will be covered in the narrative then.

UNIQUE FIND No. 52
From the collection of:
Leo & Karma Osborn
Evanston, Wyoming

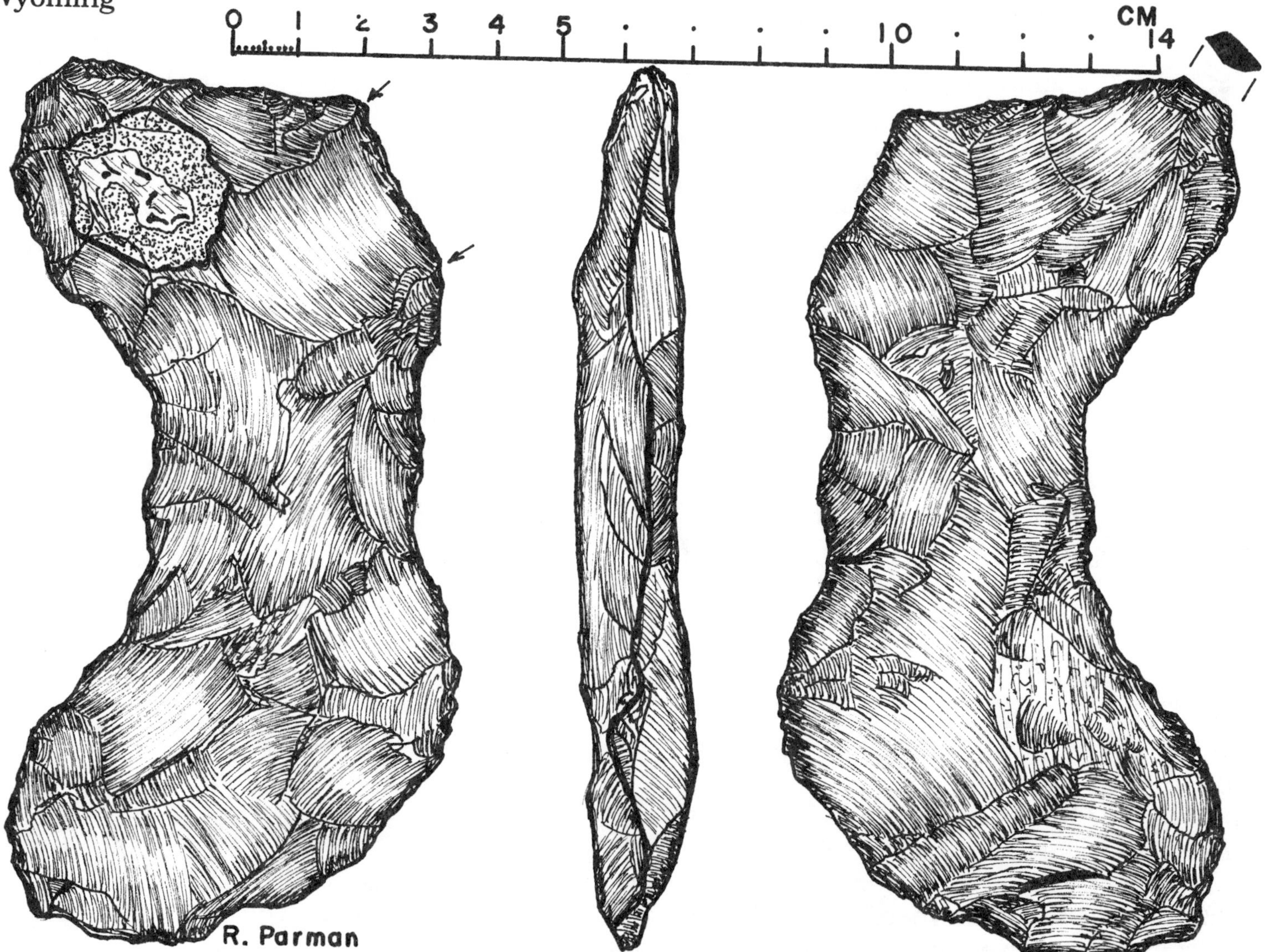

SKINNING KNIFE - HIDE SCRAPER

(Weathered - Very Old)

UNIQUE FIND

Color & Material: Laminated light tan to light brown for the half displayed in the left view; light brown to brown for the right view; light tan, irregular size and shaped inclusions throughout. A poor grade of chert with chalcedonous inclusions.

Location: Southern Sweetwater County, Wyoming.

First note the profile of a flat surface on the edge of this tool (upper right of the right view). It is possible this is a small portion of the original surface (cortex) of the stone from which this tool was crafted, intentionally left intact to be ceremonially removed at a later time. Or it was simply left in place out of respect for the earth and its materials. This is definitely a significant feature, because of the 55 tools and tool fragments taken from one campsite (Huckey Puck Site, Fremont County Archaeological Society), 27 exhibited this feature.

This feature is felt to be of only a single tribe's influence. It would be interesting to know what and when other tribes, across this continent, produced this feature in their lithic tools.

This tool is not only unique in configuration, but displays wear from use as two separate tools...a skinning knife and a two-handed draw-knife type scraper. By grasping the lower, ovoid end of the tool (as displayed in the left view) in the palm of the right hand, the edge (between arrows) with the rounded corner at the upper end would be an excellent skinning knife.

With the same side up, rotate it 90 degrees clockwise so that the two oval tips are pointing away from the body. By grasping the wings in the palms of the hands, with the thumbs at the middle (side by side) and parallel to the long axis of the tool, the slightly curved edge, toward the body, becomes a scraping edge.

With a hide draped over a log, the tool (held as described above) would be drawn along the hide toward the body, possibly to scrape the hair off or as a flesher.

A RARE ANTLER ARTIFACT No. 53
From the collection of:
Amoss Welty
Dubois, Wyoming

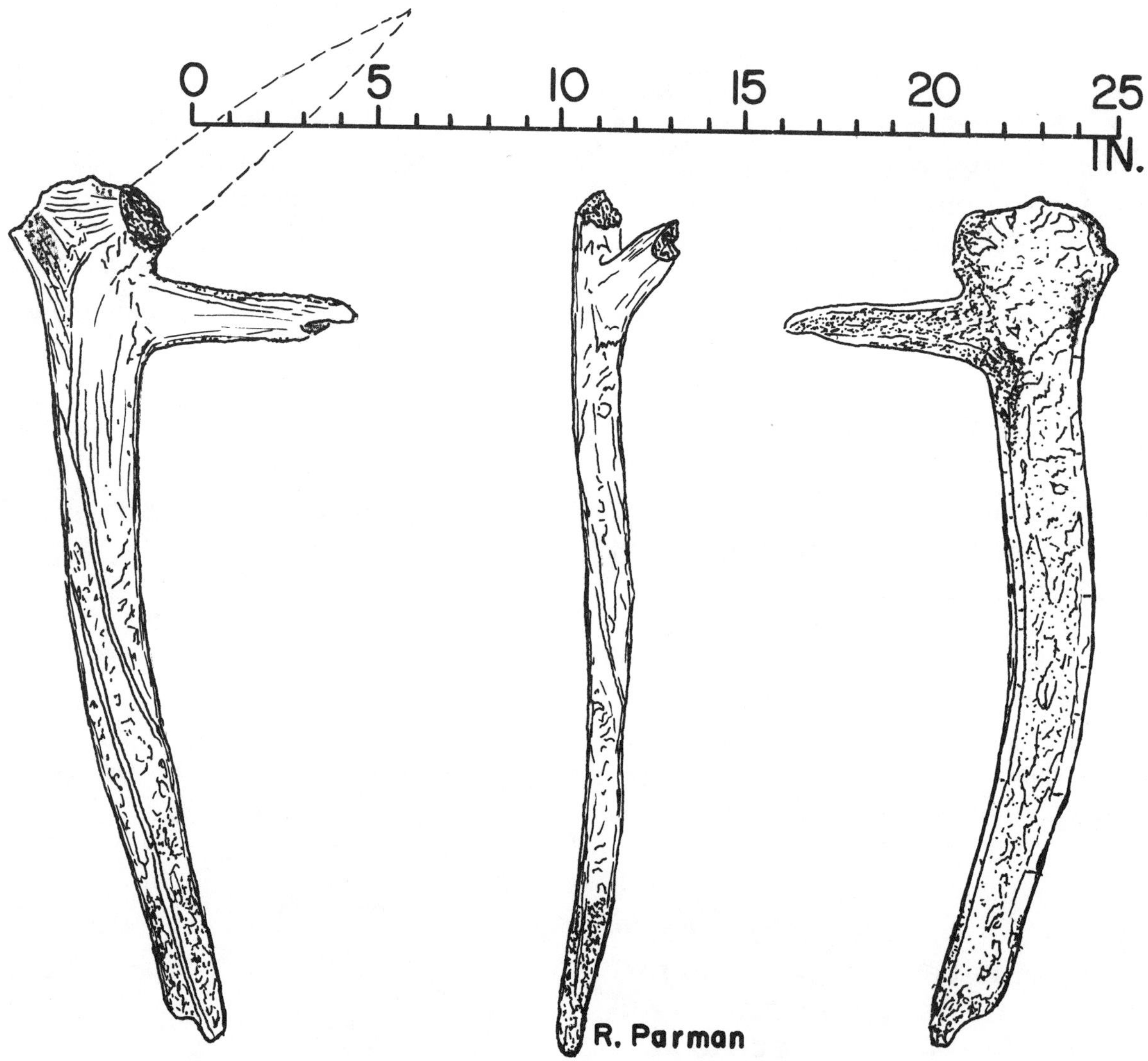

THOUGHT TO BE MEAT HOOK
(Preserved in dry cave)

A RARE ANTLER ARTIFACT

Color & Material: Natural colors of the antler of elk (Cervus alces) with exception of greyish brown staining on the rounded surface of the smaller end (lower, left and middle views), and what is thought to be rust staining (from iron contained in red cells) wherever blood was trapped in the porous, inner structure of the tool. This occurred on the point*, within the main shaft at the point's base, and where the brow point was removed. (*This point would be the bez antler.)

Crafted from a 23.5 inch (60.16 cm) length of the right antler of an elk. It consists of the upper third of the burr, (brow point removed) 5/8ths of the first point (bez antler), and the upper half of the main shaft to the first main branch.

Location: Northwest corner, Fremont County, Wyoming.

Though any artifact placed in a collector's hand will arouse some interest, this one, as Amoss Welty placed it in mine, was totally surprising. How was it possible that an antler was so smoothly divided? How was the implement used? Those two questions have come to mind repeatedly. There is more evidence on how the antler was divided. How the tool was used is open to conjecture.

The edges of the main shaft (view to right) and the point are rounded. This would indicate that a line was inscribed along the shaft and point (where the separation was desired), and then repeatedly scraped with a sharp burin point until the hard outer horn was worn through. It was then split with wedges, chopped and scraped smooth.

The rounded surface of the smaller end fits, with comfort, in the right hand. The fingers curl smoothly into the indented, core side. This would account for the staining of this surface. It also evidences lighter staining where at times the fingers of the left hand grasped the rounded surface. Held in this manner, the working point (not the brow antler that was removed but the bez antler) would point downward as a pick.

Though the point must have struck something hard at one time (a large flake was chipped from it) its surface is highly polished. Even the edges of the flaked area are polished and well rounded, indicating continued use after the flake was chipped off.

Considerable thought was given to why the working point was not left full round. It would have been much stronger and easier to make.

A RARE ANTLER ARTIFACT No. 53
From the collection of:
Amoss Welty
Dubois, Wyoming

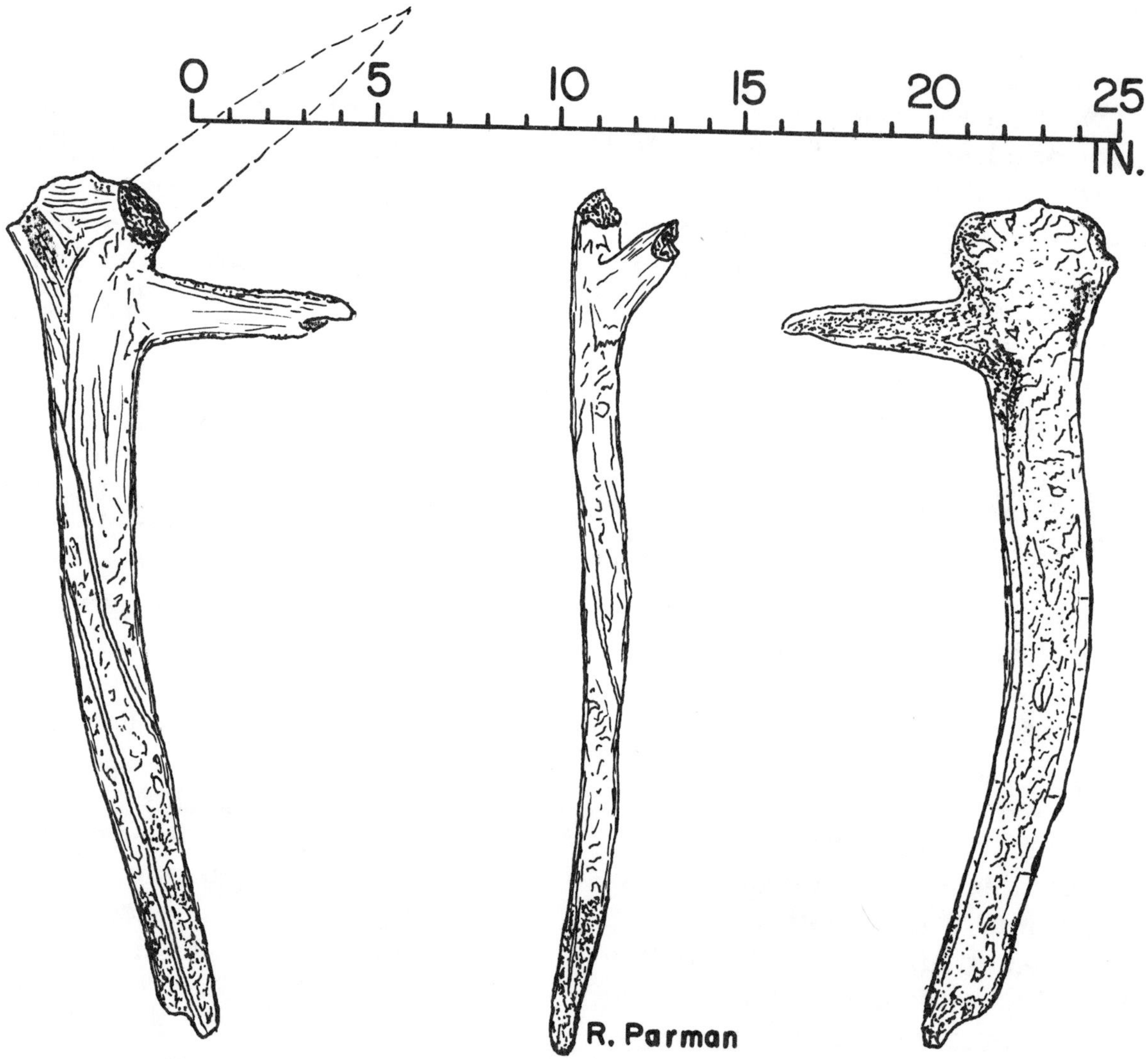

THOUGHT TO BE MEAT HOOK
(Preserved in dry cave)

Evidently, strength was not so important as the deep penetration possible with a slender point. It was decided the main shaft was split simply to make the tool lighter. It is real conjecture, but a left-handed tool could have been crafted from the remaining portion of the same antler.

One can not picture this slender point piercing the skull of a buffalo without shattering, but it would have been useful if one were to have driven the point into the flesh of the shoulder or hip, and held tension on the flesh, while another, using a stone knife, separated the flesh down to the ligaments binding the joint. It would be useful for one to hold tension on the entrails, while another stripped them from the body cavity.

One other possibility rather more gruesome...Could it have been a "slave killer?"

While visiting the museum at Dubois, Wyoming, a diorama of a sheep driveline and trap was noted. The trap consisted, in miniature, of what would have been a rectanglar wall, three to four feet high, constructed of fallen timber. It was covered by slender poles laid side by side. Sheep, driven to jump upon this trap, would have their legs fall through the poles and be suspended there for a moment. This artifact is now thought to have been used to club the sheep and pull them from the trap.

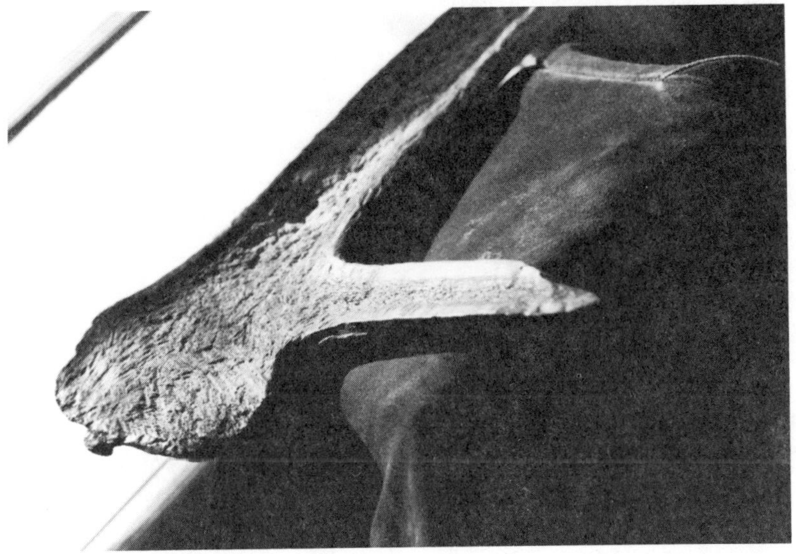

A RARE EFFIGY No. 54
From the collection of:
Mrs. Eleanor Kendall
Riverton, Wyoming

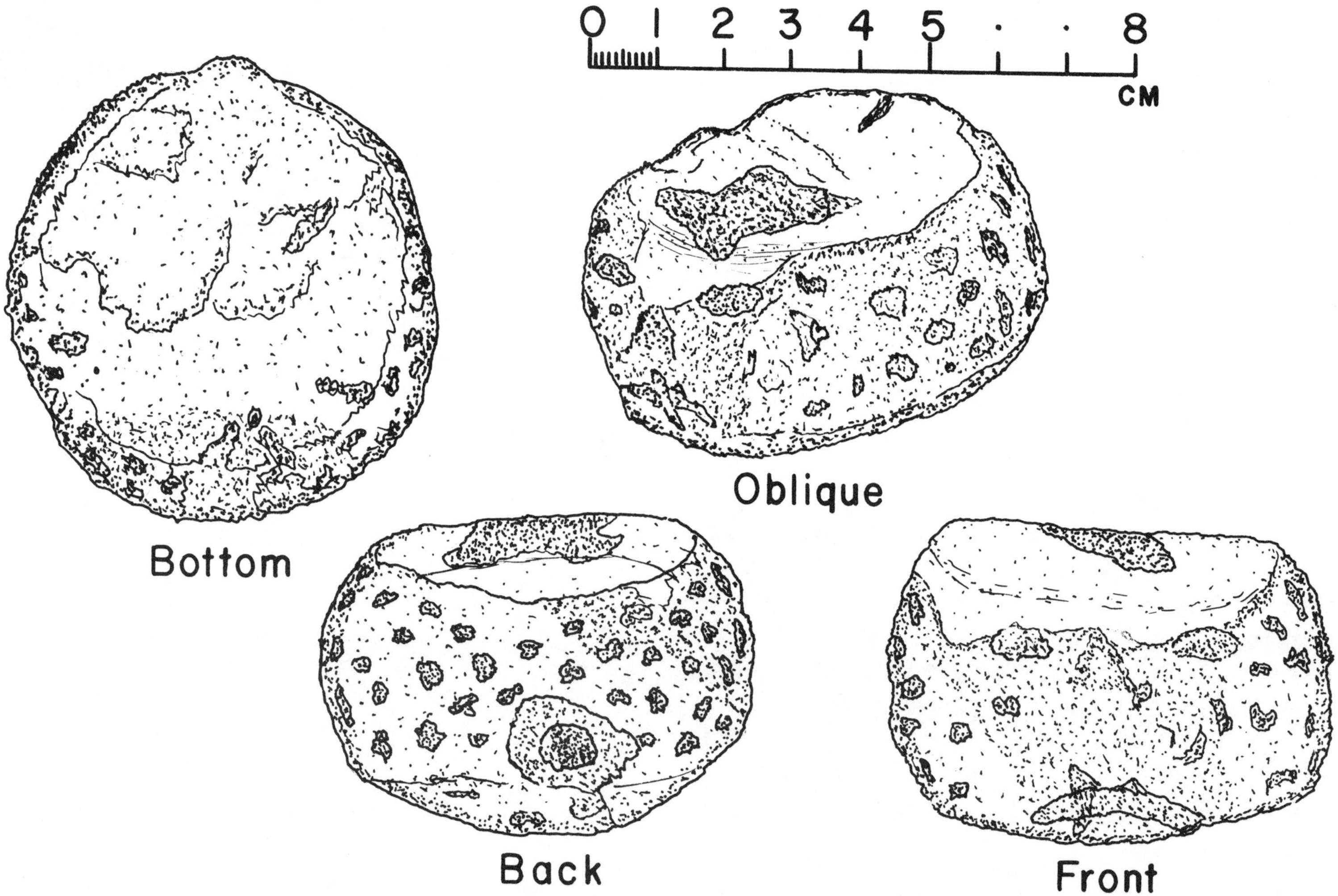

THOUGHT GAMING STONE TWO YEARS–FACE THEN FOUND
(Tail discovered days later)

A RARE EFFIGY

Color & Material: An even, flat, dirty brown with first a dark brown overstain covering the concave surface of the oblique view and most of the circumference of the edge. A second, nearly black, overstain covering the same concave surface and the edge about the face. A third overstain (actually an encrustation) that is off, or nearly white, covers the same surface as the second but is slightly reduced in area. It extends thinly over the edge and down to the level of the eyes and slightly defines the nose. This third is the lighter area of the oblique, back and front view. A fourth overlay of dull, blackish brown forms the irregular shape in the lighter area. A medium to coarse grain, angular, hard to slightly friable sandstone with slightly red, clay matrix with a trace of orange feldspar granular inclusions. Five to ten percent intergranular porosity.

Location: North central Sweetwater County, Wyoming.

This artifact could not be passed over because it could bring so much history to light if it were studied by trained, experienced paleontologists. There would be an excellent chance that it (along with the array of artifacts found with it) would reveal some plants being used as food, flora existing in the area of the site, and data concerning clan organization as long ago as seven to nine thousand years. Alberta points were found with the effigy. Secrist's Guide (third edition, p.56) gives the age of Alberta points as "7000 B.C. to 5000 B.C.".

The first dark brown overstain is thought to be a heavy patina or light rind. The second, nearly black, has not been identified but could possibly have been caused by fungal growth or another form of plant growth. Phototropism may have been the cause of the extension of the stain to the one area of the stone's edge. The third, nearly white encrustation is fungus residue. It is not known when this grew, but when it died it acted as a cement and would certainly contain identifiable fungal structures, as well as other entrapped seed, spores, and similar evidence.

Some plant fibers are visible. The "elbow" mark below and slightly to the right of the nose (front view) is thought to be the distal growth of a plant (when the stone lay on the surface), or a root (after .75 meter of alluvium covered it).

The fourth, blackish brown, irregular spot is a portion of the softer sandstone on which the effigy lay. It was cemented to it by the fungal residue.

A RARE EFFIGY No. 54
From the collection of:
Mrs. Eleanor Kendall
Riverton, Wyoming

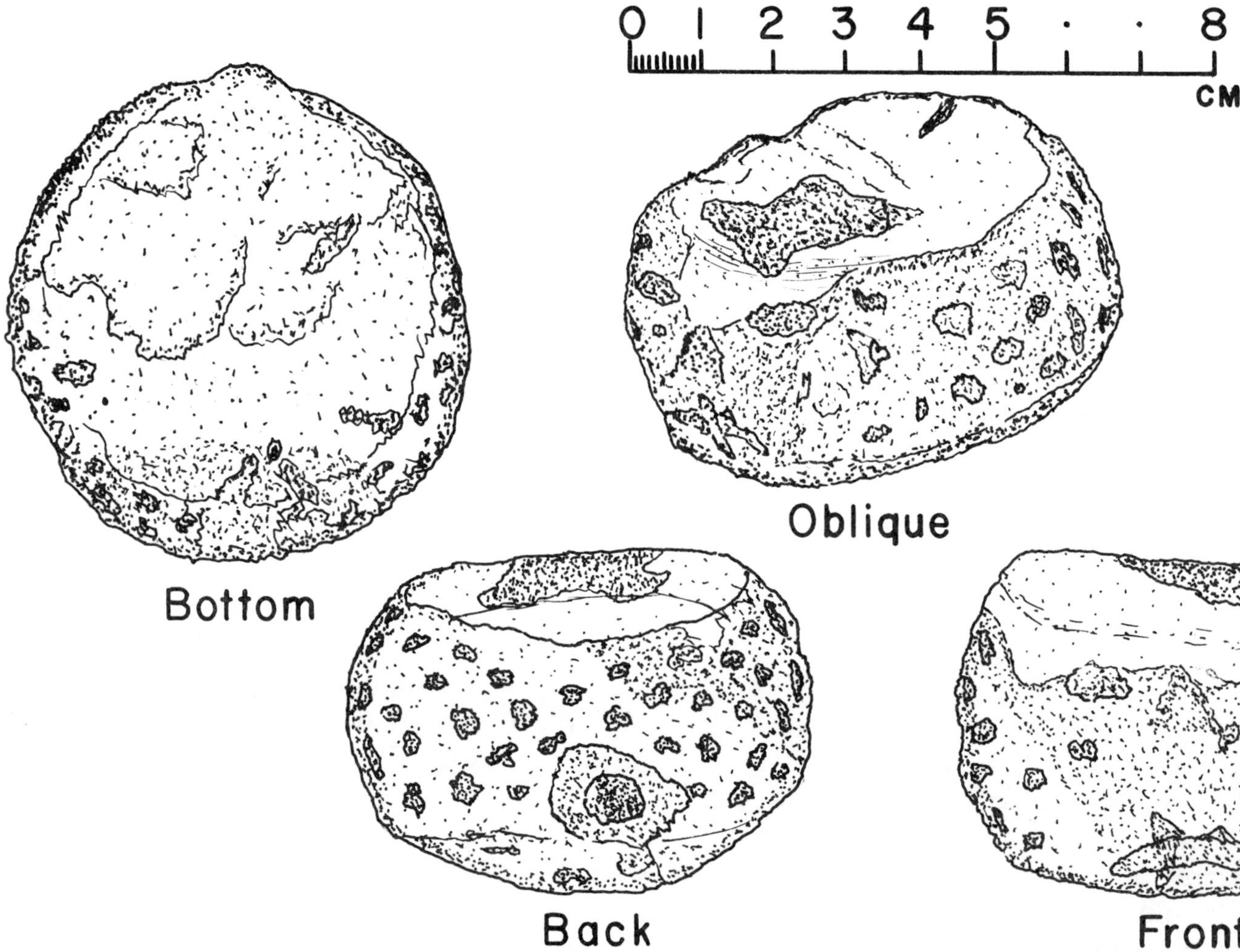

THOUGHT GAMING STONE TWO YEARS–FACE THEN FOUND
(Tail discovered days later)

Shortly after the face was discovered by Mrs. Kendall's daughter, Patt Brown, she suggested it looked much like a turtle's face. Later, while preparing the art copy for it, the author took a break and sat near it in a recliner. The stone was on the corner of the drawing table upon a sheet of white paper. Looking at it, at near eye level, and from the side, the concave top of the stone became the back of the head and neck. The convex bottom became the lower curve of the turtle's neck if it were extended. The face appeared in the proper, vertical plane and the triangular nose (no longer present but the fungus separated to grow around it) was at the proper elevation between the eyes if the neck were extended upward in the normal walking position. On examining the back of the stone the tail (previously undiscovered) became most evident, clearly visible against the white paper. This seemed to confirm a turtle effigy.

This artifact was shown to Pius Moss, an Arapaho, age 75, who teaches Arapaho language, history and heritage at St. Stephens Mission School, near Riverton, Wyoming. I asked if it would have been a child's toy or a clan symbol. He told me that the Arapaho Tribe (Northern Arapahoe) revered the turtle. In historic time, many tribes revered the turtle. Could this effigy be evidence of clan organization?

If this artifact dates back to nine thousand years before present, was there tribal organization then or simply nomadic bands? Was this a totem for an individual Indian? Or, was it a symbol representing a turtle clan?

This effigy may, in some small way, have brought a bit of the ancient past into the light of the present.

A BEAUTIFUL KNIFE, AN OLD, OLD POINT No. 55
From the collection of:
Helen Lookingbill
Riverton, Wyoming

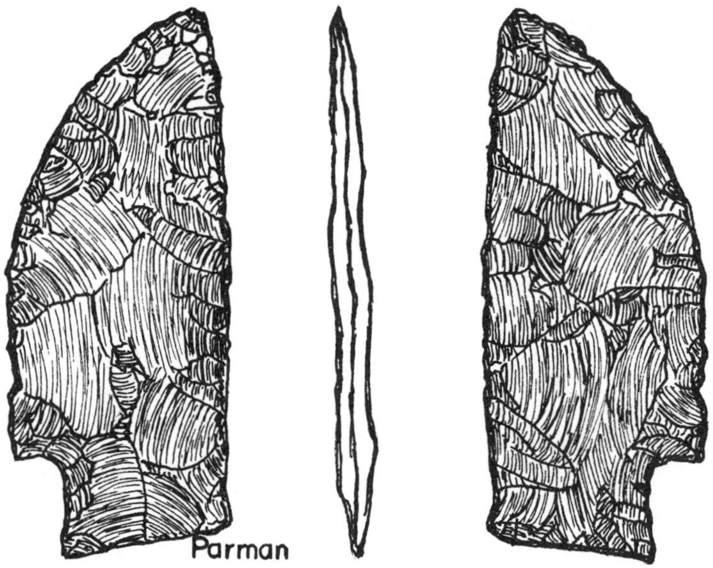

"B"

EVOLVED FROM CODY ?

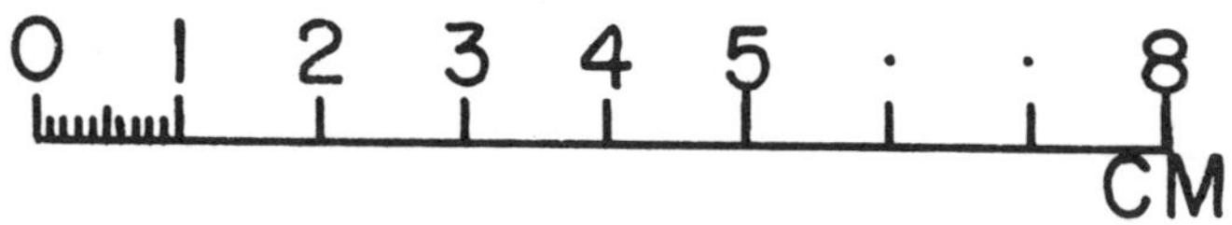

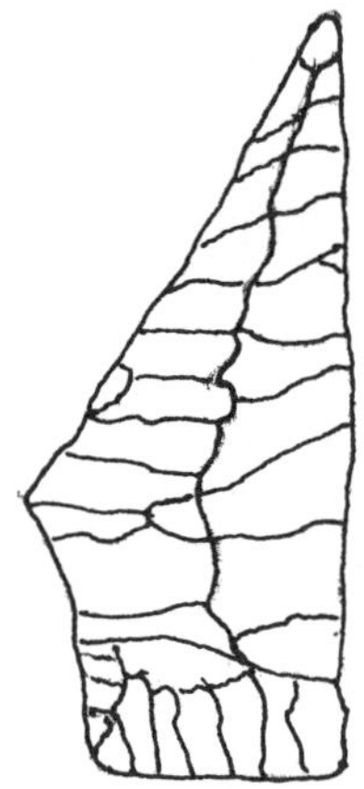

CODY KNIFE
from
SECRIST'S 3 Edition
P 107

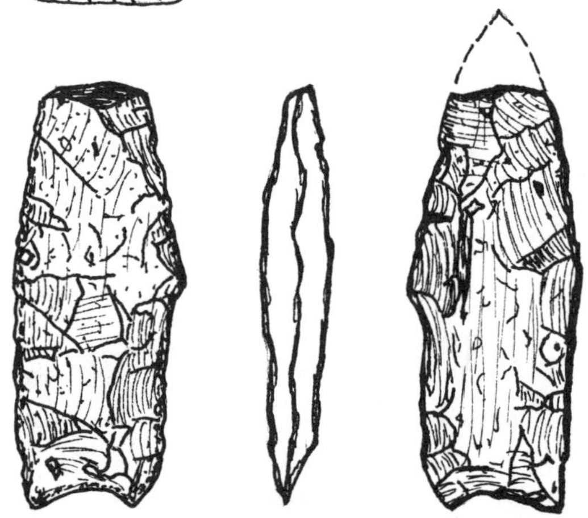

"A"

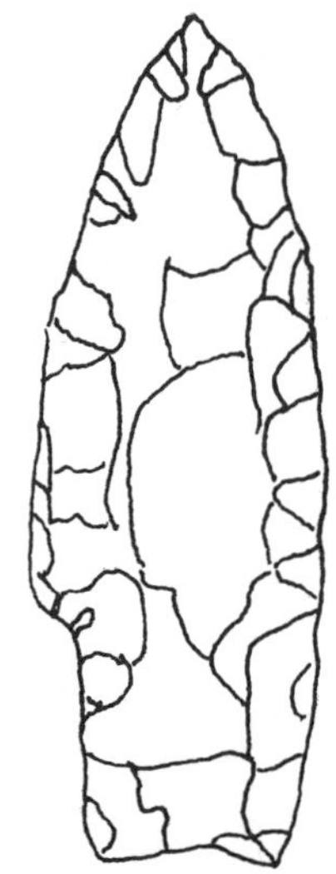

from
HIBBEN, 1941
pl 12, Ic

POSSIBLE SANDIA II

A BEAUTIFUL KNIFE, AN OLD, OLD POINT

Color & Material: A, Dull, stove black with dull, red staining in pinpoint porosity and slight crevices. Basalt. B, pastel cream with slight orange cast. Light grey-brown intrusion with dark brown, chromatographic banding of the edge of the brown area on the surface in the left view. A jasperlike chert or flint.

Location: A, southwestern Arizona. B, northwestern Sweetwater County, Wyoming.

Artifact A. The age of Sandia type points was thought to be around twenty thousand years (Hibben, 1941) but this age is now quite suspect. Whether Sandia predates Clovis (approximately 11,900 B.P.) is not yet known.

This artifact has been selected, for it most closely resembles the type example (illustrated by Hibben in 1946) of a point recovered from the Sandia Cave excavation. It was crafted of basalt, thought to have been used most frequently by Paleo Indian cultures. And it evidences extreme weathering, for the flaking is most indistinct.

Other Sandia finds have been reported as follows: one type II, from Manzano Cave (Hibben, 1941) ; two type Is and three type IIs from the Lucy site in Estancia Valley, New Mexico (Roosa, 1956) ; and possible surface finds in Alberta and Saskatchewan, Canada as well as Alabama (Wormington, 1957).

Artifact B. This knife is most beautiful and evidences an advanced stone technology. Note how thin and smooth the flat surfaces have been worked. Though it differs from Secrist's example of a Cody knife (by having a single shoulder) , most Cody knives examined by this writer have had two shoulders. The one (shoulder) on the straight back has usually been very shallow.

All examples have had straight (or very near-so) working edges. This one displays a most convex working edge, and to describe it as a Cody knife would not be correct. It is possibly an evolved improvement of the Cody knife, providing more strength to the working tip of the blade.

UNUSUAL, UNIDENTIFIED FINDS No. 56
From the collection of:
Stuart & Nancy Shepherd
Riverton, Wyoming

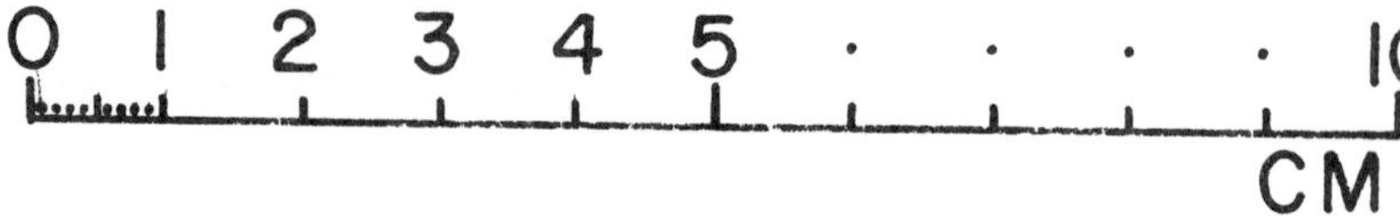

"A"

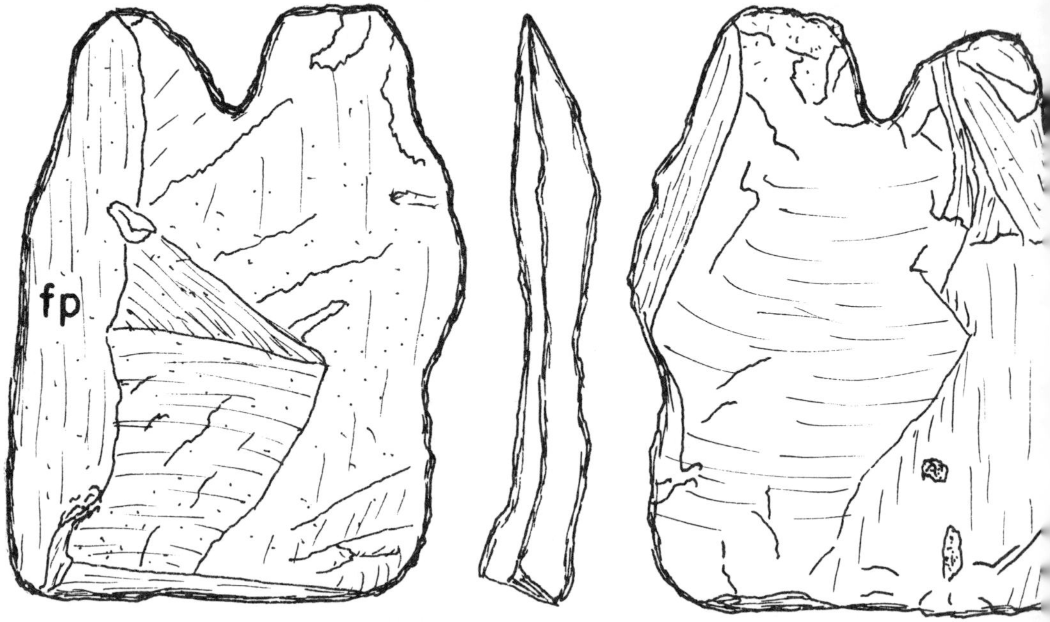

"B"

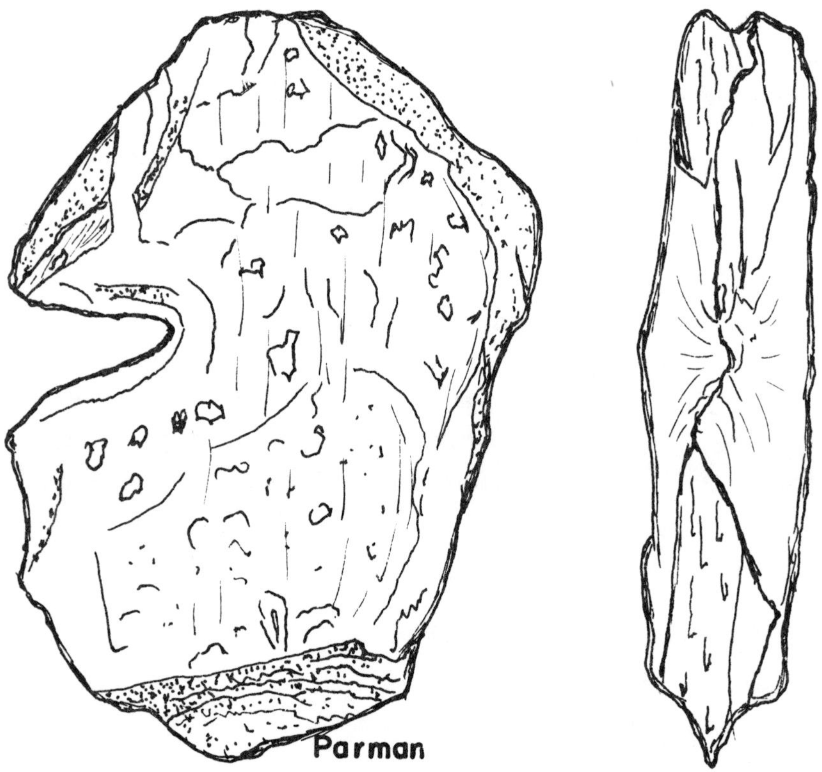

WHAT TASK CAUSED THESE TOOLS TO BE MADE

?

ARE THERE MANY OTHERS

?

UNUSUAL, UNIDENTIFIED FINDS

Color & Material: A, dull, dark black with slight grey rind. Clean, hard basalt. B, grey to dark grey with some light rind. Hard, platy, micaceous shale.

Location: Both, south of Reno, Nevada.

Artifact A was crafted out of very hard, dense basalt with one large percussion flake struck from each side at the base, or edge opposite the notch. The flat surface labeled "fp" is a natural fracture plane. It has the greatest patina of all surfaces.

There is no evidence of chipping or flaking nor indication of how the notch was cut into the stone. The interior edge of the notch does display a light grey, crushed surface that is evenly distributed in width and depth. There is no indication of wear or polishing either in the bottom of the notch or the surface bordering it on either side. This seems to rule out use as a scraper.

Artifact B was crafted of a flat, platy, shale cobble that was reduced to hand size by striking off the ends. The thin edge, on which the notch was cut, was caused by the convergence of two bedding planes forming the sides of the stone. The notch displays the same characteristics as described for artifact A.

The reason these two artifacts were selected was that the Shepherds and the author have never seen similar tools in private or published collections. They were found by the Shepherds over 500 miles, and four years, apart.

What specific task created the need for simple, hand- held, notched stones? If stripping, drawing, and scraping are ruled out by the lack of worn or polished surfaces, then it would seem that the crushed, inner edges of the notches point to something having been wedged into them. Why then, were they held in the hand? Or were they? Harvesting grass seed has been suggested. Perhaps the tool was not used sufficiently to cause a wear pattern to show in the notches.

Stuart and Nancy Shepherd would like to know if anyone might have similar artifacts, or know how they were used. Their address is: 407 South Broadway, Riverton, Wyoming 82501.

OLD ARTIFACTS No. 57
From the collection of:
Bruce W. Bergstrom
Greybull, Wyoming

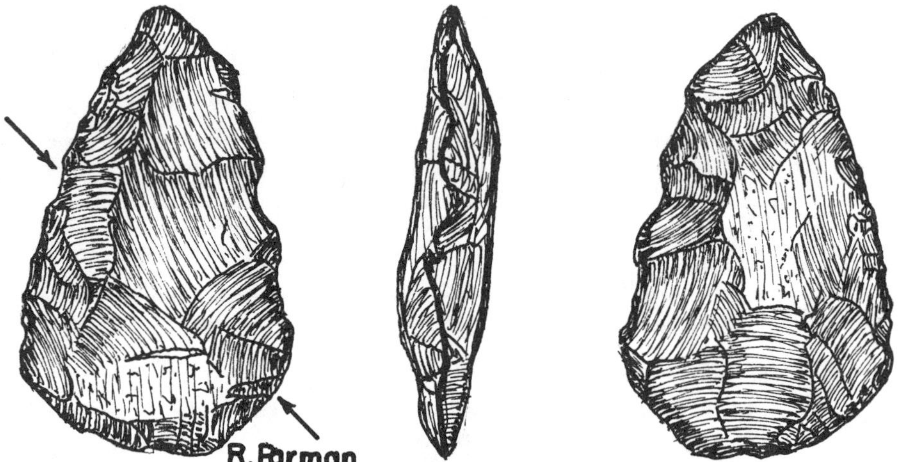

"A"

DART POINT

Examples from SECRIST'S GUIDE 3rd Edition

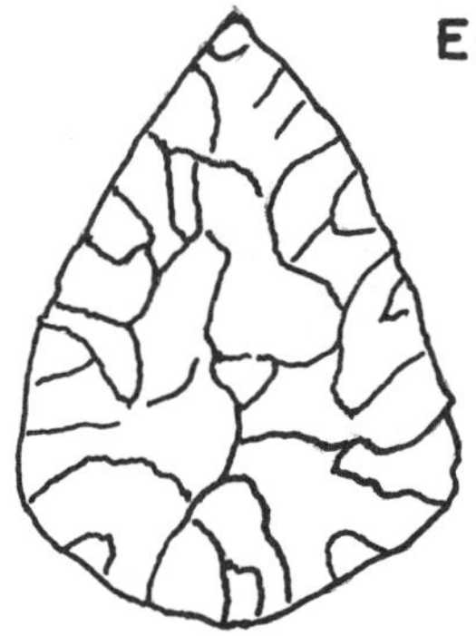

MARROW MTN.
ROUNDED BASE
p 26
(7,000 to 4,500 B.C.)

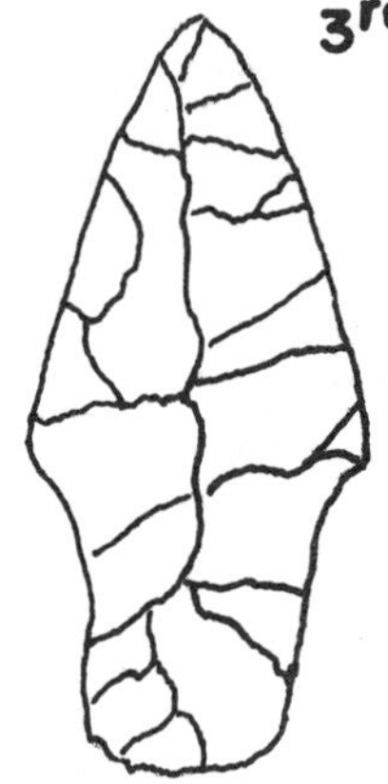

KENT
p 55
(1,000 B.C.)

ELAM
p 57
(500 B.C.)

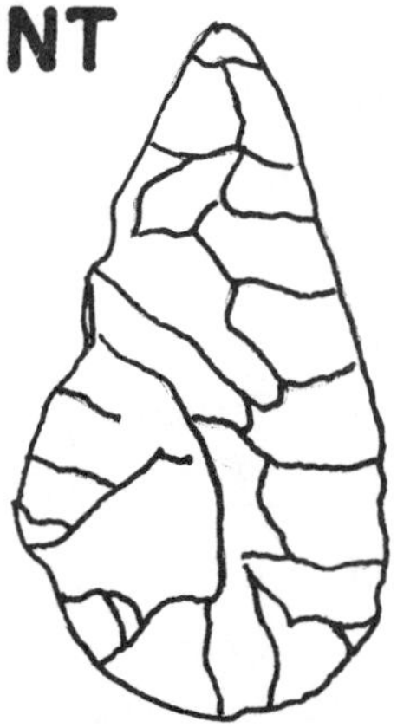

ABASOLO
R.E. Bell, 1964
p 3 Pl. 1-D
(5,000 to 3,000 B.C.)

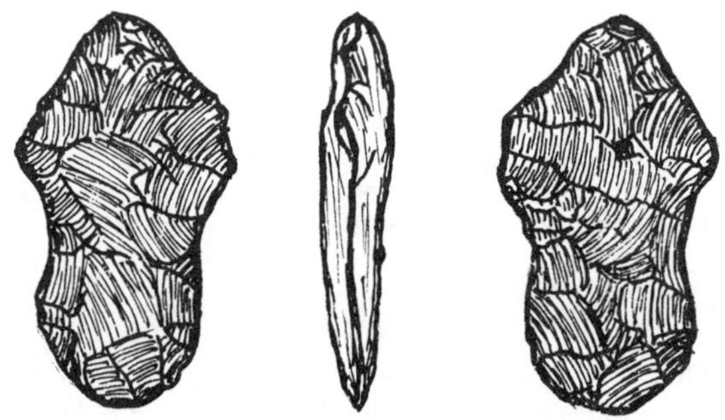

"B"

OLD ARTIFACTS

Color & Material: Artifact A, milk white with very slight blue cast. Small, irregular, white inclusions. Bone white rind covering all of surface in right view. Slightly thinner rind on side in left view. An irregular, tan incrustation 1.7 cm wide diagonally between the arrows. Agate.

Artifact B, tan with slight, brown-orange washes along length. Very faint, light orange patina. Marked weathering. Material not recorded.

Location: A, east of Meeker, Colorado. White River Mountains.

B, Lost Creek drainage, Southwest Wyoming.

Artifact A. This medium-sized dart point with its crude flaking, basal thinning, and the amount of rind formed on it, caught the authors attention. Whether identified as a Marrow Mountain Rounded Base or an Abasolo, it gets this writer's vote to be in the 5,000 to 7,000 year old range.

Artifact B. This unusual point also drew attention for its marked weathering. Some time was spent trying to determine how to classify it, too. A good friend, Mrs. Helen Lookingbill, who is very knowledgeable concerning artifacts, has suggested that it may have been used as a throwing stick (atlatl) weight. Its shape would make it easy to bind on the end of the atlatl. By adding weight, a greater force could be imparted to the spear (with dart point attached) being launched.

A SANDIA I TYPE POINT No. 58
From the collection of:
Joe & Arlene Tyrrell
Lovell, Wyoming

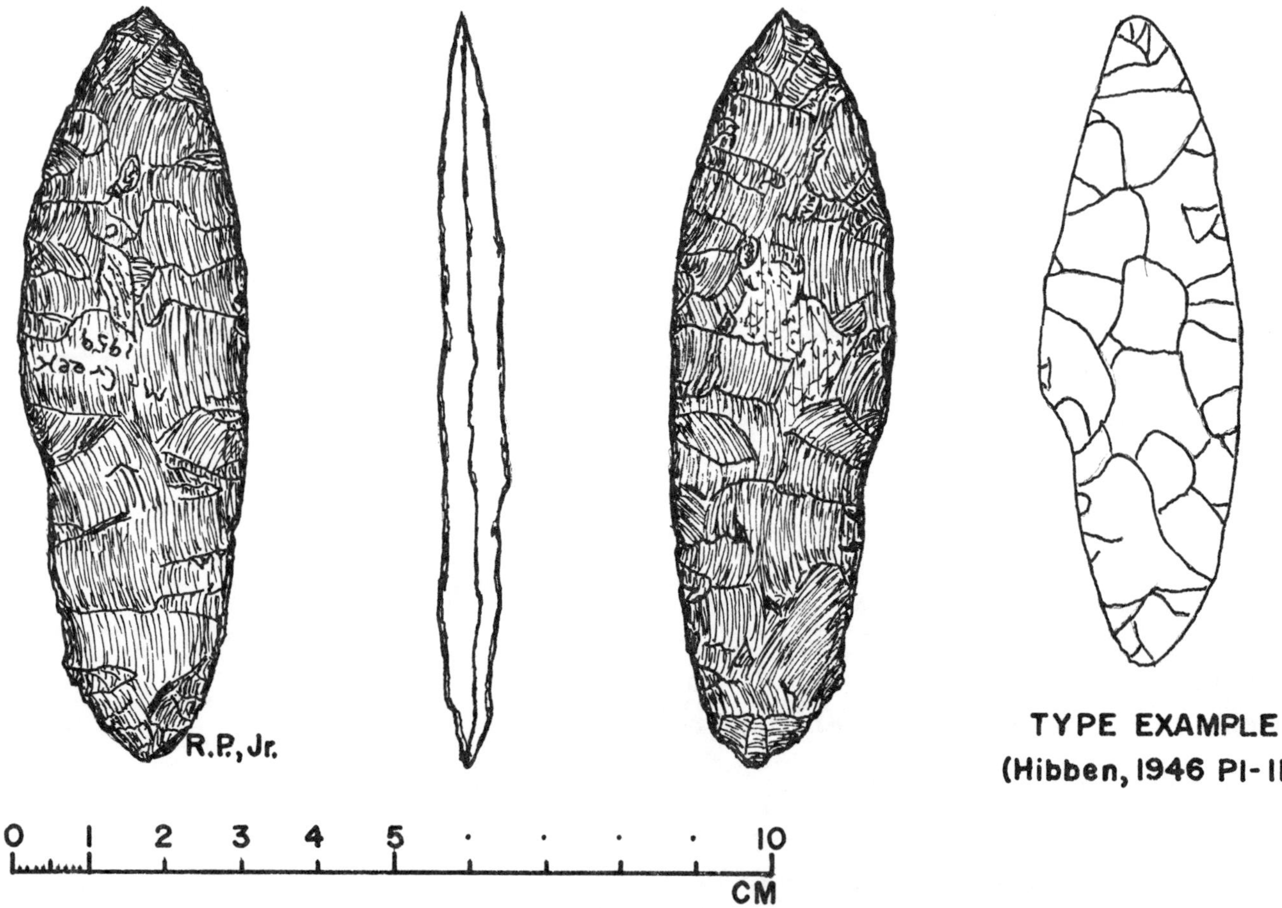

TYPE EXAMPLE
(Hibben, 1946 Pl-IIe)

STONE TAKEN FROM SAME QUARRY AS 33

A SANDIA I TYPE POINT

Color & Material: Egg shell white with very faint tan cast. A clear, shiny patina; and a light pastel, clear to tan to pink inclusion in the base approximately two centimeters wide. A chertlike chalcedony.

Location: Southeastern Big Horn County, Wyoming.

On a previous page, a possible Sandia I point (No. 33) from the collection of John Larsen of Rawlins, Wyoming, was reported. It was rather exciting to discover that this point, No. 58, was crafted from material taken from the same quarry. Particularly exciting when one considers that two points, as similar in all characteristics as these two, were probably fashioned by the same band of people if not by the same craftsman.

There has been professional controversy with respect to the validity of Sandia Cave artifacts and their published age of 20,000 B.C.

Some professionals suggested that particular artifacts (reported as Sandia) had been brought from Africa and included in those covered in the initial Sandia cave report. There is evidence that contradicts this theory however.

Marie Wormington, a noted authority, reported surface finds of Sandia points in Alabama, Alberta and Saskatchewan. The initial site of discovery was near Albuquerque, N. Mexico. Private collections examined throughout Wyoming, have included five Sandia-like points. These surface finds were taken from near a line running from Rawlins, Wyoming, at the southern border to Lovell, Wyoming, at the northern border. One additional Sandia point was taken in western Arizona.

This evidence leads one to believe there was a Sandia culture, for an area as expansive as that from which these finds have been reported could not have been "salted".

FRAGMENT OF VERY OLD KNIFE No. 59
From the collection of:
Ed Fowler
Riverton, Wyoming

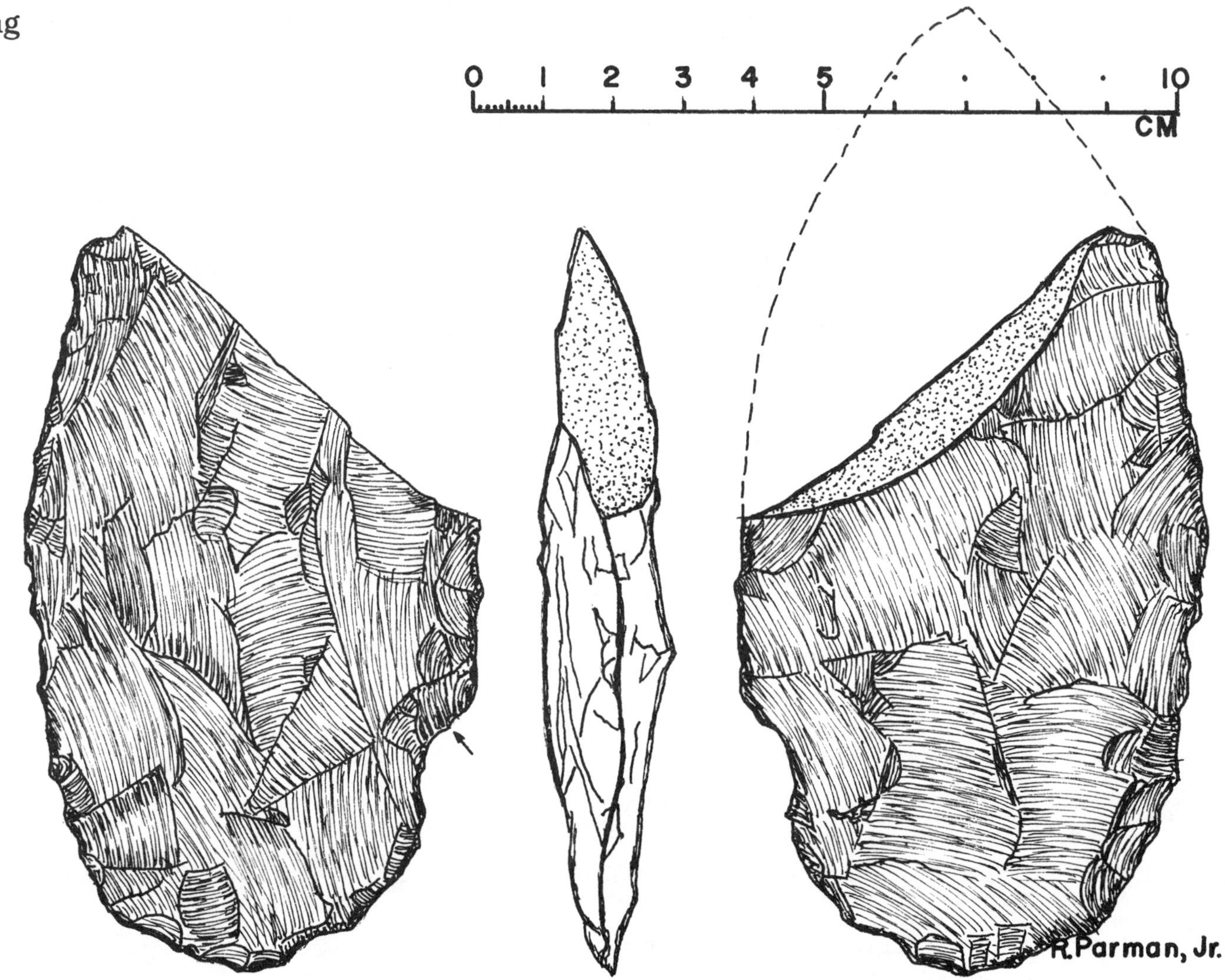

TRADEMARK FOR A BLADESMITH

FRAGMENT OF VERY OLD KNIFE

Color & Material: Pale, dull orange with slight brown cast. Very thin, light tan rind covering the surface in the left view (except its ridges and edges). Fairly heavy, light tan rind covering entire surface (except the extreme edges) in right side view. Fine-grain quartzite with reduced depth of color caused by argillaceous (clay) impurities.

Location: Cultivated lowland on west bank of Wind River, northeast of Riverton, Fremont County, Wyoming.

Ed Fowler was rather pleased to have found this knife fragment on his land. Knowing that a maker of knives occupied his land thousands of years ago had a personal significance to him. Fowler is a bladesmith (this stone knife is his trademark) whose knives are shown throughout the state, and measure with the best. He holds the distinction of forging the first two Damascus steel knife blades in Wyoming.

This large knife fragment, that was plowed up, has the distinctive, single shoulder of the Sandia. Is this a true shoulder, or just the appearance of one caused by a shaft scraping notch?

The fairly heavy rind does indicate age, but one has no way of knowing how long the knife lay exposed or buried. The size might indicate this tool had been used as a chopper. Sharpening would reduce its size until it could be used as a knife. More reduction might have eventually caused it to become a dart point.

A dart point predates the bow & arrow and is usually somewhat larger than the arrow point. It was a affixed to the "foreshaft" and this assembly was called the "dart". It was used in conjunction with the throwing stick called the "atlatl".

UNUSUAL FINDS No. 60
From the collection of:
Barbara Swenson
Hanna, Wyoming

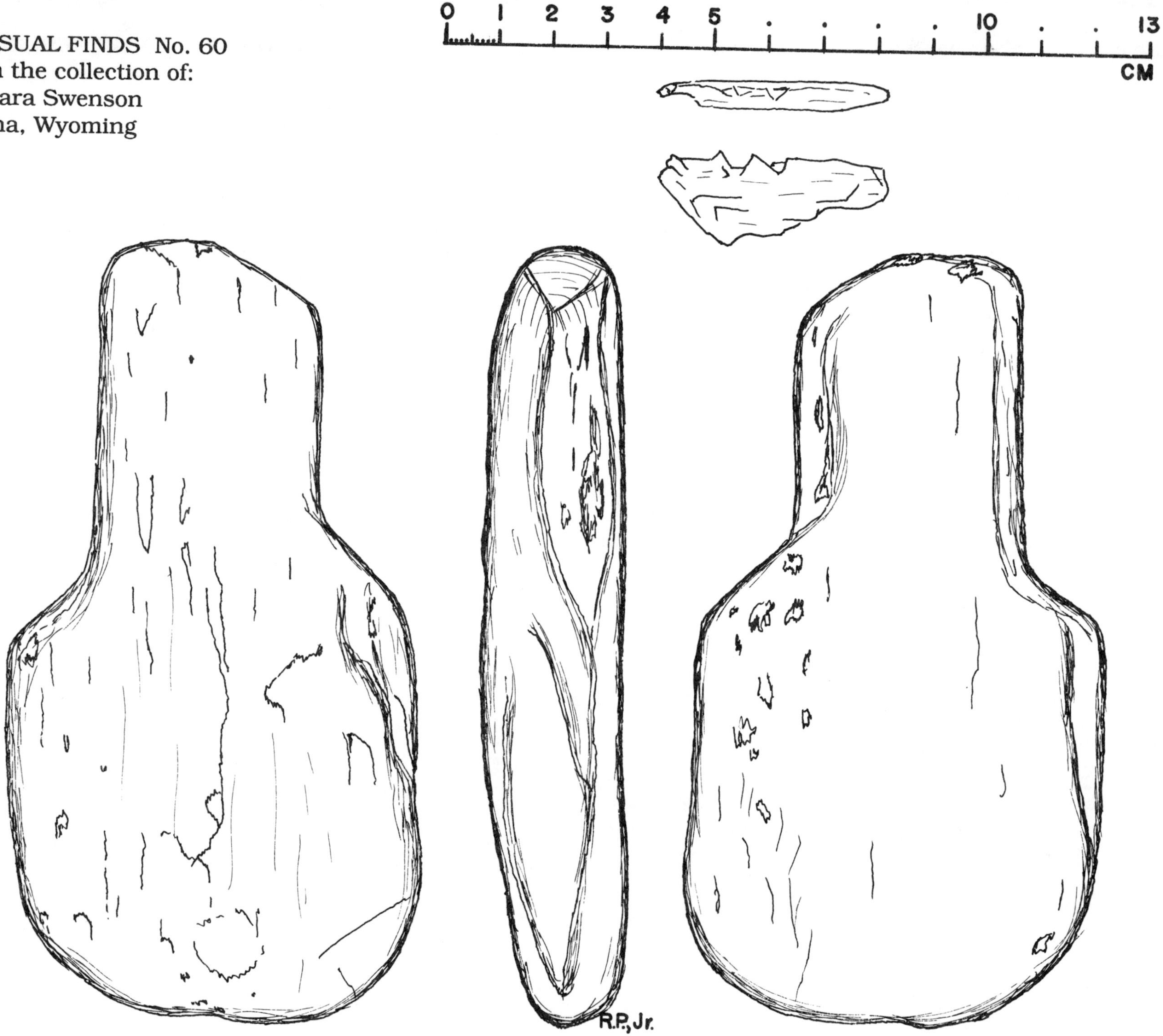

UNUSUAL FINDS

Color & Material: Tan to light brown; with slightly darker brown, stainlike color along the left edge of the right view. A heavy patina over all surfaces except the edges of the handle.

Location: Near Hanna, in southeastern Carbon County, Wyoming.

The paddle, at first thought to have been totally shaped by nature, was carried to the site where it was found. It was not indigenous to that area. When I saw this artifact, Mother's butter paddle came to mind. How was pemmican blended? Berries, seed, nut meats and jerked meats had to be blended together evenly in order to preserve the meat. It also had to be packed into containers for storage. It would be like working whey out of butter, working the salt into it, and packing it, with the butter paddle, into the butterbox. Could this stone have been used for that purpose?

There is an excellent possibility that the handle of the paddle was shaped by man in the same way as the artifact in No. 91.

A BEAUTIFUL CLOVIS POINT No. 61
From the collection of:
Brandon McNamara
Rawlings, Wyoming

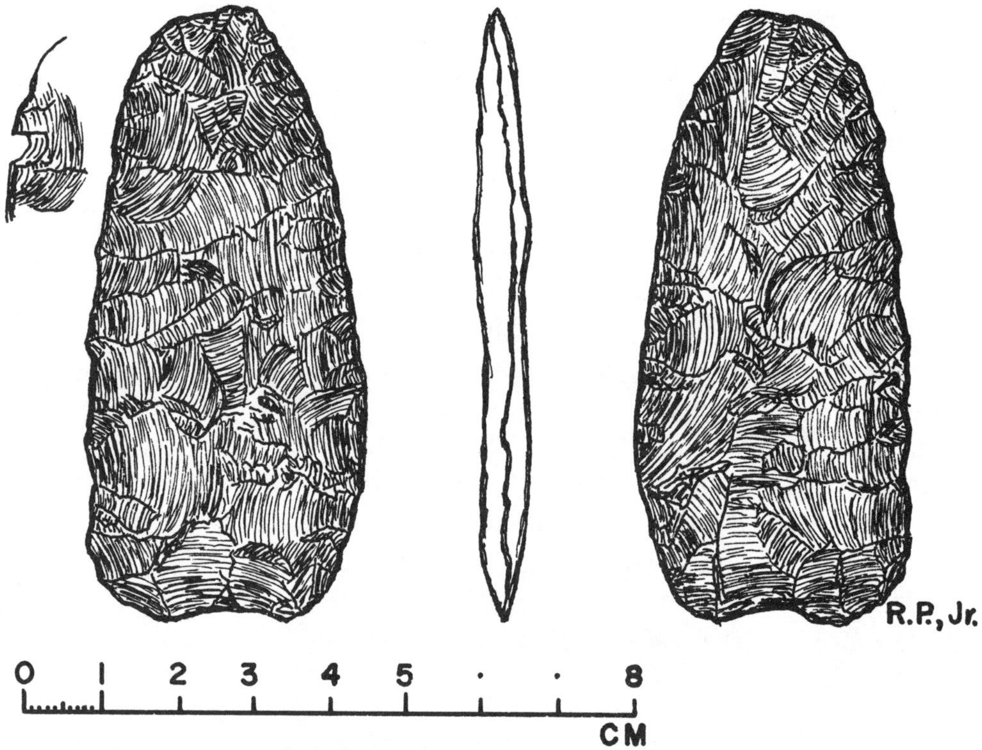

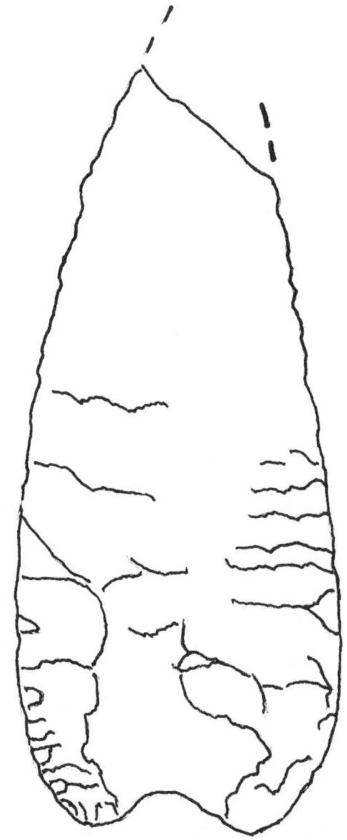

TYPE EXAMPLE
Plains Chronology
Reher & Hughes

FOUND IN SAME AREA AS BUTCHERED MAMMOTH

A BEAUTIFUL CLOVIS POINT

Color & Material: Pastel tan with pale blue and lavender inclusions at the mid-section. It has an overall tan cast and clear, shiny patina. A chert-like jasper with chalcedonous inclusions.

Location: Approximately six miles south of Rawlins, Carbon County, Wyoming.

This beautiful point closely matches thc description of Clovis points compiled by Dr. Charles Reher and Susan Hughes at the University of Wyoming. However, this point does not evidence the grinding they mentioned. It is not known how important grinding is to identification; otherwise this point exhibits the features they have listed, which are: 1. Large lanceolate with slightly convex lateral edges; 2. Base ranges from straight to highly concave; 3. Grinding along base & lower lateral edges; 4. Irregular percussion flaking with some pressure flaking along margins; 5. Flute is present on one or both sides, usually extending less than halfway up the length.

There are two dated mammoth sites in Wyoming. One is the Colby Site, east of Worland (approx. 11,200 years before present) where Clovis points were found. The other is the Union Pacific Mammoth Site (11,280 B.P.) , southwest of Rawlins where a butchered mammoth was found but no points.

It is of interest that this point was found in the same general region as the U.P. site.

OLD CODY KNIFE, UNIDENTIFIED POINT No. 62
From the collection of:
Darrell Gothard
Rawlins, Wyoming

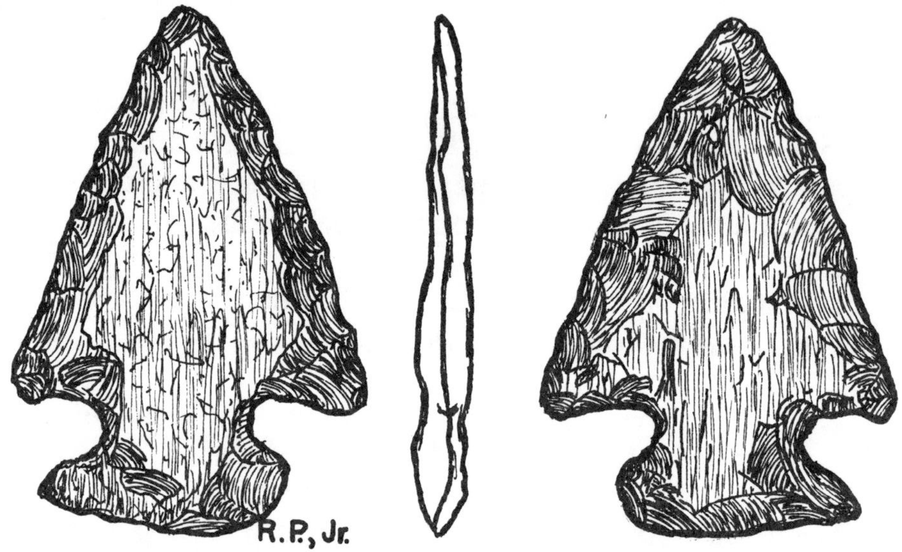

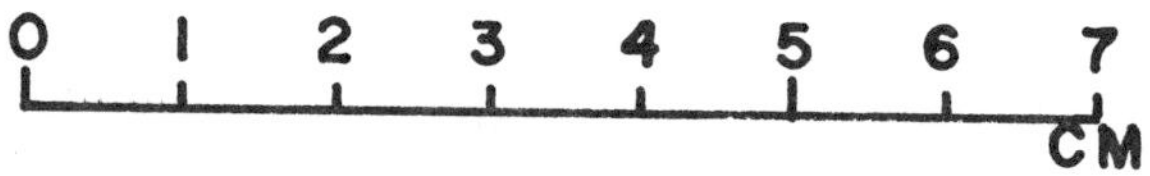

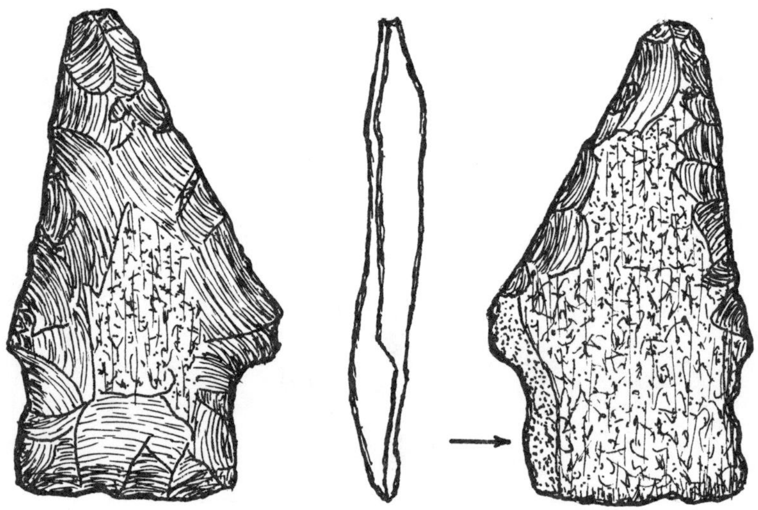

CODY KNIFE

(→ Ground Surface)

Jack's Reef Or Brewerton

(Corner Notched)

?

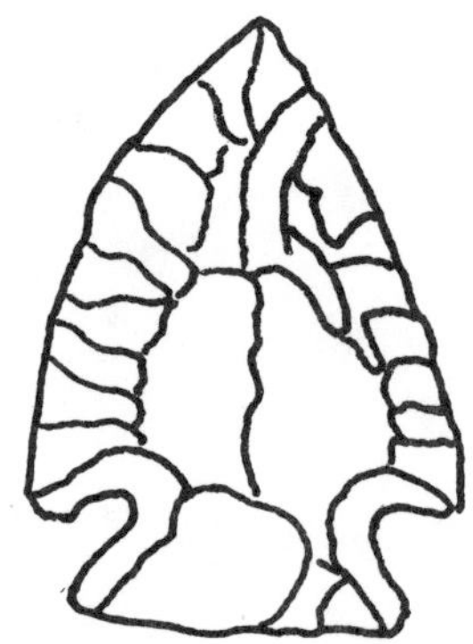

JACK'S REEF

TYPE EXAMPLES from Secrist's Guide

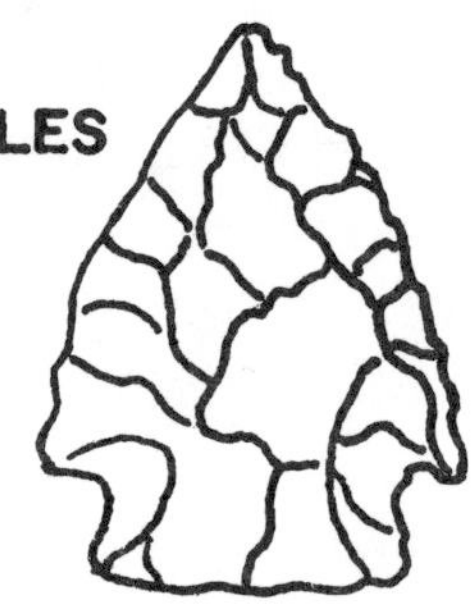

BREWERTON

OLD CODY KNIFE, UNIDENTIFIED POINT

Color & Material: Cody knife, light tan and lavender laminated through the longest dimension with faint fractures essentially diagonal across the laminae. A slight orange appears in the fractures with thin, pale orange rind over all surfaces. Fine to medium-grain quartzite.

Point dark, dull, clean olive-drab (army) with hard, shiny glaze and thick, dull orange rind on unflaked surfaces. Chert.

Location: Knife, north of Rawlins, northwest Carbon County, Wyoming.

Point, north central Carbon County, Wyoming.

This knife was taken from the east side of a north-south ridge with fire pots nearby. No teepee rings were noted.

The tip appears to have been broken and subsequently reworked. The ground surface on the larger shoulder (right view) appears to be from use. Cody knives have been dated about 9,000 years before present. This one may have been used as a shaft scraper; the grinding was to sharpen the working edge.

The point (possibly a stemmed knife) could not be identified. The two examples shown are markedly separate in age. The Brewerton points date from 5,000 B.C., but the Jack's Reef points are from only 500 B.C. to 500 A.D. The old appearance and crude flaking causes one to lean toward identification of Brewerton (notching more alike, also). Other finds in the area would help in this identification.

UNIQUE THROWING STONE No. 63
From the collection of:
Brandon & Laura McNamara
Rawlins, Wyoming

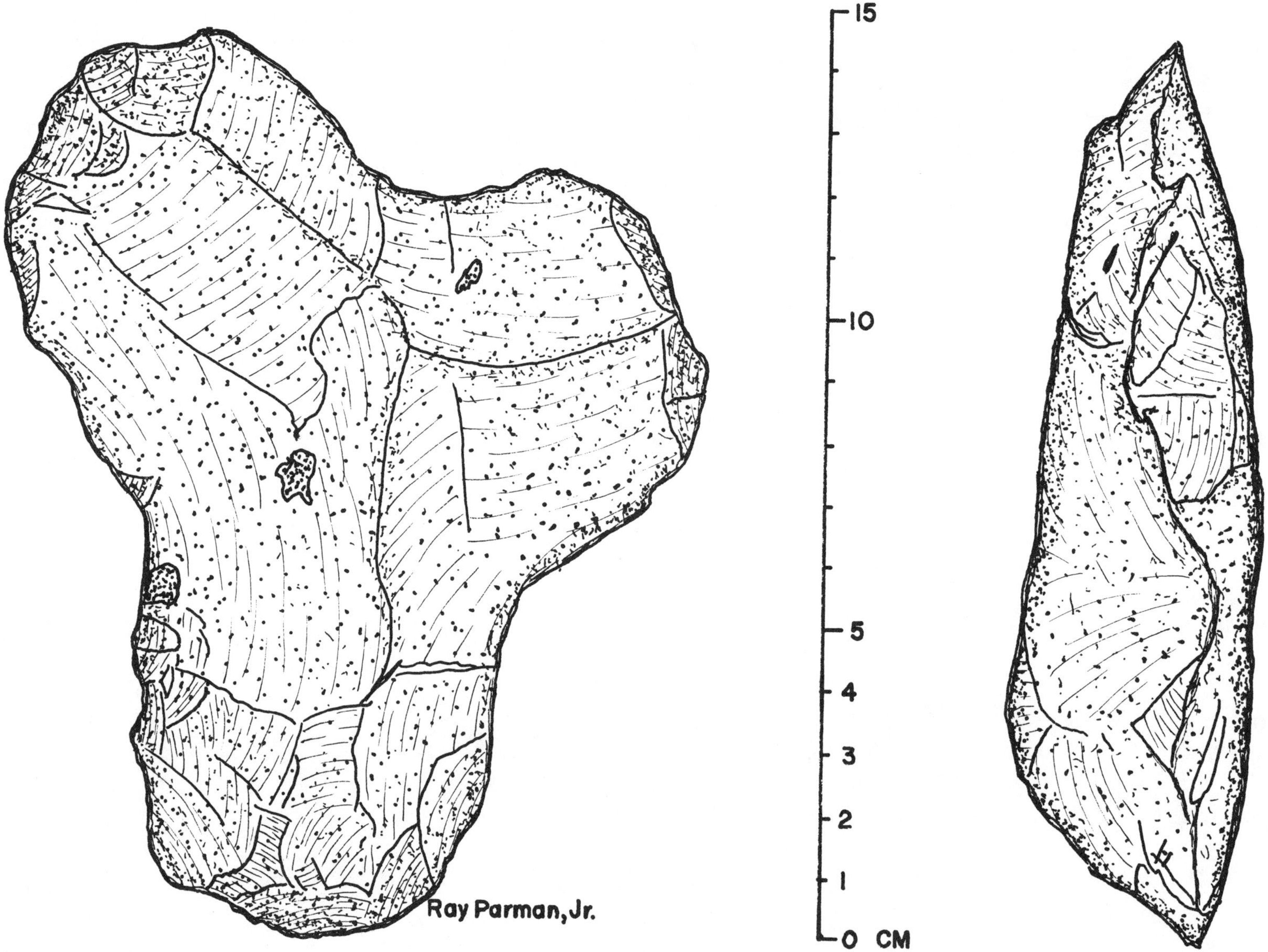

USED FOR SMALL GAME

UNIQUE THROWING STONE

Color & Material: Light grey with pale lavender cast and slightly darker grey, visible laminations. Dark, dirty brown patina on the obverse side. The reverse side has a very heavy patina and the spots are dark lavender inclusions. Medium to coarse-grain quartzite. The inclusions are unknown.

Location: The artifact was taken from a burn area in aspen woods on the foothills of Limestone Mountain, northwest of South Pass City in southwestern Fremont County, Wyoming.

The author has never seen an artifact such as this one. It is conjecture to call it a throwing stone; however, there is no evidence of use in any other way. The wooded terrain in which it was found, would have been the most suitable for its use as a throwing stone. In open flat land it would be difficult to get sufficiently close to game for a throwing stone to be used.

The weight and contour of this stone serves two purposes. Held in any position, the contour privides an excellent grip. Once thrown (spinning), it would provide a stable trajectory. The weight would provide a stunning blow, if not a killing one. Coupled with contour, the weight would quite likely break legs if the body of the animal was missed.

This stone was probably used with small game, but it is also possible to see this stone bringing down a deer.

UNUSUAL HOE OR SCRAPER No. 64
From from the collection of:
Sandra Warren
Evansville, Wyoming

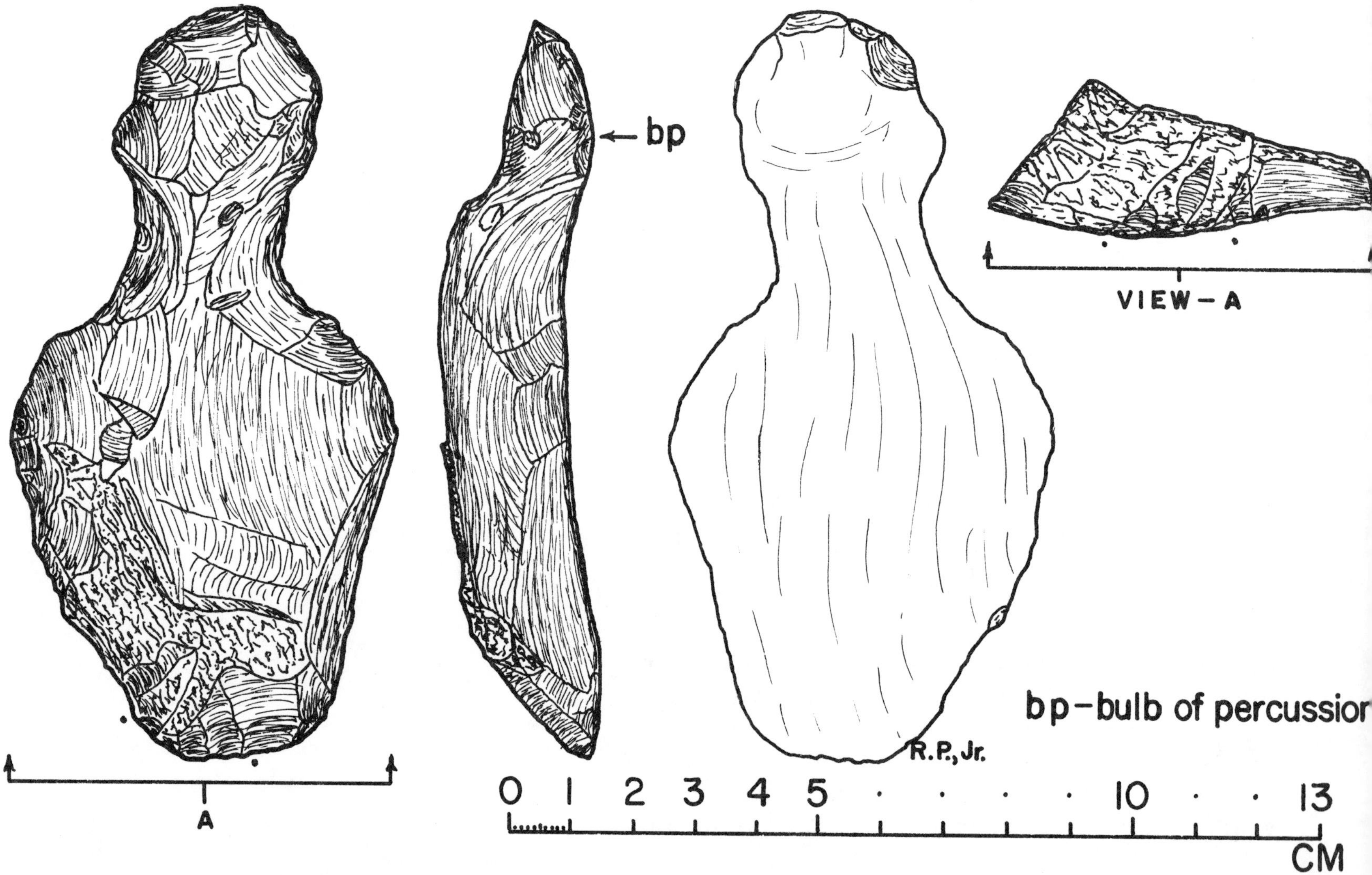

THOUGHT NOTCHED FOR THONG-NOT HANDLE

UNUSUAL HOE OR SCRAPER

Color & Material: An even, clean tan with the exception of a dark brown overstain that is almost covered by a thick, lighter tan encrustation (a rind remaining from the original outer surface of the stone) displayed on the lower left edge of the left view. A slightly impure grade of chert quarried near the area the artifact was found.

Location: Southwestern Wyoming

There are unusual characteristics and features of this artifact that brought about its selection for publication. It has been examined by an archaeologist (name unknown) who identified it as a notched hoe, and estimated an age of 10,000 years.

It has been crafted from a large percussion flake (bp) and mainly shaped by percussion flaking (evident by the numerous, large, curved, flake surfaces displayed in the left view).

Note the alignment of the notches (left view) with the abrupt change in the surface contour of the ridge between the notches displayed in the edge view (upper end left side). The ridge continues across the notches. In view of this, it is thought that the attaching of a thong, not the hafting of a handle, was intended.

The archaeologist's description should be given strong consideration. However, examination discloses no nicking or scratching that would occur on the flake faces of the working end if it were used as a hoe. The edge between the dots (lower left view and view A) does display the tiny, crushed flaking parallel to the edge that occurs when an edge is used for forceful scraping.

Many (including this writer) have looked at notches shaped as those displayed by the artifact, and immediately thought of hafting a handle to it. This may not have been true.

Whether held in the fingers or grasped in the hand, this tool fits with comfort in either hand. If a thong were attached with the knot on the surface displayed in the view, the thong would appear (in this left view drawing) as inverted Y with the knot resting against the shoulder of the ridge previously mentioned.

Those of you who have used nail clippers will realize how placing the loop of chain around a finger helps to hold the clippers firmly. The attached thong works the same way. If the thong is wrapped first around the palm of the hand, then drawn tight when the tool is grasped, it may be held more firmly.

SPLENDID EAGLE EFFIGY No. 65
From the collection of:
Norene Thompson
Cokeville, Wyoming

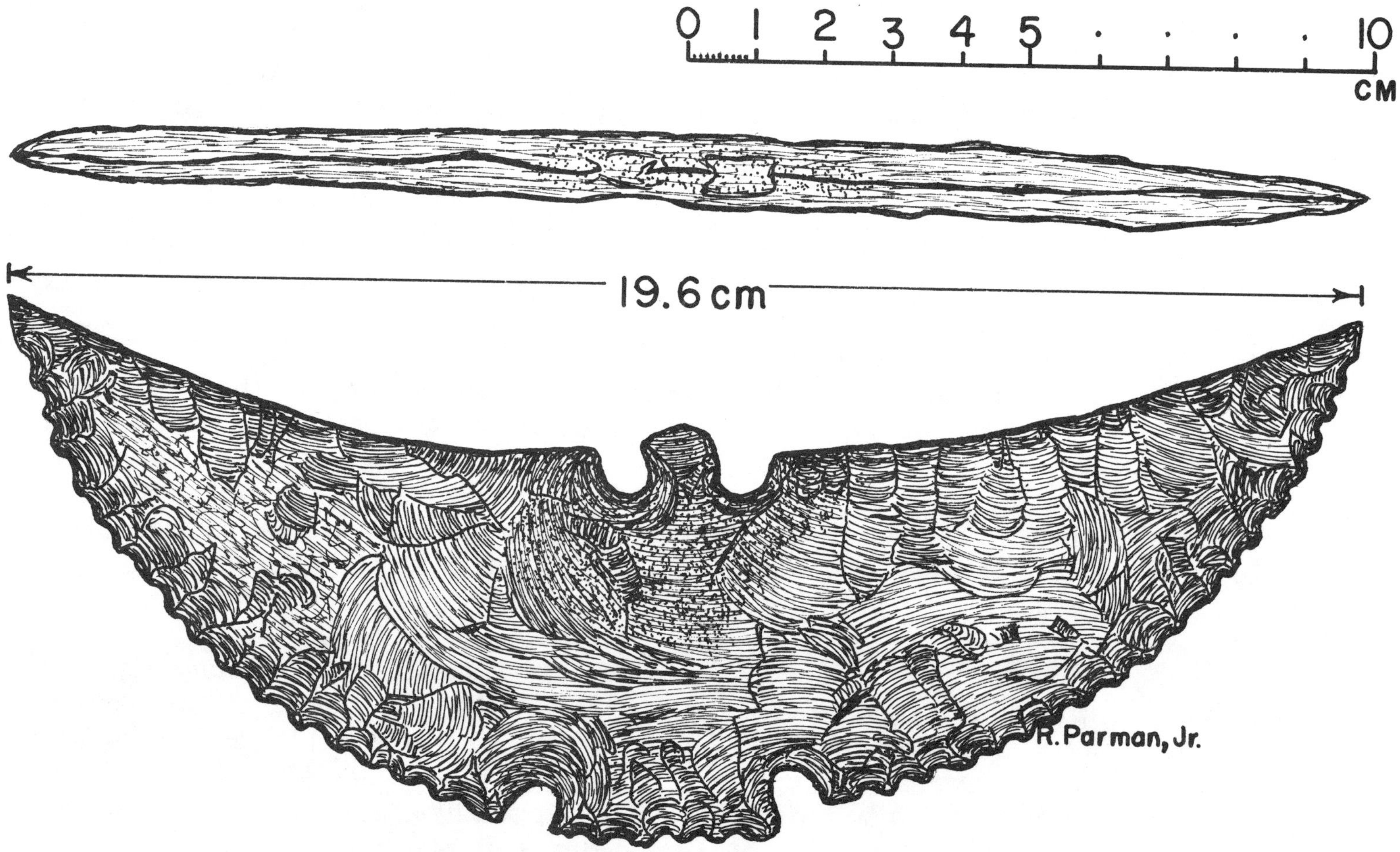

PROBABLY COMANCHE CEREMONIAL

SPLENDID EAGLE EFFIGY

Color & Material: A dull, pastel gray with a slight tan cast. The reverse side has a very slight orange patina in the depths of the flakes. A slightly darker, greyish brown, washed inclusion appears about the head and shoulders of the wings. Material from the same quarry as Patt Brown's Ceremonial Crescent reported in No. 37. Patt Brown's crescent was described from memory and should have been called orthoquartzite, the same as this Eagle Crescent. Both have slight traces of pale blue and white chalcedonous inclusions.

Location: This artifact was found in New Mexico in 1969.

Many consider all elaborately crafted,large artifacts such as this crescent and that of Patt Brown's, to be "fakes". They immediately mention "grey ghosts" and are critical of publishing artifacts of this nature. They have failed to note that the crescent (described in No. 37) was taken, as a surface find, in flat prairie land. Also, the Smithsonian determined from photographs that the artifact was probably Comanche Ceremonial.

While holding this magnificent crescent, one perceives a feeling of wonder. How skillfully the selected stone was crafted so the head and shoulders would be accented. Surely the craftsman's mental image was of the bald eagle. Did he simply find this stone? Or, did the eagle imprisoned within it, cry out to him? However it might have been, this magnificent eagle now soars freely in the boundaries of our imaginations.

Patt Brown's crescent (see No. 37) was taken to Cokeville, Wyoming in order that the two might be compared. They could very well have been crafted by the same person. Another crescent has been reported from South Dakota; a color photograph of it was sent to Patt. It is essentially identical to the one reported in No. 37. The stem is narrower and the material appears to be from the same quarry also. It is also possible the Comanche had discovered an excellent trade item.

FANTASTIC CEREMONIAL PIECE No. 66
From the collection of:
Jim Farver & Family
Rawlins, Wyoming

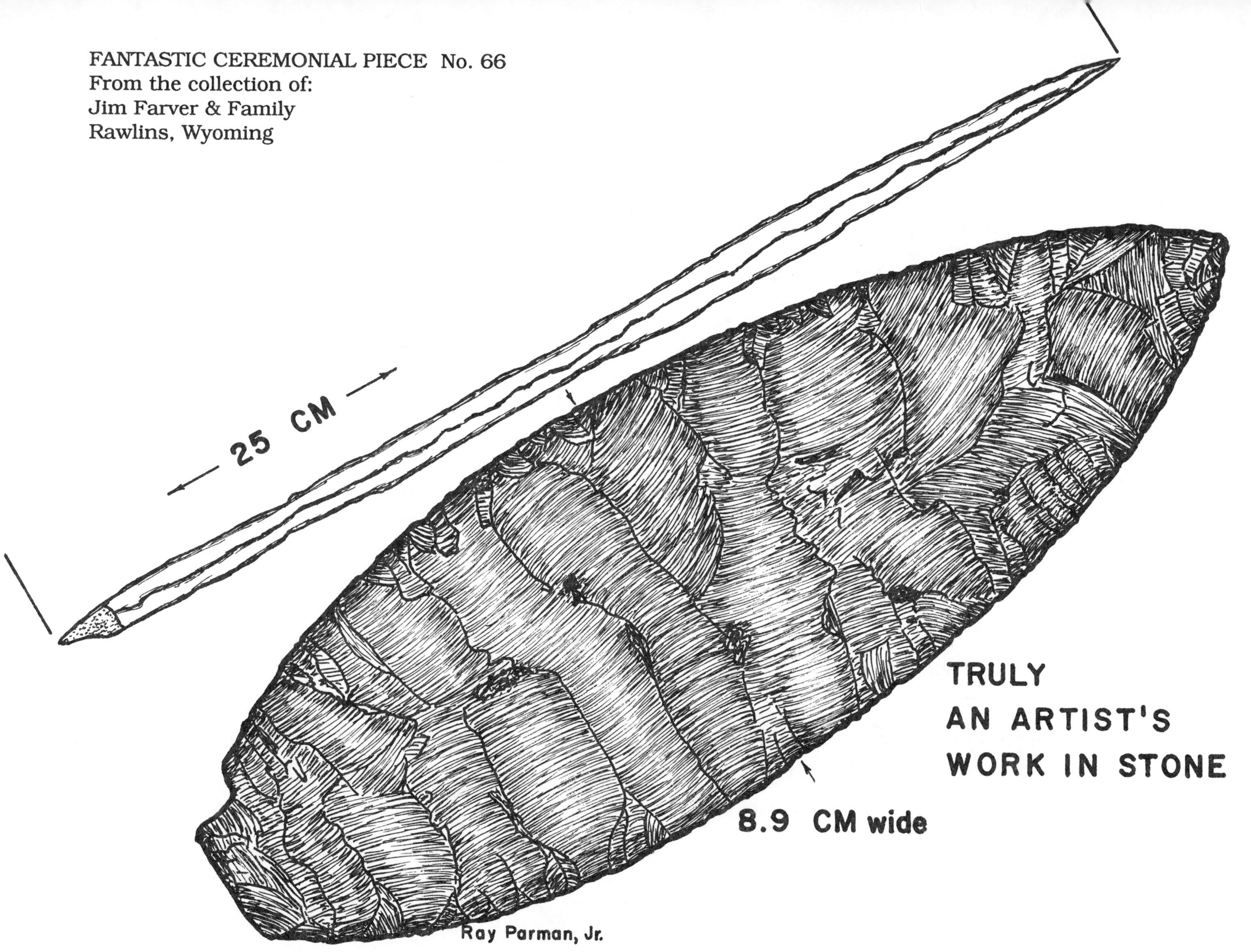

FANTASTIC CEREMONIAL PIECE

Color & Material: Medium greyish brown with diagonal lines slightly darker across the widest dimension. Chert.

Location: Lying half exposed in a near vertical position, the artifact was found on a friend's ranch in northern Carbon County, Wyoming, by Jim Farver's son, Mike.

It is thought this beautiful ceremonial lance tip has been crafted of chert taken from one of the quarries in central Uinta County, Wyoming. It is predominately brown and has many characteristics of the "tiger chert" from that area of the county.

The edge view, coupled with the large, transverse percussion flaking, discloses the truly remarkable feature of this piece. It is amazing what skill was needed to bring this wide blade to such a thin profile. Normally, thickness is limited to about one fifth of the width. This piece is just slightly over one tenth.

The observations of two professional archaeologists who have examined it express this writer's feelings about it quite well...."the craftsman's hallmark".

When showing this piece to me, Jim demonstrated one of its features. Placing it on a desk blotter, he traced one edge with a pencil from point to base. He then turned it over and aligned the opposing edge near the first trace. There was no more than two millimeters separation between the two lines. The perfect symmetry is interrupted only by the slight damage that has occurred to the base. This was probably caused by the hoof of an animal.

Its lack of notches, plus the transverse flaking and profile, leads one to believe it is of Paleo origin. Some day we may know.

UNIDENTIFIED ARTIFACT No. 67
From the collection of:
Richard Snook
Wheatland, Wyoming

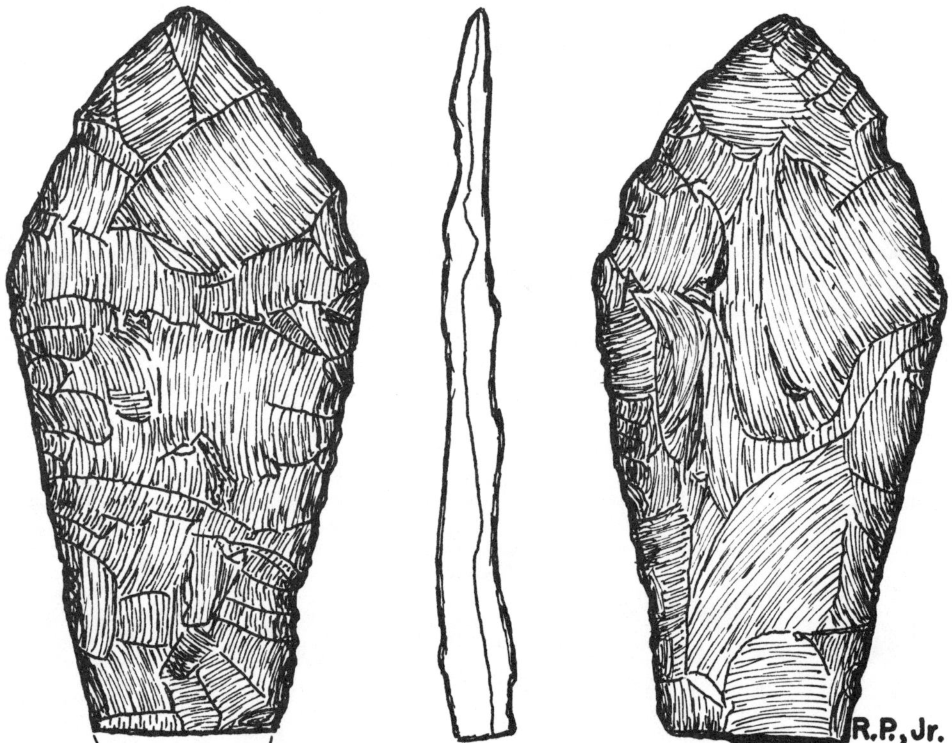

A LARGE DART POINT OR KNIFE ?
(Owner would like to know.)

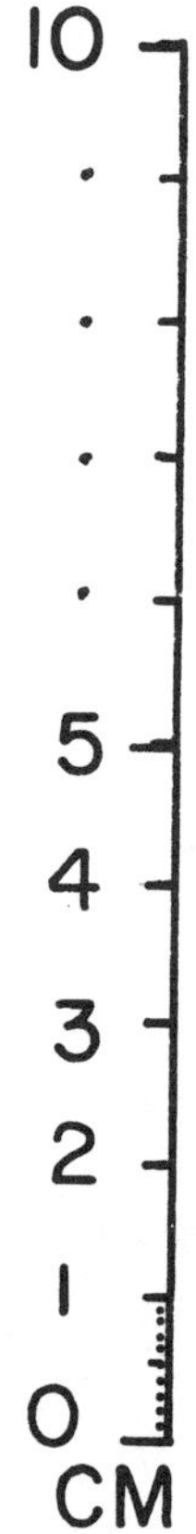

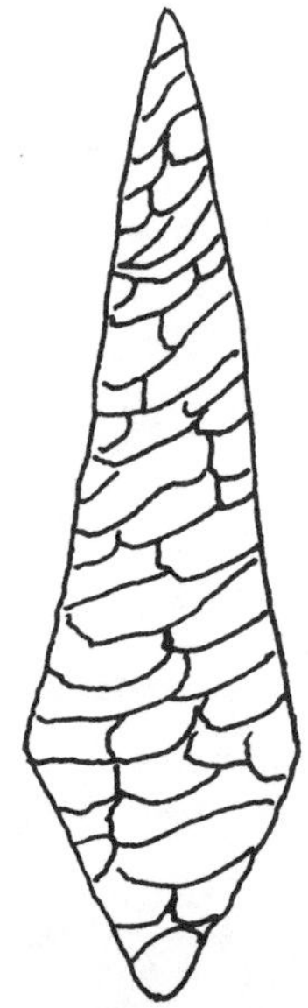

EXAMPLE
Triangular Based Knife

Secrist's Guide 3rd Ed.
(p. -107)

UNIDENTIFIED ARTIFACT

Color & Material: An even light brown with slight orange cast and thin brown patina on the surface in the left view. Extremely fine grain orthoquartzite

Location: Northwestern Platte County, Wyoming.

When Richard Snook, of Wheatland, Wyoming, enclosed a sketch of this artifact, Hell Gap seemed to be almost definite. Once in hand, it became a puzzle. The flat end has definitely been broken off, for there are halves of pressure flakes along the broken edge that could not have taken their configurations without the additional stone having been present.

The example to the right (not drawn to scale) is a triangular knife described in Secrist's Guide as indigenous to most of the United States, but actual finds are scarce.

The question is...Is this a large dart point (or lance tip) with the tip broken off, or a triangular knife with the blade broken?

If anyone has a complete triangular knife with similar configuration as this fragment, or a similar, identified point or lance tip, please write to: Mr. Richard Snook, 1405 19th Street, Wheatland, Wyoming

OLD KNIFE BLANK No. 68
From the collection of:
Otto Wismiller
Torrington, Wyoming

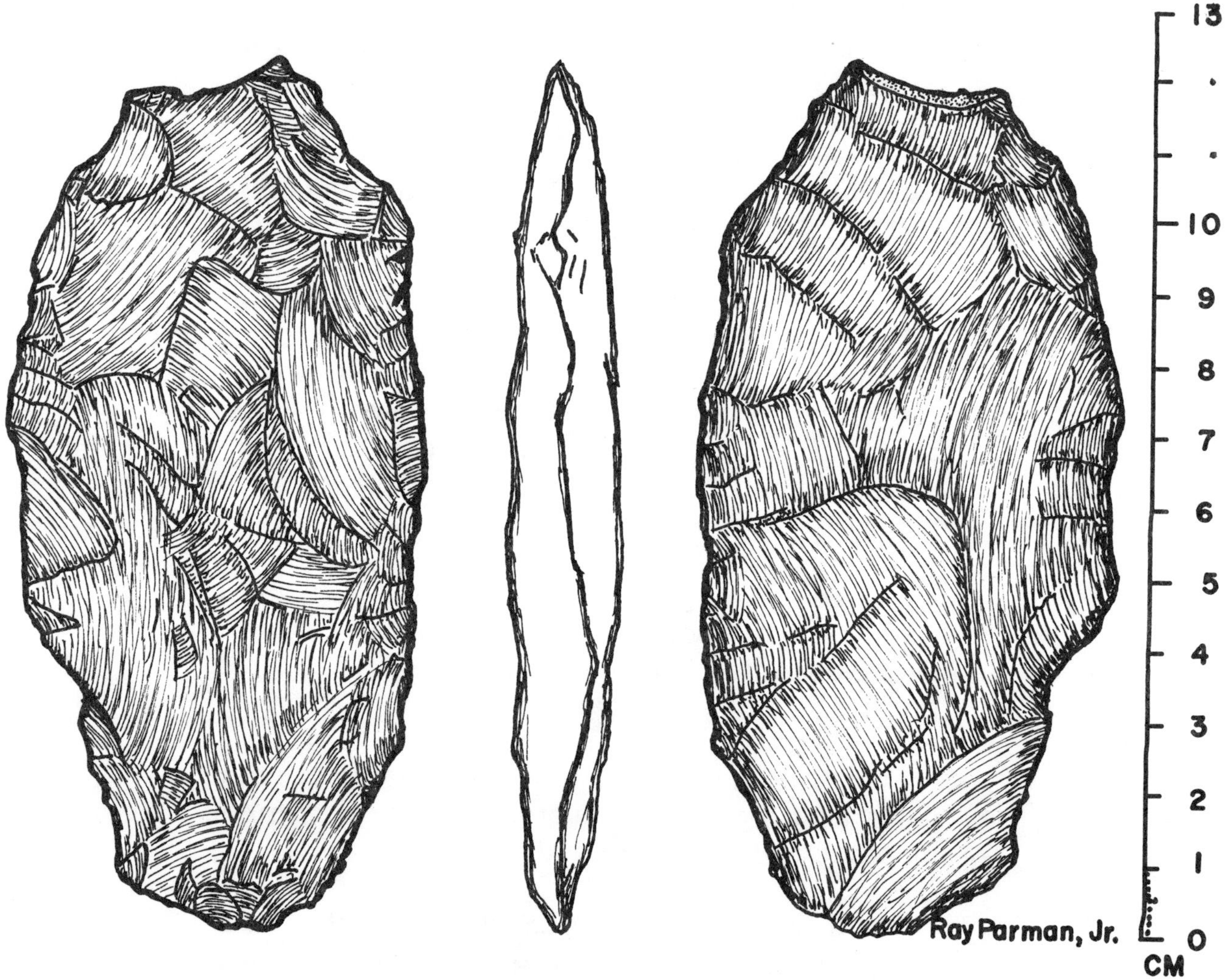

OLD KNIFE BLANK

Color & Material: The color of this material is not visible, for the entire artifact is covered by a heavy rind. The rind appears to be about one millimeter thick and has a rose colored cast to the surface displayed in the right view. The surface displayed in the left view has a light orange cast. Over all, it is light tan to brown. The rind also covers the surface exposed when the tip was broken off. Probably chert.

Location: Ten miles north of Hartville, northeast Platte County, Wyoming.

This knife was selected for its apparent age indicated by the heavy rind. This rind is not a deposit of minerals upon its surface, but an alteration of the material from which it was crafted. Oxygen, and many othe trace elements of the atmosphere, chemically reacted with the stone (probably chert), and altered its surface to a depth of approximately one millimeter.

This knife (or knife blank) also displays the single shoulder that is an asymmetrical configuration associated with Sandia cave artifacts. One other feature indicating extreme age is the very indistinct flaking on the surface displayed in the right view.

It has been sufficiently weathered to remove all but the major ridges between the flakes.

Dr. Frank C. Hibben (Sandia Cave Report, 1941), responded to a letter written to the University of New Mexico asking for information concerning the Sandia Cave excavation. Quoting a portion of his letter: "There was originally some question concerning the dating of the Sandia level (Crane, 1956). Another Sandia site, at Lucy, New Mexico, has demonstrated that the original datings were fairly accurate. We now have dates from Lucy and elsewhere that range from 23,000 to 26,000 B.P. The Lucy site was excavated by Dr. William Roosa of the University of Northern Illinois. He has published a number of articles on this site..."

UNFINISHED BURIAL PIECE No. 69
From the collection of:
Otto Wismiller
Torrington, Wyoming

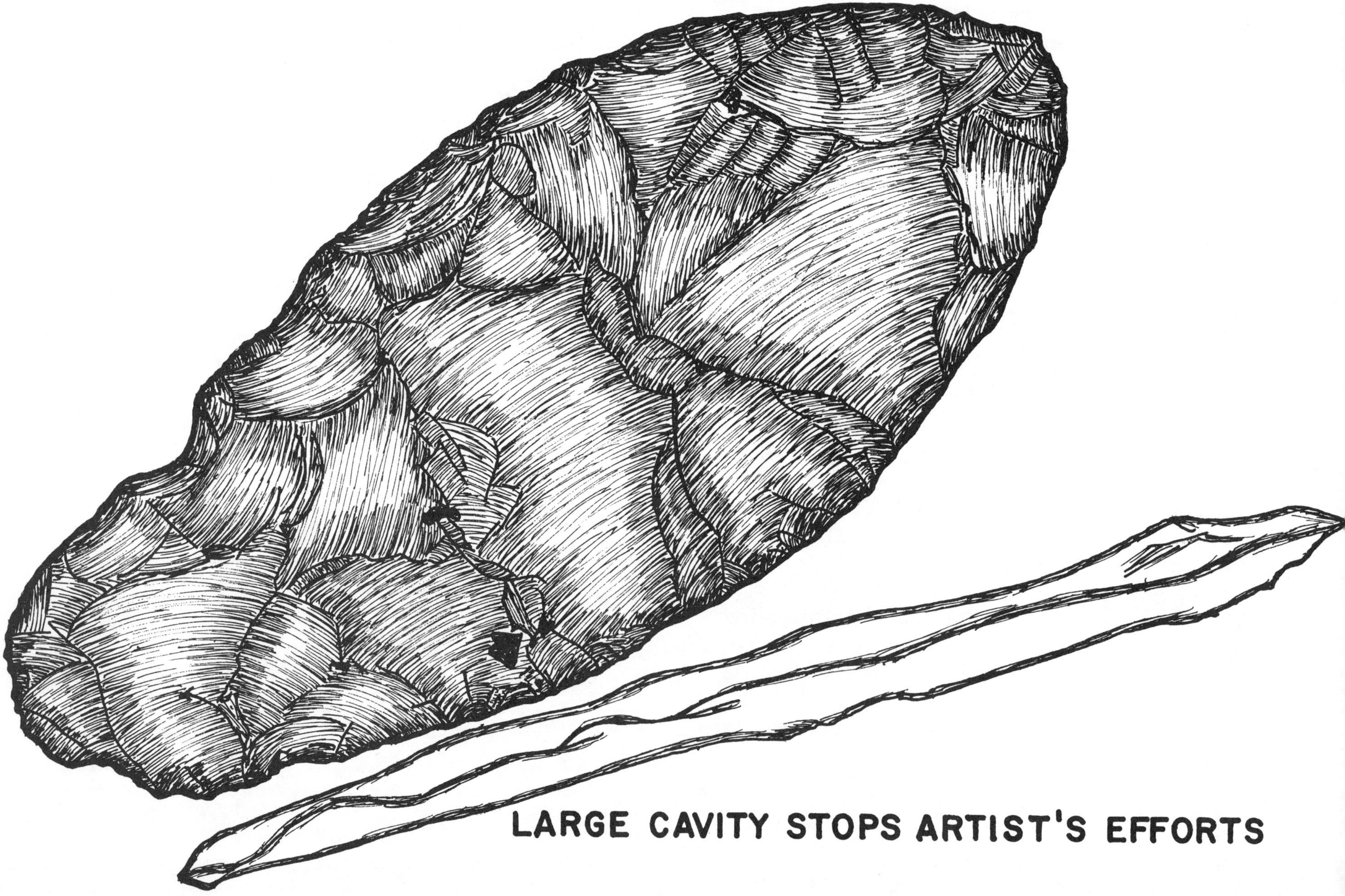

LARGE CAVITY STOPS ARTIST'S EFFORTS

UNFINISHED BURIAL PIECE ?

Color & Material: Predominately light yellowish tan. Varicolored; orange, pink, purple and blue. A chert, jasper, and chalcedony brecia.

Location: Seventeen miles north of Hartville, northeast Platte County, Wyoming.

This large chopper was crudely crafted and displays the single shoulder characteristic of Sandia Cave artifacts.

Otto Wismiller also submitted a smaller, single shouldered knife blank that appeared on the preceding page (No. 68) . These two in Otto's collection, along with those previously appearing in this book seem to indicate a rather extensive Sandia culture.

The size of this artifact is most unusual. It is believed by this writer that it was intended to have been worked to a thin configuration as a ceremonial piece. This thinning progressed until large, vugular, pore spaces were discovered within the stone.

There are two smaller holes (in black) on the side displayed, and a very large one on the reverse side. The large one will almost accommodate the first joint of one's little finger, and extends very nearly to the other side.

It is thought that ceremonial prospects were eliminated by these pore spaces. In view of this, it was simply used as a common butcher knife, meat cleaver, or hide scraper. The edge opposite the notch has been altered by its use for chopping and scraping. When invited to the Wismiller's home, the author had Barbara Swenson's pemmican paddle (No. 60) with him. When it was mentioned that his Mother's butter box and paddle had come to mind (while showing the paddle), the author was escorted to the fireplace mantle where there was a matched box and paddle on display. Many thanks to Mr. & Mrs. Wismiller.

BEAUTIFUL, OLD KNIVES No. 70
From the collection of:
Mr. & Mrs. R. D. Hone
Kemmerer, Wyoming

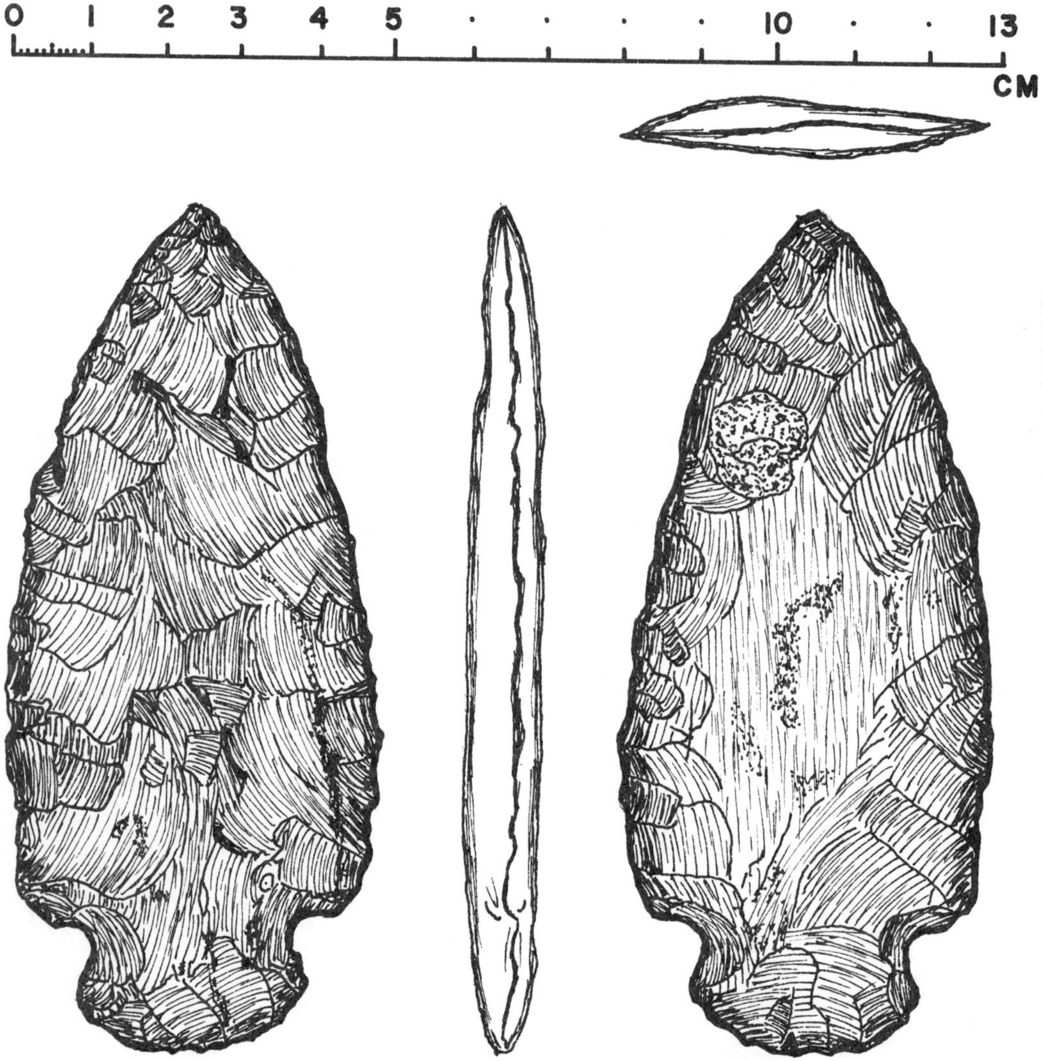

RESEMBLES SAN PEDRO & WILLIAMS

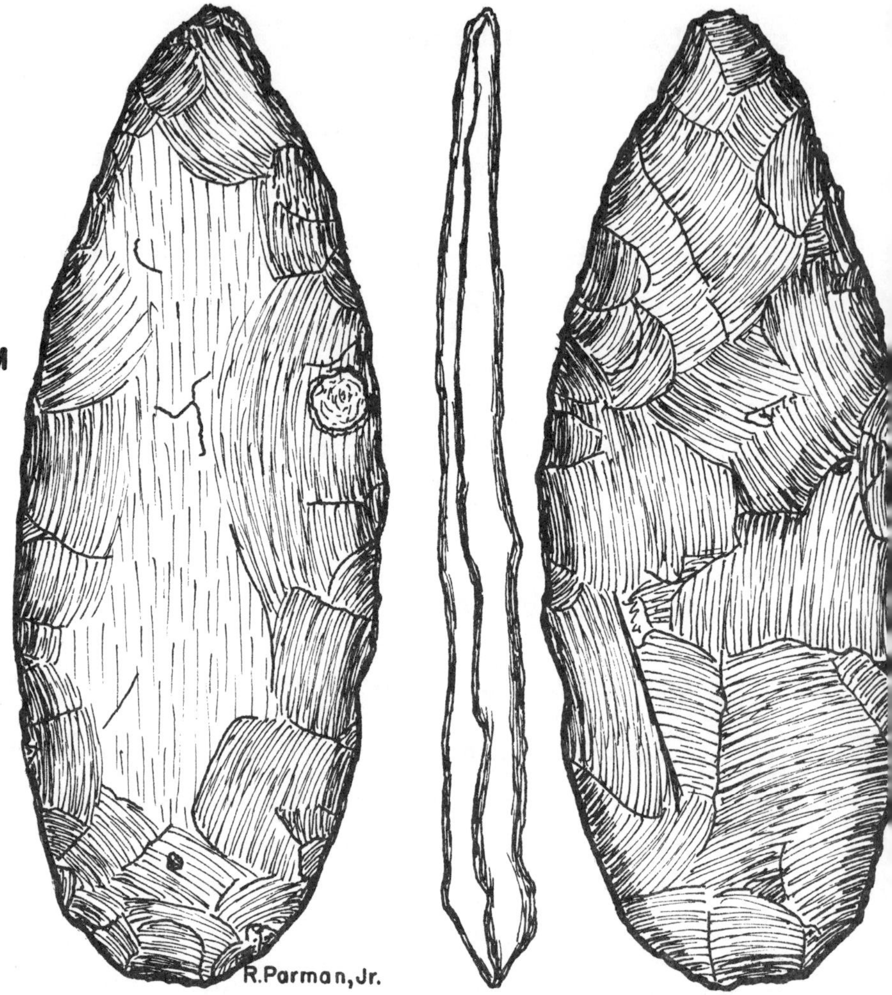

RESEMBLES LERMA & REFUGIO

BEAUTIFUL, OLD KNIVES

Color & Material: Stemmed knife, an even, light tan with the slight areas of pinpoint porosity being a slightly darker brown. Chert.

Plain knife, dark brown with a heavy, light tan and brown patina covering all but the major ridges between flakes. This patina is irregularly splotched on the side displayed in the left view. Chert.

Location: Central Uinta County, Wyoming.

These two knives were selected from the Hone's beautiful collection because they are both crafted of chert taken from the same quarry at markedly different periods of time.

The four possible point types involve ages from 4,000 B.C. to 1,000 A.D. From Secrist's Guide, their ages are: Williams (stemmed) 4,000 B.C. To 1,000 A.D.; San Pedro (stemmed) 1,000 B.C. to 500 A.D.; Refugio 2,000 B.C. to 1,000 A.D.; Lerma 2,000 B.C.to 200 A.D.

It is interesting that the stemmed knife resembles the older types, yet does not have a rind or patina. Has it been buried in dry soil, and thus protected?

The plain knife displays marked weathering on the side in the left view. This weathering has removed almost all of the flaking.

The plain knife was found very near the artifact reported on the next page (No. 71).

UNUSUAL & RARE EFFIGIES No. 71
From the collection of:
Mr. & Mrs. R. D. Hone
Kemerrer, Wyoming

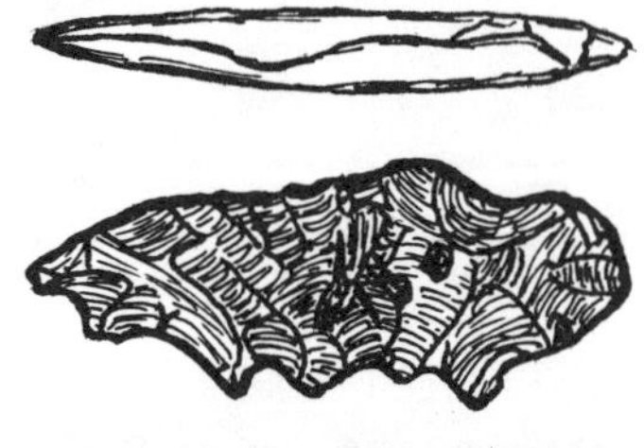

WHITE BUFFALO
(VERY RARE)

Example

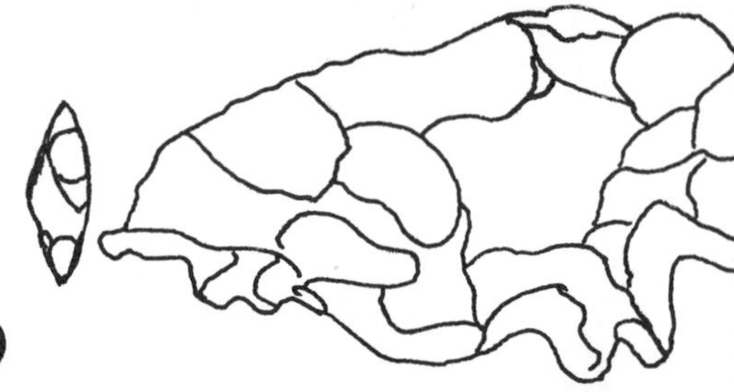

Secrist's Guide p. III

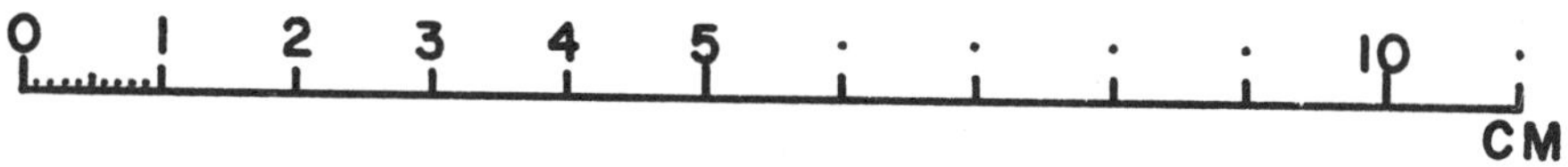

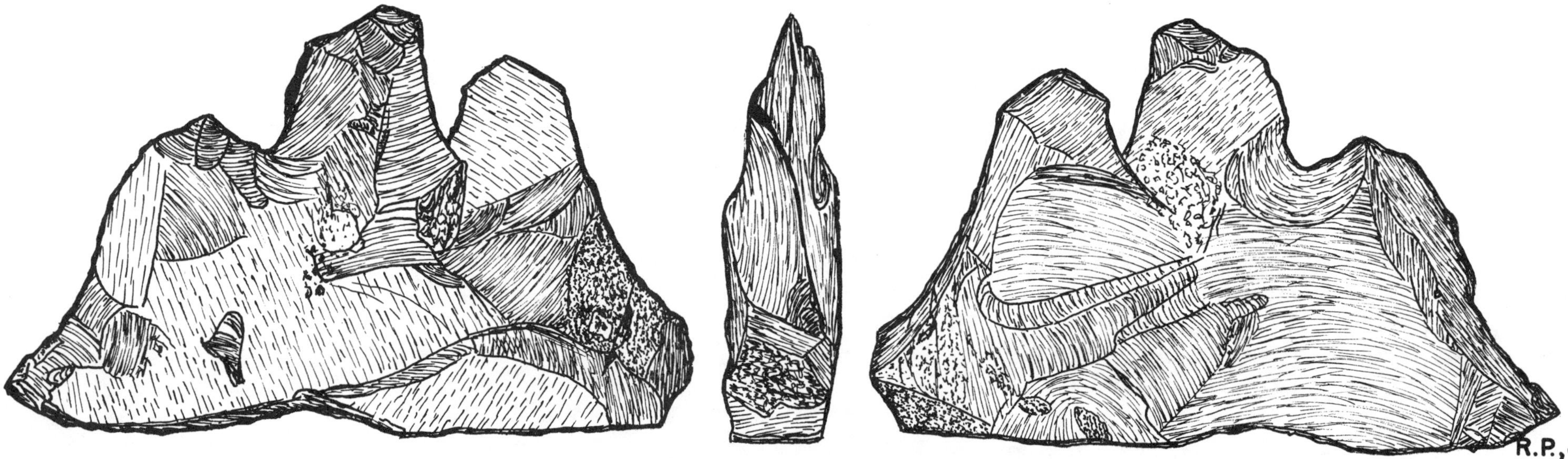

R.P., Jr.

PROUD EAGLE STANDING ON ROCK
(FOUND NEAR LERMA TYPE KNIFE - 70th Ed.)

UNUSUAL & RARE EFFIGIES

Color & Material: Eagle, a dark brown with tan banded at center, and to the right edge of the left view. The tan bands having formed an orange rind on all sides. Clear, hard chert with rinded, chalcedonous banding.

Buffalo, bone white with two round spots, 1.5mm in diameter, 7mm apart; one pale blue, the other light tan, one on each side. Very thin, tan patina and brown staining in slight, curved fractures. Chalcedony.

Location: Both artifacts, southwestern Wyoming.

This simple, stylized effigy (eagle) was found upright on a large boulder. Another artifact, an unstemmed knife (No. 70) was found nearby.

The chert from which it was crafted has been identified as "tiger-chert" and comes from one of several quarries in central Uinta County in southwestern Wyoming.

It is the nature of this chert (and many others) to have numerous, irregular fracture planes throughout the body of the formation. This causes unusually shaped fragments of chert to be found. This has happened with this artifact.

A percussion fragment (percussion points are evident) has been removed from each side to give the gentle, concave curve to the outer edges of the wings. The notch to the right of the head (left view), below the beak, is naturally formed. While the right shoulder was rounded by the removal of two pressure flakes, the left shoulder was rounded by removing ten to twelve tiny pressure flakes from the outer edge. The removal of four large ones formed the inner edge of the wing and the left side of the neck. Approximately six flakes were removed to form the head and beak.

If the native American who crafted this effigy is the one who placed it upright on the boulder (where it was found), it is hoped that the spirits he revered have not been too disturbed. Perhaps this effigy should be placed upright, out of doors, and in a place of prominence.

The small effigy to the buffalo appears almost identical to one illustrated in *Secrist's Guide to Identification*, p. 111. It has been crafted from nearly white chalcedony. This could be significant as an effigy to the Great White Buffalo noted in historic, native American lore.

A tribal shaman may have performed a ritual chant over this effigy to assure a good hunt.

REMARKABLE, HAFTED HAMMER STONE No. 72
From the collection of:
Jim & Angel Leachman
Lower Wishram, Wasington

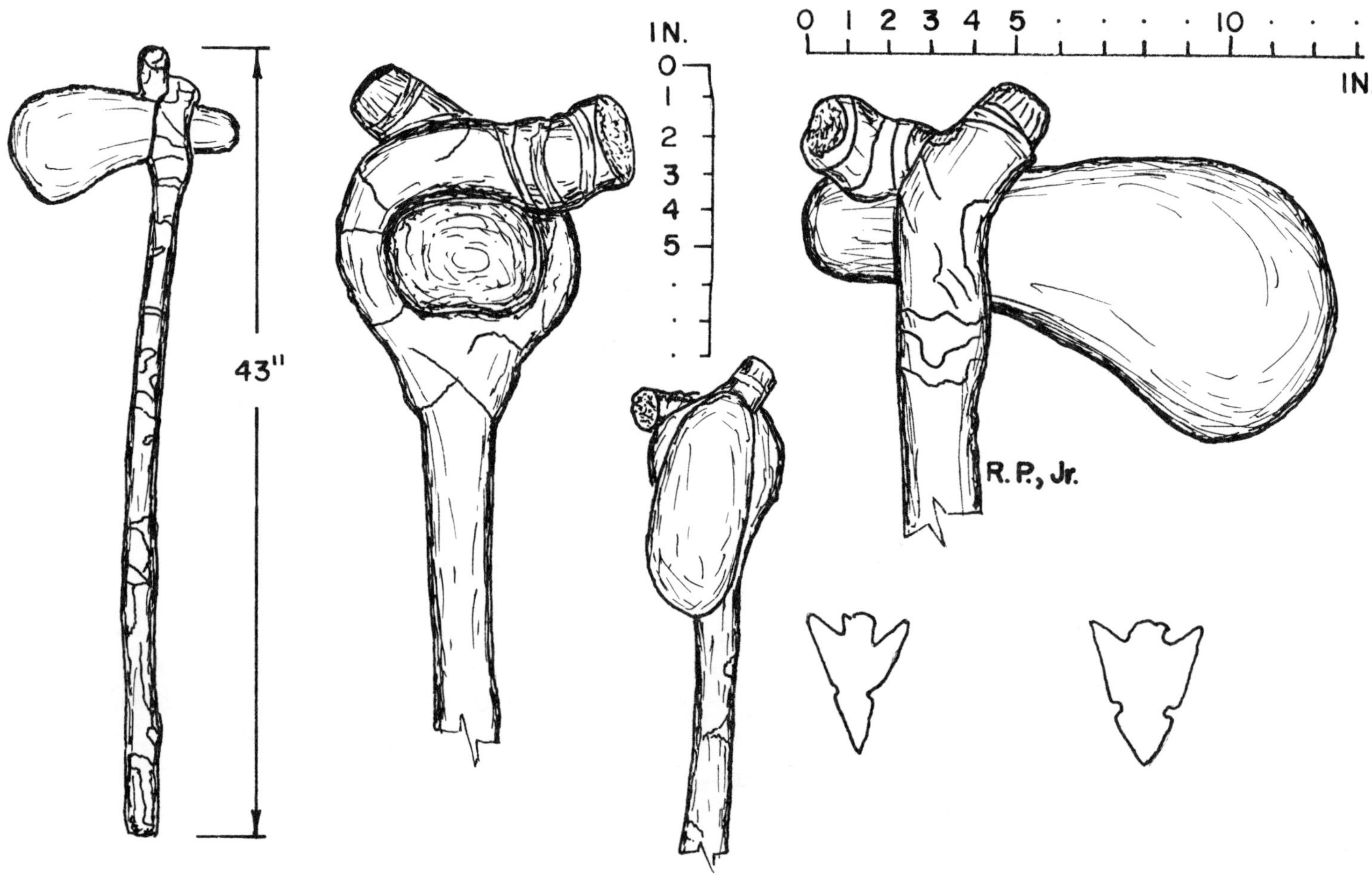

REMARKABLE, HAFTED HAMMER STONE

Color & Material: Stone, light grey with traces of dark grey, spotted rind. Fine grain, siliceous sandstone.

Handle, a thin, reddish maroon bark with slight, yellow cambium showing through the bark in irregular areas. Thought to be a chokecherry branch.

Location: Unknown.

The hafted hammer (pounder might be a better description) was so unusal that it had to be published. Jim recently purchased it for their collection, so it is not known which of the Pacific Northwest tribes would have been associated with it.

A suitable, river cobblestone was selected, grooved, and placed in the fork of a chokecherry branch. The two, smaller branches were then bound around the stone with leather thongs (grooves of restricted growth, caused by the thongs, are visible), and the two branches continued to grow.

With (tree ring dating), the exact year this artifact was crafted could be determined. Without this dating, this artifact could not be considered truly authentic.

The use of this "tool" was questioned, and Jim thought it might have been used in connection with processing redwood bark to be braided into fish nets. One would assume that it was used to remove bark from the trunks of the trees.

There is no evidence of it having struck anything hard. It could also have been used to dispatch trapped animals or spawning fish.

TREASURED FINDS No. 73
From the collection of:
Howard Geike
Edgerton, Wyoming

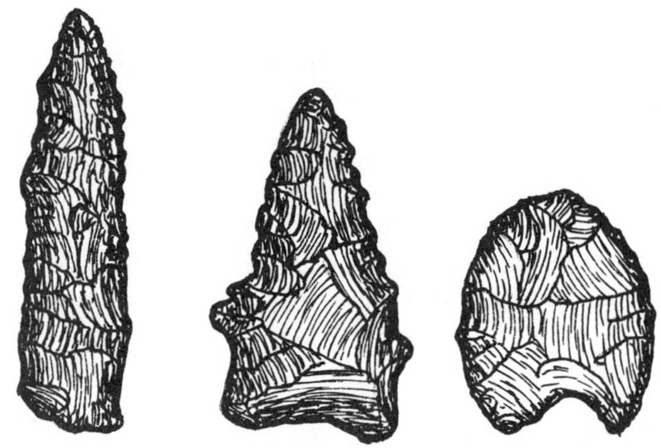

SEARCY
(4,000 B.C.)
p 51

KIRK
(4,000 B.C.)
SCARCE
p53

GREEN RIVER
(4,000 B.C.)
RARE
p 24

Page No. From Secrist's Guide

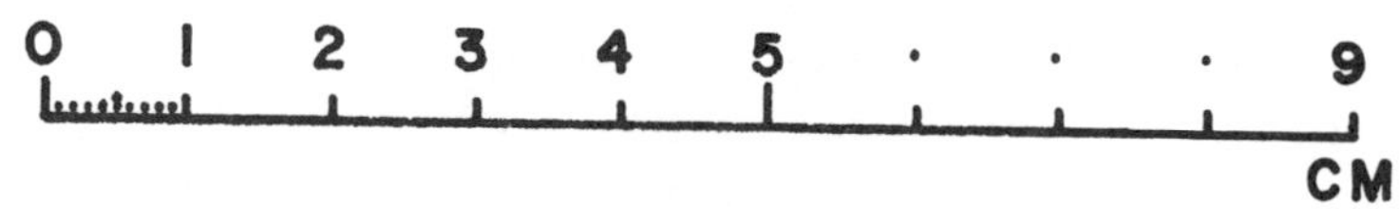

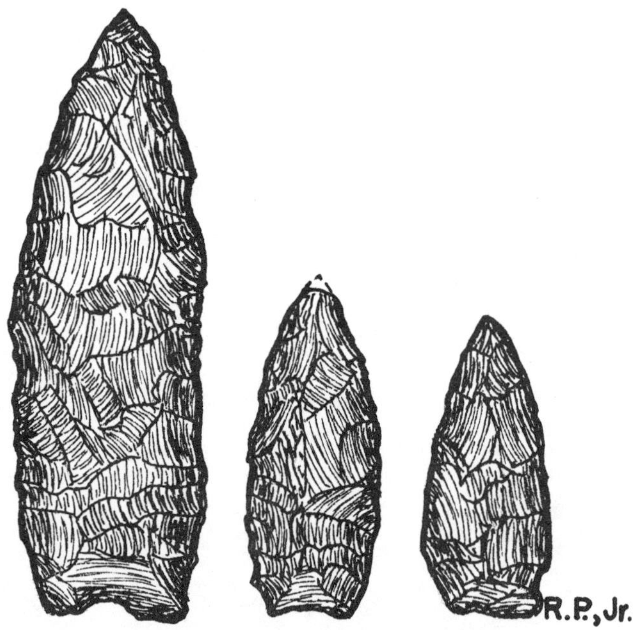

POSSIBLE CLOVIS POINTS
(No. 3 Re-worked)

TREASURED FINDS

Color, Material and Location: Searcy, maroon with pale, pastel blue inclusions. Chert. Northeast Natrona County, Wyoming.

Kirk, pale green. Very shaly quartzite with chalcedonous inclusions. Northern Sioux County, Nebraska.

Green River, pastel tan with orange cast stain on all but two horns (protrusions lower sides). Chert. Northern Natrona County, Wyoming.

Large Clovis, pale grey with very slight green cast and light, dull red inclusion. Orthoquartzite. Northern Natrona County, Wyoming.

Medium Clovis, very light, translucent tan with white patination of flake ridges on one side only. Agate. Northern Natrona County, Wyoming.

Small Clovis, dull orange with heavy lichen damage to the side opposite the one illustrated. Orthoquartzite. Northern Natrona County, Wyoming.

Author's note: All Clovis points are heavily weathered.

To find three "first of types" in one collection, at the end of a happy day (called to go on a well-logging job) was almost too much. Howard Geike of Edgerton, Wyoming, wrote to me in February of 1985, and enclosed a photograph of several points and knives from his collection. The time spent with Howard, viewing his collection, was a great pleasure.

The Kirk point practically leaps up and shouts "Here I am!", when its distinctive shape penetrates the consciousness. It has a distinct, small barb ? immediately above the larger. One wonders what its purpose might have been.

The Searcy is not a positive identification. This one appears to have been notched, but it is quite possible that the usual shouldered stem had broken off, and the new base was slightly reworked. There is no change in the patina at the new base, so the rework was done when the point was young.

The Green River is right out of the book, for this one displays all of the characteristics mentioned in the identification guide. This was a pleasant discovery for Howard. He learned the Green River point is noted as indigenous to Southwestern Wyoming, and finds are quite rare.

TREASURED FINDS No. 73
From the collection of:
Howard Geike
Edgerton, Wyoming

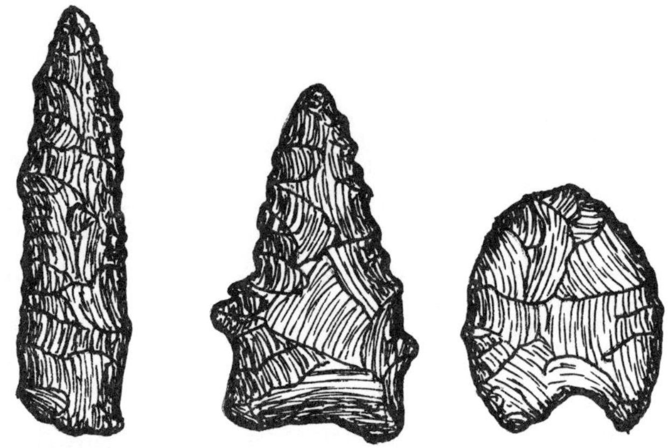

SEARCY	KIRK	GREEN RIVER
(4,000 B.C.)	(4,000 B.C.)	(4,000 B.C.)
p 51	SCARCE	RARE
	p53	p 24

Page No. From Secrist's Guide

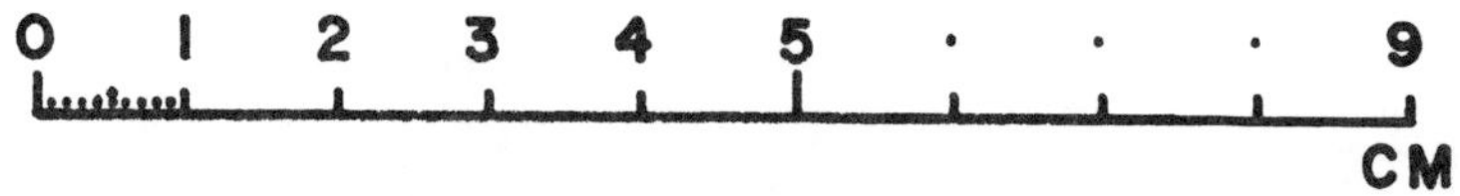

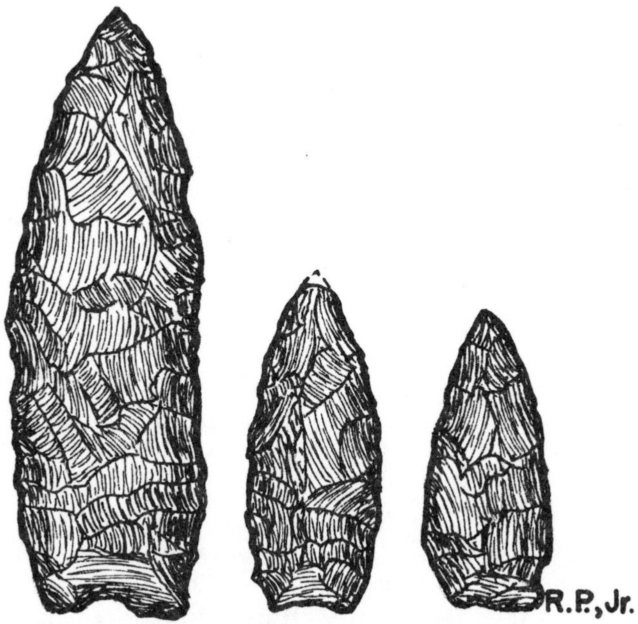

POSSIBLE CLOVIS POINTS

(No. 3 Re-worked)

The possible Clovis points illustrated do not display fluting of the base in more than a token way and might make this tentative identification incorrect. However, their apparent weathered features (very faint flaking and highly patinated surfaces) causes one to accept the Clovis-like blade shapes without too much hesitation. The smallest of the three has the more aged appearance and is thought to be a Clovis point tip, notched at a later time.

This smaller point has also suffered extreme lichen damage. The acids produced by the lichens have almost totally removed the flaking ridges on the side opposite the one displayed. There is ongoing, scientific research called lichenometry, whereby the younger limit (most recent in time) of a point's age might be determined.

Again, the importance of cataloging surface finds is stressed. Methods of dating that will be developed in the near future, will make cataloged, private collections valuable sources of archaeological data.

BEAUTIFUL, OLD POINTS No. 74
From the collection of:
Mary Hickford
Midwest, Wyoming

Type Example
Secrist's Guide
3 Edition, p 28

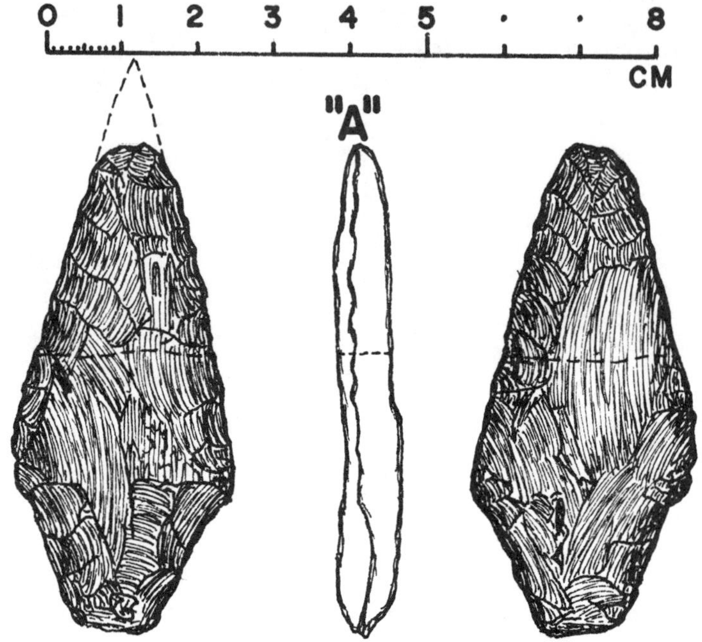

POSSIBLE MORRILL

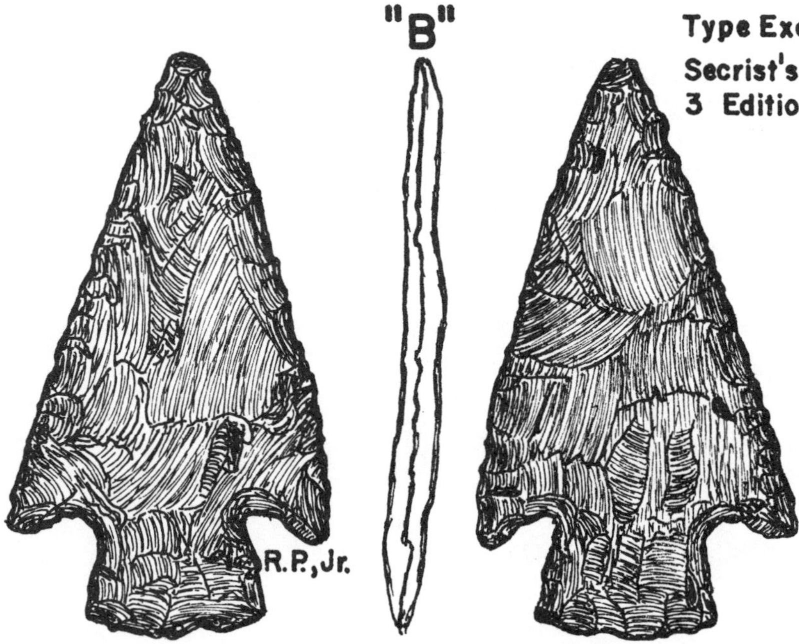

CASTROVILLE

(4,000 B.C.-1,000 A.D.)

Type Example
Univ. of Texas
Cat. No. IC-33-10h

BEAUTIFUL, OLD POINTS

Color & Material: A, tan, clean fine grain quartzite.

B, grey with numerous brown inclusions. Light brown patina on side displayed in the right view. Moderately weathered chert.

Location: A, northeast Natrona County, Wyoming.

B, southwestern Fremont County, Wyoming.

The possibility of A being a Morrill point is fairly strong even though the stem is more contracted, and the point is blunt compared to the type example. From Secrist's Guide description, "Workmanship is crude and point is thick. Found over most of the United States and are plentiful".

With this in mind, Morrill was decided. The tip could have broken off, and rework blunted it. The dashed lines across the middle denotes a break line. This point was two separate finds that fit together. Fortunately, there were no missing chips and the joint is almost invisible.

The description of "one barb often longer than the other" and "average 2.5 inches in length", coupled with the similarity of the craftsmanship of artifact B to the type example, give fairly strong identification. The Castroville is usually found east of the Rocky Mountains. This one almost got away, for it was found just west of the Continental Divide.

Mary Hickford of Midwest, Wyoming, has written that on a trip to the same general area of these finds, she has found what could be a Green River point and an ususual stone axe. These will be reported later in the book (See Nos. 89 & 91).

Sincere appreciation is expressed to Mary for writing and submitting thsese finds.

OUTSTANDING, OLD POINTS No. 75
From the collection of:
Dorothy Nickerson
Midwest, Wyoming

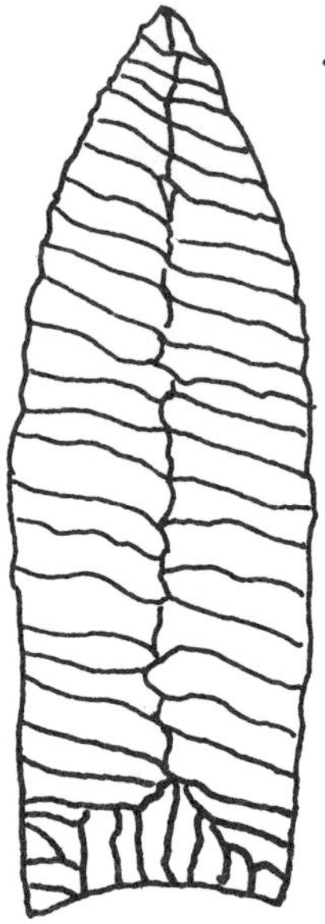

TYPE EXAMPLE
from
Secrist's Guide, 3rd Edition
p. 40

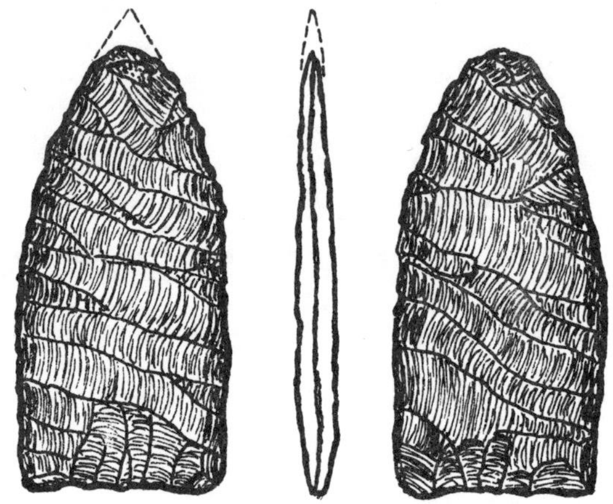

ANGOSTURA
(Re-Tipped)
(8,000 B.C. to 4,000 B.C.)

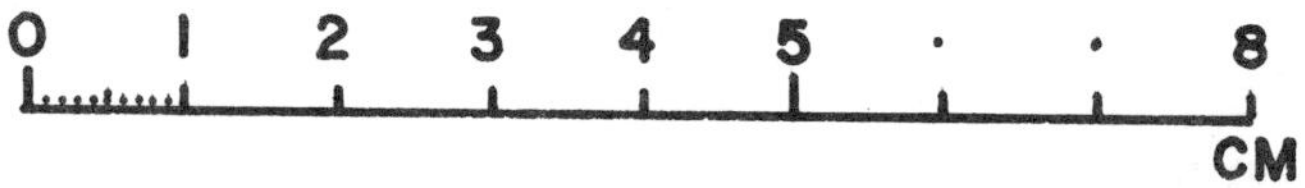

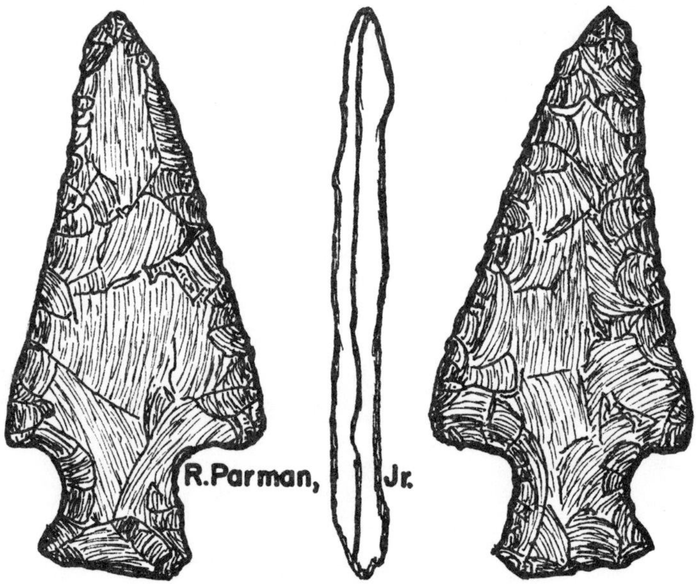

EPPS
(1,300 B.C. to 200 B.C.)

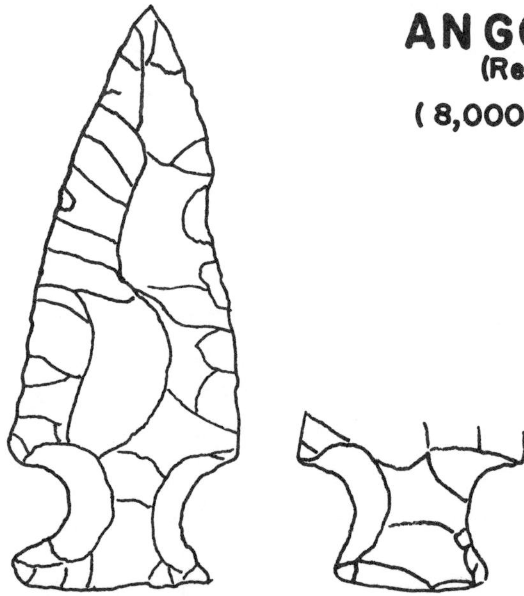

TYPE EXAMPLE
Carl Alexander
Collection
EPPS, LOUISIANA

OUTSTANDING, OLD POINTS

Color & Material: Angostura, brown with abundant bone white, pinpoint to 1 mm diameter dots evenly throughout. Translucent chalcedony with abundant oolites.

Epps, chocolate brown with very small, faint, chalcedonous washes throughout. Clean, hard chert.

Location: Angostura, northeast of Farson in Sweetwater County, Wyoming.

Epps, southeastern Sublette County, Wyoming.

The Angostura point is markedly weathered and the flaking is very faint. According to Secrist's Guide, the type example shown is not typical. The flaking is usually transverse oblique, and the example is collateral oblique.

This artifact's tip is blunted and is thought to have been reworked after the tip broke off. Otherwise, it strongly resembles the example shown. Angostura points are found over most of the United States, but are not too plentiful.

The Epps point was named by Ford & Webb (1956) from specimens found at the Poverty Point site in northeastern Louisiana. The stem of a second example has been illustrated, indicating that the shortened tangs of Dorothy's Epps point is well within the range of this feature. The blades of both the artifact and the example are otherwise almost identical. Dorothy, thank you so much for making these available.

BEAUTIFUL, OLD, RIO GRANDE POINTS No. 76
From the collection of:
Karmel S. Hibdon
Kaycee, Wyoming

"Rio Grande" A Proto-Archaic culture complex of the Southwest. Believed to be rooted in the earlier Agate Basin complex of the Northern Plains. These finds provide additional confirmation.

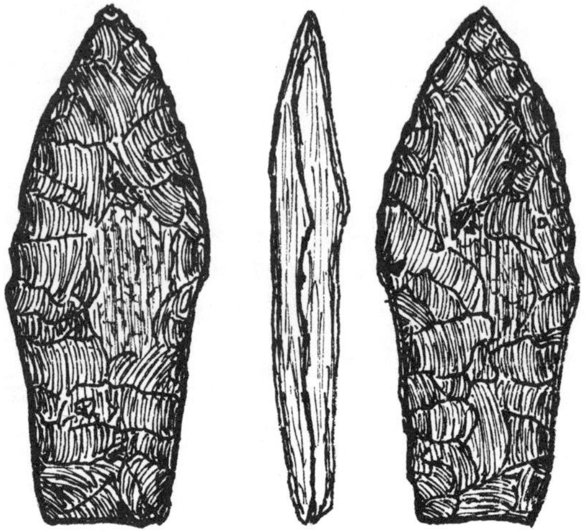

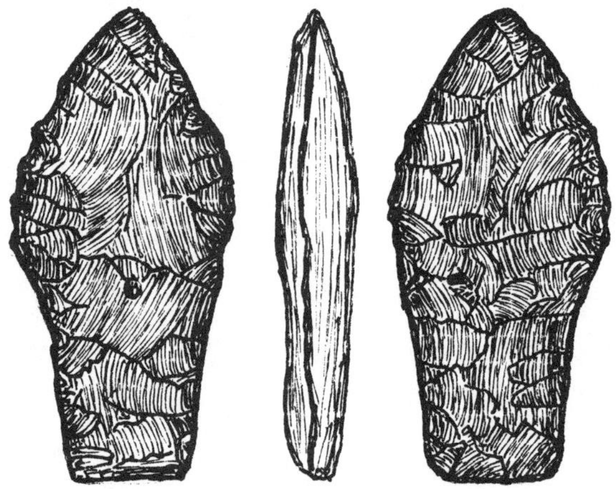

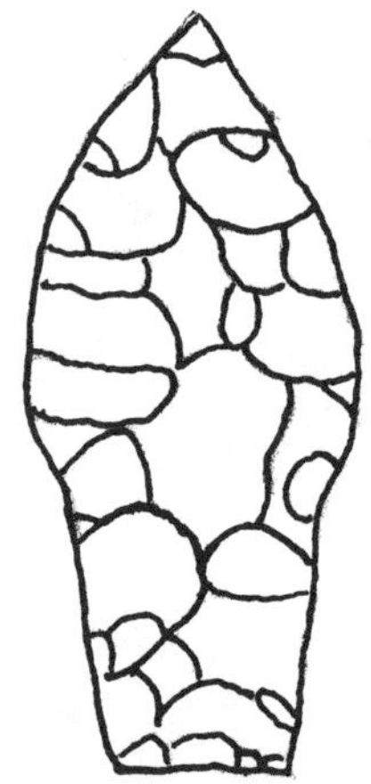

Type Example
(J.C. Conklin collection)
(El Paso, TX)

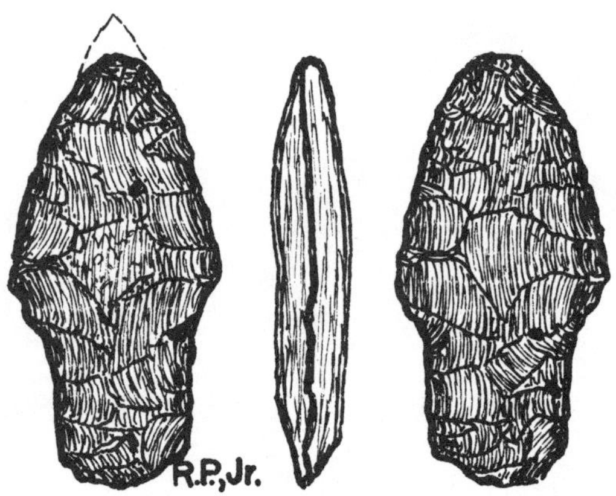

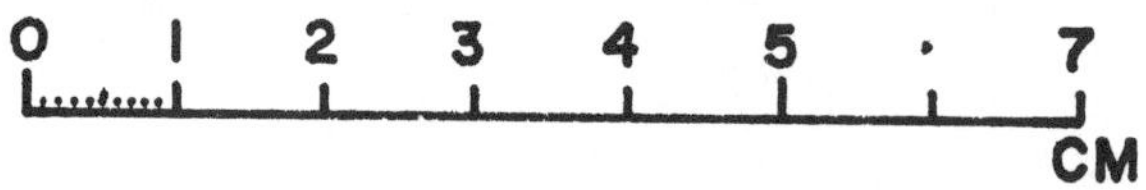

BEAUTIFUL, OLD, RIO GRANDE POINTS

Color & Material: Small, pale greyish tan with lavender cast and lavender banded diagonally across the point. Chert.

Medium, pale tan rind, or patination, on translucent brown with slight green cast. Agate or chalcedony.

Large, light tan with strong, pale, pastel green cast and minute black inclusions. Chert.

Location: The smaller point (lower left) Western Johnson County, Wyoming. On Doyle Creek.

The two larger points were probably from the south end of the Big Horn Mountains where Mr. Hibdon did most of his hunting.

Mr. Hibdon's collection was most remarkable. Three large shelves within an old, glass and oak department store showcase about six feet long. Each shelf held knives, ceremonials, arrow points, dart points, and effigies representing tribes from the Arctic to South America. All of the artifacts, as well as the shelves were the same color. An even layer of dust indicated that not one of the artifacts had been touched in years. Clovis, Folsom, and many other types were displayed in perfect condition. The similarity of the Rio Grande to the Hell Gap point (known to be old) caused the author at first to think these were possible Hell Gap points. It was later they were identified as Rio Grande points. The following information about Rio Grande points comes from Gregory Perino, (Oklahoma Anthropological Society, Special Bulletin No. 3, 1968) "Rio Grande" a proto-archaic culture complex of the Southwest, believed to be rooted in the earlier Agate Basin complex of the northern plains.

The fact that these points were taken from the Big Horn Mountains supports this theory.

Many thanks to Rome Taylor for permitting the removal of the glass top. By turning over selected artifacts, colors stood out in marvelous contrast. Exposures 13 through 24 were taken. It was a 12 exposure roll of film in the camera. Must get back there!

BEAUTIFUL, OLD, McKEAN POINTS No. 77
From the collection of:
Glenn & Mavis Lund
Kaycee, Wyoming

(McKEAN Point type named by R. Page Wheeler from examples found at Keyhole Reservoir site N.E. Wyoming, 1952)

"3"

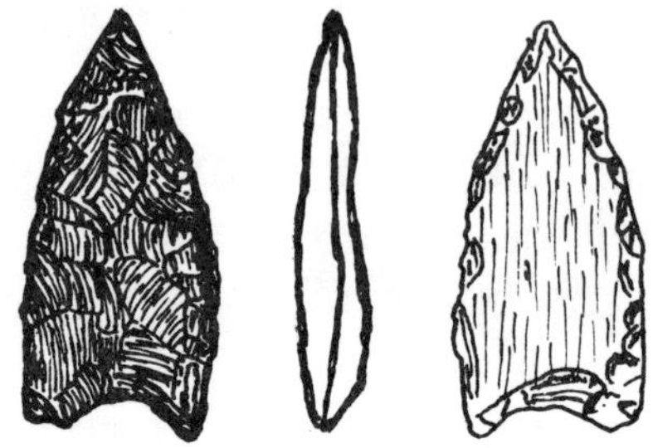

(AGATE)

"2"

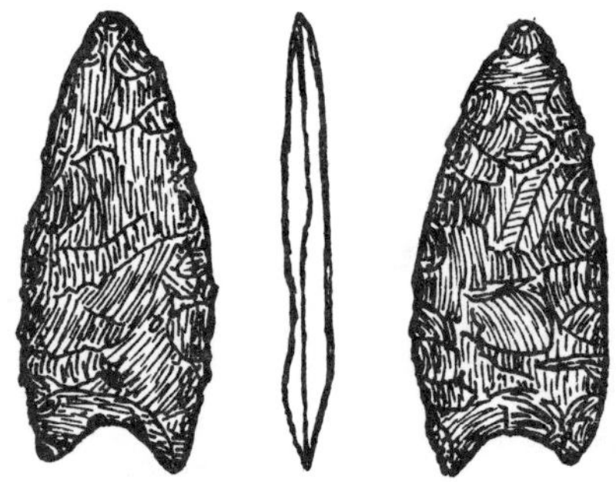

(JASPER or CHERT)

"1"

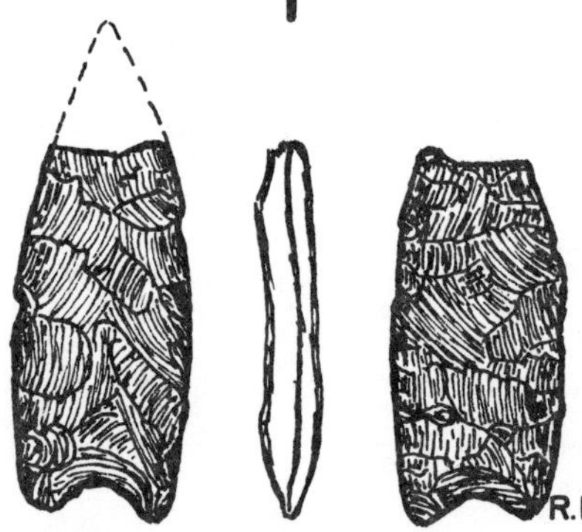

R. Parman, Jr.

(ORTHOQUARTZITE)

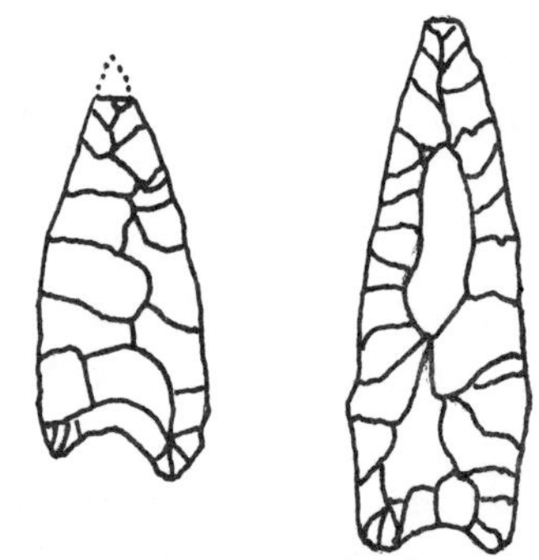

Type Examples from Keyhole Reservoir (cat. no. 48CK7-26,10)

McKEAN POINTS NAMED IN WYOMING

BEAUTIFUL, OLD, McKEAN POINTS

Color & Material: No. 1, pastel tan with pink cast. Minute brown and lavender inclusions. Orthoquartzite.

No. 2, base (mid sec. down) dull black. Tip beef liver brown. Jasper.

No. 3, milk white, translucent agate.

Location: All three, southwest of Kaycee, Johnson County, Wyoming.

The Lund's collection is totally of their efforts. Each artifact has been found by either Glenn or Mavis, and they have been most successful. The collection is beautiful to see.

The McKean points illustrated were selected because their type has been accurately carbon dated at Signal Butte, Nebraska (Wheeler, [1956] suggests an age of 3500 to 4000 B.P.). In Angostura Basin, South Dakota, charcoal was found along with three Mckean points. Carbon dating of this charcoal (Crane, 1956) were 3630 +/- 350 and 4230 +/- 350 B.P.

The Mckean point has been found in Wyoming, Montana, South Dakota, and western Nebraska. They have also been found in collections taken from western Oklahoma. Probably most of the western United States could be involved.

One feature that should be noted is that each of these points has been crafted of distinctly different material.

Authors note: In May of 1989, while visiting good friends L.V. & Pat Baker, Safari Ranch, Elk City, Oklahoma, the author was present when a McKean point was recovered while making a surface survey.

BEAUTIFUL STEATITE PAN No. 78
From the collection of:
Ray Parman, Jr.
Riverton, Wyoming

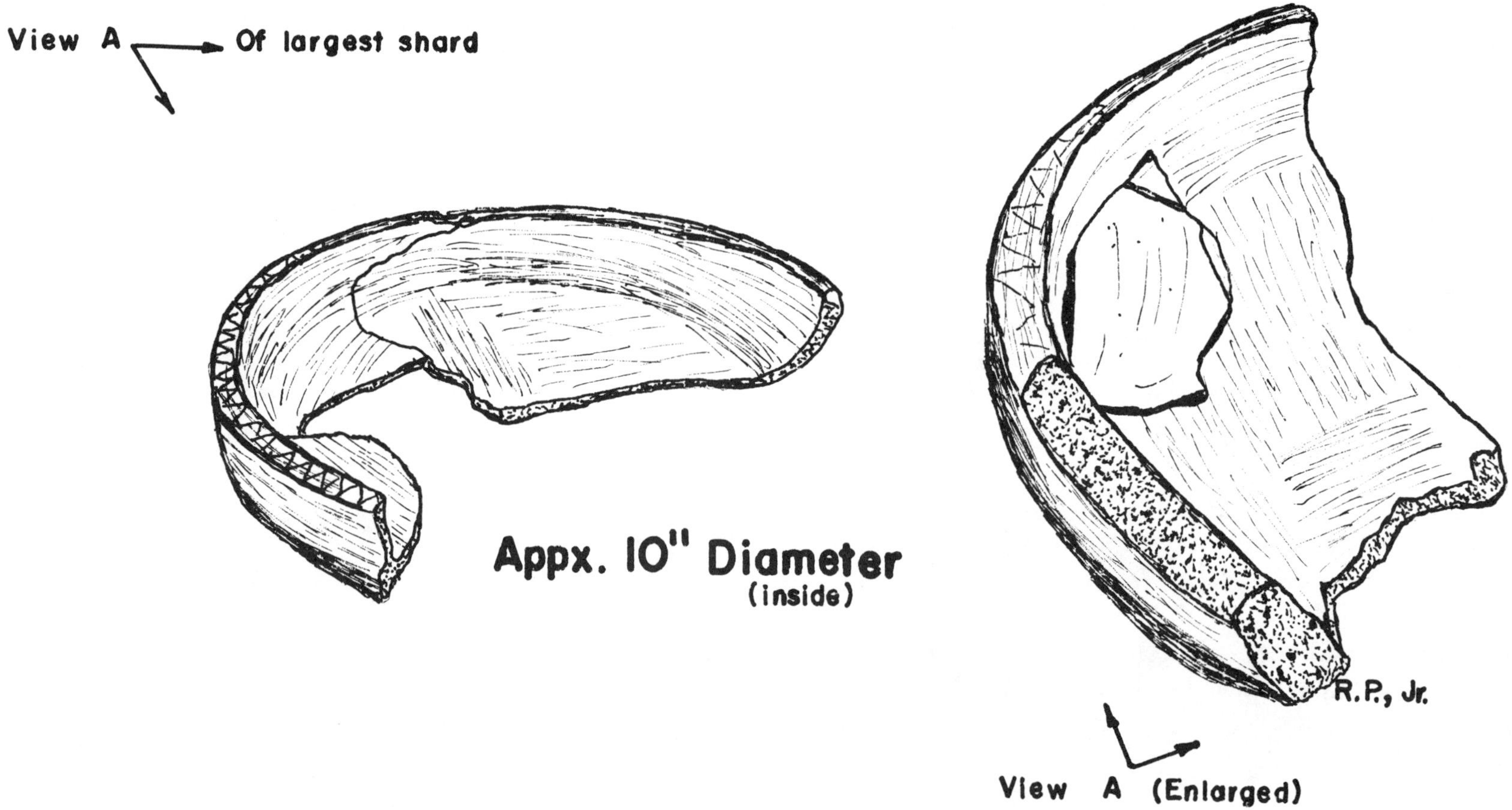

BEAUTIFUL STEATITE PAN

Color & Material: Generally a dark greyish appearance that in strong light has a deep, forest green cast. The shard to the left (of the three displayed together) is somewhat lighter due to altered exposure to the elements after the pan was shattered. The steatite is thought to be from a quarry in the Wind River Mountains. Other quarries are located in the Teton, Big Horn and Laramie mountain ranges.

Location: Found south of Rawlins, Wyoming during a surface, geological survey in 1959.

These shards represent one of the most exciting discoveries this writer has ever experienced. One of the purposes of publishing this material was to help private collectors learn more about the artifacts in their collections. This discovery was beyond all expectations. Earlier, a chert, burin-scraper from Jim Osbourne's collection was selected because of the ususual wear pattern along its edges. While studying it (particularly how the edges had been polished), It was decided that something ridged had been scraped; steatite (soapstone) came to mind. A call to Jim confirmed that steatite shards had been found at the same site. It was published as a "Possible Tool for Working Steatite" (See No. 34) in December of 1984.

In April of 1985, Jim made the shards available; it was then discovered, by microscopic examination, that striations on the scraper matched those found on the shards. Not only the identification of the tool's use was correct, but there was proof that the scraper had been used to make this particular "pan".

The word "pan" has been used because, for other than small cups, small shallow bowls, pipes and ceremonial pieces, steatite was most frequently used by native Americans to craft boiling pots that were eight to twelve inches deep.

It is possible this particular steatite artifact was crafted in the seventeen hundreds or early eighteen hundreds, after the utility of the frying pan became known among the tribes.

The rickrack design is continuous across the upper edges of the three shards. It displays considerable wear and nicking as though it were damaged from use. A portion of the side of the larger shard displays light scratches laying out the rickrack pattern. The ornamentation was added after the pan had been used.

The steatite's dark color, and hardness, indicate the pan had been used to fry foods. Steatite pots, used for boiling fluids, did not reach temperatures sufficient to harden steatite in this manner.

BEAUTIFUL, UNUSUAL ARTIFACTS No. 79
From the collection of:
Mr. & Mrs. R. D. Hone
Kemmerer, Wyoming

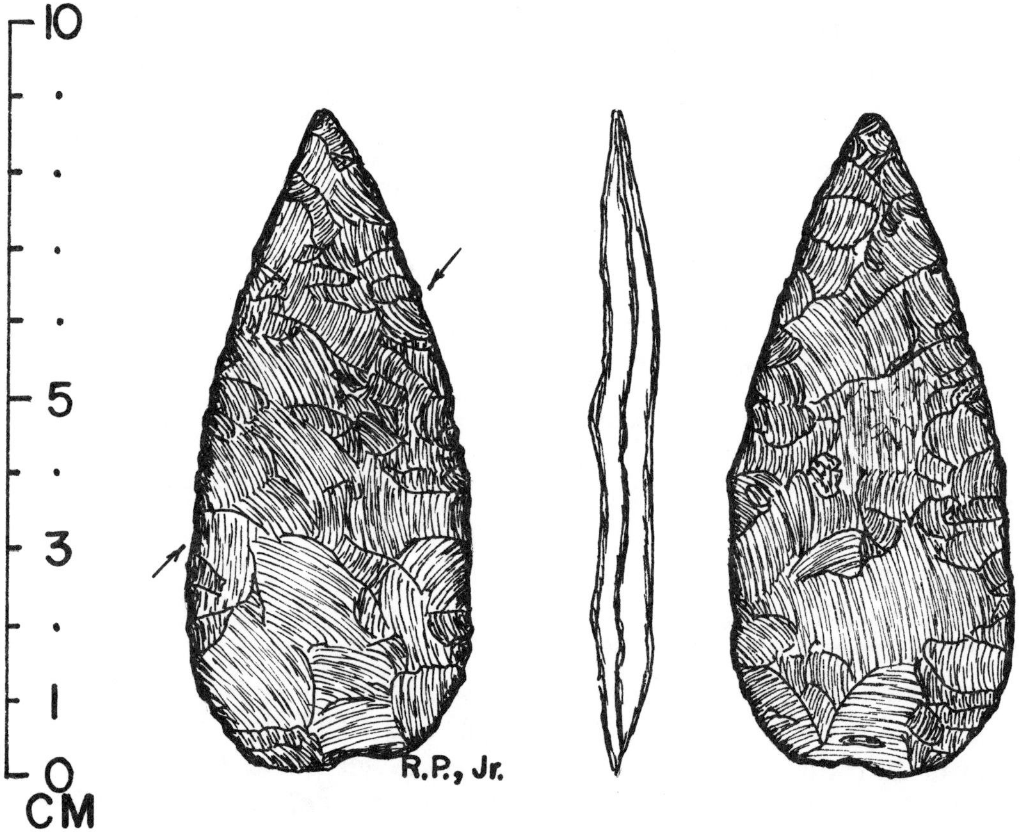

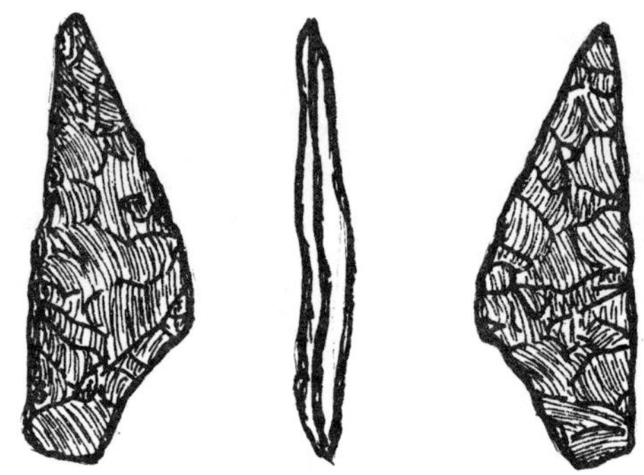

Tiny Cody Knife
?

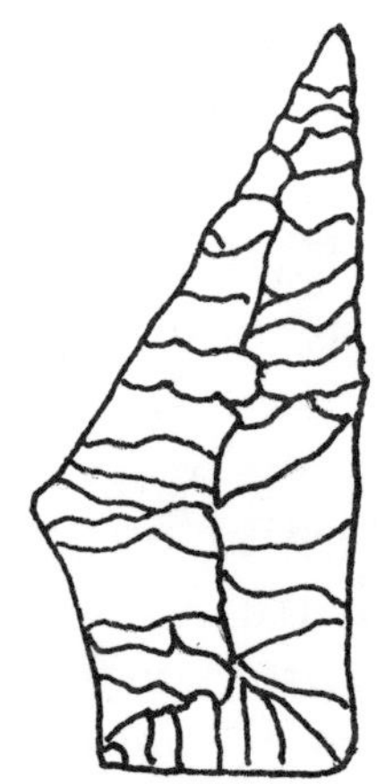

Type Example
Secrist's, p.107

BEAUTIFUL, UNUSUAL ARTIFACTS

Color & Material: Clovis point, light, translucent, pastel greyish brown with reddish brown intrusion along left edge and diagonally across tip (between arrows), on side displayed in left view. Chert.

Small Cody knife, slightly translucent brown with rind, giving the appearance of cocoa with scum forming on top. Chert.

Location: Central (Clovis) and south (Cody knife) Lincoln County, Wyoming.

It is known, from the distribution of flakes and broken points recovered at Folsom sites that the process of fluting points was frequently unsuccessful and resulted in the body of the point breaking laterally. The earlier stone technology of the Clovis culture did not attempt extensive fluting of their points; therefore, many Clovis points are found that have little, or no fluting.

This beautiful point from the Hone's collection is thought to be one. The shape of the body and the manner in which it was flaked, make this very possible. It is weathered and appears old.

The small knife is so Codylike in appearance, old and weathered, that one wonders if it might be older than the Cody Complex and its forerunner.

The Hone's collection is truly remarkable. When last at their home in early August, the author was shown five artifacts taken from one site. Together those five artifacts vividly display an event in the past. This event will be described in Nos. 93-1 and 93-2 later in this book.

A REMARKABLE, OLD FIND No. 80
From the collection of:
Jim Miller
Evanston, Wyoming

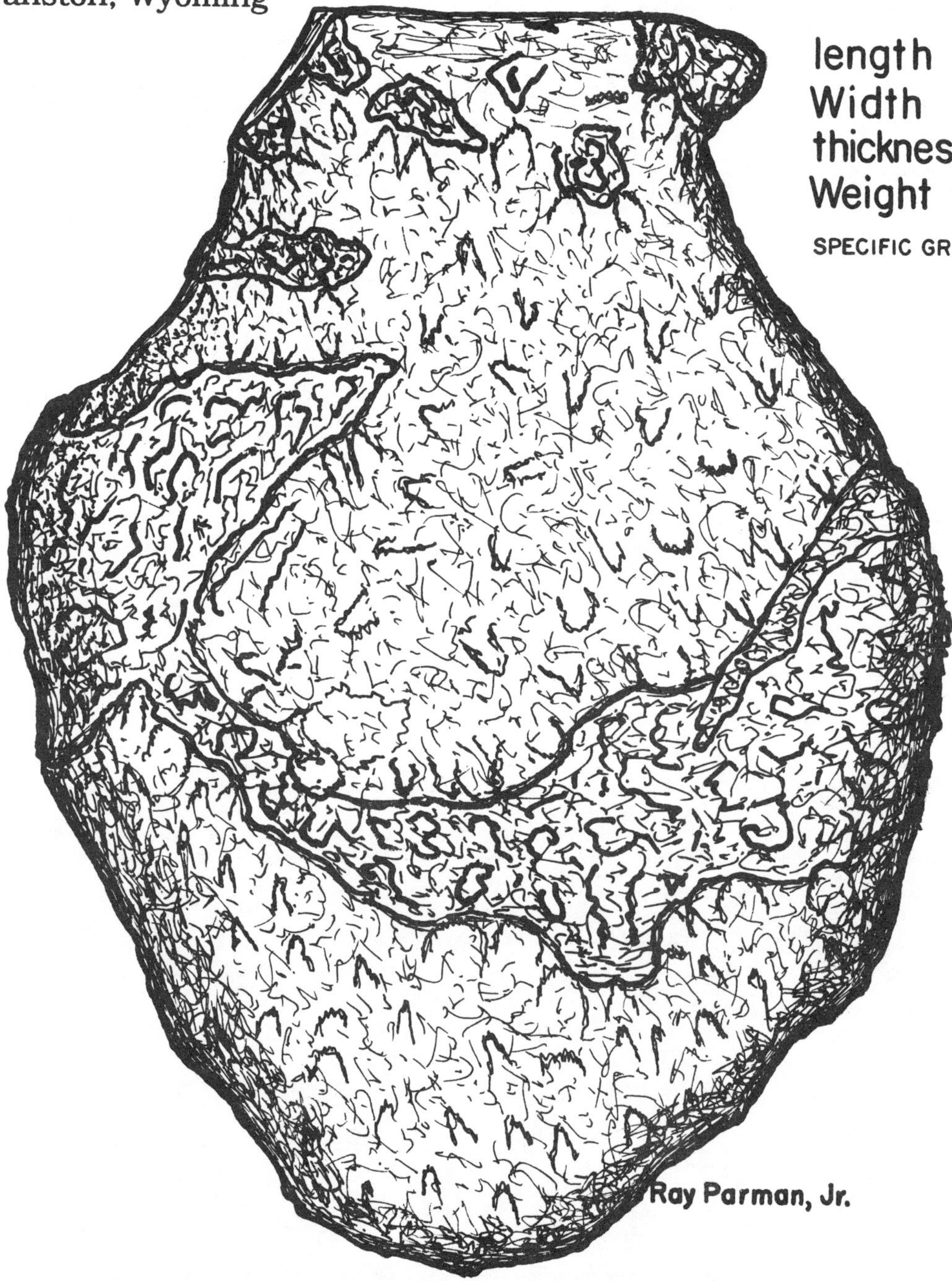

length	17.4 cm-6.8"
Width	12.9 cm-5.0"
thickness	8.8 cm-3.5"
Weight	2.6 Kg-5.8 lb

SPECIFIC GRAVITY 3.17

0 1 2 3 4 5 6 7 CM

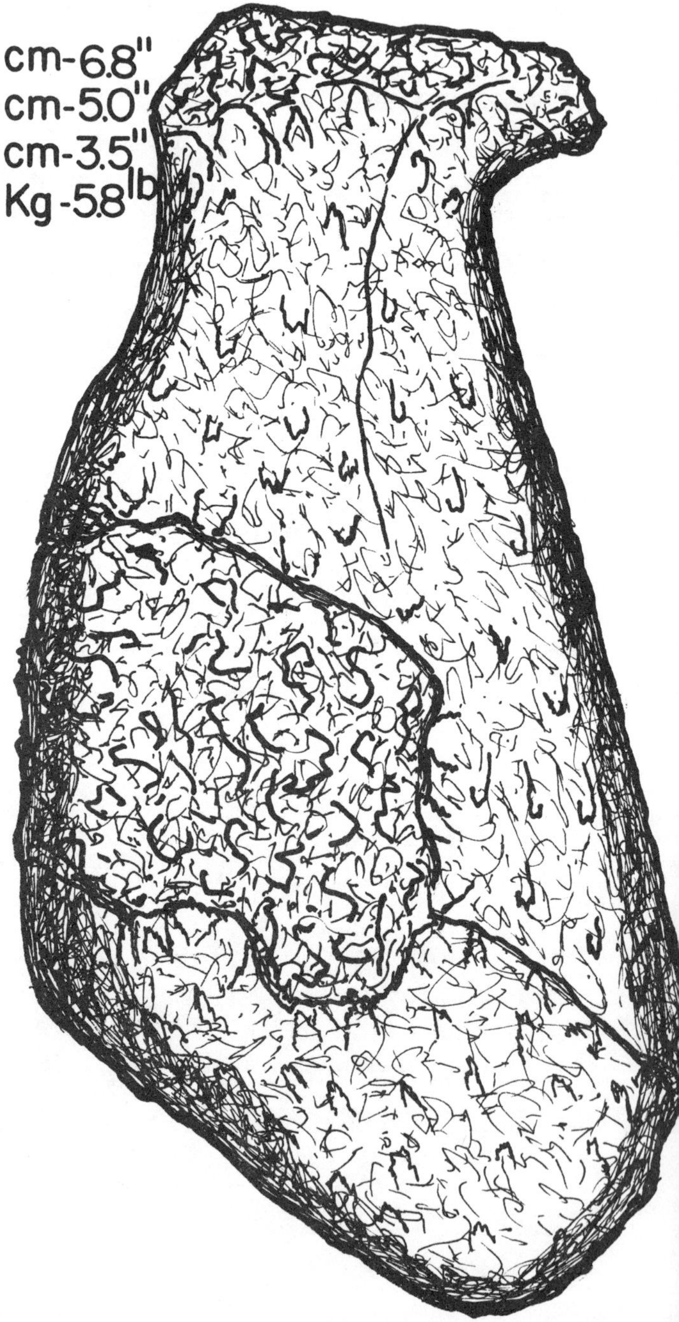

A REMARKABLE, OLD FIND

Color & Material: An even, dull black. Diorite.

Location: Northeast of Shoshoni, Fremont County, Wyoming.

Time has erased almost all evidence that this stone was shaped by man. Was it crafted before the hafting of a handle was known? Artifacts of this nature have received little attention or publication in the past. Surely others exist; comparative studies could elicit valuable data.

After about forty-five minutes (when this stone was first examined), there was a near firm decision that it was shaped entirely by nature. There was no evidence of specific flakes having been removed. If it had been utilized as a hand held pounder, there was no visible evidence of crushing or wear on what would have been the working end. The first of what was to be a flood of evidence, then came to light.

Three Vs in a row, near the neck of the stone, were so aligned and equal in size that they did not look natural. After close examination disclosed other Vs in similar alignment (points toward higher surfaces and open ends toward lower surfaces), it was discovered that approximately seventy percent of the surface of the stone had been pecked away. The stone had been shaped by man! (The lighter areas of the drawings display areas where the stone has been pecked away.)

This shaping was so specifically directed toward overall size and contour, with the detail of the surface contours so controlled, that these findings were determined:

1. A specifically shaped stone (in this case a teardrop volcanic bomb) was selected. Its shape was then enhanced so that when pivoted from the shoulder and elbow, the arc through which it would travel extended through the stone to the center of the working end.

2. The larger end was reduced to a rounded point so that more force per area could be transmitted through the working end.

3. It was to be held in the left hand and was shaped for that use. The size of the extended hand it was crafted for would have had a span of nine inches from the tips of thumb and little finger.

4. The neck was shaped to fit the triangle formed by the thumb and the first finger.

5. An area of the convex side of the stone was reduced approximately three millimeters to fit the last three fingers of the left hand.

A REMARKABLE, OLD FIND No. 80 (Cont.)
From the collection of:
Jim Miller
Evanston, Wyoming

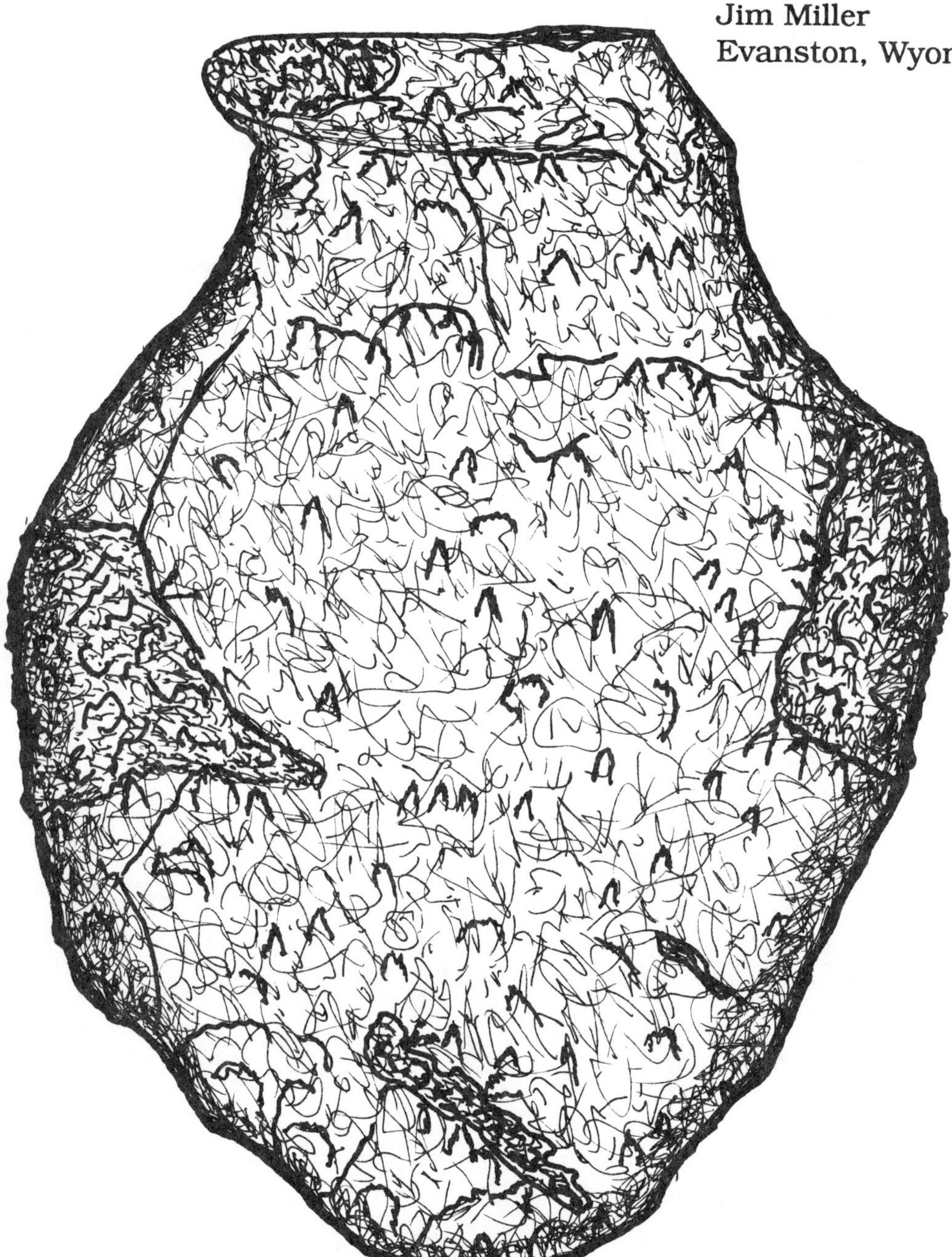

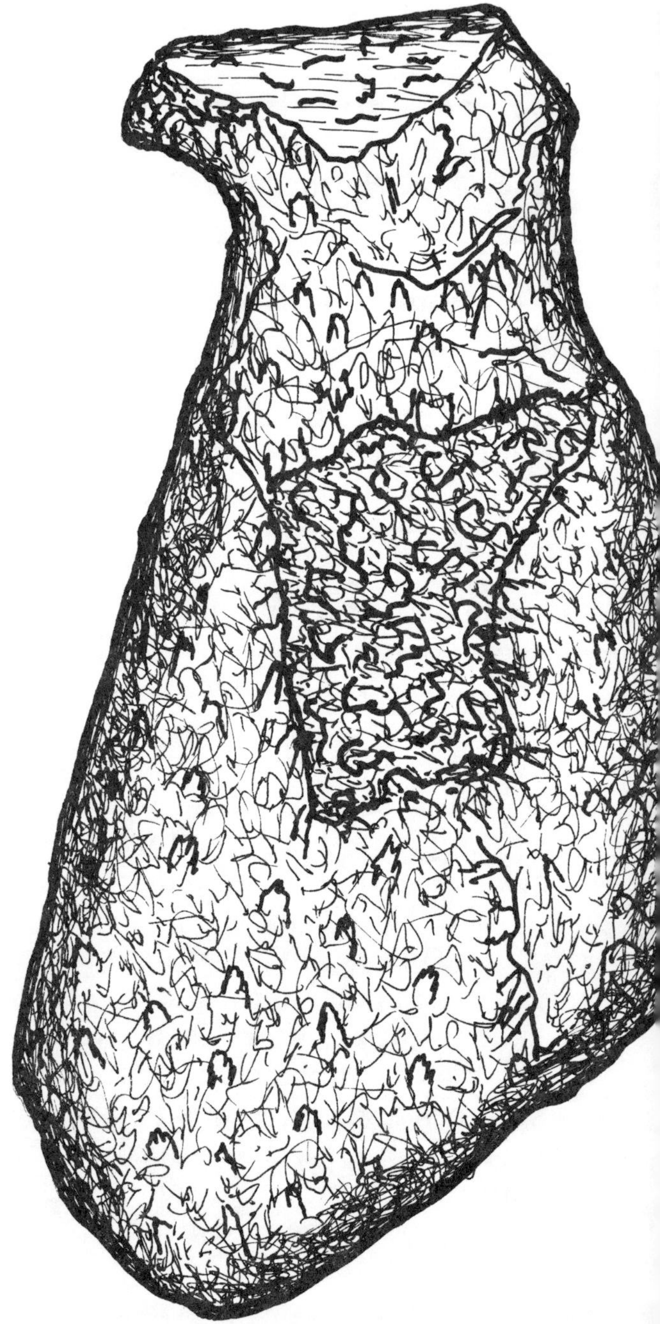

6. Part of the reduced area described in No. 5 was further reduced so that the ends of the fingers would provide a better grip.

7. A slight groove, extending away from the narrow neck, was reduced (pecked away) where the first finger must lay. With the hand in this position, the first finger will not flex around the neck.

These seven features not only preclude natural shaping, but also give evidence of a rather advanced mental capability of the one who crafted this weapon. It is somewhat assuming to use the term weapon. However, the lack of crushing or wear on the working end seems to indicate this.

With the help of William G. (Bill) Davis at Prairie Gems in Riverton, Wyoming, it was possible to determine that a pointed hammerstone of jade would reproduce the characteristic Vs on a diorite nodule having a surface similar to that of the artifact. Hammerstones of chert, agate, and jasper shattered when struck against diorite, so it is likely that a jade hammerstone was used to craft this artifact.

It appears that this is a most advanced specimen of a hand held weapon. Could it have come from a period of time when the handle had not been invented? If so, it does not fit the accepted theory that the first man to enter this continent was capable of crafting Clovis artifacts.

FORERUNNERS TO MODERN KNIFE No. 81
From the collections of:
Mr. & Mrs. Melvin Moen and Jacob Jacoby
Riverton, Wyoming

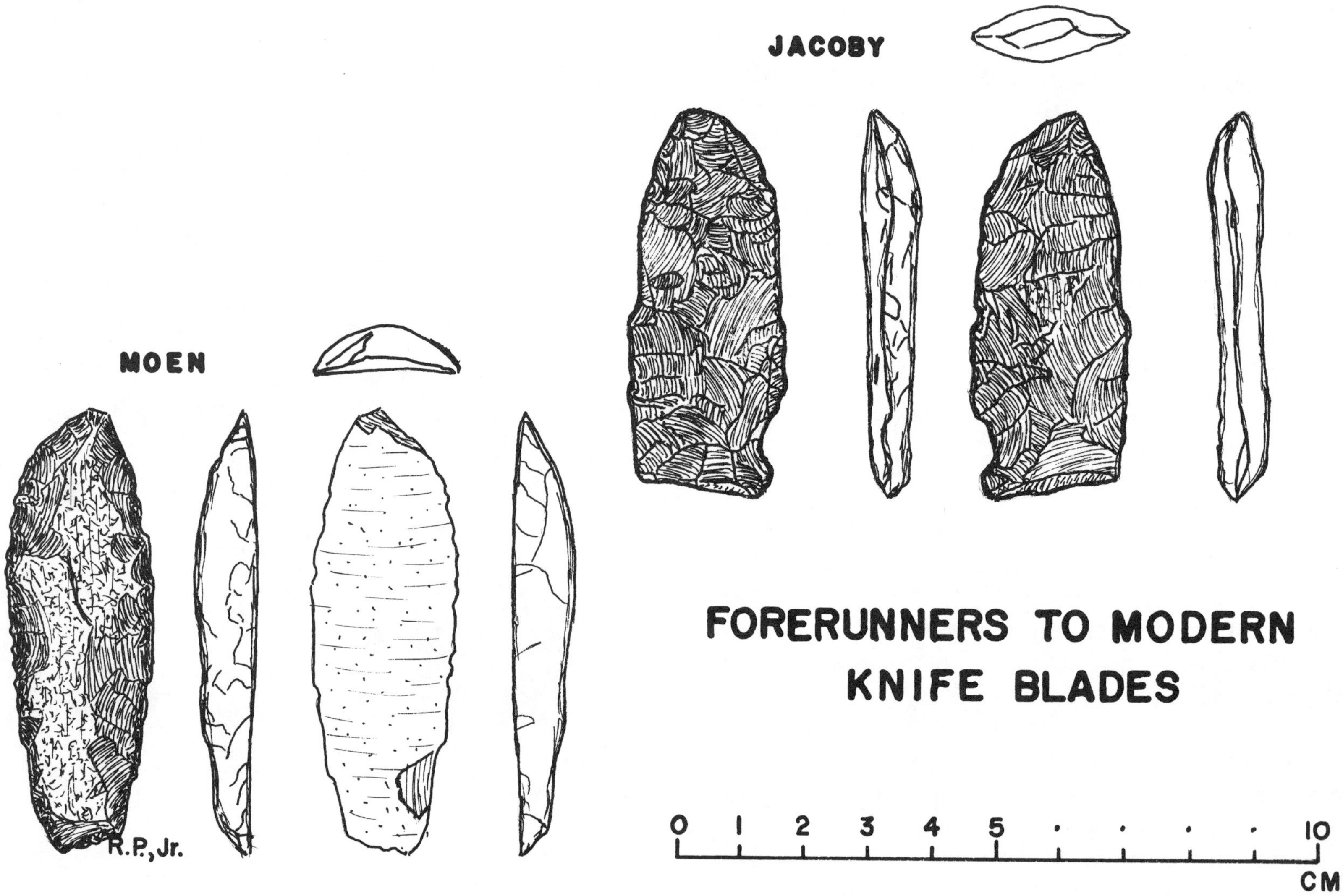

FORERUNNERS TO MODERN KNIFE

Color & Material: Moen, an even light grey with pale tan patina on convex side and very pale patina on the flat side. Quartzite.

Jacoby, bone white with very faint brown patination over all surfaces and four, small, pale orange, washed inclusions. Chert.

Location: Moen, northeast of Jeffrey City, southeastern Fremont County, Wyoming.

Jacoby, northeastern Oklahoma.

Mel and Veronica Moen showed me a recent find that raised interest, first for its remarkable resemblance to a modern pocket knife blade, and then for the faint shoulders creating a stem on the smaller, blunt end.

The next day John Jacoby brought one of his father's finds to my attention, and there was the "knife blade" again! This blade had a single notch with a slight, raised shoulder on the opposite edge.

Clearly both of these blades were crafted with the intent of being hafted. With handles, they would have been very efficient knives.

Ed Fowler, a local bladesmith, was very helpful in determining why the author thought of a "knife blade" when seeing these two artifacts. One of his books illustrated profiles of the five most common blade types; spear, spey, sheepfoot, case, and pen. These two exhibit, with near exactness, the features of the "spey" blade type, the most widely used of the five blade types.

Both artifacts evidence marked weathering, expecially the Jacoby knife that shows damage from use as well. Both are thought to be quite old.

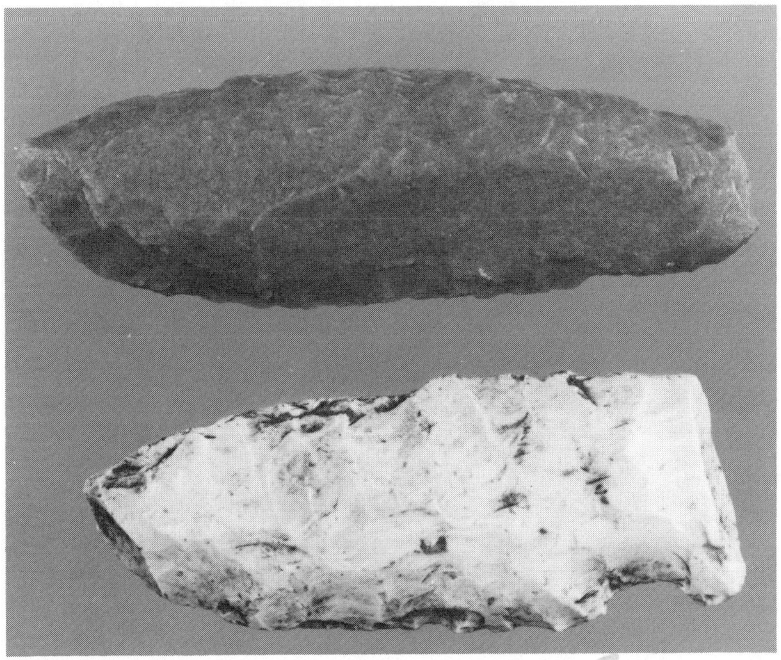

OLD, RARE POINTS No. 82
From the collections of:
Stuart & Nancy Shepherd
Riverton, Wyoming, &
Don Bradley
Casper, Wyoming

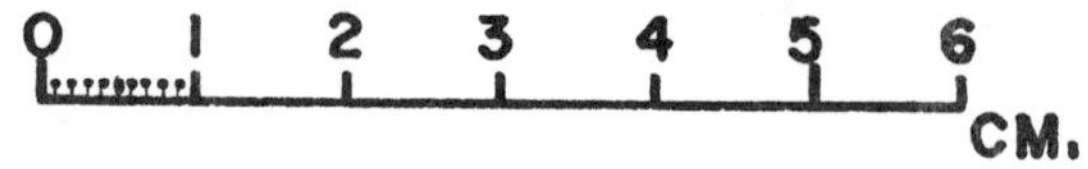

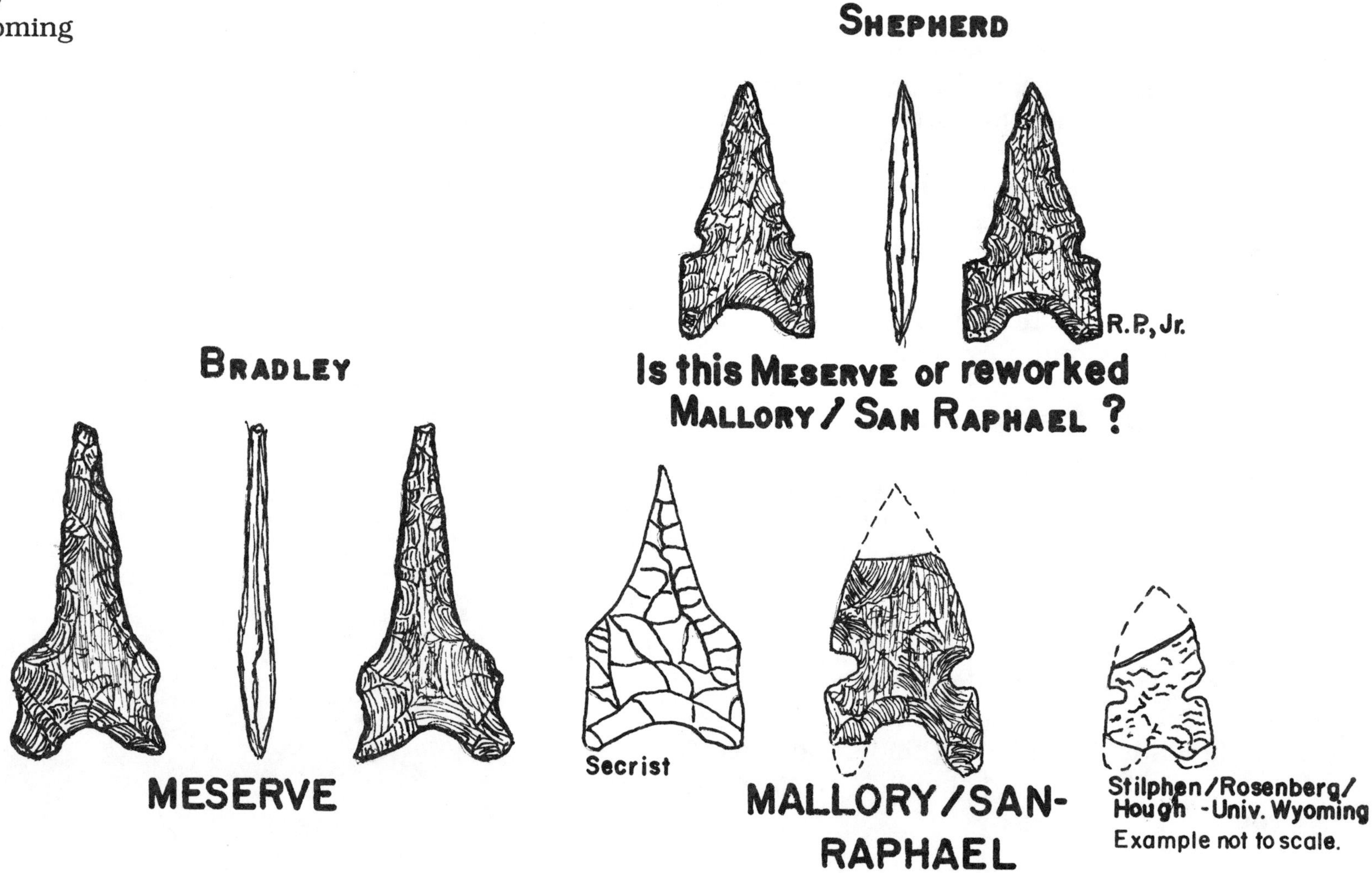

FOUR TO NINE THOUSAND YEARS OLD

OLD, RARE POINTS

Color & Material: Bradley Meserve, heavy, dull tan patina with slight, pastel orange cast overall. Agate and chert brecia with chalcedonous intrusions.

Shepherd Meserve, tan to light brown, with light brown from notches to tip. Slightly argillaceous quartzite.

Shepherd Mallory, light brown, slightly argillaceous quartzite.

Location: Bradley Merserve, southwest of Green River, Utah.

Shepherd Meserve, southern Fremont County, Wyoming.

Shepherd Mallory, western Carbon County, Wyoming.

The work of Stilphen, Rosenberg, and Hough, of the University of Wyoming, made the identification of these points eventually possible. Stuart and Nancy brought their two points to my attention one evening, and, in view of the similar bases, it was first thought there was some relationship between the whole Meserve and the fragment of the Mallory.

The next morning, Helen Lookingbill traveled to Casper with the author to call on Don E. Bradley, who had submitted an unfluted Clovis point (See No. 84) . When he placed his Meserve point in the author's hand, it was exciting because the Shepherd's point immediately came to mind. At this point, identification was unknown and there was thought of naming it the "Shepherd-Bradley" point.

All of these points evidence marked weathering, particularly the two Meserves. The sides displayed in the left views of both have had the flaking almost worn away.

There will be questions arise about reworking a Mallory to obtain a Meserve for the Meserve predates Mallory by about two thousand years. The native who reworked his Mallory may have desired the characteristics of the Meserve with regard to penetration.

The slender blade of the Meserve point is thought, by this writer, to have been for better penetration of thicker hides. The point, having the entire kinetic force of the shaft affecting such a small surface area, could pierce the hide more easily. The slowly expanding, sharp edges would then slice, knifelike, to enlarge the hole before the momentum of the shaft (foreshaft of the atlatl) was lost.

TANNING STONE No. 83
From the collection of:
Robert J. Thomas
Evanston, Wyoming

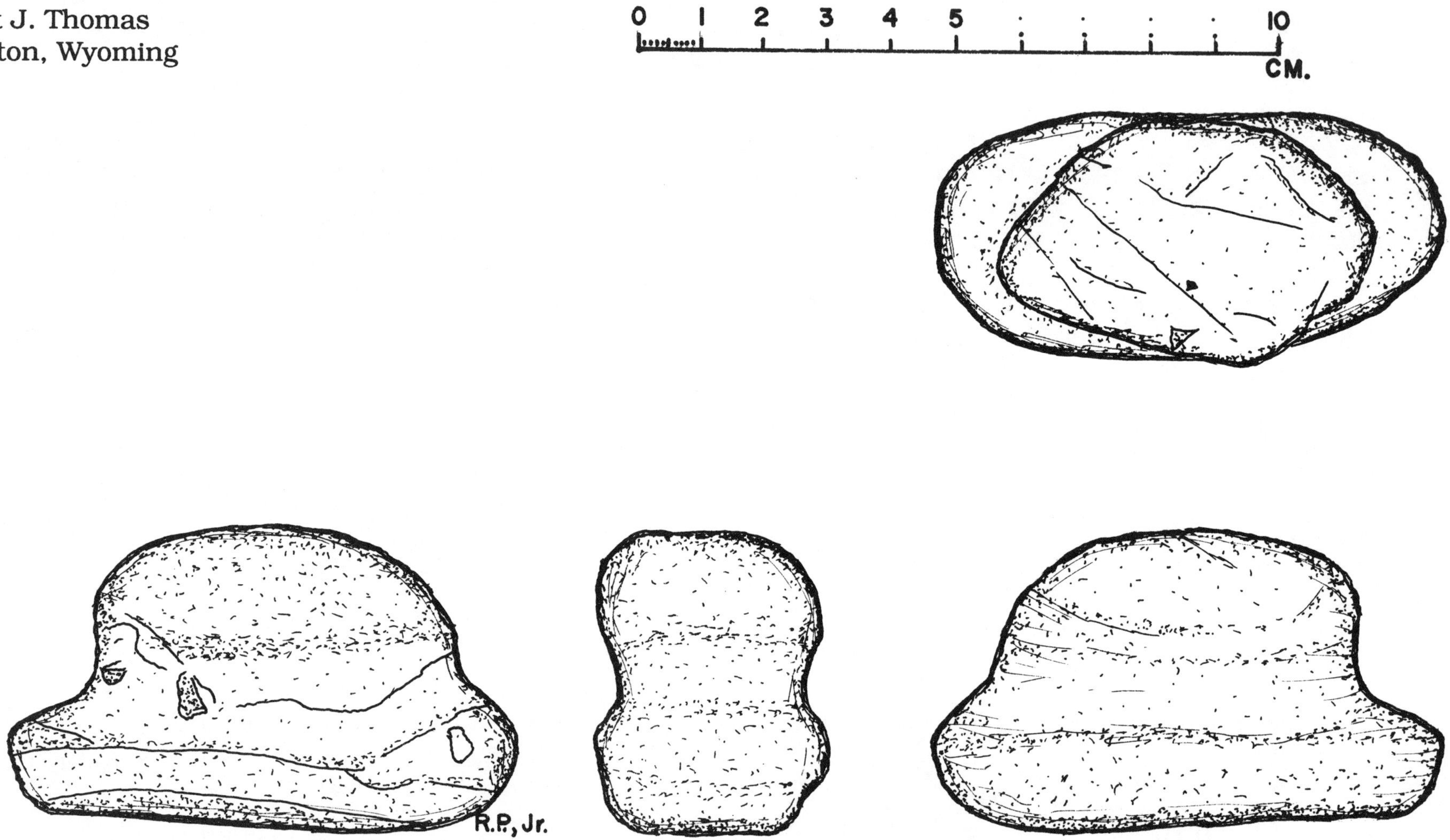

TANNING STONE

Color & Material: Light greyish, dirty brown with slight, irregular areas of darker brown. Orange inclusion on side in view to left. Argillaceous siltstone with feldspar inclusion.

Location: North of Evanston, southern Uinta County, Wyoming.

The forces of nature that shaped this stone could not be determined with certainty, but it is thought that flowing water crafted the primary contours while the stone was still attached to the sedimentary layers below.

Though highly conjectural, it is possible that the native who utilized this stone forcefully removed it from the siltstone pedestal.

It was first thought this was a small mano and very likely it was used in much the same way, but with no metate involved. The lower surface does evidence slight polishing, but faint variations in the plane of the surface indicate that it was not rubbed against a rigid, stone metate.

Probably, it was used in the preparation of hides for clothing.

A RARE FIND No. 84
From the collection of:
Don E. Bradley
Casper, Wyoming

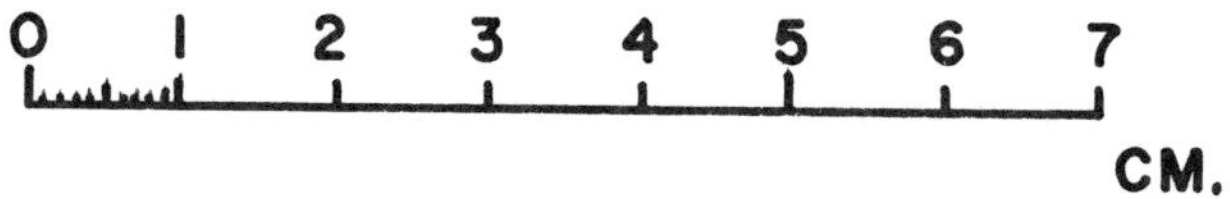

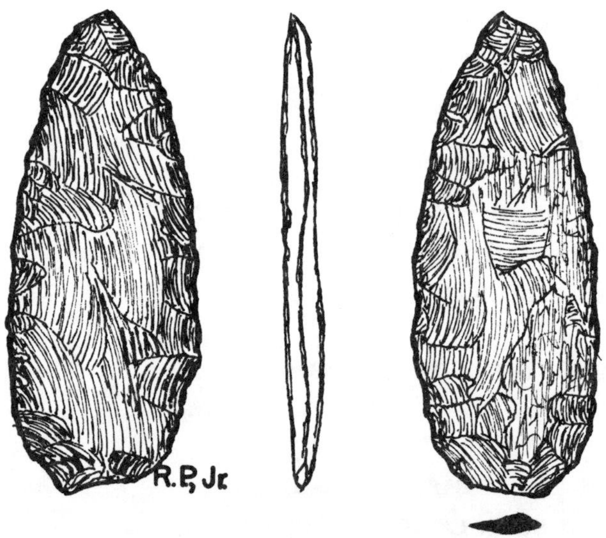

UNFLUTED CLOVIS

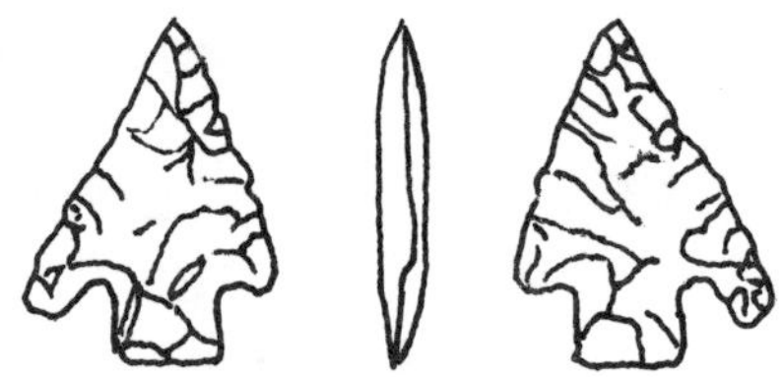

UNIDENTIFIED POINT

A RARE FIND

Color & Material: Clovis, pale lavender, slightly translucent, with slight trace of dull orange wash across tip and black, threadlike inclusions. Faint patina along right edge of side displayed in the left view. Moss agate.

Unidentified, light, translucent, calf-liver brown with two small inclusions that are brown. Agate.

Location: Both taken from Red Desert area of southwestern Wyoming.

It is always a pleasure to hold a specimen of moss agate, but to find it crafted into an old and unique Clovis projectile point, is rare indeed.

The Clovis point has been named for types found in association with extinct animal remains near Clovis, New Mexico. It was assigned to the Llano Complex by Sellards (1952). Since then, it has become one of the most extensively researched point types. Specimens have been found in sites over the entire North American continent. Nearly all of these sites have been dated from ten to twelve thousand years before present.

The identification of Don's point as a Clovis is not entirely certain. However, in view of marked weathering that has almost removed the flaking on the side displayed in the left view, and of there being an eleven thousand, eight hundred year old site (Pine Spring, Sharrock, 1966) immediately to the west of where it was taken, the identification has strong support.

A unique feature of this point is that a fluting platform had been prepared (profile below right view), but it had not been used.

Although crafted in this asymmetrical form, the small point to the right could not be identified. While possibly used as a slitter, it would have been quite small for that purpose. If crafting had been symmetrical, then the artifact would be a typical Columbia River gem point.

AN OLD, BEAUTIFUL KNIFE No. 85
From the collection of:
Steve & Mary Ann Holmquist
Shoshoni, Wyoming

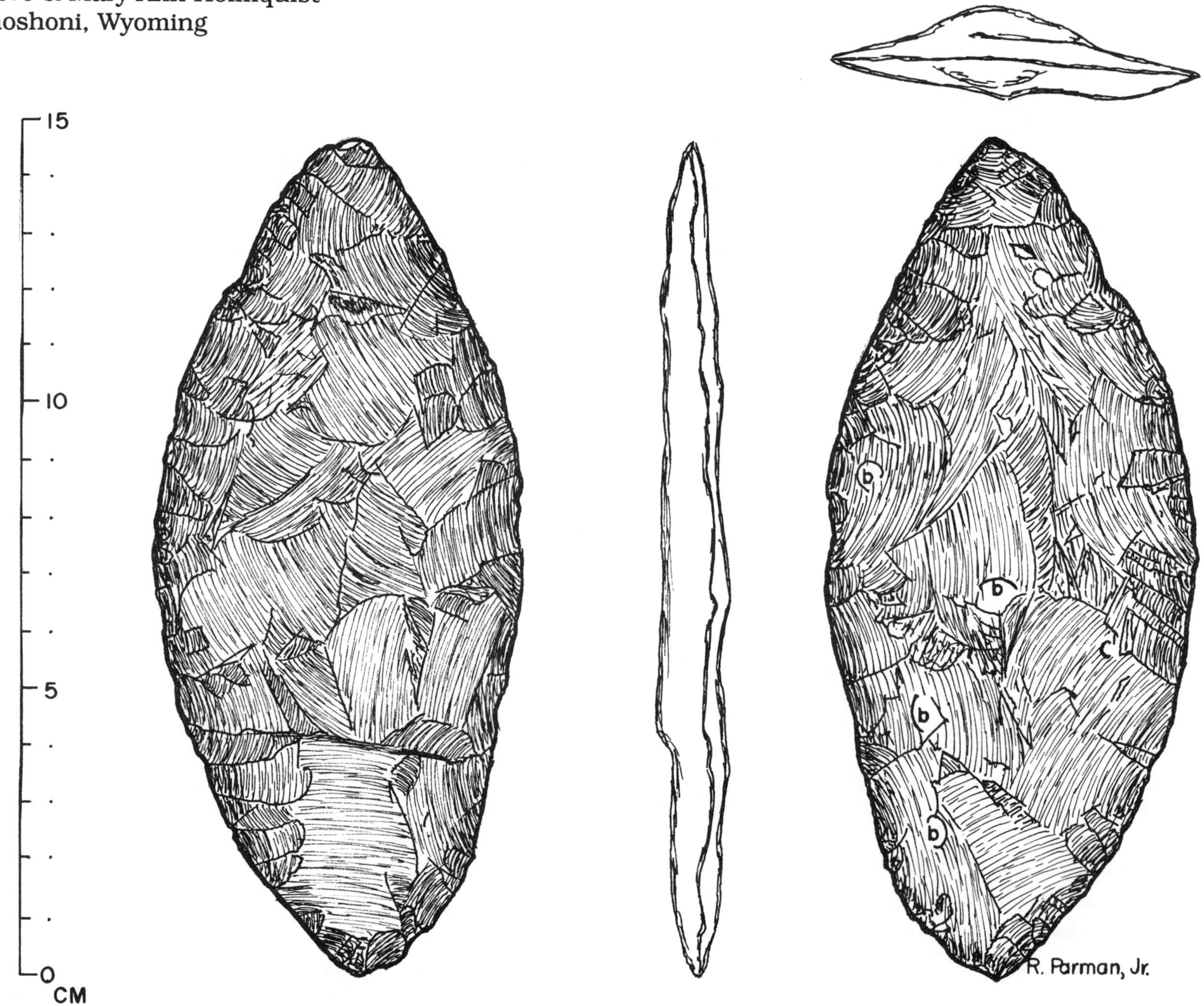

AN OLD, BEAUTIFUL KNIFE

Color & Material: Cocoa-brown with faint blue cast and extremely faint, blue and grey laminations through the longest dimension. One pronounced, reddish-orange ferrous oxide stain near the smaller end of the view to the right. There are several small, similar stains overall. Quartzite.

Location: Northeastern Fremont County, Wyoming.

This beautiful knife was crafted from a large, percussion flake struck from a bruised, river cobblestone. Faintly visible on the surface displayed in the right view, are distinct, rounded fractures. These occur when a stone, tumbling downstream, is struck by, or strikes another stone. From the size and shallowness of these rounded fractures, it is thought that the material of this knife was removed from the cobblestone. The surface displayed to the right would have been approximately eight millimeters below the cobblestone's surface.

The relatively thick, center ridge markedly contrasts the thin, sharp edges. In view of these thin edges, it is thought that the knife saw little use and was never resharpened.

The patination of this knife's surface could best be described as a clear, satin finish varnish. There is no distinction between the patina on the body, and that on the faint, small pressure flake scars that sharpened its edges. This would strongly indicate that the entire knife was crafted from cobblestone to finished knife in a very short period of time.

Weathering has softened the contours of all flaking ridges, and the small, pressure flake scars are only faintly visible. Many of these pressure flake scars were so small that they could not be illustrated in the drawing. In view of this weathering, this knife is thought to be very old.

The caption under the drawings, stating the knife was made from the material of choice, concurs with recent experiments conducted by Dr. George C. Frison, et al., in Africa. Using knives of several materials, they skinned and butchered several elephants. Their conclusion was that quartzite knives were far more functional than those of other materials.

DIGGING STONE No. 86
From the collection of:
Steve & Mary Ann Holmquist
Shoshoni, Wyoming

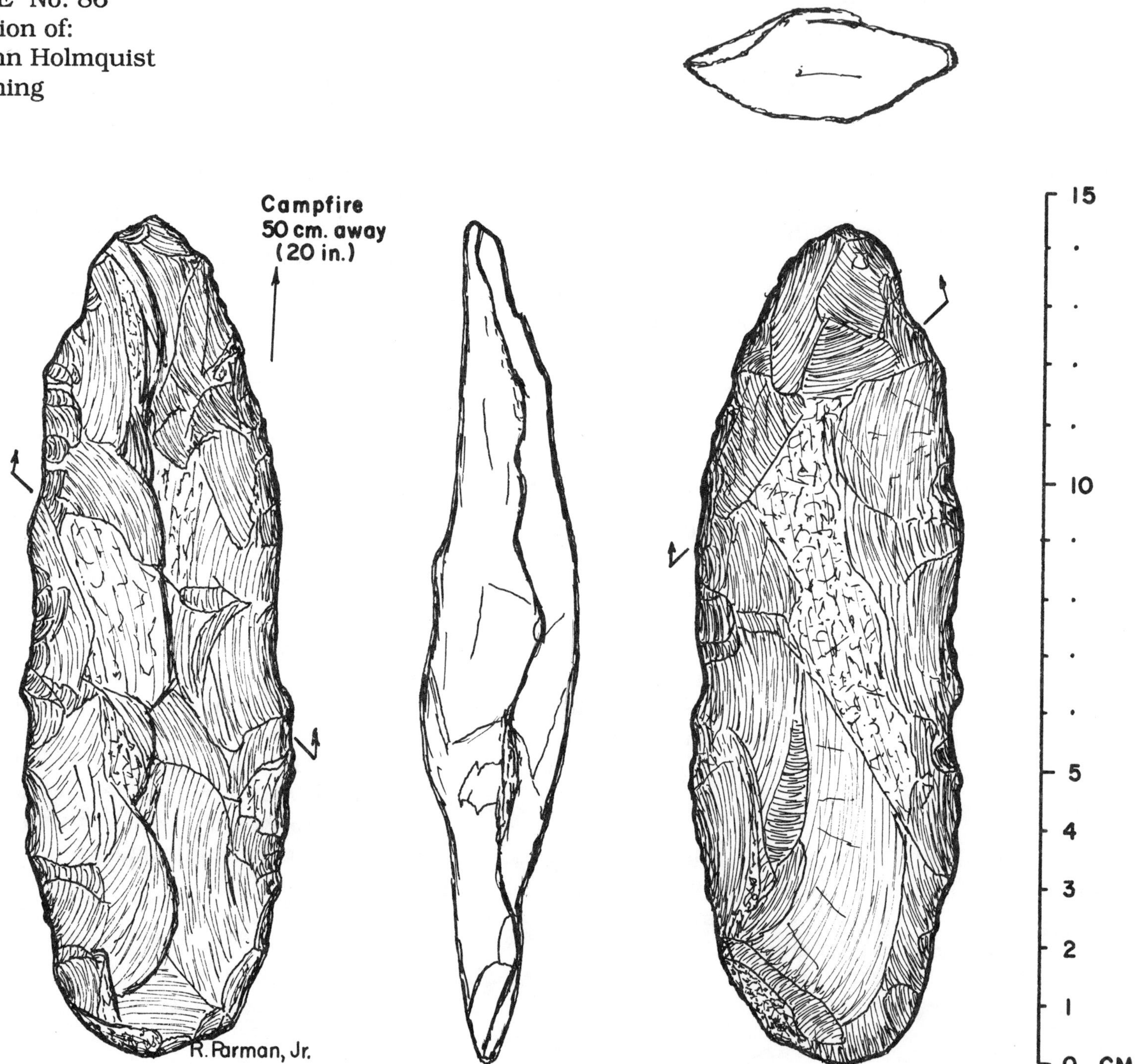

DIGGING STONE

Color & Material: Deep, dull, reddish-brown with slightly blackened surfaces above the arrows on both sides. A very dense, hard orthoquartzite evolved from argillaceous siltstone.

Location: Northeastern Fremont County, Wyoming.

This is another first for this writer. When Steve placed this artifact in my hands, there was an immediate awareness of its use..."A digging stone!" As expected, both ends evidenced marked, crush flaking parallel to their edges.

The digging stone was crafted entirely by percussion flaking. The more pointed end would have been most funtional for penetrating the soil. Then the rounded end would have been used for raking the soil back from the hole.

The blackened area of the smaller end is aligned so distinctly that one is able to determine the artifact's position in relation to the fire that blackened it (see arrow by left view).

Could this artifact have been crafted for the singular purpose of digging a pit in which a campfire was to be built? One can picture a native, on his knees, digging with the stone. He then sits back on his heels to rest, and places the stone by his knee. Once again, he leans over to draw out (with his hands) the last soil from the pit. The stone tool simply remained by the fire.

A UNIQUE, REMARKABLE SCRAPER No. 87
From the collection of the late
Eleanor Kendall, submitted by Patt Brown
Riverton, Wyoming

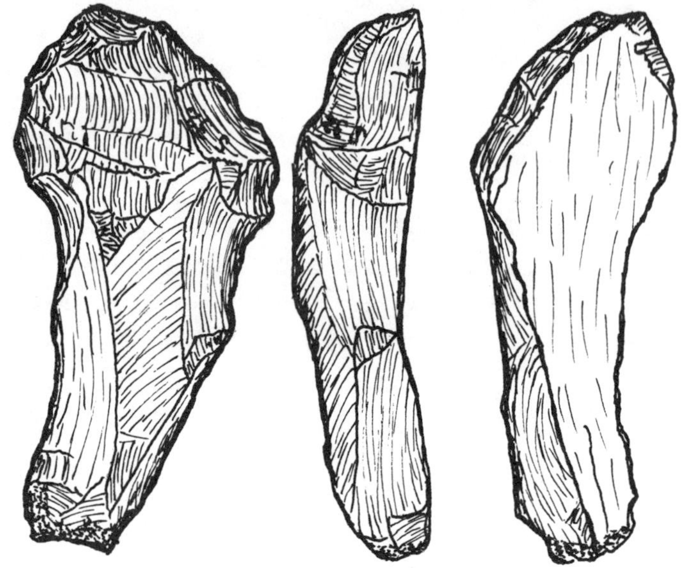

S-32 ROTATED 45°

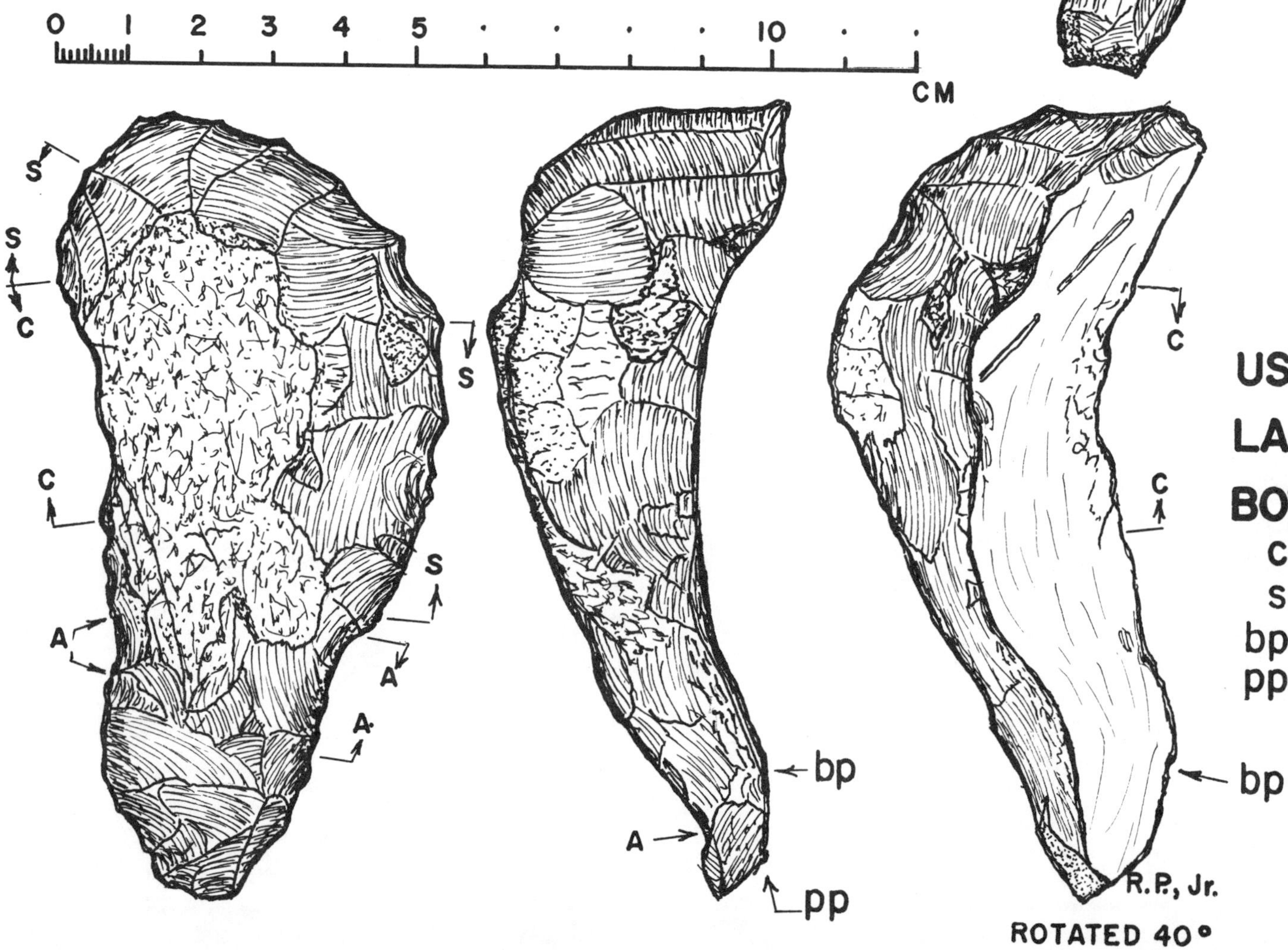

ROTATED 40°

USED TO CRAFT A LANCE SHAFT OR BOW ?

c- chopping edge
s- scraping edges
bp- bulb of percussion
pp- point of percussion

A UNIQUE, REMARKABLE SCRAPER

Color & Material: Large scraper, deep, liver-brown with slight maroon cast. Large, irregular area of the convex surface (left view) bearing marked patination; thick, light tan, calcium carbonate incrustation with a tan to brown stain appearing as a patina. Two slender, wormhole-like chalcedonous inclusions on concave side (visible in right view); a few pinpoint to one millimeter, black inclusions. Chert.

Small scraper, light grey with light tan patina on all surfaces; thick, tan, calcium incrustation on the small end. Quartzite.

Location: Large scraper, Orcgon Butte region, southwestern Wyoming.

Small scraper, south face of Cedar Ridge, approximately nine miles east of Lost Cabin; Fremont County, Wyoming.

This large scraper is unique in both size and contour. While it was examined, numerous features came to light. The color of the material and the two, wormhole-like inclusions kept the author's attention until it was determined where they had been observed before.

This scraper is another artifact crafted from chert taken from the same quarry as Mike Henry's thumb scraper and knife that were published as No. 21.

This particular chert is of such quality that it is described as " flintlock chert ". It is very likely that long, slender flakes, removed from the face of the larger end of this scraper, were utilized as flint pieces placed in the hammers of flintlock guns.

The arrow labeled " pp " (smaller end, center view) is the point of percussion struck on a portion of the core platform, displayed as the dotted area of the smaller end (right view).

It is not positive, but strongly indicated, that the edges between the arrow (A) of the left view have been contoured and ground, so that a thong could have been attached. The knot would have rested in the hooked contour opposite the bulb of percussion (bp right view). This is marked "A" also.

This thong would be wrapped around the palm of the right hand, so that the final length (attached to the tool) was drawn tightly across the palm. With the thumb and first finger gripping the smaller end (convex surface toward

A UNIQUE, REMARKABLE SCRAPER No. 87
From the collection of the late
Eleanor Kendall, submitted by Patt Brown
Riverton, Wyoming

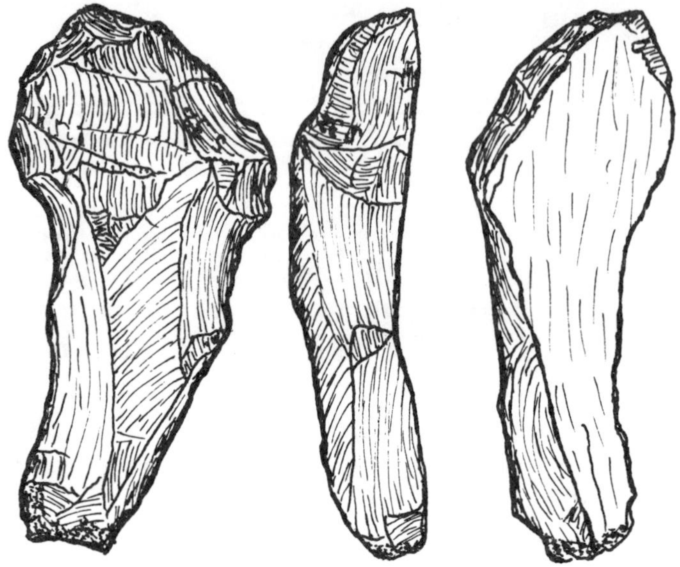

S-32 ROTATED 45°

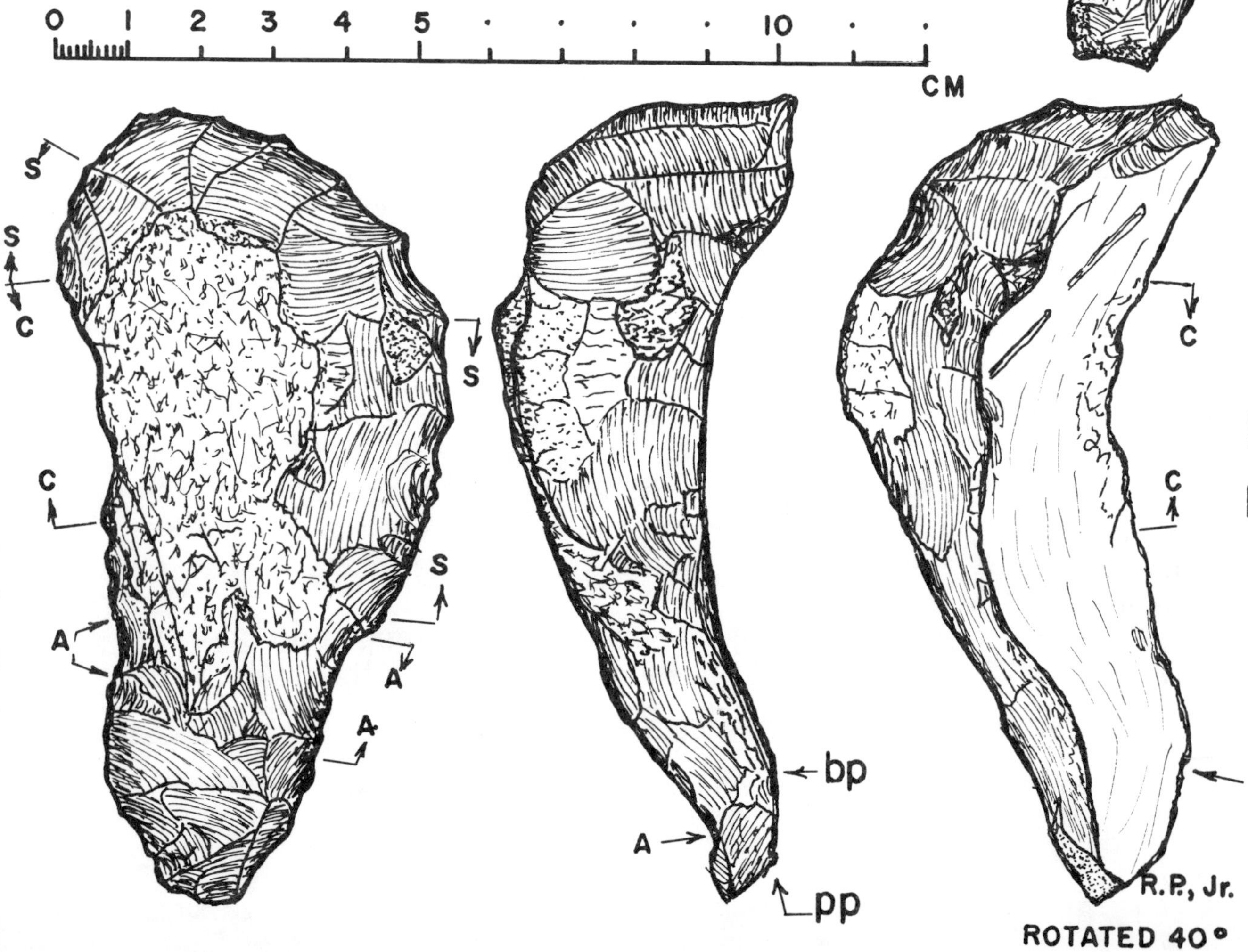

ROTATED 40°

USED TO CRAFT A LANCE SHAFT OR BOW ?

c- chopping edge
s- scraping edges
bp- bulb of percussion
pp- point of percussion

thumb) it would have been an effective adz, or small axe. This would account for the damage on the concave surface, illustrated between the arrows "C" of the right view.

The edges between the arrows marked "S" (left view), have been worn smooth by scraping in a direction away from the concave surface. In view of there not being a definite line of smooth surface, it was most likely used to scrape green wood, or to flesh hides.

The small scraper (S-32) from the author's collection, has been included because of its similar contours. It was very likely used in the preparation of small hides.

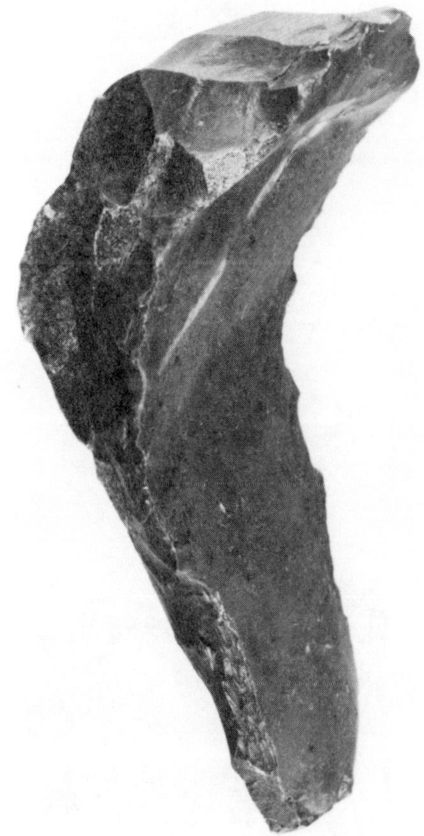

POSSIBLE SANDIA I & II FRAGMENTS No. 88
From the collection of:
Lee & Fern Whitlock
Whitlock Ranch, Sweetwater, Wyoming

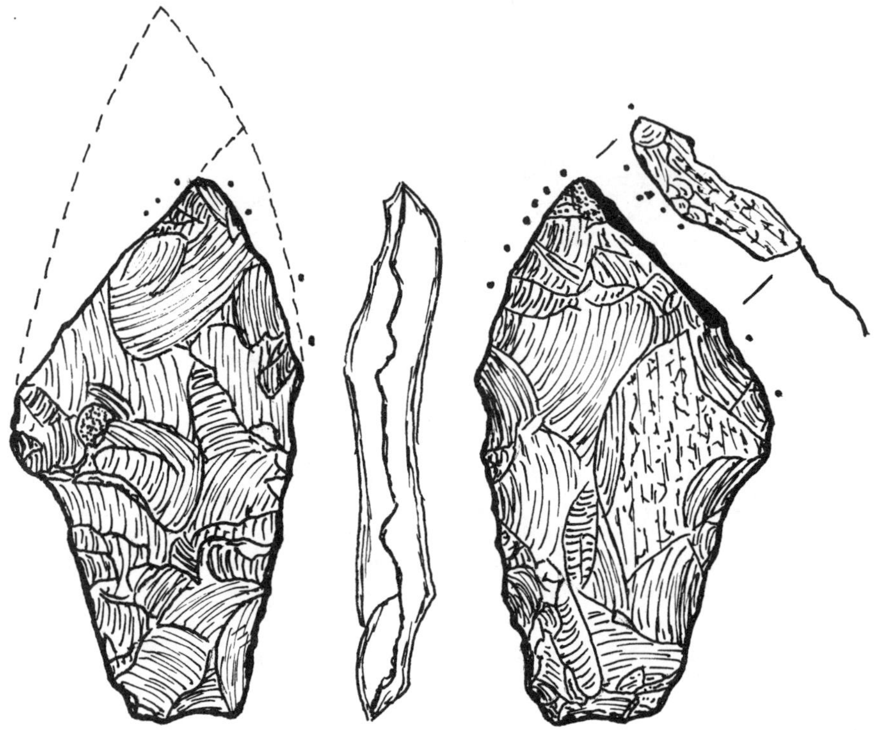

SANDIA II
(REWORKED)

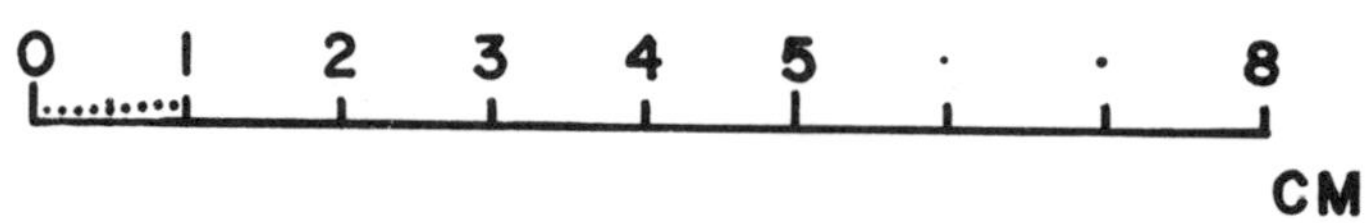

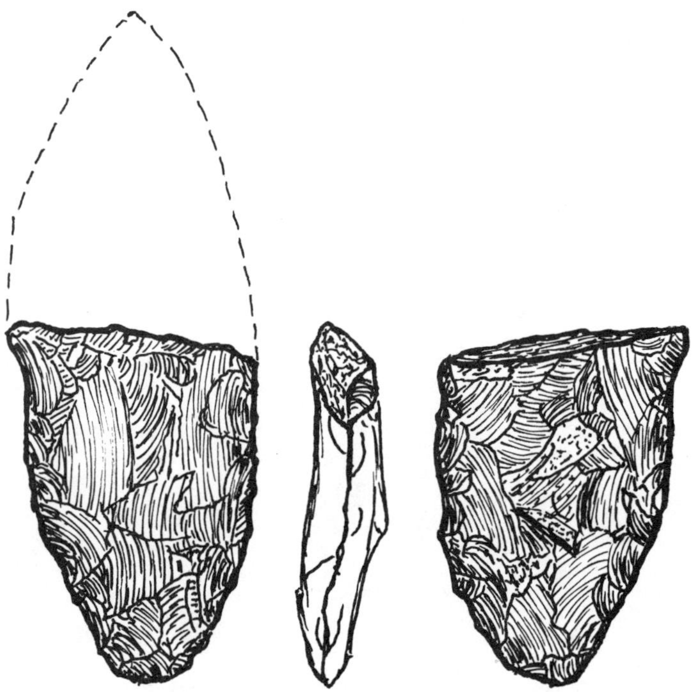

SANDIA I

POSSIBLE SANDIA I & II FRAGMENTS

Color & Material: Sandia I- A, a brown so dark as to appear black. Three slightly lighter, reddish-brown inclusions; two perpendicular to the long axis (one of these exposed on the fracture plane), and the third, an irregular spot near the end of the stem. Faint, pale green, washed inclusions parallel to the long axis and visible on the surface displayed in the left view. Chert. Sandia II, milk (1%) white agate with faint white patination over most of the surfaces. Two areas with heavy patination; several, pressure flake surfaces having little, or no patination.

Location: Both artifacts were found in vicinity of the Whitlock Ranch, east of Sweetwater Station; southeastern Fremont County, Wyoming.

These two artifacts were selected solely to record additional Sandia finds. The more probable of the two is the Sandia I fragment, because the Sandia features (listed in No. 40) are markedly present. In view of the lack of weathering, and the even patination of all its surfaces, it is thought that the fragment was buried until just before it was found.

The edge view has been rotated slightly to expose one of the two inclusions previously mentioned. The inclusion is distinct, and the point was broken along a plane of the inclusion's surface.

It is possible this point was a burial piece that was broken in a ceremonial or ritualistic manner.

The Sandia II is identified only tentatively, but it does evidence rework and varied patination. Both of these features are indicative of age. It is thought that the original Sandia II point broke along a single diagonal plane; the heaviest patina occurs on a remaining portion of this plane (displayed in drawing to right).

On this surface, there are five tiny flake scars that have less patina. Another area of heavy patination appears on the right central portion of the surface as displayed in the right view.

At a more recent time, small pressure flakes were removed (indicated by each dot) to rework the broken point into what was thought to have been a hafted knife. These pressure flake scars show the least patination.

Appreciation is expressed to Lee and Fern Whitlock for making these available for publication.

A RARE, GREEN RIVER POINT No. 89
From the collection of:
Mary Hickford
Midwest, Wyoming

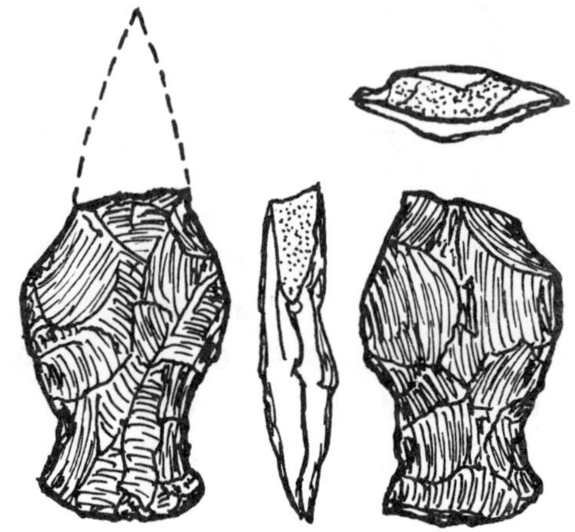

TRINITY
(2000 TO 1000 B.C.)
?

Example
Secrist's 3rd
P. 70

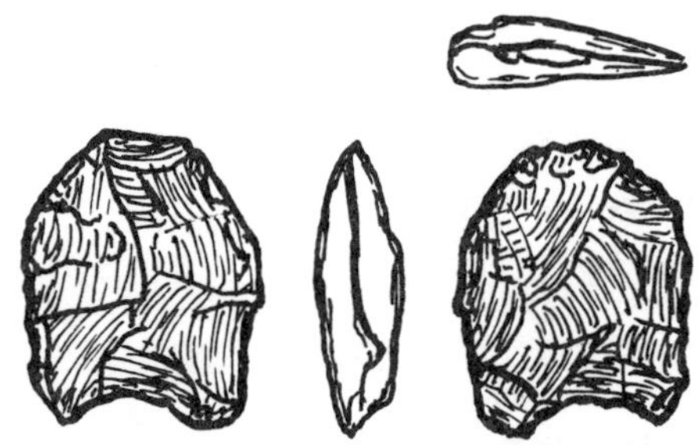

GREEN RIVER
(5000 TO 3000 B.C.)
RARE PROB. UNFINISHED

Example
Secrist's 3rd
P. 24

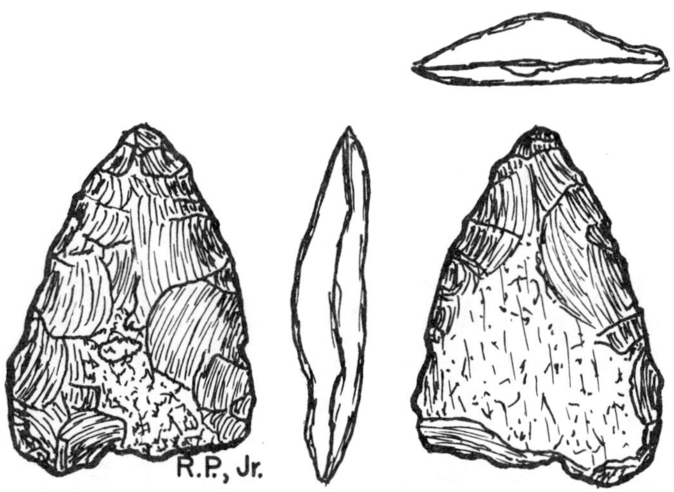

UNKNOWN

A RARE, GREEN RIVER POINT

Color & Material: Green River, irregular, light greyish-tan and very light brown, translucent with slight lavender cast; having several brown, pin-point inclusions and two, white, small, round (2.5 mm & 3.0 mm dia.) fossil casts. Chert.

Trinity, light tan with abundant, minute, irregular, grey speckles. Chert.

Unknown, from the same quarry as those above.

Location: All from southwestern Fremont County, Wyoming.

The unknown projectile point is thought (by this writer) to be contemporary with the Green River point. It would have been utilized with the atlatl and a heavy shaft to kill heavier game such as buffalo, elk and moose. (The Green River point would be used the same way, but with a lighter shaft, to bring down deer and antelope). This point was crafted using a natural fracture plane (unflaked surface at base of left view) that essentially left the base "fluted" or thinned for ease in hafting it to the foreshaft.

The Green River has been described (Secrist's Guide, 3rd Ed.) as a small sized dart point and as being rare. It was named for the Green River region in southwestern Wyoming, near where this specimen was found. Normally, the Green River point is fairly thin. This one has a protrusion at the base of the left tang, on the side displayed in the right view. The slender, darkened area (across the tang) is the marked shoulder of this protrusion. While holding this point, one gets thc impression that if the one remaining flake had been removed, then the point would have been completely finished.

The Trinity is not whole; the dashed lines display its expected configuration. Secrist's Guide describes it as a "small to medium sized dart point" and as being "fairly plentiful".

The material of these three artifacts is thought to be from the same quarry in central Uinta County, Wyoming.

Congratulations to Mary Hickford for the "rare" Green River find. An unusually shaped pounder, found on the same hunt, will be featured in No. 91.

BEAUITFUL KNIFE, SLITTER & CLASSIC LANCE TIP No. 90
From the collections of:
Ralph & Patricia Rhodes
Lander, Wyoming &
Helen Lookingbill
Riverton, Wyoming

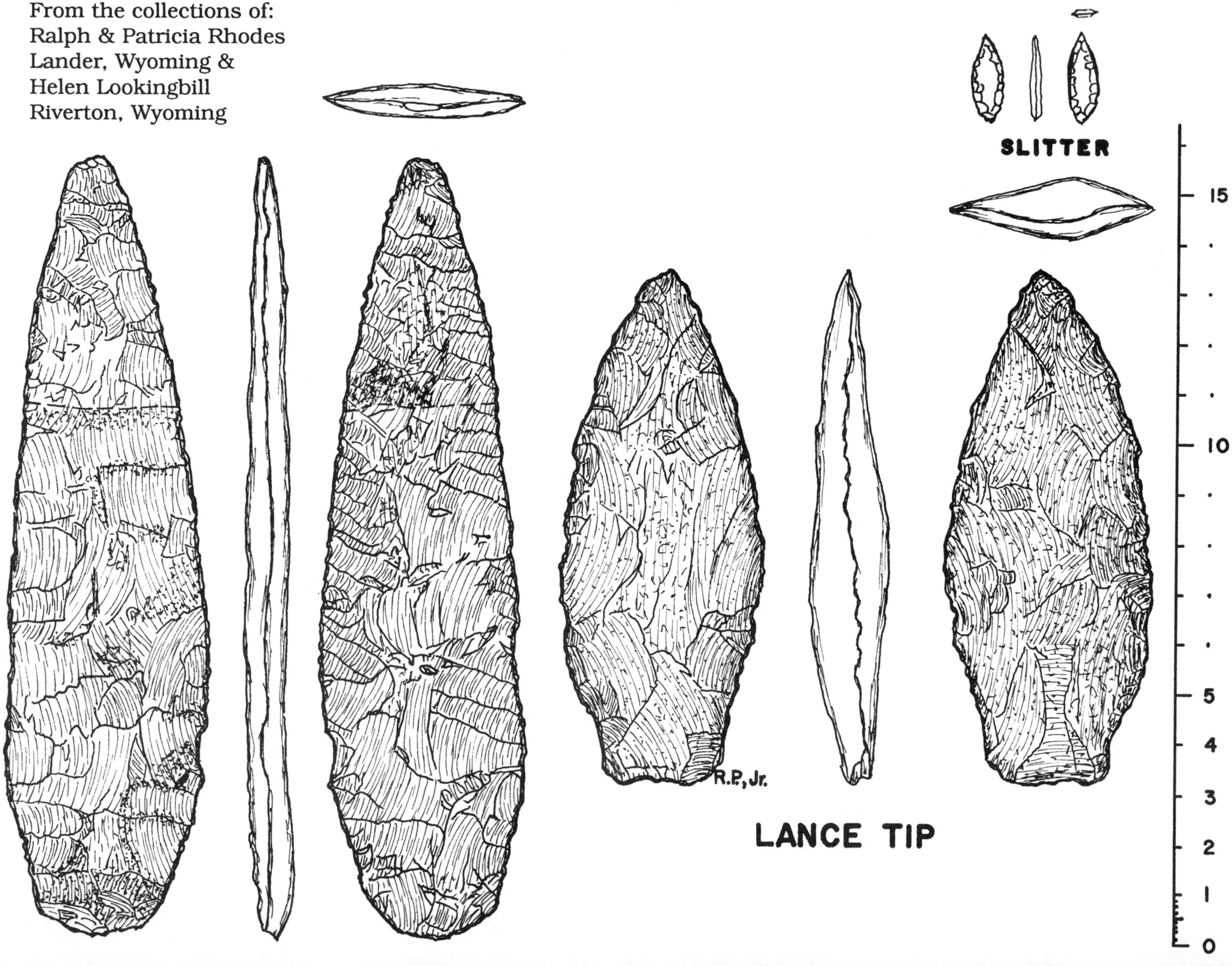

BEAUTIFUL KNIFE, SLITTER & CLASSIC LANCE TIP

Color & Material: Knife, an even, light grey with faint tan patina from the fracture line (dashed line near pointed end) to rounded end on surface displayed in left view, and from the fracture to the pointed end in view to right. The surfaces on opposite sides of those described, have an irregular brown to dark brown, contact stain, and slight incrustation. Quartzite.

Lance tip, an even, light brown with pale green cast. Slightly translucent with abundant, small, light orange-brown inclusions. Quartzite.

Slitter, dark, translucent brown with slight red cast. Agate.

Location: Knife, Red Desert, southwestern Wyoming.

Lance tip, southwestern Fremont County, Wyoming.

Slitter, Eastern Idaho, just west of Yellowstone.

It was a pleasure to hold this knife. The faint, oblique, collateral flaking (visible on the surface displayed in the right view), coupled with the random percussion flaking of the reverse side, leads one to believe it is quite old. Oblique flaking (diagonal) is found on Allen, Angostura, and Hell Gap points. These are Paleo Indian points, and range from 6,000 to 9,000 years old. The flaking ridges of both sides are markedly rounded, indicating considerable wind erosion. It is characteristic of quartzite that cutting edges are very sharp, even after long exposure to the elements.

After the knife was broken (dashed line near tip), one of the two fragments was flipped over. The brown stain and incrustation were the result of the transfer of soil or mineral particles from the surface on which the fragments had lain.

The lance tip from Helen Lookingbill's collection was selected to contrast the knife. Many hold a knife and call it a "Spear Point". This lance tip is classic in configuration. It displays: a short, strong stem that has been thinned for hafting to a shaft; a fairly thick body so that the side thrust forces of striking a rib will not break it; and a strong, sharp point for effective penetration.

The slitter is another rare find. It was this artifact that the Rhoads first brought to my attention. Tiny pressure flakes were removed from

BEAUITFUL KNIFE, SLITTER & CLASSIC LANCE TIP No. 90
From the collections of:
Ralph & Patricia Rhodes
Lander, Wyoming &
Helen Lookingbill
Riverton, Wyoming

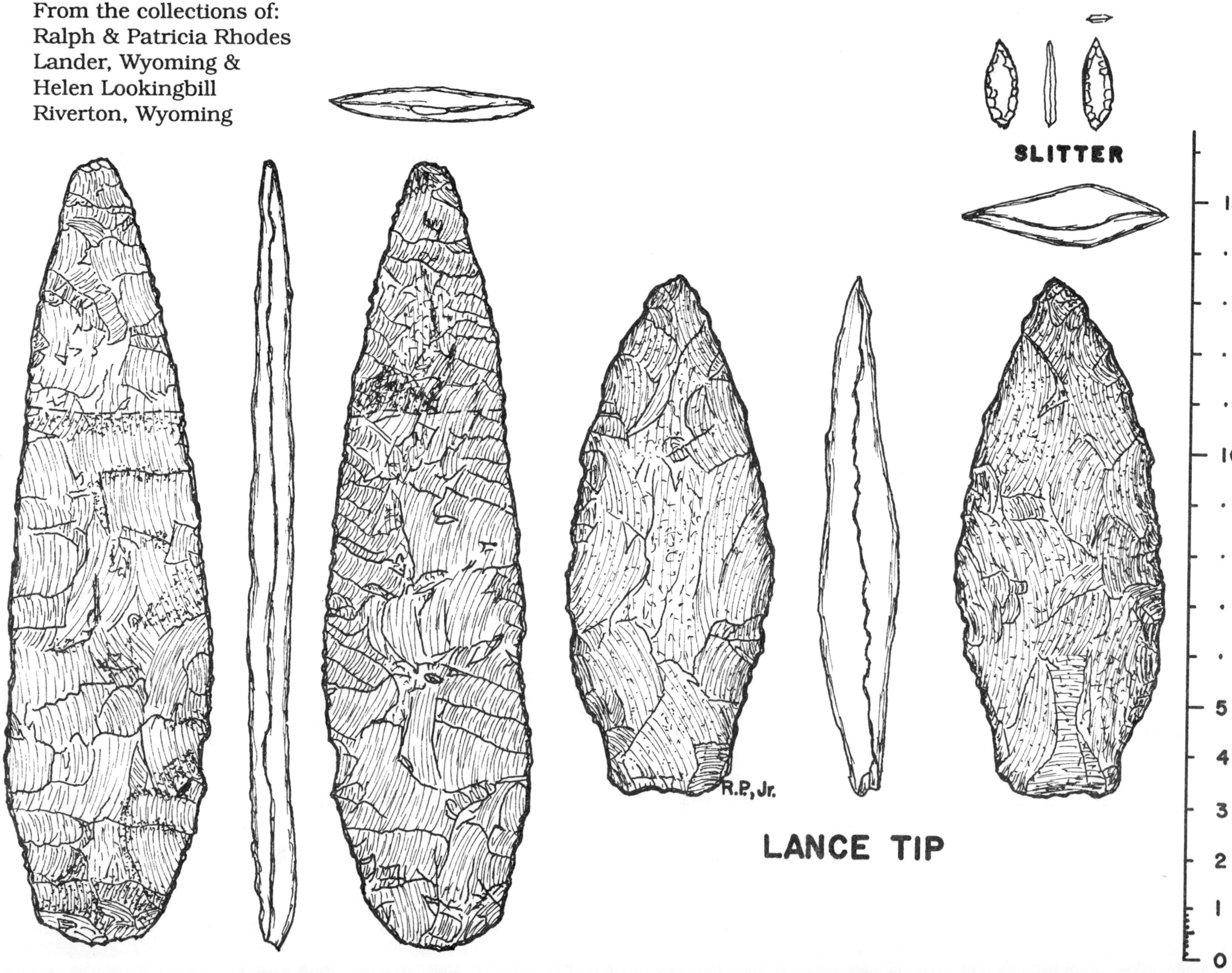

all edges on both sides. It may have been held between the thumb and first finger and used as a small knife. It may also have been pressed into a small, growing twig of suitable wood (probably a hardwood), until new growth surrounded slightly more than half its length. The twig would then be cut away, sinew wrapped about it next to the stone, then fashioned into much like an Exacto knife of today.

Many thanks to the Rhoads and Mrs. Lookingbill for making these rare and classic finds available.

UNUSUAL STONE POUNDER No. 91
From the collection of:
Mary Hickford
Midwest, Wyoming

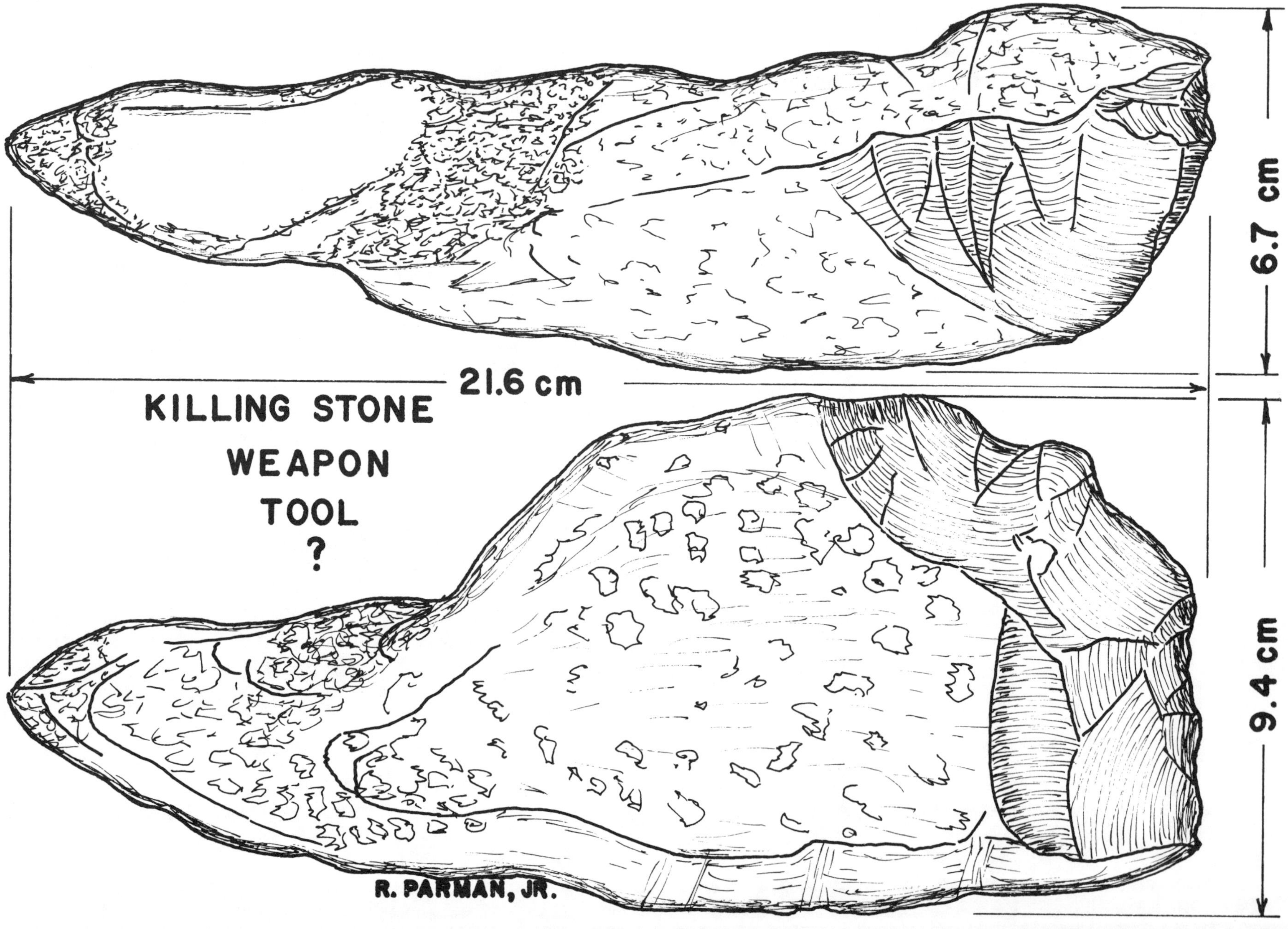

UNUSUAL STONE POUNDER

Color & Material: An even brown with light tan rind appearing as the lighter, unflaked areas of the drawings. Numerous light tan, predominately circular, irregularly shaped, percussion fractures over the convex surface and very densely over the concave surface (visible along the upper edge of the view above). Quartzite.

Location: Southwestern Fremont County, Wyoming.

The hunter kneeled behind one of the larger sage bushes that grew near the bank of a stream behind him. He was aware that the others had been successful because he could hear and feel the herd coming. The stone tipped dart was already affixed to the end of the shaft that he had placed along the top of his throwing stick. Grasping this in his hand, he raised it slightly above his shoulder as he rose to his feet. He crouched low, and waited, alert. A moment later, he lifted to his full height. Two powerful steps gave his body momentum, and with the third, his arm followed a graceful arc over his shoulder. The stone tipped shaft flew true.

The old buffalo lagged behind. It was late in the afternoon, and he had been ready to lie down and rest, when the herd he was with had been startled by strange creatures and even stranger noises. The stampede had begun over a mile back. He struggled to keep up with the others, but they thundered on ahead. He stumbled, but had regained his footing just as the heavy shaft drove a stone tipped dart deep into his right shoulder. Terrifying pain coursed through his body as the wooden shaft turned and twisted with each powerful thrust of his leg. It lessened somewhat as the shaft fell away. The pain might save his life, for it called forth even more adrenalin, and the old buffalo was drawing on its last reserves. He continued to run but his strength was failing rapidly.

Suddenly, another strange creature rose before him, to his right. To turn away, the buffalo thrust this right leg forward, and his full weight came down upon it. The leg failed and his massive shoulder plowed heavily into the ground. The last of his strength brought him to his feet. At that instant the hunter reached him. In the late afternoon sun, a killing stone follows another graceful arc, and the old buffalo's pain is no longer.

Perhaps six thousand years later, another hunt comes to a climax against this same stream bank. This time, the hunters are on horseback.

UNUSUAL STONE POUNDER No. 91
From the collection of:
Mary Hickford
Midwest, Wyoming

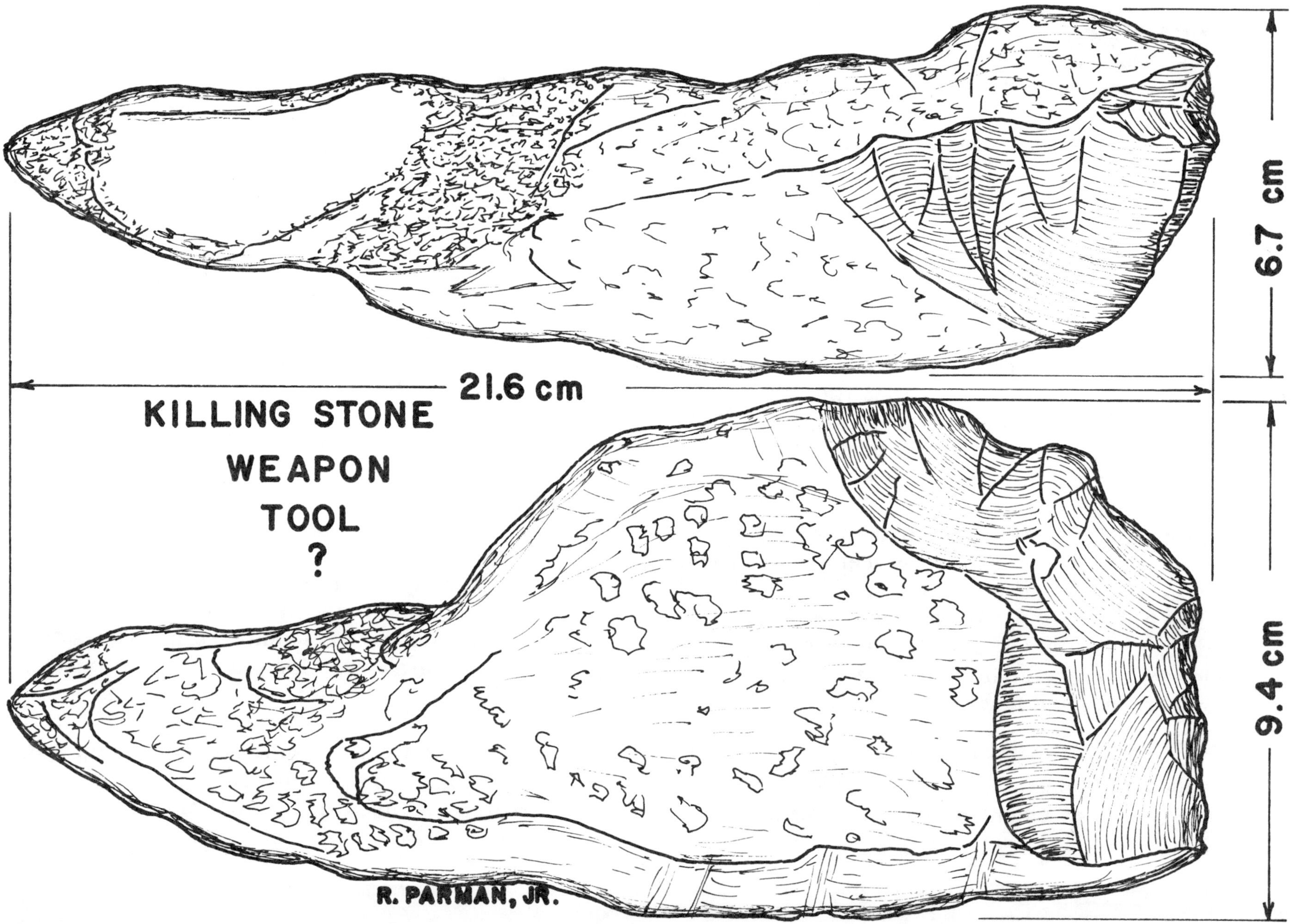

Not one, but several buffalo fall prey to many arrows. Tribal women are now moving among them, dividing into two, sometimes three about each animal. There is much work to be done, and large choppers and knives will be needed. One of the women readily finds a rounded cobblestone--it will make an excellent hammerstone. Her eyes scan the ground about her-- it is the handle of the killing stone that catches her eye. Its size, shape, and the quality of the stone becomes more apparent as she picks it up. She realizes then that the handle is the work of one who lived long ago.

Using the hammerstone, it is only a moment later that the larger end of the old killing stone is sharpened into a chopping edge. Yet another moment later, the two women with her finish crafting knives, and their work on the downed animal gets under way. As the sun passes two fingers, the hide is removed, and knives flash repeatedly in the late afternoon sunlight. The flesh falls away from the heavy shoulder and hip joints, and she again reaches for the chopper. As her hand folds around the handle, thoughts of the hunters who lived long ago enter her mind.

The graceful arc of long ago forms as a vivid image as she raises it over her head. The same arc brings the chopper down upon the neck of the femur.

Her work done, this woman drops to her knees. With last thoughts of the long ago hunters, the stone tool is again placed gently upon the ground.

Mary, it was two hundred years later that you lifted this treasure from the ground and brought it to us. Thank you for making these images of the past possible.

A CLASSIC TOMAHAWK No. 92
From the collection of:
Ralph & Patricia Rhoads
Lander, Wyoming

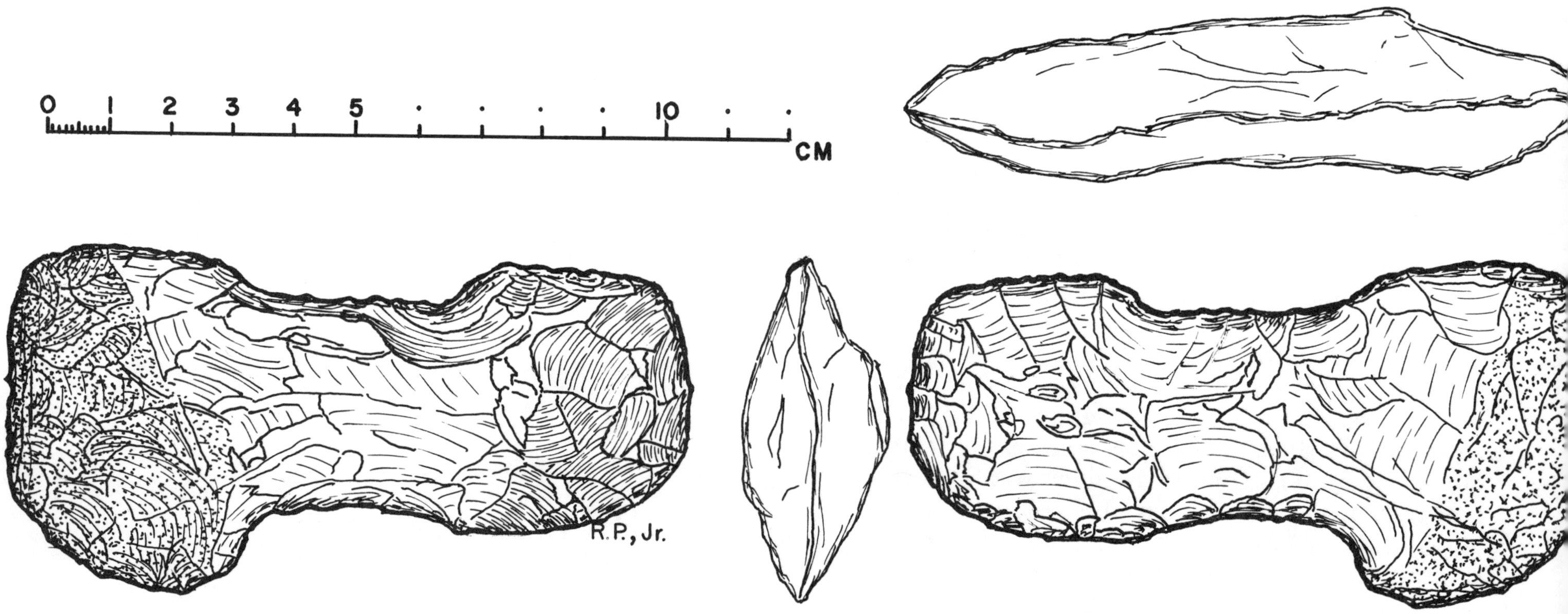

FORERUNNER OF MODERN HAND AXE

A CLASSIC TOMAHAWK

Color & Material: Body and small end, bone white with dull, light brown stain in some flake bottoms, grading to dark brown in others. Light tan patina over all. Larger end, (darker area) coal black with surface sheen of coal. Chert.

Location: Northwestern edge of Fremont County, Wyoming.

This artifact is truly a classic. It is an extremely rare find as well.

Information about, and images of the tomahawk have been related, by writers and artists, from our earliest contact with Native Americans on the Eastern Shores. Since the early years in grade school, when we cut them from craft paper just before Thanksgiving, all of us have an image of the tomahawk in our minds.

When Ralph and Pat placed this one in my hands, the old memories of tomahawks flooded back. It is with difficulty that I see only the head, because the imaginary handle is always there. A cluster of feathers dangles from it, as well.

It was crafted from the same type of bone-white chert as John Larsen's Sandia I point (No. 33), and the Tyrrells Sandia point (No. 58).

The larger, black end displays marked crushing fractures, running parallel to the edge that shows use. One wonders about the number of long bones that were broken for the marrow, the number of skulls that were opened, and whether they were animal or human. It was very likely both.

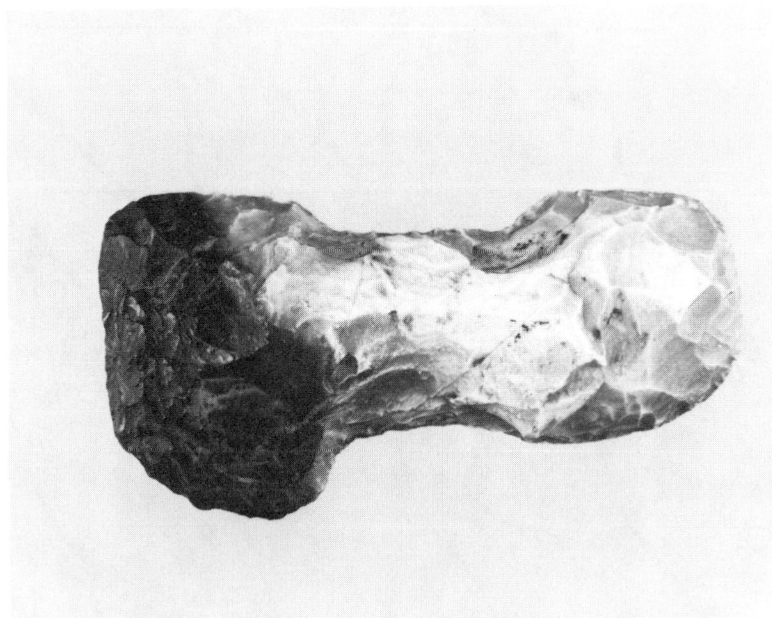

UNUSUAL & BEAUTIFUL KNIVES No. 93
From the collection of:
Bob & Stella Hone
Kemmerer, Wyoming

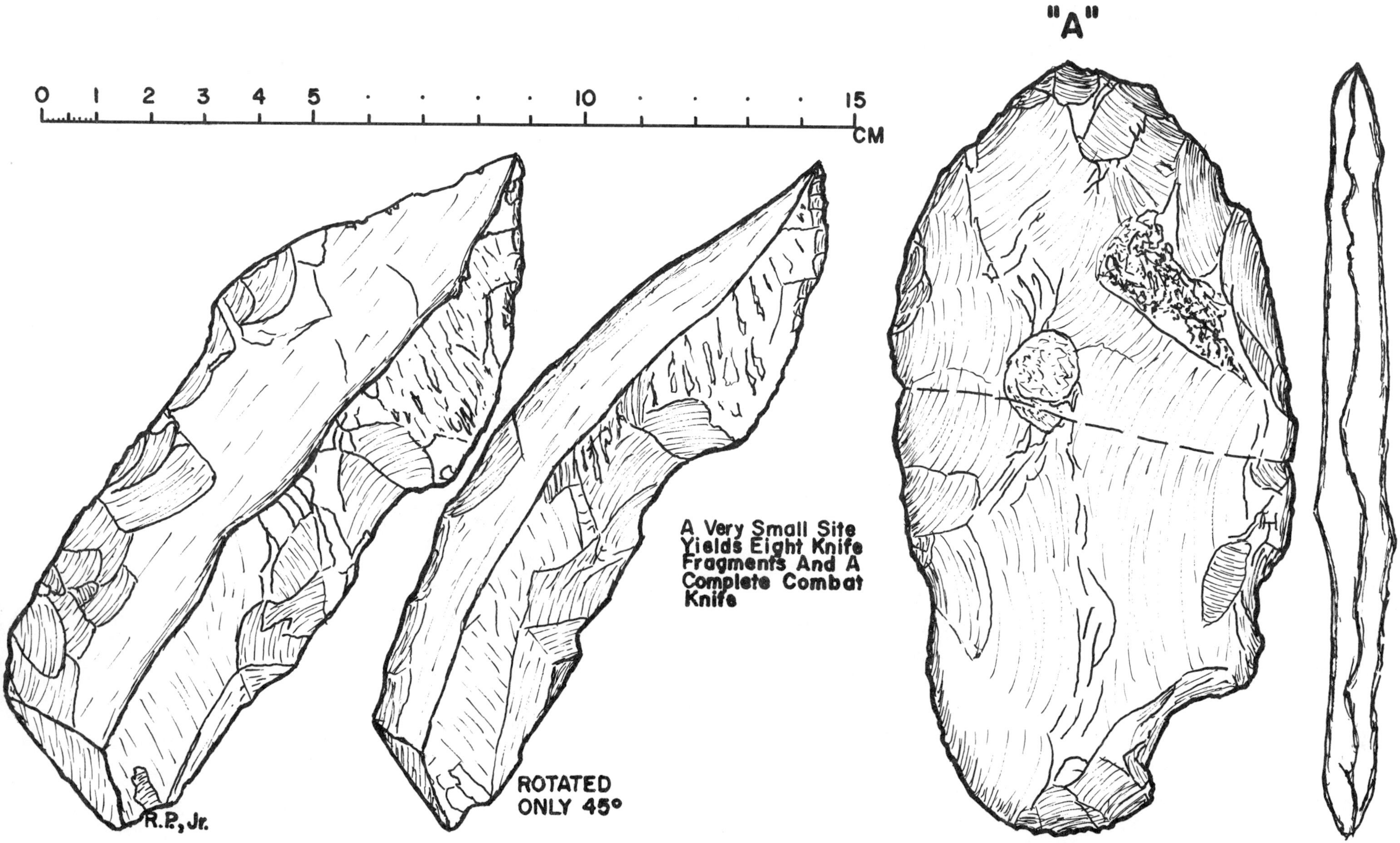

CAMP KNIFE

UNUSUAL & BEAUTIFUL KNIVES

Color & Material: Combat knife, generally light tan but having irregular, greyish-brown inclusions in wave-like form appearing diagonally across the handle. These inclusions have a faint blue cast. Patination is greater on the concave surface, but it has caused all surfaces to display colors that are soft or pastel in nature. The narrowest, plano-convex surface of the blade is the original cortex (surface) of the cobblestone from which the knife was crafted. It evidences a heavy, light brown rind. Chert.

Knife "A", crafted from the same chert as the combat knife. Dark greyish browns are predominate with the whorls covering the whole blade.

Location: Both knives, southern Uinta County, Wyoming.

These two artifacts, and an additional three that are covered on the next few pages, make up a single assemblage* that is one of the more exciting and thought provoking finds submitted to this writer. The integrated knife blade and handle (combat knife), along with eight knife fragments, were found within two to three meters of each other. The site was about one-third of the way up the sloping side of a high, flat mesa.

A brief description of the specific features of each artifact will be given first, followed by a discussion of two of the more probable explanations for this grouping of artifacts.

Close Combat Knife. There was not adequate space to illustrate a side view; however, it would have appeared much like the right half of the right view without the apparent, upward curve of the tip. The right edge of the blade evidences damage from use while the left edge does not. Gripped in the left hand, the notch displayed in the middle of the right edge fits the thumb. The fold between the first and second joints of the fingers matches the alignment of the left edge of the handle when it is gripped tightly. The blade edges are relatively thin and sharp, while the body is backed by a ridge. The overall appearance is that of a "close-combat" knife.

Knife "A". This knife displays the single shoulder of the Sandia I projectile points. This could be significant. The larger of the two notches (lower right edge of side view), displays a great amount of wear from scraping. Its size suggests that it was used to scrape the shafts of throwing-

*assemblage: artifacts that are considered to be associated with each other through common feature, site, material, use, etc.

UNUSUAL & BEAUTIFUL KNIVES No. 93
From the collection of:
Bob & Stella Hone
Kemmerer, Wyoming

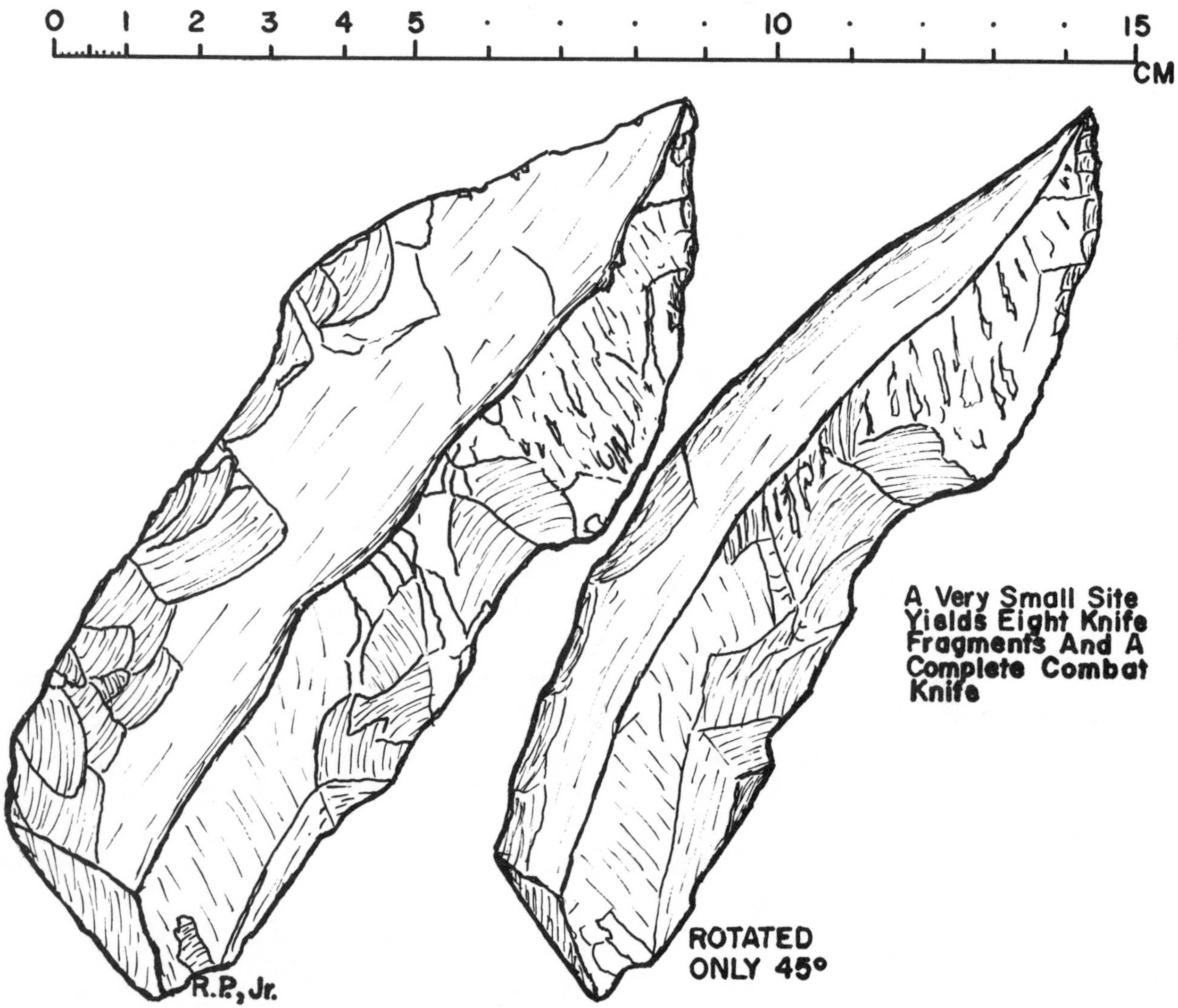

A Very Small Site Yields Eight Knife Fragments And A Complete Combat Knife

"A"

CAMP KNIFE

spears or atlatl shafts. The round spot is a cast of a nodule that was encased within this chert. It is about five millimeters deep. The irregular area, slightly above and to the right of the spot, is a field of some type of crystals that were encased within the chert somewhat like the center of a geode. The break that separated the two halves of this knife follows one of the many fracture planes within this chert, that recemented while still in the bedded formation.

When Bob and Stella Hone first placed these knives before me, the appearance of the complete knife and the fact that the four others had been intentionally broken, caused them to relate the following scenario: Two bands had fought; the victors then destroyed the tools of the defeated ones, so they would not have them in the after-life.

If this event took place, it is thought that these knives were not at the hunting camp, but at a site where the women were butchering an animal that had fallen from the hunt. They would have dropped their knives and fled as the raiding band appeared on the scene.

On the following pages the remaining three knives of this assemblage, and another possible scenario, will be featured as No. 93 continues.

SIX KNIFE FRAGMENTS No. 93 (Cont.)
From the collection of:
Bob & Stella Hone
Kemmerer, Wyoming

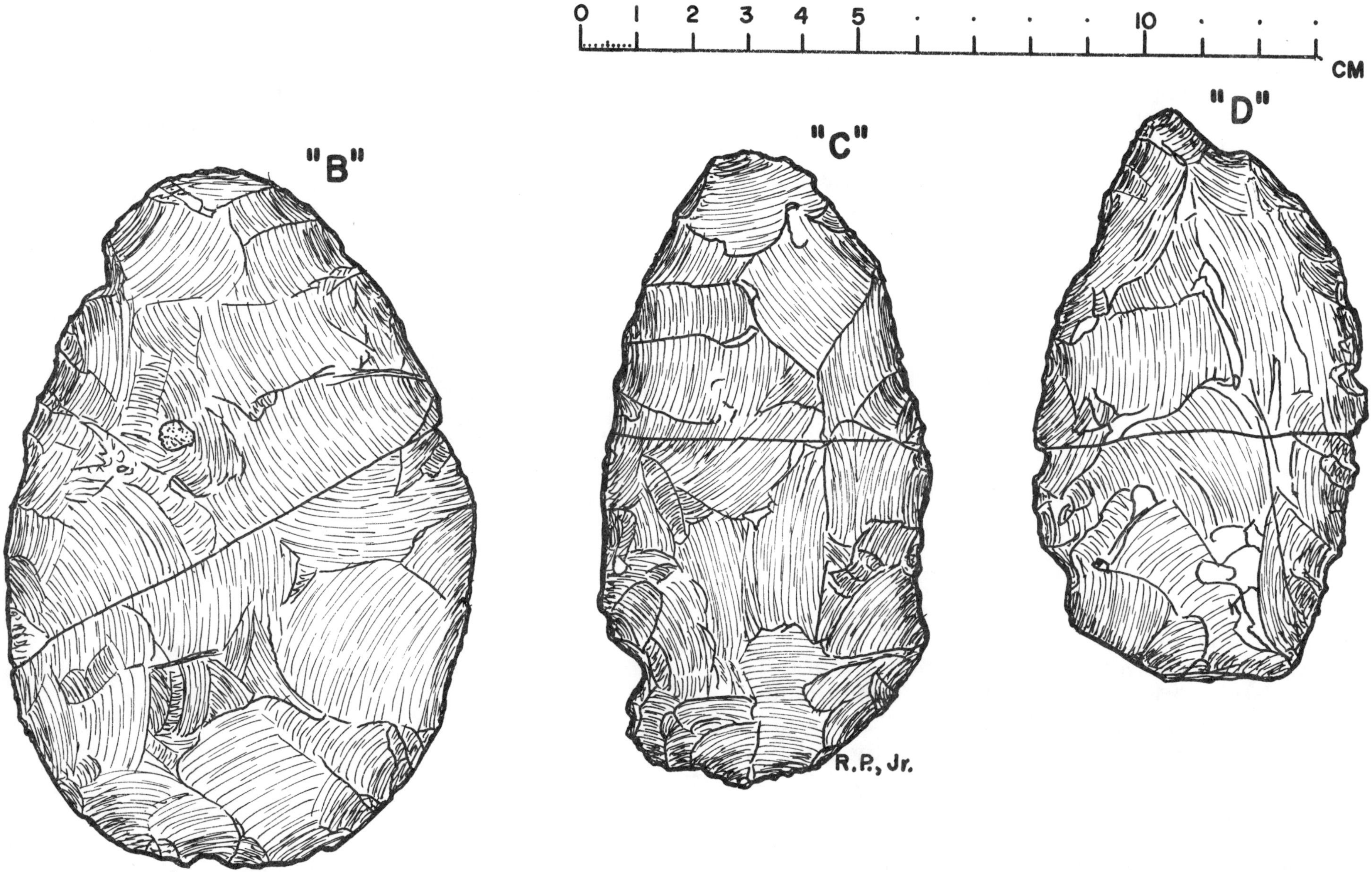

SIX KNIFE FRAGMENTS

Color & Material: Knife "B", generally light tan with irregularly shaped, light blue-grey to dark blue-grey inclusions and several ovoid fossil casts. Heavy tan patination on the side displayed and very faint patination on the reverse side. Chert.

Knife "C", pastel tan with faint blue cast. Traces of dark blue-grey at both ends. Light pastel tan patination from the break to the more rounded end on the side displayed, as well as from the break to the pointed end on the reverse side. Chert.

Knife "D", same description as knife "C". These three knives, and the other two of this assemblage, are of material from the same quarry. *Author's note: When patination occurs on the opposite sides of the halves of these knives, it indicates the halves of the knives were turned with opposite sides up. Patination was greater on the lower sides of these halves.*

Location: Southern Uinta County, Wyoming.

The larger of these knives evidences marked wear along both sides with no rework (sharpening by removal of pressure flakes). The smaller two evidence wear on their left edges (as displayed) and rework on their right edges.

Separately, with the exception of their beauty, these knives are not too remarkable. However, the previous two knives, along with these three, were found as one complete knife and eight fragments, within two to three meters of each other. The site was about one-third of the way up the sloping side of a high, flat mesa. About two kilometers away, fire pits were found at the end of the mesa. It would have been about seven kilometers to reach water. It is probable that the fire pits were at the site of the hunting camp. The knives would indicate a possible butchering site for one of the animals killed in the hunt. It is easy to envision a wounded buffalo, bearing several lances (or atlatl dart tips) in its sides, driven up the steep side of the mesa to drain the last of its energy. Then it would have been safe to use a killing stone.

As Bob & Stella suggested before, a raiding party may have been responsible for these knife fragments. There is another possibility that may account for this array of fragments:

In the early 1970's, Mr. & Mrs. Robert McFadden of Rock Springs, Wyoming, assisted in the excavation of the Beaver Valley Site in Beaver County, Pennsylvania. The dig was conducted by the Carnegie Institute. By telephone, Mrs. McFad-

SIX KNIFE FRAGMENTS No. 93 (Cont.)
From the collection of:
Bob & Stella Hone
Kemmerer, Wyoming

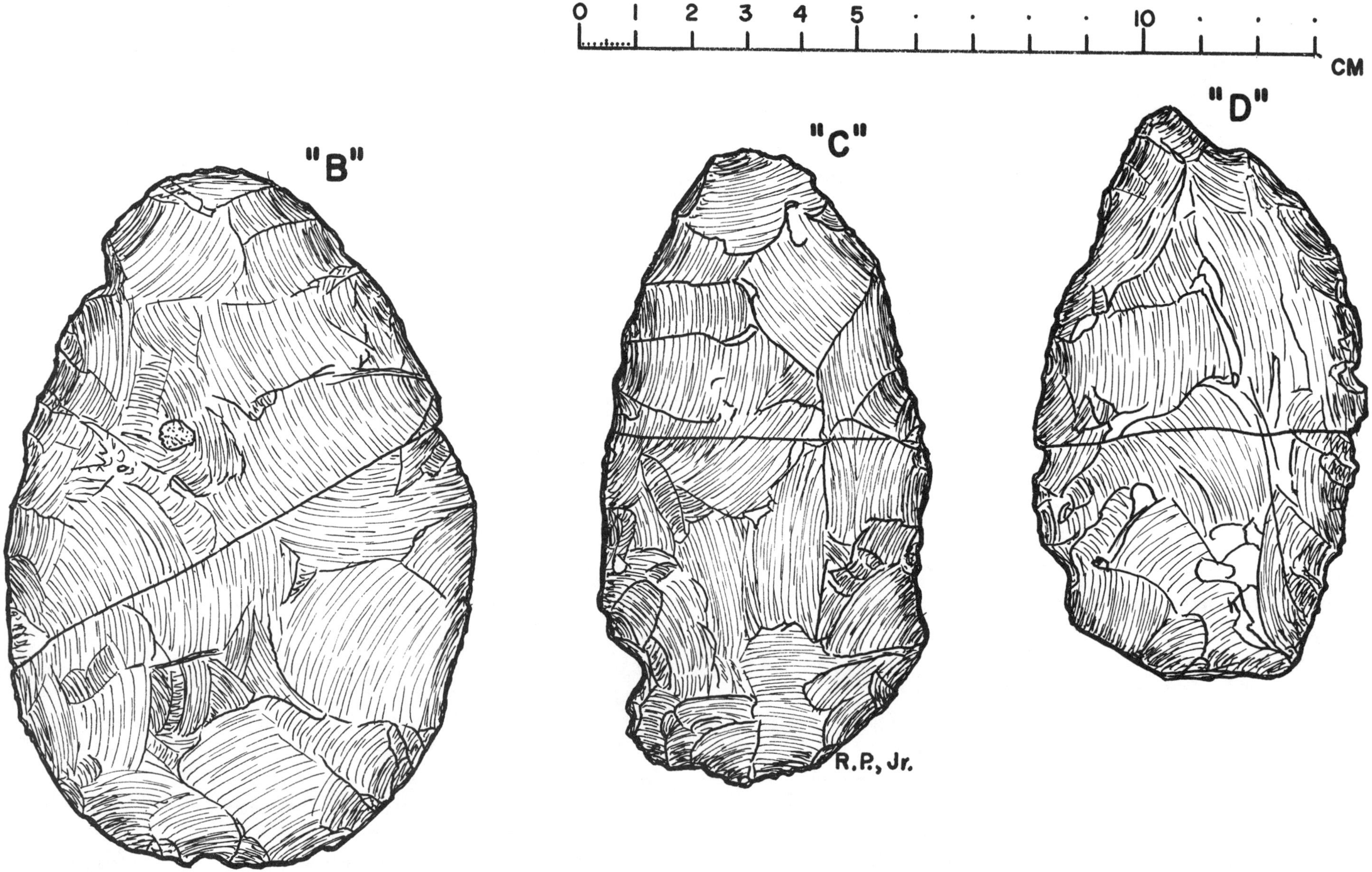

den stated that burials had been recorded there. Among the burial pieces, projectile points and knives were found intentionally broken.

It is very possible that a burial site may have eroded from the top of the mesa (frequently selected for burials), and these broken fragments moved downward to the site where they were found.

Most heartfelt appreciation is expressed to Bob & Stella Hone for making these remarkable finds available for publication.

RARE ANTLER ARTIFACT No. 94
From the collection of:
Ralph & Patricia Rhoads
Lander, Wyoming

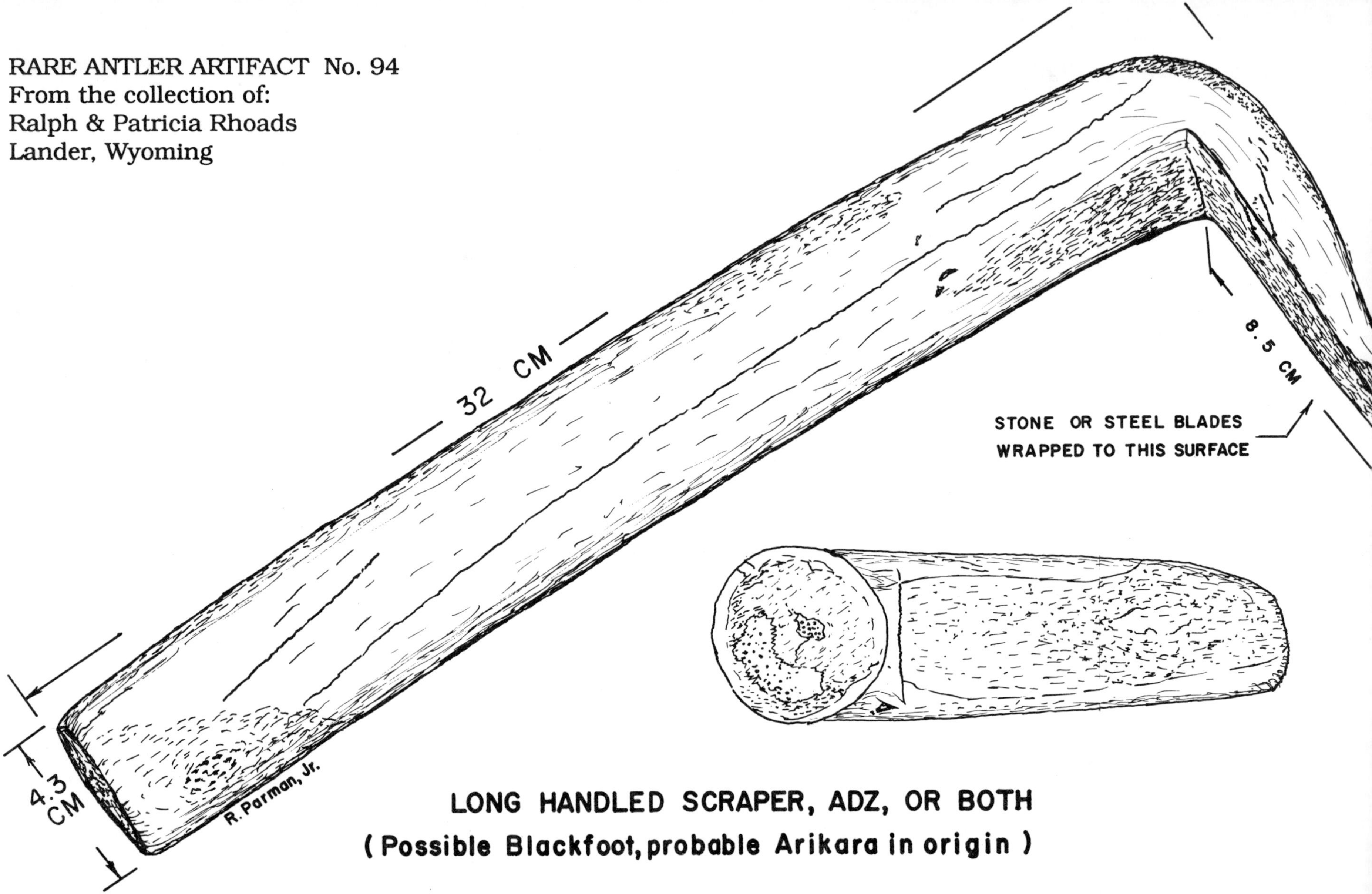

LONG HANDLED SCRAPER, ADZ, OR BOTH

(Possible Blackfoot, probable Arikara in origin)

RARE ANTLER ARTIFACT

Color & Material: Light brown with faint orange cast to the patina formed by the oils from the hands that have handled its surface. A segment of the left antler of an elk (Cervus alces) from a point proximal (toward the body) to the bez antler, (whose core is visible where it was removed-lower left end) to just distal (away from body), including a portion of the antler royal that forms the hooked end of the tool.

Location: South Dakota.

The ingenuity and resourcefulness of the Native American is readily reflected by this somewhat rare artifact. By its design and selection of a specific portion of an antler, the inherent strength of the antler has been retained, even though a portion of the stronger, outer surface has been removed.

The shaded area along the curved surface at the upper right end depicts the porous core of the main shaft where the distal portion was removed. The curved arm is formed by the distal, outer surface of the antler royal. One half of the proximal portion of this antler was removed to form the platform on which stone blades were first attached. After steel was introduced, it was frequently utilized for blades.

George Mile's book, *Indian and Eskimo Artifacts of North America*, displays four of these handles on page 101. One of the three handles that were fashioned from antler material is of Blackfoot origin. The fourth handle, made of wood, came from South Dakota; therefore, its origin is probably Arikara. Coming from South Dakota, this particular artifact is most likely Arikara in origin as well.

The Museum at Saint Michael's Mission in Ethete, Wyoming, has several antler artifacts of this nature that are thought to be from the Arapahoe tribe, but of a later time period. These handles have steel blades and have been ornamented with what appear to be upholstery tacks.

A tool of this nature, fitted with a relatively thick-bodied, stone blade extending about three centimeters beyond the tip of the arm, would have been most useful for the hollowing out of a log canoe. One must have respect for the industry of Native Americans.

Appreciation is expressed to Mr. & Mrs. Rhoads for making this beautiful artifact available to us.

PEMMICAN No. 95
From the collection of:
Orville & Nadine Corbett
Casper, Wyoming

0 1 2 3 4 5 10
CM

Weight: 160 grams (5.7 oz.)

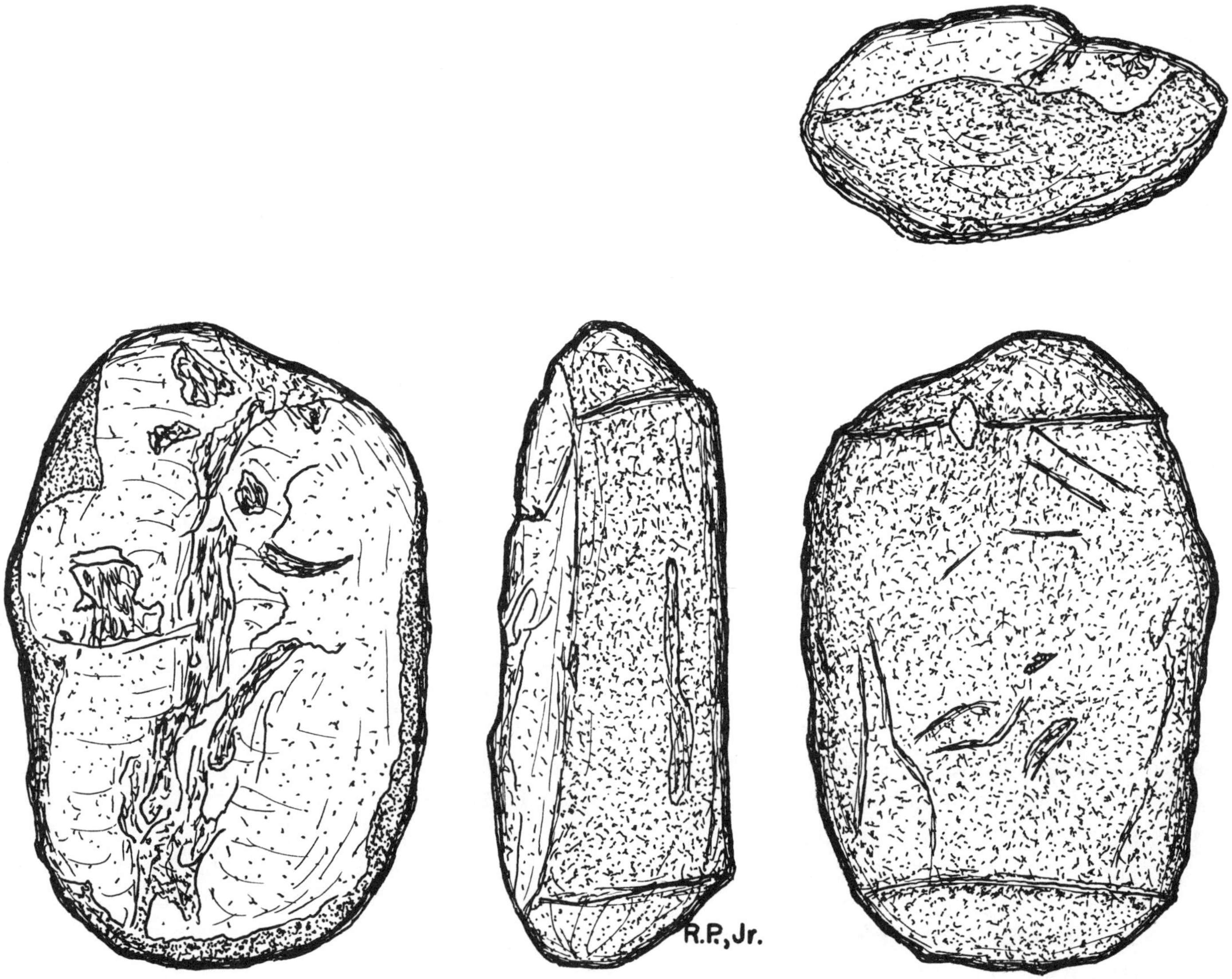

PEMMICAN *: From CREE INDIAN words "pemikkan" (fat meat) & "pimiy" (fat).

PEMMICAN

Color & Material: Light tan with slight grey cast and dark greyish-brown rind. Pemmican with rind of leather residue.

Location: East of Teapot Dome Naval Oil Reserve; south of Edgerton, Natrona County, Wyoming.

For simply preserving meat through the winter, Native Americans relied primarily upon a drying process to produce "jerky". To fulfill the higher energy needs of rapid travel, cooperative hunting, and battle, a food concentrate was prepared and packed into small, leather containers called parfleches. This concoction has come to be known as "pemmican"; it consisted of dried meat, ground finely, then mixed with a paste of suet and whatever wild berry was available, Its preparation was not an easy process; therefore, amounts were limited. Mountain men readily realized its high nutritional value and lasting qualities. It became one of their important trade items. One would never dream that such an artifact could exist today, that would so vividly display the characteristics of a parfleche, and the pemmican it had once contained. Early in 1986, Mrs. Idabel Cramer of Lander, Wyoming, wrote to suggest that this treasured find from her brother's collection should be shared. Mrs. Nadine Corbett of Casper, Wyoming, was contacted, and arrangements were made to view this pemmican at their home. It will not be forgotten.

Having read histories of the West, particularly of Colter, Bridger, and other Mountain Men, my mind had formed an image of pemmican as somewhat like a fine-textured fruitcake. Examination of this artifact has altered that image. The individual ingredients had been ground so finely, and blended so evenly, it appeared as an homogeneous mass. For a humorous note, when this artifact was first published in the newspaper, this last word appeared as a typo and read...homogeneous "mess".

The configuration of the parfleche is readily apparent. Two ovalshaped end pieces (with their inside surfaces brought together and their edges to the outside) were sewn to a rectangular strip of leather. This would make the inside as smooth as possible. As the pemmican was packed into the parfleche, it extruded into the seams, forming the ridges appearing on the surfaces displayed in the center and right views.

The artifact lay, with the surface displayed in the right view, buried in the soil. The dark brown stain covering this surface is the residue

PEMMICAN No. 95
From the collection of:
Orville & Nadine Corbett
Casper, Wyoming

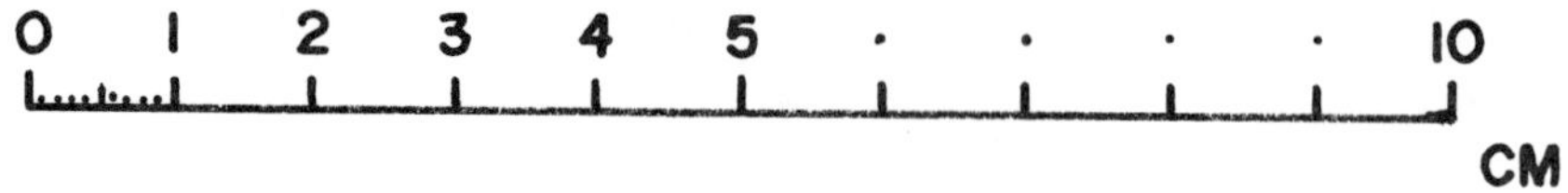

Weight: 160 grams (5.7 oz.)

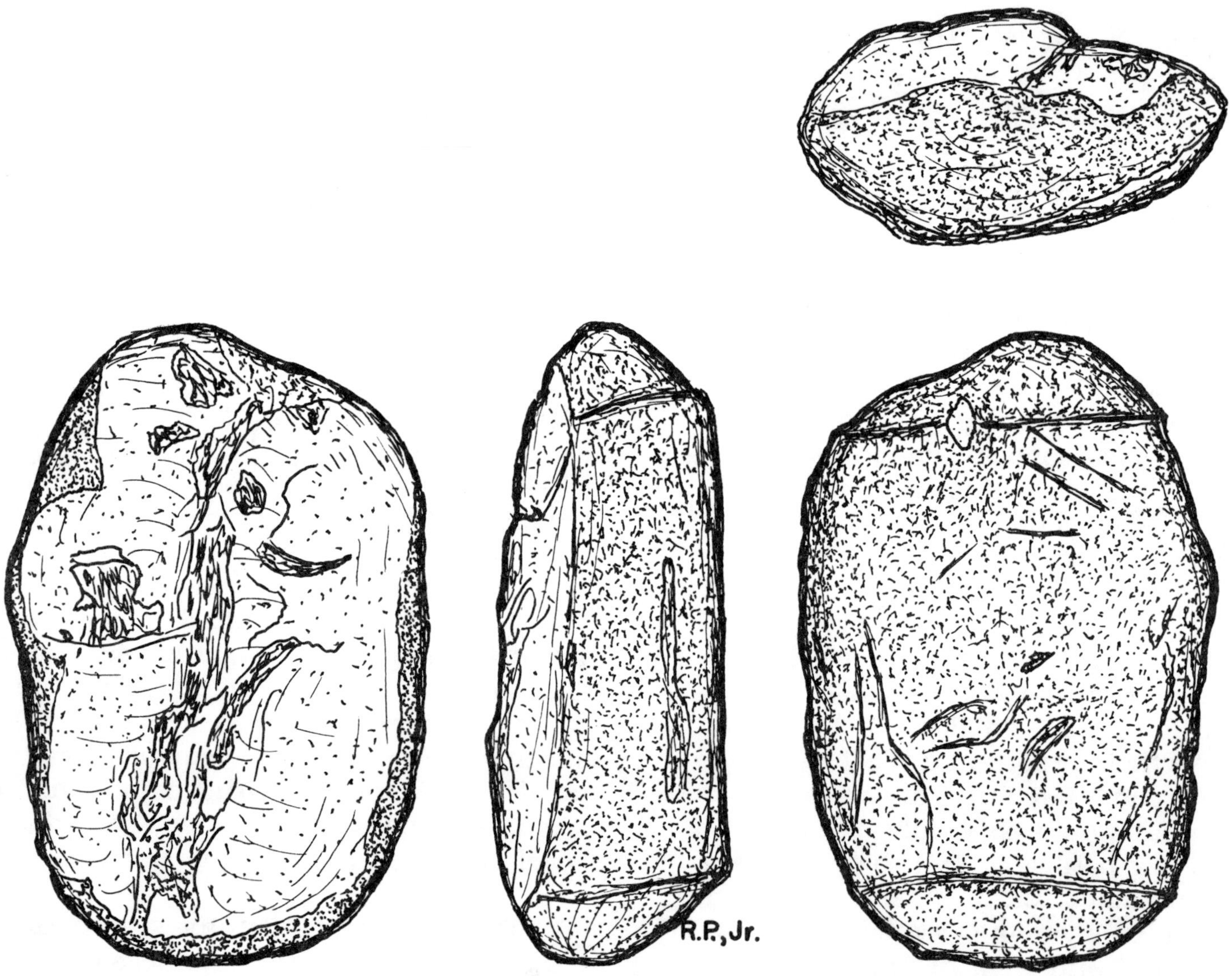

PEMMICAN *: From CREE INDIAN words "pemikkan"(fat meat) & "pimiy"(fat).

of the rotted leather. The irregular dark areas of the other side are residues of the inner layer of leather, that was pressed into the pemmican as the covering flap was closed over it. Wind erosion has cut away the stain from the higher, rounded surfaces of this side (left view). The elements have leached all pigments from the exposed pemmican, leaving it a light greyish-tan. Its appearance was very much like that of felt.

The light, diamond shaped spot (upper end of right view) is where a small sample was removed for laboratory analysis at the University of Wyoming. The Corbetts were informed by the university that thcir artifact was indeed pemmican.

Appreciation is expressed to Mrs. Cramer for suggesting that this find be shared, and to Mrs. Nadine Corbett for making it possible.

RARE CEREMONIAL MANO No. 96
From the collection of:
Ron & Joanne Harvey
Lander, Wyoming

17.3 cm long
9.0 cm wide
4.2 cm thick

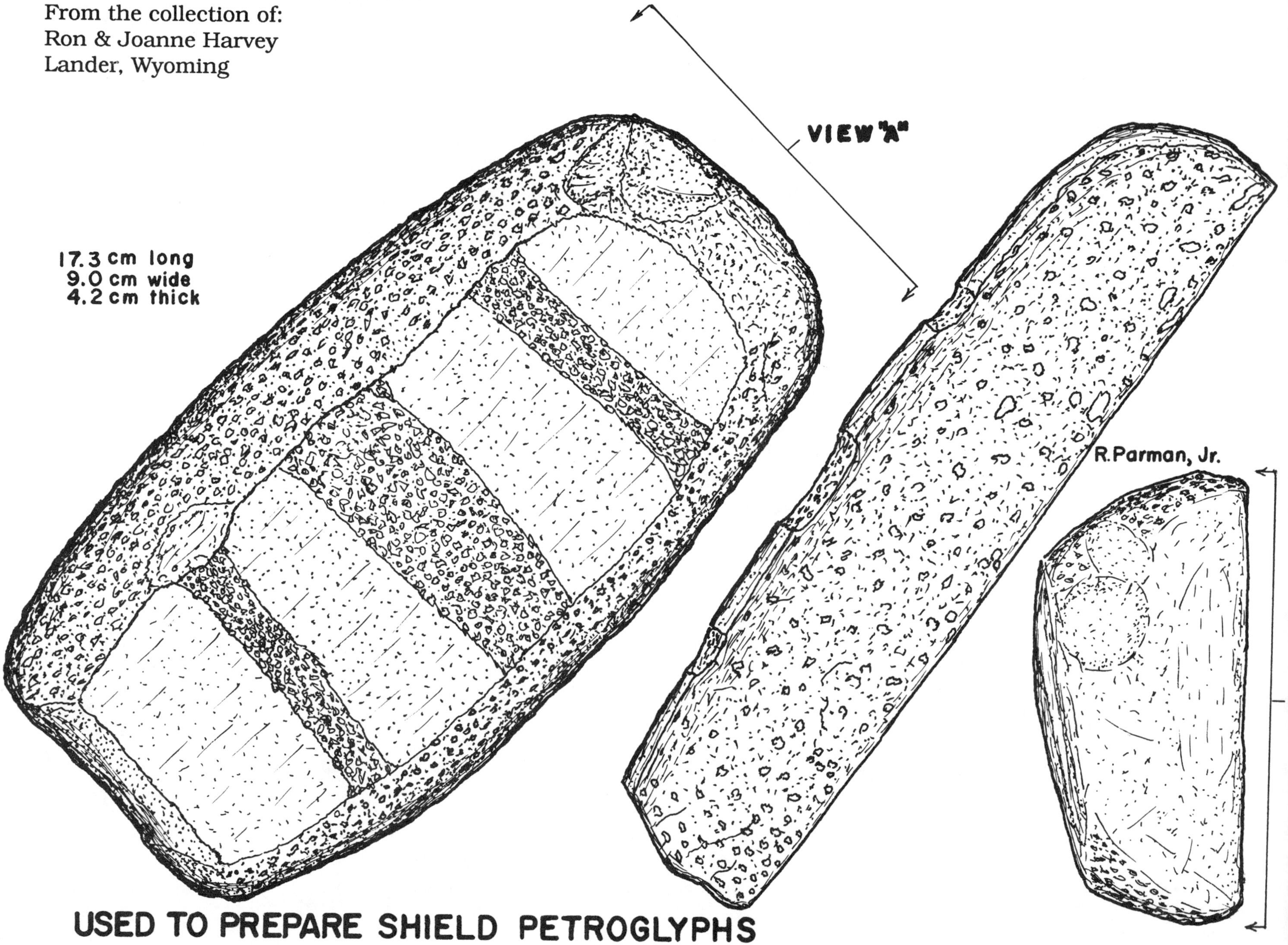

USED TO PREPARE SHIELD PETROGLYPHS

RARE, CEREMONIAL MANO

Color & Material: Reduced surfaces are tan to light brown with a slight rose cast. Slightly darker stainlike patina on superior surfaces. A near white, light tan incrustation covers the left half of the upper end (left view), the upper half of the left edge, and most of the surface of the lower half of the same view. Siliceous (very hard) sandstone.

Location: Red Desert region of southwest Wyoming.

Two features of this mano catch one's attention immediately. A third soaks in a little later, with examination.

Adornment becomes apparent at first sight. The wide band, and the two narrower, one on either side, have been pecked into the convex surface. The second feature is the "essentially flat" working surface. Actually, the surface curves 1.5 mm through the longest dimension and .5 mm laterally. Manos, used in conjunction with grinding bowls (metates), usually have curved (convex) working surfaces. Why has this mano a flat surface? The third feature was discovered to be pecked surfaces along both sides. It is assumed this was to provide a better grip.

With regard to the flat working surface, the first deduction was that it had been used in a circular motion. A reciprocating (back and forth) motion was used most frequently in conjunction with the metate. As this was being discussed among several friends, Mrs. Lucille Adams who, with her late husband Jim, extensively researched Native American petroglyphs, suggested the most probable answer - shield petroglyphs.

Petroglyphs are symbols composing messages or art forms that have been pecked or abraded into sandstone and limestone bluffs. Shield petroglyphs are distinct because the surfaces on which they were placed have first been ground smooth. It is highly probable that this mano was used for this purpose.

Decorated manos are rare finds. Adorned manos with a flat working surface are extremely rare, leading one to assume that shield petroglyphs were placed on bluffs during a ceremony of significance.

The last feature discovered was that the flat working surface had been pecked over its entire surface. The pecking was intended to make

RARE CEREMONIAL MANO No. 96
From the collection of:
Ron & Joanne Harvey
Lander, Wyoming

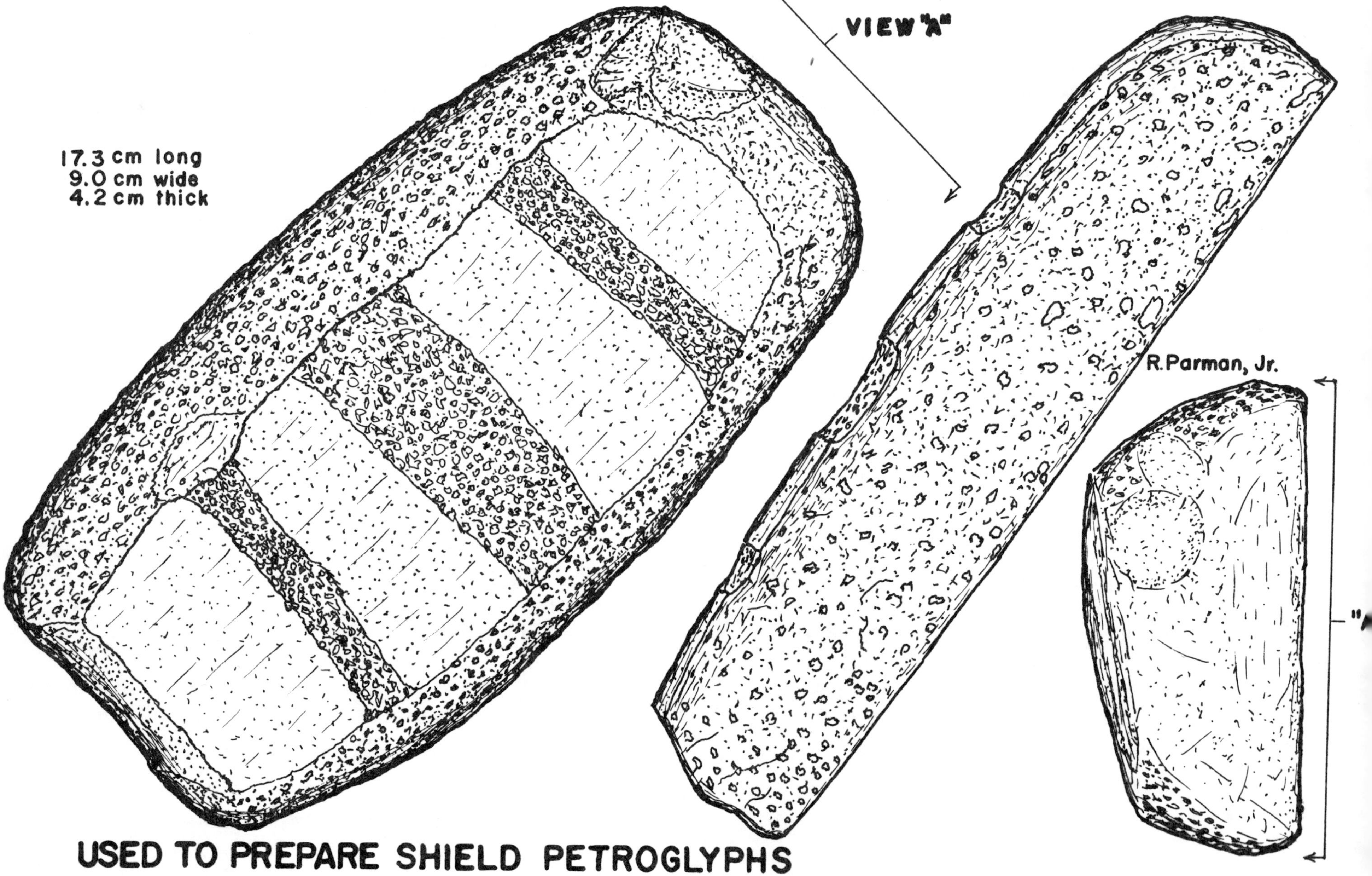

USED TO PREPARE SHIELD PETROGLYPHS

the working surface more abrasive. The mano was used after this pecking, because a band across the middle was worn smooth again.

This mano was used in recent centuries, for the holes pecked into the surface were very small in diameter. Only a metal point could have made them so small and deep. A stone point, so small, would surely have shattered.

RARE, BEAUTIFUL POINTS No. 97
From the collection of:
Mrs. Louise Turk
Kaycee, Wyoming

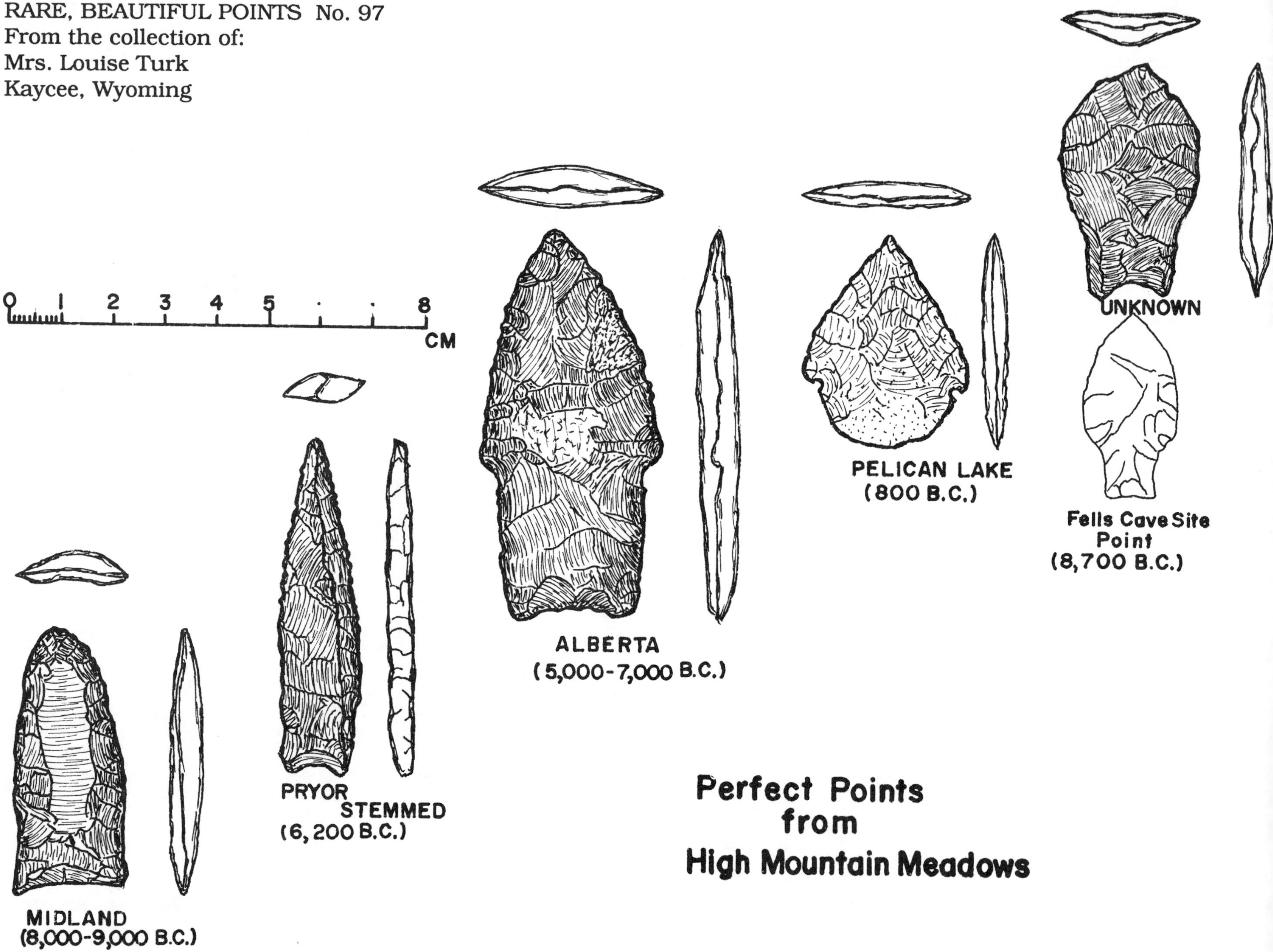

Perfect Points from High Mountain Meadows

RARE, BEAUTIFUL POINTS

Color & Material: Midland, light, translucent brown at base, edges and tip with light blue through the body. Irregular shaped tan inclusions and bone white patination on the side displayed. Very faint patination on the reverse side. Chalcedony.

Pryor Stemmed, light pastel lavender with clear, varnishlike sheen on side displayed except lower half of the left edge. That edge, and the reverse side are a dull, greyish pastel lavender. Chert.

Alberta, calf liver, reddish-brown with faint maroon cast. Abundant light tan inclusions surrounding the right barb and extending down the right edge of the stem (side displayed). Agate or possibly translucent chert.

Pelican Lake, bone white with light tan patina on side displayed. Very fine-grain quartzite.

Unknown, maroon with dull, light brownish-grey patination over all surfaces. A very fine-grain, argillaceous siltstone.

Location: All, Big Horn mountain region of Wyoming.

The Midland point was named for specimens found at the Sharbaur site near Midland, Texas. They are found chiefly on the high plains of North America. Specimens have been reported from Texas northward to Manitoba. They have been found at sites with Folsom points.

The Pryor Stemmed point has been named by Wilford M. Husted for a type found at Bottleneck Cave located on the Big Horn River (now Yellowtail Reservoir) in Big Horn county, Wyoming. These points are very rare and are readily recognized by the distinct beveling of the right edges of both faces. This is thought to be a sharpening process.

The name for the Alberta point was suggested by Marie Wormington for a distinctive point found in Alberta, Canada. It is associated with the Cody complex and is thought to be the northern version of the Scottsbluff projectile point. One of the four examples pictured in the *Oklahoma Anthropological Society Guide No. 2* is identical to this one. The points of both are exactly the same amount off center.

RARE, BEAUTIFUL POINTS No. 97
From the collection of:
Mrs. Louise Turk
Kaycee, Wyoming

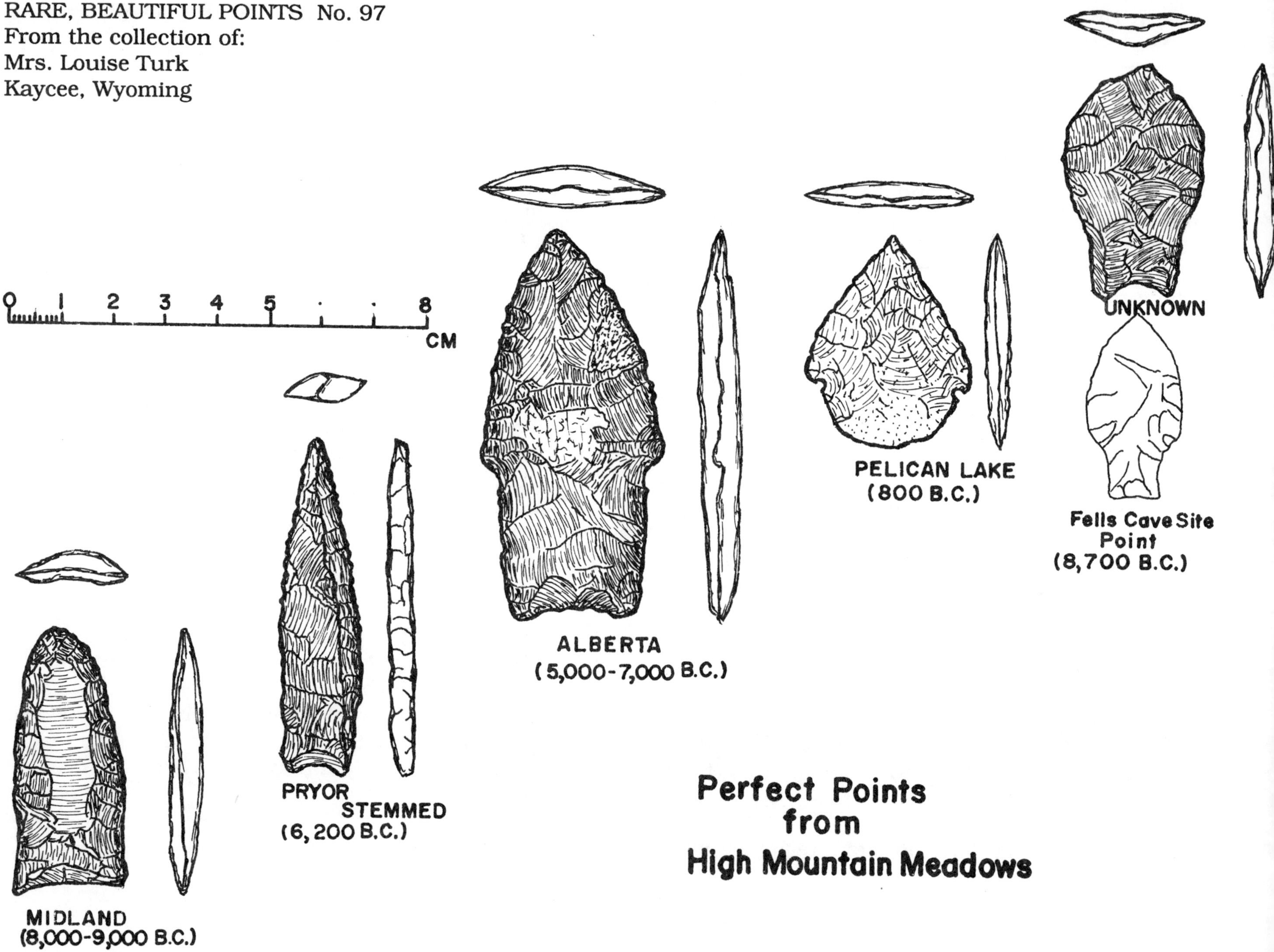

**Perfect Points
from
High Mountain Meadows**

The Pelican Lake point was named by Wettlaufer at the Mortlach site in central Saskatchewan. There is great variance in the configuration of points of this type. All are corner notched, but notch depths and widths are markedly variable. Since the author viewed the unknown point in Mrs. Turk's collection, an additional two have been noted in other collections. A photograph of a point taken from Fells Cave (Southern tip of South America) in *American Genesis* (Goodman, 1981) illustrated a point very similar. Its outline has been included.

HIGH ALTITUDE FINDS No. 98
From the collection of:
Larry & Marta Amundson
Riverton, Wyoming

Type Example
HANNA
(P-22, p.45)
O.A.S. Bulletin 4

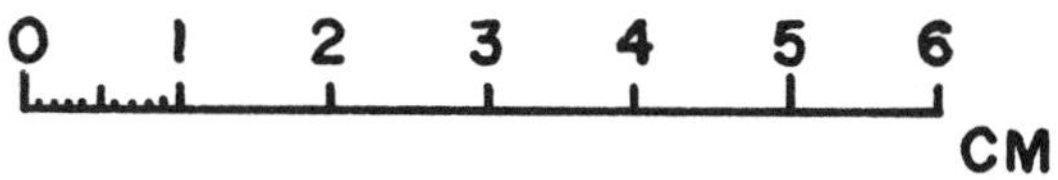

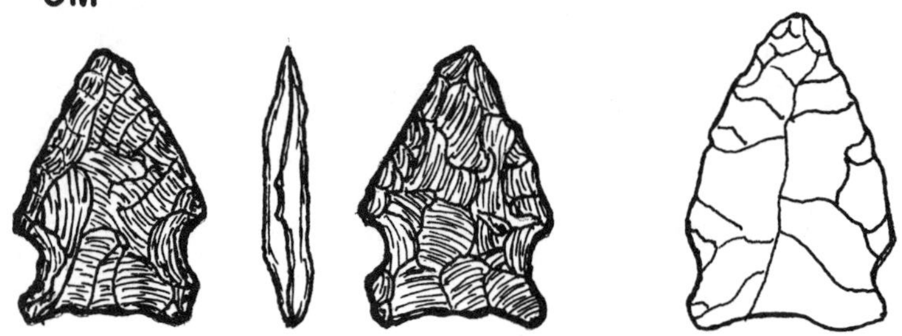

Type Example
BESANT
(Pl-4, p.9)
O.A.S. Bulletin4

Taken From The
TERMINAL MORAINE Of
HELEN GLACIER
Elevation - 11,000'

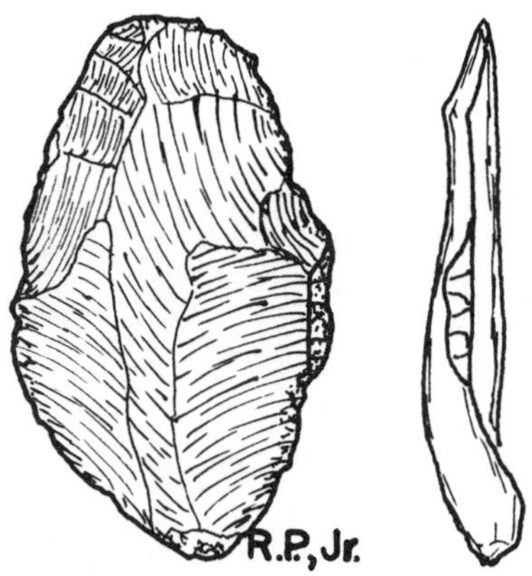

SMALL KNIFE

HIGH ALTITUDE FINDS

Color & Material: Knife, pale, translucent tan with slight blue-white, washed inclusions. Chert.

Besant, slightly translucent brown. Very dense, clean orthoquartzite.

Hanna, dark, black-brown quartzite.

Location: Western edge of Fremont County, Wyoming. West northwest of Fort Washakie, Wyoming

There is geological evidence that for a period of about two thousand years, the mean temperature of the High Plains region of this continent was from seven to ten degrees higher than at present. This span of time has been called "The Altithermal", and it occurred sometime between four and seven thousand years ago.

During the Altithermal, which could be described best as an extended draught, the grasses of the high plains were stunted, if not killed. Subsequently, the grazing animals (buffalo, elk, deer, and antelope) were greatly reduced in number. With the pressure created from this sudden disappearance of their food source, the surviving herds were forced to higher mountain meadows in search of adequate grasses.

Considering these finds were taken from the terminal moraine immediately below the foot of Helen Glacier, the author feels it is safe to assume that bands of Native Americans followed the movement of these herds.

Though positive identification has not been made, two type examples of similar points have been included with the drawings.

A point of interest...The elk (Cervus alces) liked the higher elevations so well that it decided to remain. It is very likely that a band of natives remained as well and subsequently became known as the "Shccpcaters".

Appreciation is expressed to Larry & Marta for making these available.

HALLMARK POINT, OLD CLUB HEAD No. 99
From the collections of:
Chuck & Barbara Amadio, Lander, Wyoming
Patt Brown, Riverton, Wyoming

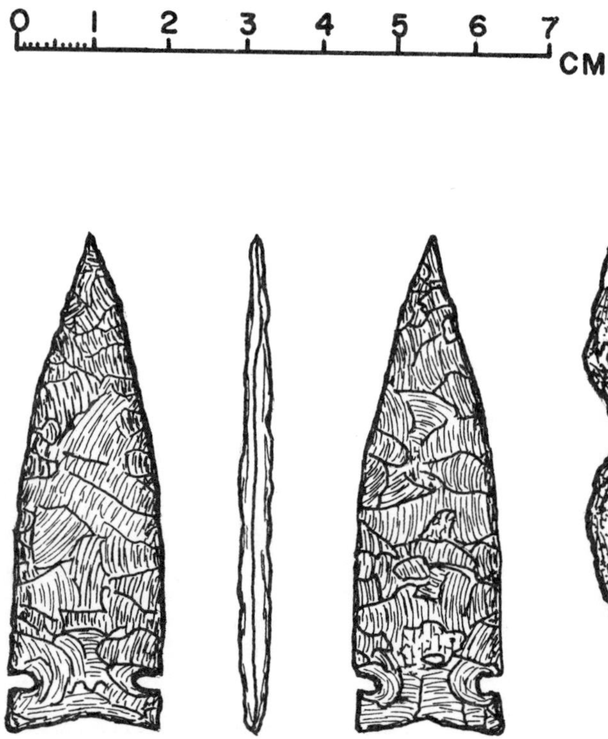

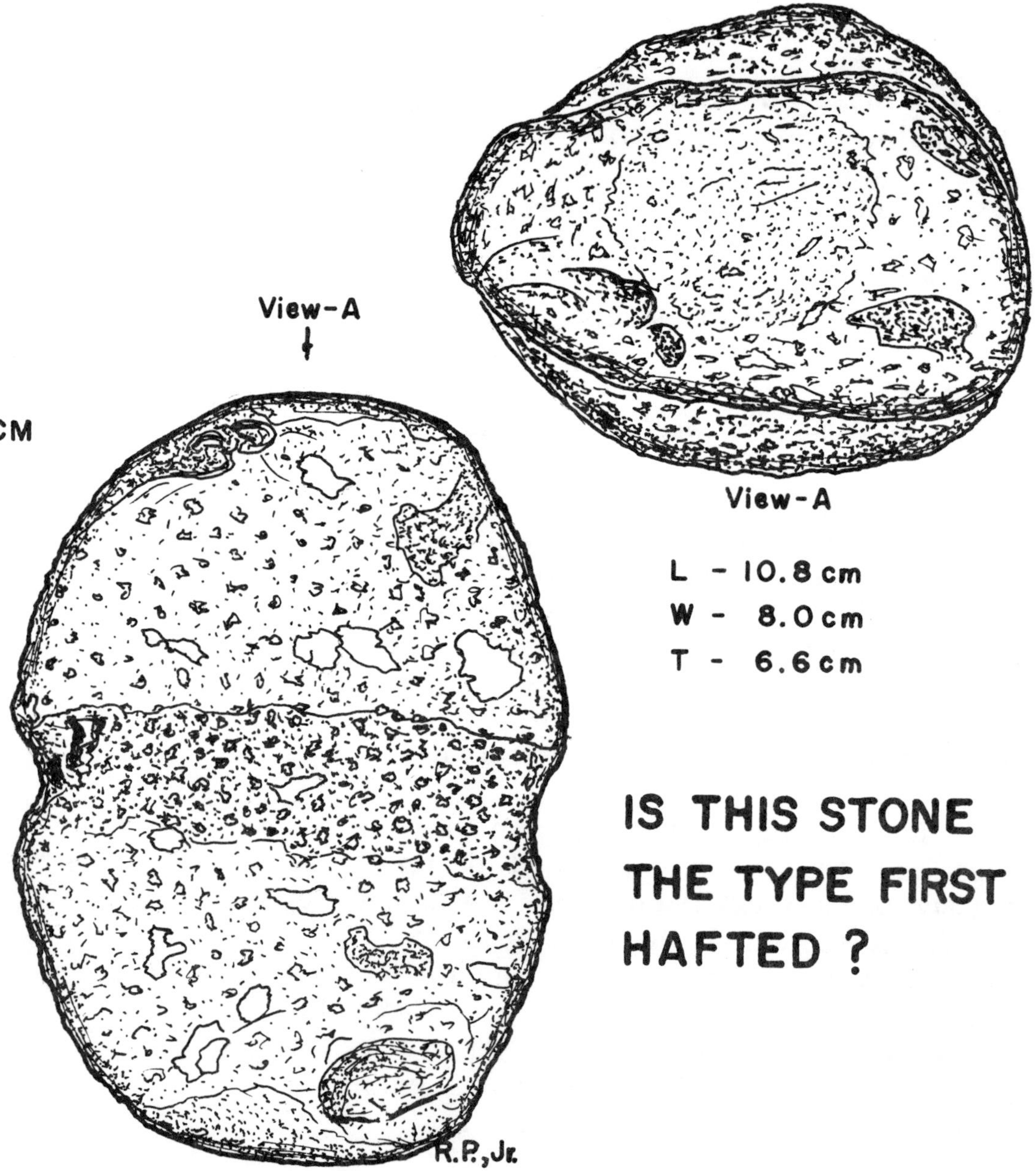

L - 10.8 cm
W - 8.0 cm
T - 6.6 cm

IS THIS STONE THE TYPE FIRST HAFTED ?

HALLMARK POINT, OLD CLUB HEAD

Color & Material: Point, light, brownish-grey with very faint green cast. Light, bone white patination on one side and incrustation on the other. Chalcedony.

Club, dull, light brown on reduced surfaces to a dull greyish, slightly darker brown on superior surfaces. Abundant inclusions grading from pale blue-white to white and few tan. A hard, argillaceous sandstone with feldspar inclusions.

Location: Point, shoreline of Pathfinder Reservoir; Natrona County, Wyoming.

Club, Red Desert region of southwestern Wyoming.

Chuck & Barbara's collection was a true pleasure to view. Their respect, love, and care of each find was readily apparent in their artistic display. Excellent finds, representing many Paleo Indian projectile points (Clovis, Folsom, Eden, and Alberta) were among the many beautifully displayed artifacts.

Chuck selected this beautiful point to photograph and submit by letter. Is it a Hallmark burial piece?

Author's note: Shortly after this point was first published, the point type was named by Dr. George Frison. See No. 106

The club head was selected from Patt Brown's remarkable collection because it displays such extensive weathering. The pecking that shaped the groove and part of its overall contour has almost disappeared. It is thought by this writer, that a stone of this size and material, and shaped in this manner, could represent man's first efforts to improve his previously, hand-held stone weapon (see No. 80) by placing a handle on it. True, clubs of this type were made in recent times. This one, though it is pure conjecture, could be fifty thousand years old.

Many thanks to Mr. & Mrs. Amadio, and to Patt Brown for sharing these finds.

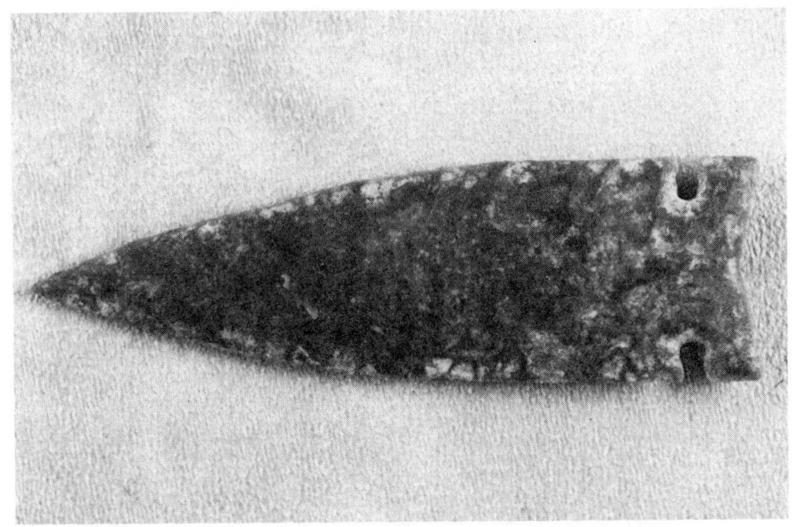

OLD, PUZZING ARTIFACT No. 100
From the collection of:
Patt Brown
Riverton, Wyoming

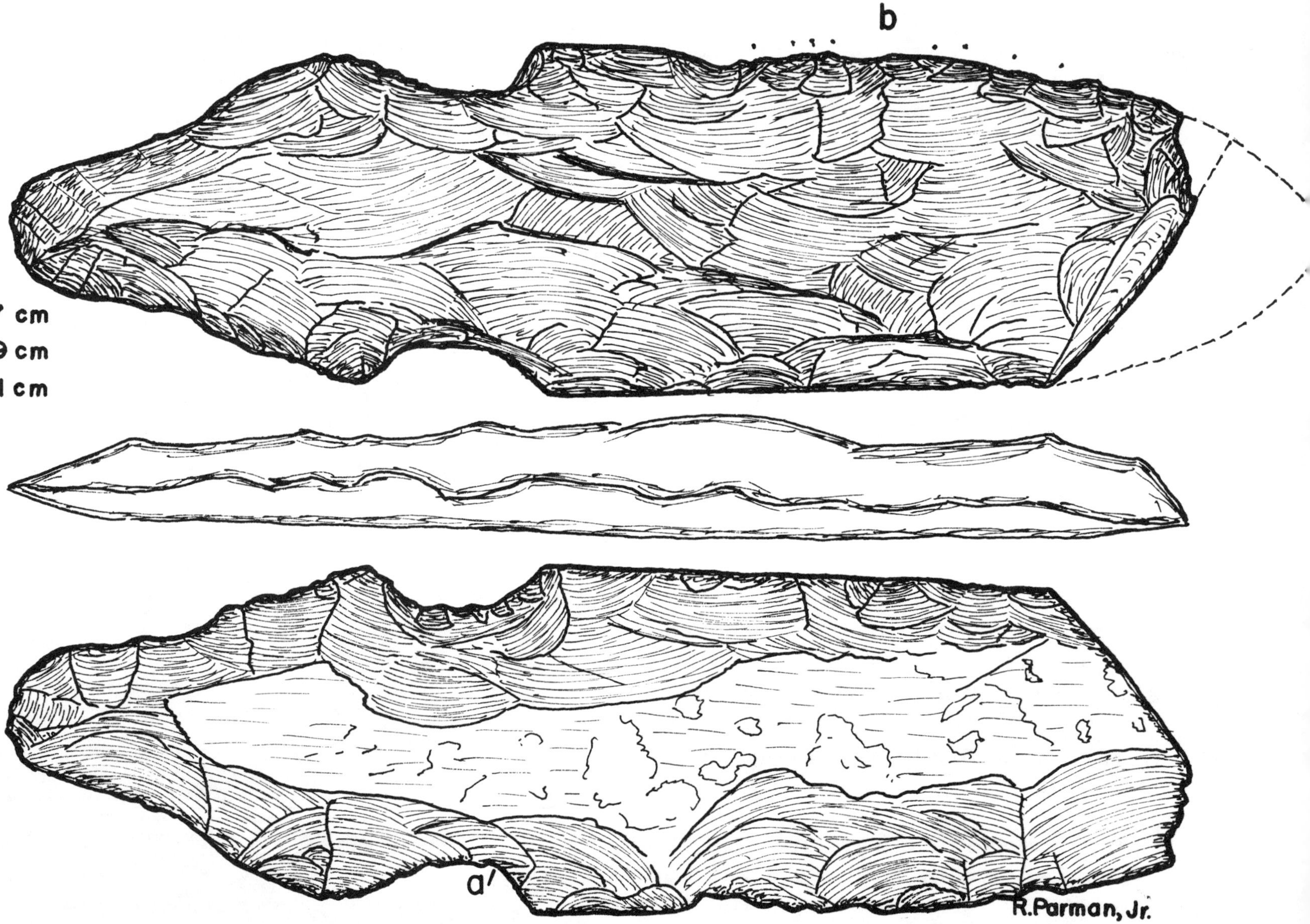

LENGTH - 19.7 cm
WIDTH - 5.9 cm
THICK - 2.1 cm

Found With TURTLE EFFIGY & ALBERTA POINTS

OLD, PUZZLING ARTIFACT

Color & Material: Side displayed in upper view, dull, pastel, light brown with light brown patina on flake surfaces grading to a darker brown on flake ridges and raised, flake surfaces along the center. A random network of tiny, nearly white markings over all this side and extending into the stone.

Side in lower view-light, pastel brown on flake surfaces along the edges and small end. Central, flat surface having a dark, reddish-brown rind. All flaked surfaces have a heavy patina. An argillaceous (shaly), siliceous siltstone having a mudstone appearance. The network of tiny cracks formed when the original silt dried.

Location: North central Sweetwater County, Wyoming.

"This artifact", in Patt's words, "has been a one hundred and twenty percent question mark!". It is thought to be from 7,000 to 9,000 years old because it was found with the Turtle Effigy (No. 54) and an Alberta projectile point.

First, the two notches have such sharp edges it is probable that they were not intended for hafting. The binding would be cut. If notched for a thong, it too would be cut. If the notches were for shaft scraping, why are they asymmetrical (one sloping side and one steep) in the same manner, yet reversed on opposite sides?

Patt suggested one possibility: that it was attached by the larger end to a large thrusting spear, leaving the smaller, barbed end as the working point. The larger end has been thinned; the smaller appears as a lance tip. Thrust between the ribs, it could then be twisted ninety degrees, locking the barbs behind the inner surface of the ribs. This would hold the ribs apart, assuring a pneumothorax and subsequent collapse of the lung.

A thrusting spear (if tipped with stone, called a lance) would have been the weapon of choice when confronted by a large animal such as mammoth or mastodon. Considering the size of these animals, it is very likely that any confrontation would be limited to when the animal was in a vulnerable situation e.g. deep sand or bog. If this lance tip was locked into the ribs (as previously mentioned), the shaft could be pulled away, another tip inserted, and thus used repeatedly. With both lungs in a collapsed state, no animal however large, would be able to survive.

UNUSUAL SKINNING KNIFE No. 101
From the collection of:
Ray Parman, Jr.
Riverton, Wyoming

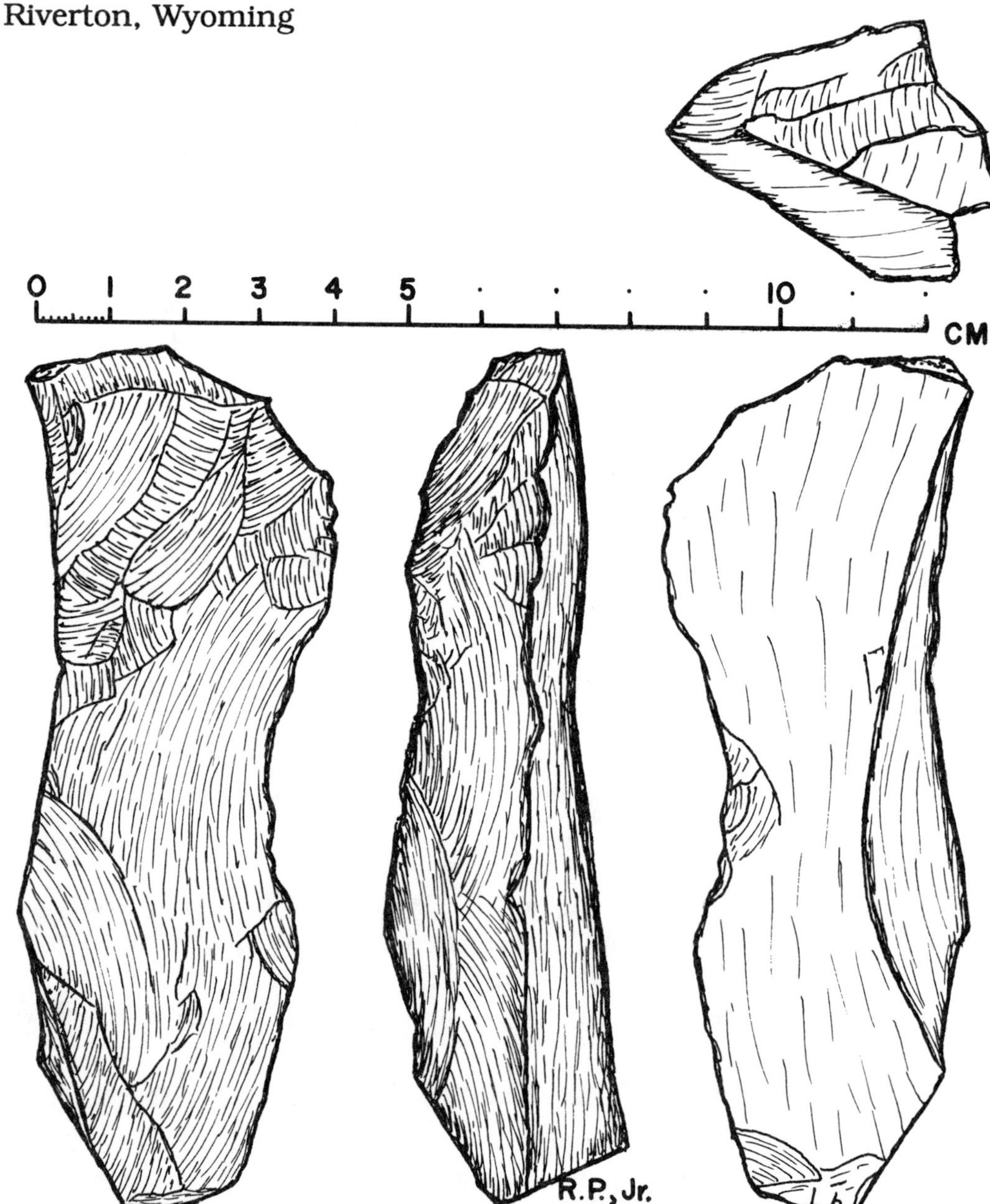

FLAT SURFACE FOR THUMB

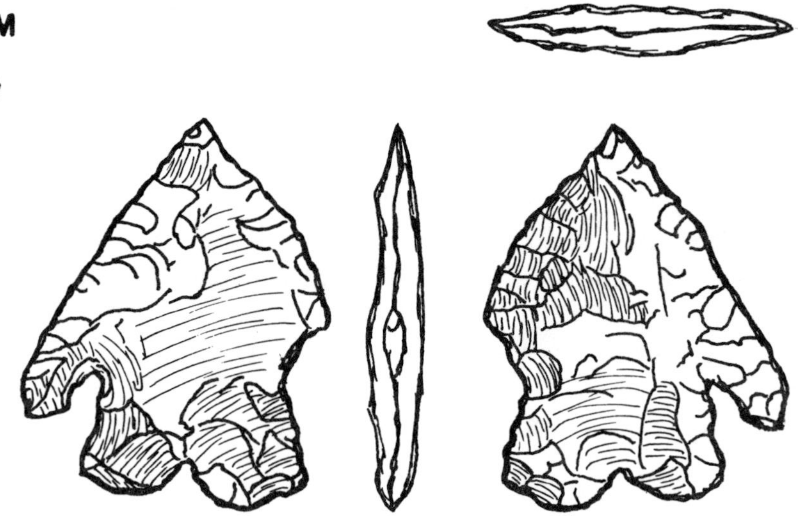

CALF CREEK
?

UNUSUAL SKINNING KNIFE

Color & Material: Knife, light, greyish-tan with banding of light blue chalcedony along the long axis. Quartzite.

Point, bone white with slight blue cast through lower half and tan through the upper. A thin (2mm wide) intrusion of chalcedony between the two halves. Chert.

Location: Knife, western edge of Natrona County; northwest of Arminto, Wyoming.

Point, unknown. From Western Trading Post of Denver, Colorado.

The skinning knife has been selected from the author's collection (Cat. No. 2T) to illustrate again that certain tools were crafted to be held exclusively in either the right or left hand. When this knife is placed with the side displayed in the right drawing facing upward in the palm of the right hand, the first finger grips the left edge immediately below the curved, cutting edge. The thumb then rests upon the flat surface along the back of the knife, and extends only slightly beyond the end.

When the knife is held in this manner the long axis of the thumb is in perfect alignment to the force of the cutting edge. There is no comfortable or effective way that it could used in the left hand.

It is believed that the two ribbed points extending beyond the cutting edge (one broken tip), were crafted to snag the small bundles of tendons that arise from an animal's body and attach to the inner surface of the skin. (With these, the animal is able to twitch the skin to frighten away biting insects.) These points would assist in separating the hide from the carcass.

The point, shaped in this manner, could not be found in any of the four Oklahoma Anthropological Society Guides or in Secrist's Guide. It was noted for sale in the Western Trading Post of Denver, Colorado, and purchased simply because it resembled the point selected as the logo of the author's newspaper column. At the time, it was thought to be a Calf Creek point with a notched base. It has subsequently been identified as an Elko eared point.

Mrs. Helen Lookingbill of Riverton, Wyoming, has in her collection a Calf Creek point that was crafted from the same material, and it is possible that it has been crafted from the same core. It is definitely from the same quarry. The

UNUSUAL SKINNING KNIFE No. 101
From the collection of:
Ray Parman, Jr.
Riverton, Wyoming

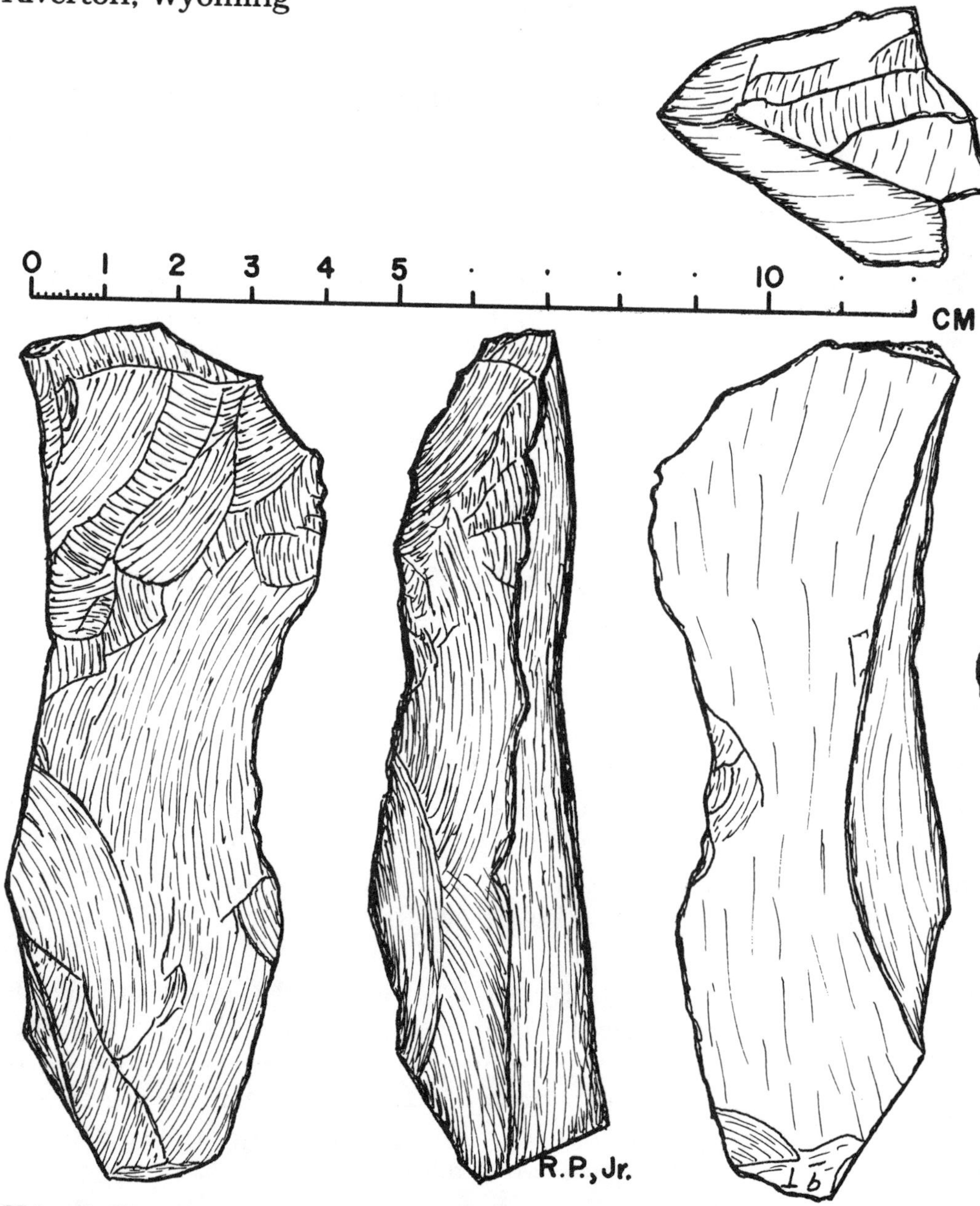

FLAT SURFACE FOR THUMB

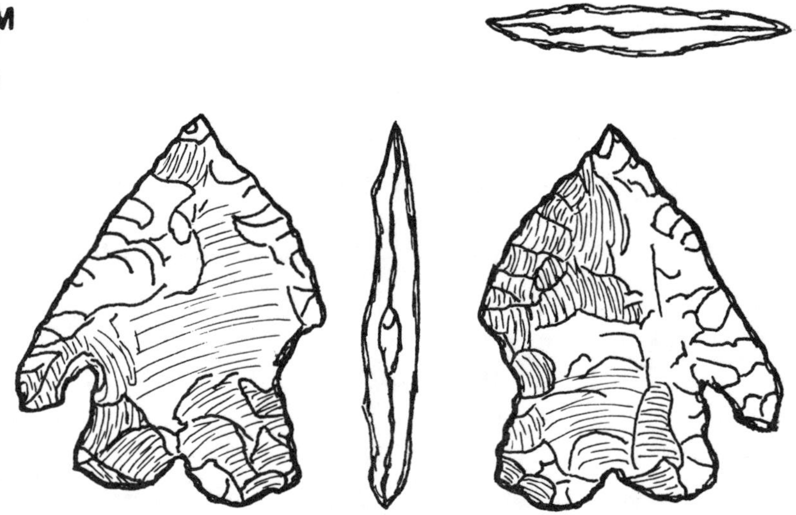

CALF CREEK
?

Lookingbill Calf Creek point is from Arkansas, where Calf Creek points are found. With this similarity, there is most probably close association between Elko Eared and Calf Creek points.

A base notch of this type, from Jim Bartlett's collection in Casper, Wyoming,was found in southern Wyoming. The Jamerman's point of this type (No. 20) was found in central Wyoming, and the Vaughn's (No. 23) was taken from the northwest corner of Moffat County, Colorado.

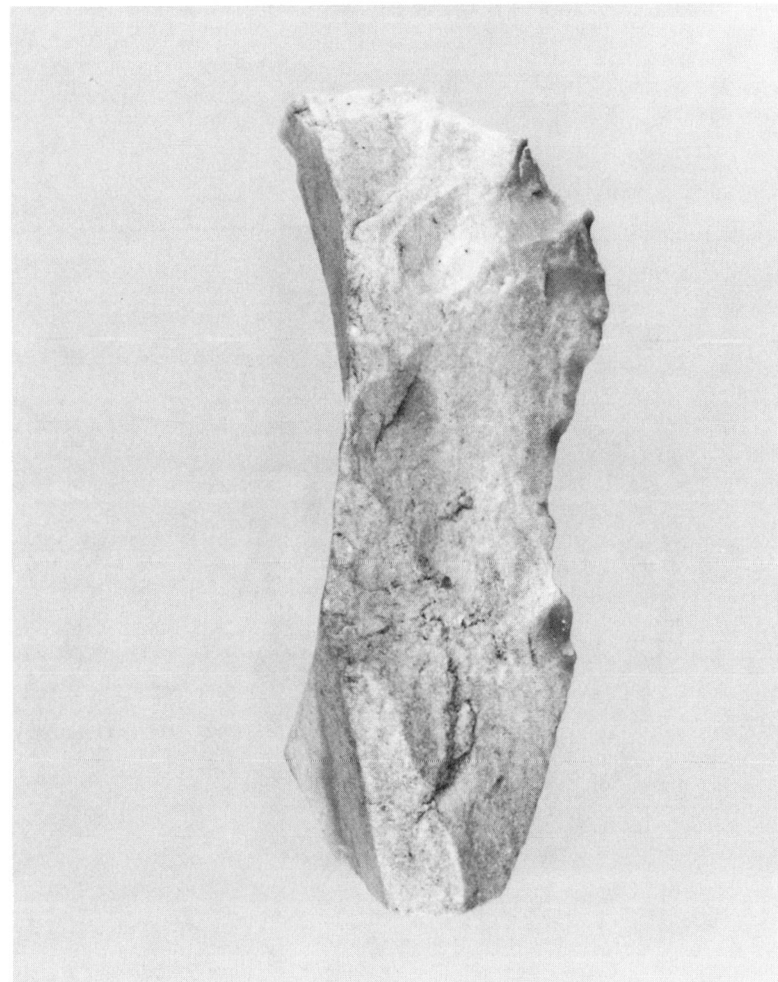

THROWING STONES No. 102
From the collection of:
Ralph & Janet Johnson
Farmington, New Mexico

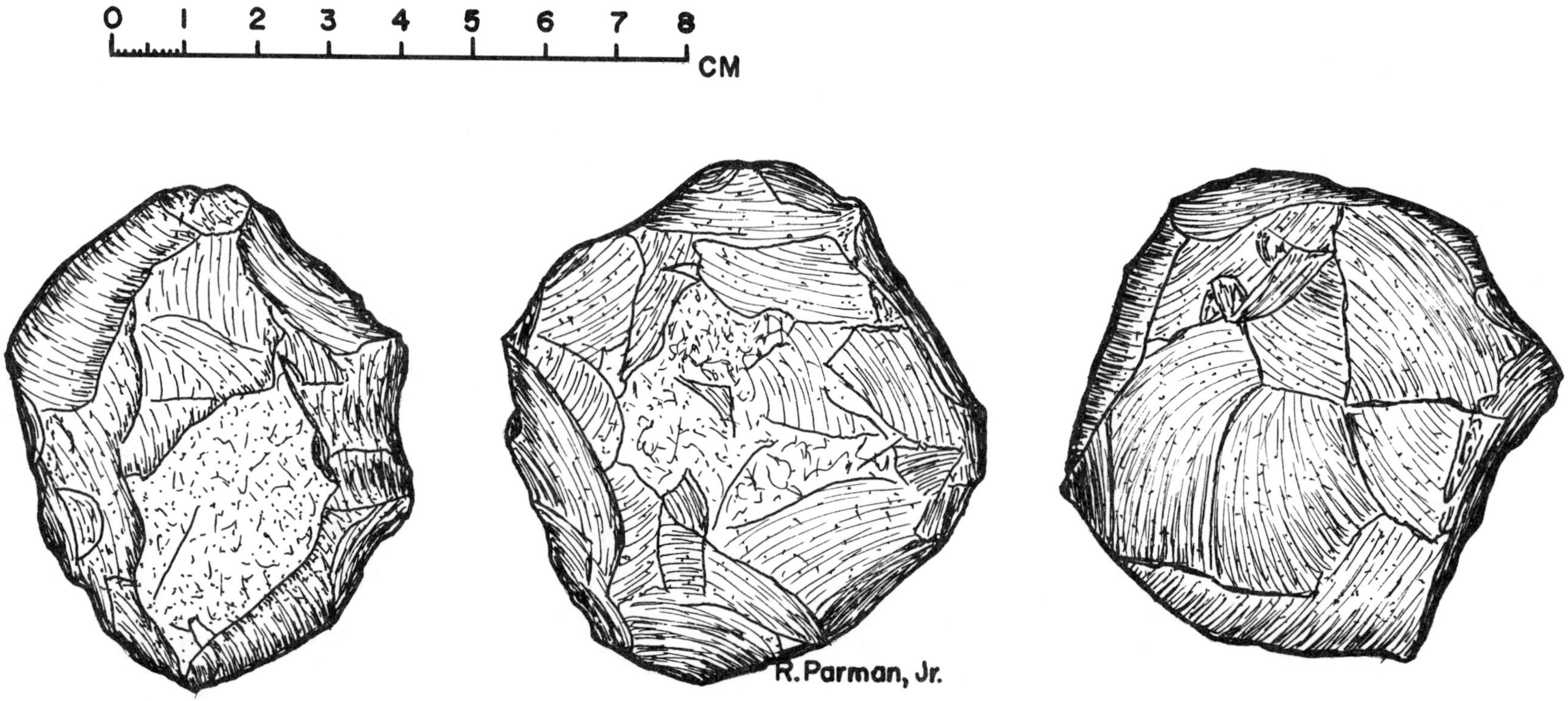

SIMILAR STONES FOUND IN GRAVE
ANASAZI BURIAL

THROWING STONES

Color & Material: Left to right, black, finely micaceous, hard, siliceous siltstone; pastel, grey-green, argillaceous siltstone; light tan and brown mottled, grey streaked, hard, siliceous, siltstone.

Location: Charnel House site, Montezuma County, Colorado. Taken from fields nearby.

Only one view of each of these stones was drawn, because whatever way you look at them, they look the same. No matter which way one picks them up, they feel the same too.

For years stones of this nature were picked up by collectors in New Mexico and Colorado. They were thought to be odd cores with no particular meaning. During the excavation of an Anasazi burial, a leather pouch of similar stones was recovered. The pouch was fitted with a shoulder strap, strongly indicating the stones were intended for throwing.

Ralph and Janet Johnson sent four of these stones to the author. They were placed in a small bag. Reaching in for one would always provide a proper grip for throwing. As Ralph suggested, if one is tossed in the air and caught, the grip is right for throwing.

There is feeling that many rabbits fell prey to these stones accurately thrown at a moving target.

ASSEMBLAGE OF OLD POINTS No. 103
From the collection of:
Becky & Dick Woods
Riverton, Wyoming

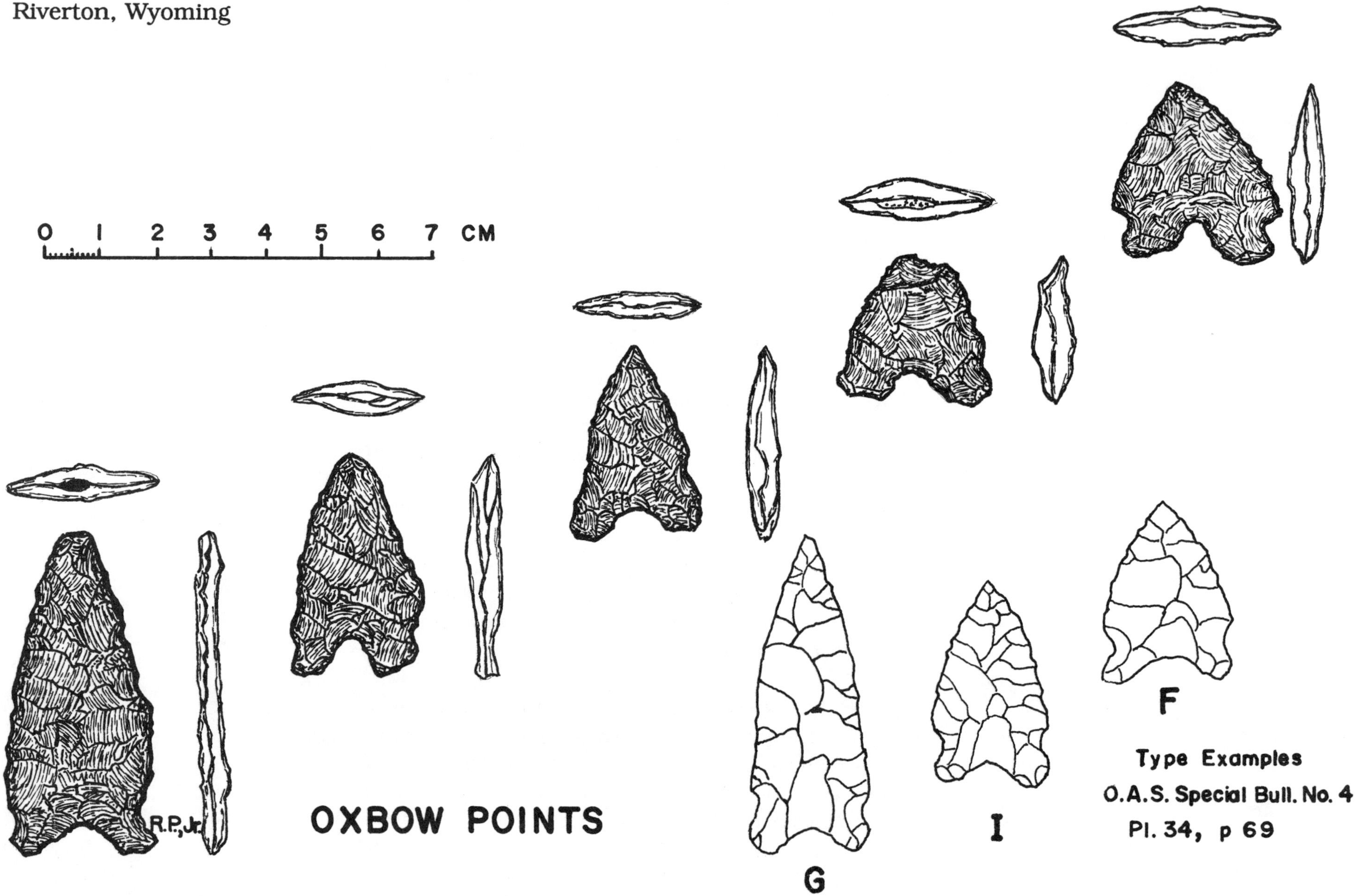

OXBOW POINTS

Type Examples
O.A.S. Special Bull. No. 4
Pl. 34, p 69

ASSEMBLAGE OF OLD POINTS

Color & Material: All, transparent to translucent, black obsidian.

Location: All five from one small valley in southwestern Mineral County, Nevada.

Becky Woods responded to the author's column. It was pleasant to view a fine, small collection right here in Riverton, Wyoming.

The Oxbow points were selected from their collection because they were such fine examples of the type. The *Oklahoma Anthropological Society Bulletin No. 4* illustrated nine examples of the Oxbow point. The Wood's points matched them very closely, both in size and flaking.

The amount of research imparted by the O.A.S. bulletins concerning point types, makes them a valuable addition to a personal library.

The following is their description of the Oxbow point type:

"The Oxbow point was named by Nero and McCorquodale (1958:82) for examples found at the Oxbow Dam site near Oxbow, Saskatchewan, Canada.

"Description: Oxbow points are small to medium size dart points having distinctive concave bases and side notches. Blade edges are convex, and flaking is random across both surfaces.

"Distribution: They are found in Canada in the provinces of Saskatchewan and Alberta with distribution southward into Montana, the Dakotas, and Wyoming (and are now known in Nevada).

"Age & Cultural Affiliation: Oxbow points were found in a middle to late archaic context with an average C-14 date of 5,200 +/- 130 years B.P. (before present)".

Examples G & I are in the James Barnett collection in Calgary, Alberta, Canada and were found near Strathmore, Alberta, Canada.

Example F is in the Glenbow Museum collections, Calgary, Alberta, Canada and was found near Estavan, Saskatchewan, Canada.

OLD, CRUDE CHOPPER No. 104
From the collection of:
Ray Parman, Jr.
Riverton, Wyoming

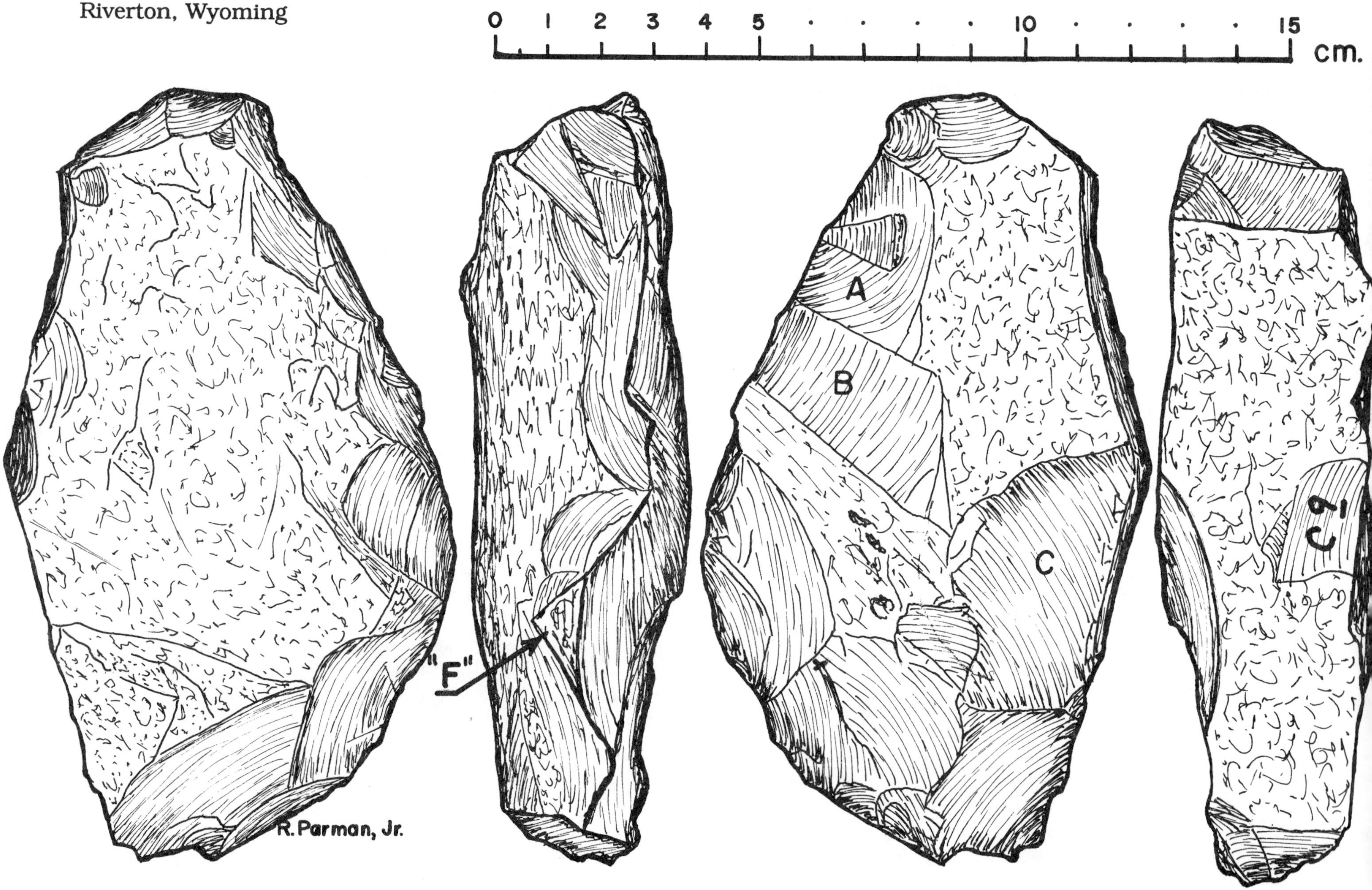

OLD, CRUDE CHOPPER

Color & Material: Dark brown with slight maroon and orange casts. Clear, shiny, varnish like patina. A very hard, argillaceous siltstone (commonly called ironstone).

Location: Northeast of Shoshoni; Fremont County, Wyoming.

The chopper lay almost totally buried (only a portion of the surface displayed in the left view was exposed). It was found on top of a flat mesa, near the edge where the surface sloped from erosion caused by surface runoff. Scrub junipers that grow on the sides of these mesas were only fifteen feet away.

At the time this tool was dropped, there must have been a greater annual rainfall than present. Tall grasses and better ground cover would have trapped wind blown sand, burying the artifact. When the climate reversed to the arid conditions present today, the ground cover was reduced, allowing erosion to expose one centimeter of the artifact's upper portion. When it was found, about three centimeters of soil still covered the surface on which this chopper was dropped. What period of time was necessary for three centimeters of soil (eolian) to build up on the top of a mesa? Whatever time was needed for this to occur, would be the minimum age for this chopper.

The unflaked surfaces of this tool have a marked patina. The three flake surfaces (A,B,& C) have more patina than the balance of the flaking. It was reflaked most likely to sharpen the working edge. Even the most recent flaking has a heavy patina.

Another feature of interest is the unflaked edge ("F"). Note the caption below the illustrations. It is hoped that the Fremont County Archaeological Society, Huckey Puck site, will yield a carbon date for this feature.

TWO RARE POINTS No. 105
From the collection of:
Becky & Dick Woods
Riverton, Wyoming

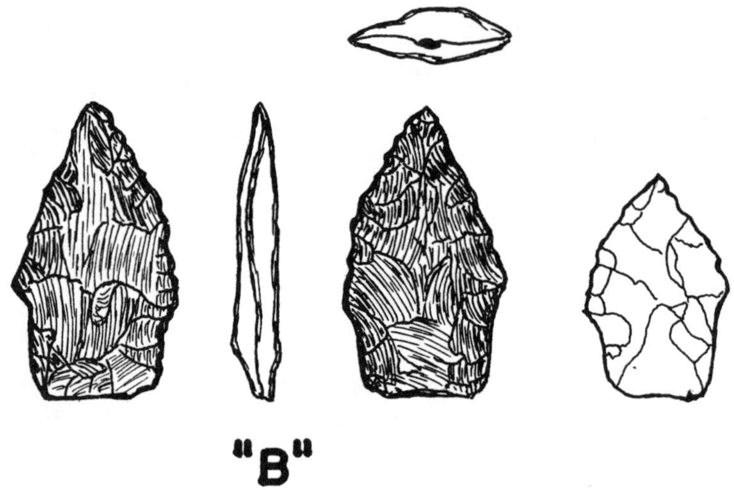

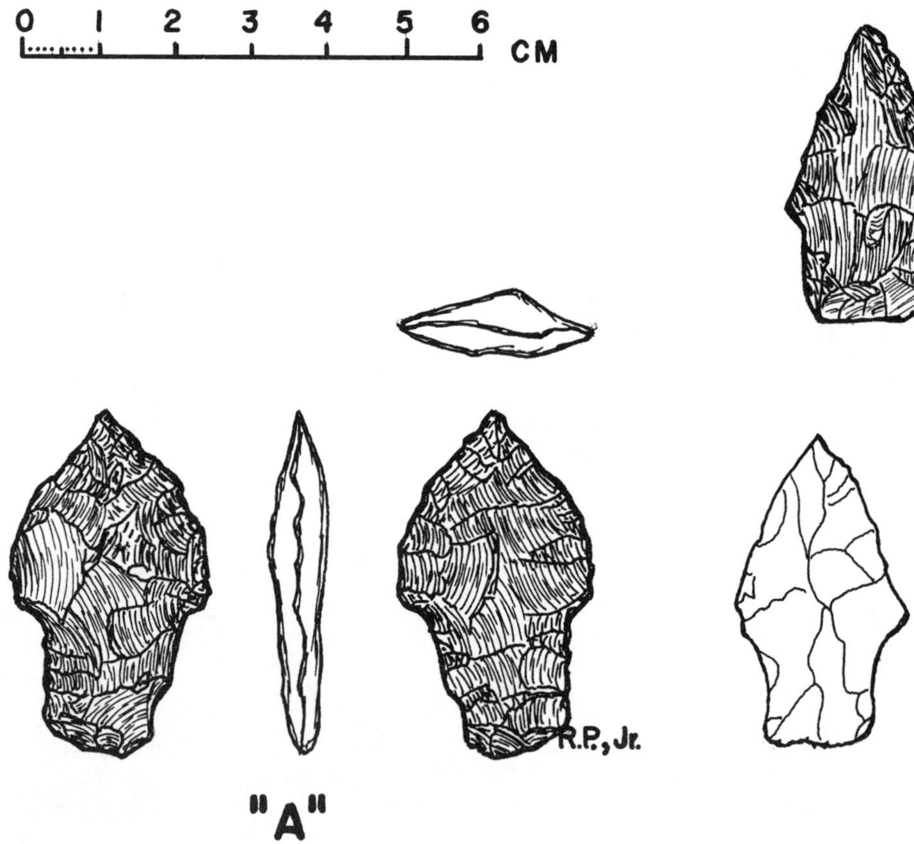

TYPE EXAMPLES
O.A.S. Special Bull. No. 2
Plate 12, p 25

DALLAS POINTS - Normally Found in TEXAS & OKLAHOMA

TWO RARE POINTS

Color & Material: "A", dark brown and brown mottled. Chert.

"B", white with light pink inclusions. Chalcedony.

Location: "A", Carter basin between Lyman and Kemmerer; Lincoln county, Wyoming.

"B", west central Sweetwater County, Wyoming. About thirty miles east of where "A" was found.

These two points were selected from Becky and Dick Wood's collection because they are not common in Wyoming. The type was first found and named by W.W. Crook, Jr. and R.K. Harris (1954) from examples taken in the vicinity of Dallas, Texas.

The following information is from the *Oklahoma Anthropological Society Special Bulletin No. 2:*

"The Dallas appears to be associated with Archaic periods and is well represented in the Carrollton and Elam foci (central location) of Texas. A suggested date range for this type would be from 2000 B.C. up to about 500 A.D.

"The Dallas point is almost identical to the Carrollton point with exception that Carrollton always has more pronounced, or sharper, shoulder".

There is one Dallas point in the late R.B. Parman's collection taken from western Oklahoma. These are the first noted from collections in Wyoming that have been viewed by this writer.

Many thanks to Mr. & Mrs. Woods for making these available.

NEWLY NAMED POINT No. 106
From the collections of:
Helen Lookingbill, Riverton, Wyoming
Darlene Hollings, Lander, Wyoming

"A" & "C"

"B"

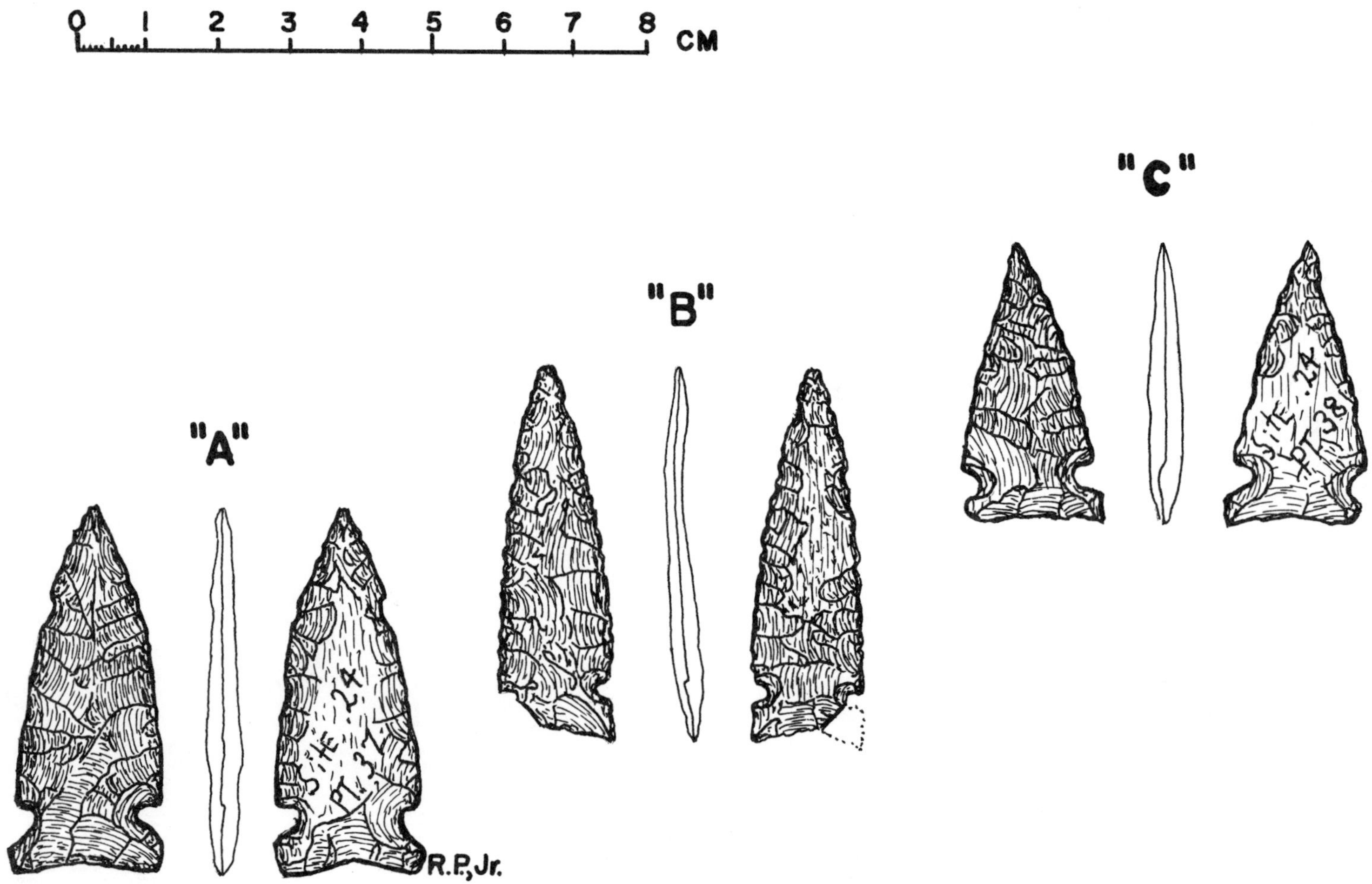

LOOKINGBILL POINTS

NEWLY NAMED POINT

Color & Material: "A" & "C", light grey chert.

"B", pale grey with slight blue cast. Chert or chalcedony.

Location: "A" & "C", North of Dubois; northwest Fremont County, Wyoming

"B", Red Desert region; northeastern Sweetwater County, Wyoming.

Work at the Lookingbill site north of Dubois, Wyoming (elevation 8,500 feet), was sporadic through the years from 1972 until 1981. It is rather inaccessible due to its elevation; ground water at the lower levels of the excavation has made the work difficult.

Two important discoveries near the lowest level (approximately 7,000 years B.P.) are manos and fragments of metates. This is an early date for the grinding industry, and further excavation may rewrite textbooks.

Dr. George Frison, University of Wyoming, is the director of the excavations of this site. He has indicated that the site has great potential for further exciting discoveries (excavations in 1988 have disclosed a Clovis level). No extensive excavations will be undertaken until there is adequate funding to provide the services of several top men in field archaeology and the equipment needed to remove the ground water.

In recognition of Helen Lookingbill's contribution to Wyoming archaeology, it is most fitting and fortunate that a distinctive, side-notched, projectile point, from the Early Plains Archaic level, should emerge from the Lookingbill site. This beautiful artifact has now been named the Lookingbill Point.

Author's note: See No. 99

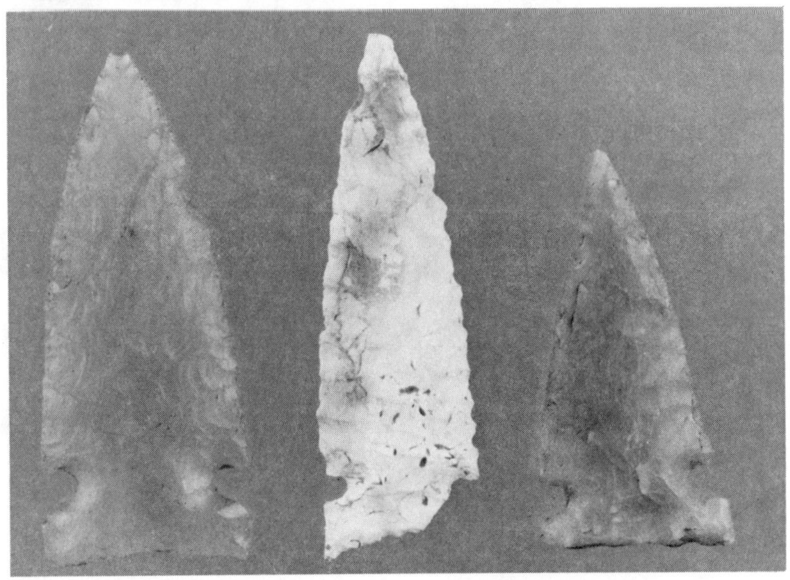

RARE & UNUSUAL POINTS No. 107
From the collection of:
John & Anna Sharp
Crowheart, Wyoming

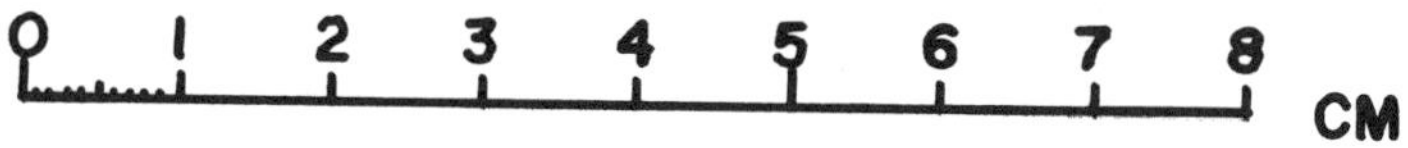

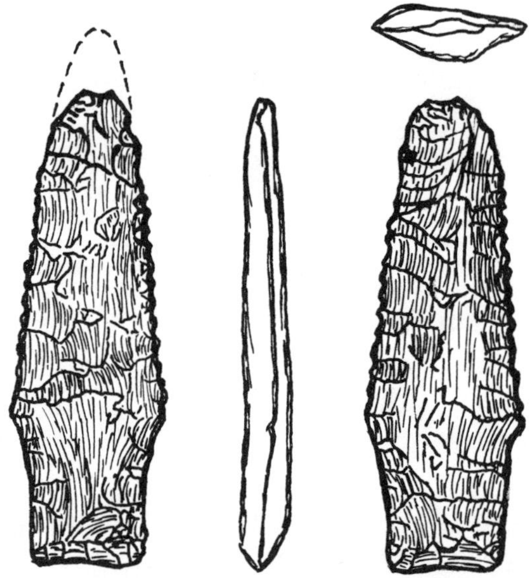

PRYOR STEMMED
(RARE)

TYPE EXAMPLE
O.A.S Bulletin No. 4
Plate 37, p 75

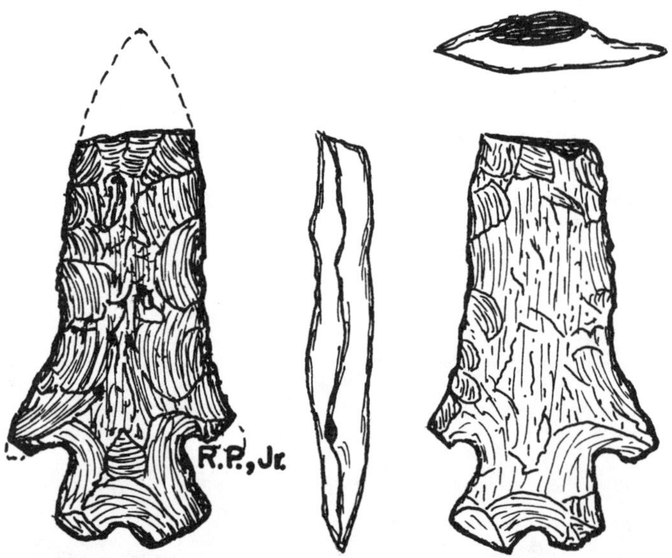

BOTH DECATUR & HANNA
?

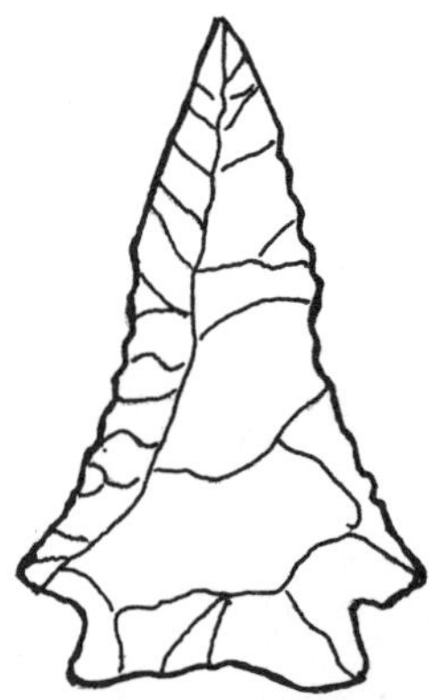

DECATUR
Type Example
O.A.S. Bull. No. 2
Plate 14, p 29

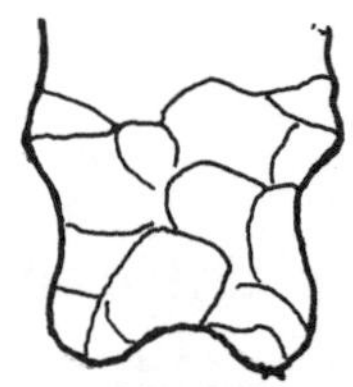

HANNA
Type Example (partial)
O.A.S. Bull. No. 4
Plate 22, p 45

RARE & UNUSUAL POINTS

Color & Material: Decatur, Hanna, light grey with faint, varnishlike patina over all surfaces. Very fine-grain quartzite. Pryor Stemmed, light grey with faint green cast. Heavy varnish-like patina on side displayed in the left view. Chert.

Location: Both, northwest Fremont County, Wyoming.

These two points were but a small part of John and Anna Sharp's fascinating collection. Part of this collection was found in their front yard.

The Hanna based, Decatur like point was one taken from the front yard. There is a strong possibility that a Paleo-Indian site is located in front of their home. Light tilling brought many points to the surface, and several of them have the Hanna-like base. This particular point was the only one having both the recurved edges and the flare toward the stem.

Of all the points listed in the author's new identification guide *, covering four hundred types, there are about twenty types having recurved edges. Twelve of these are from the Mississippi and Tennessee valleys. Four are centered in Arkansas and the other two in Texas. How does a blade or body of this configuration get tied to a Hanna-like base? It is very likely that this point has not been named yet.

The Pryor Stemmed point is a beautiful example of the type, even though it has suffered impact crushing of the tip. After the artwork for these two points was completed, several Pryor Stemmed points were noted in three additional collections. Maybe the adjective "rare" should not have been used.

Thank you, John and Anna, for sharing these.

* *Selected Preforms, Points and Knives of the North American Indians*, Gregory Perino, 404pp, hardback $40-$2 postage, 1509 Cleveland, Idabell, Oklahoma 74745

RARE FINDS No. 108
From the collections of:
Patt Brown, Riverton, WY
Henry Jensen, Lysite, Wy

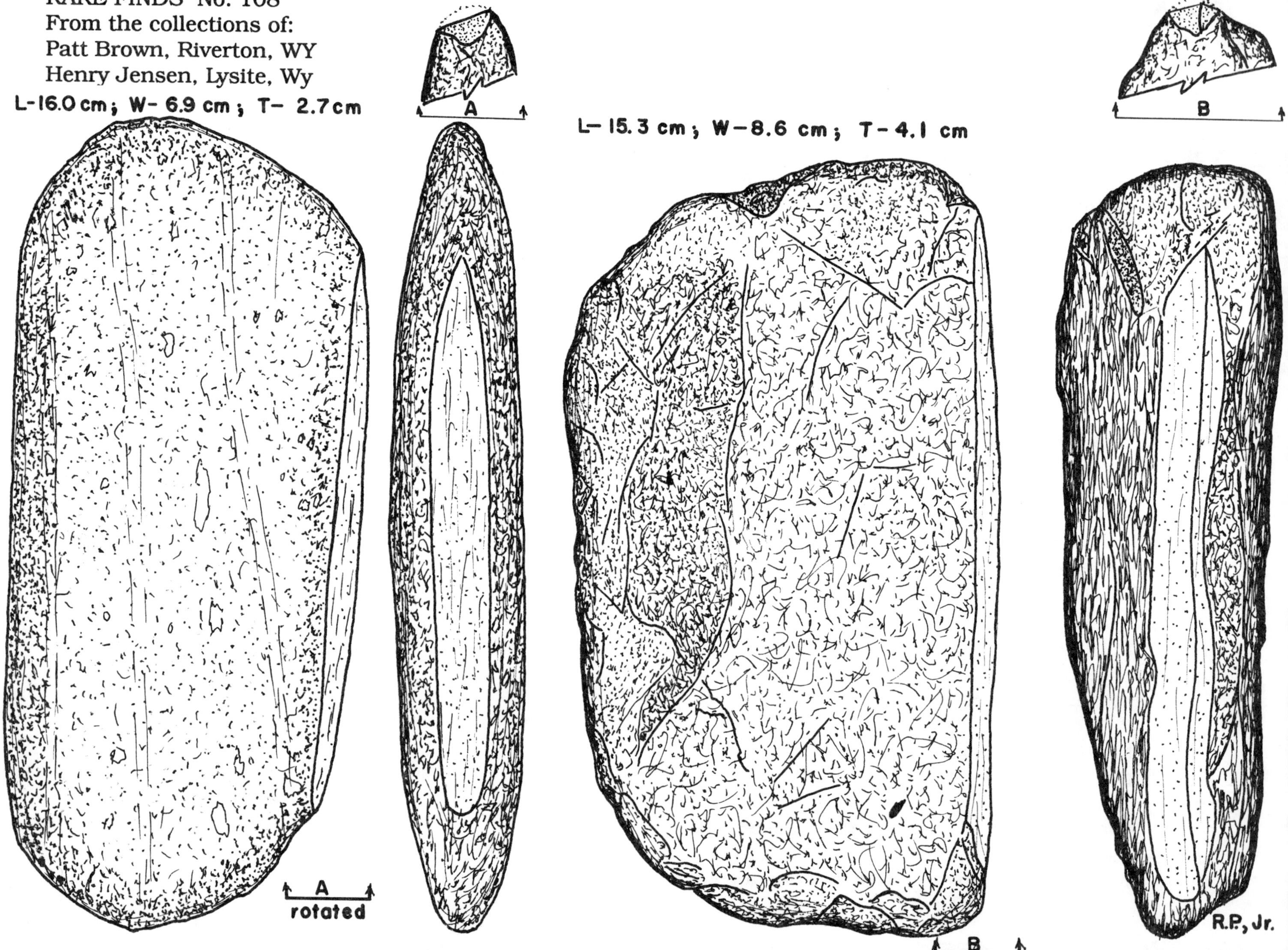

HIDE STONES

RARE FINDS

Color & Material: Brown A, medium, tannish-grey with slight green cast. Six, dark grey, paired laminae in bedding planes perpendicular to the wide surfaces. Medium-grain, hard siliceous sandstone with moderate, pinpoint and vugular porosity.

Jenson B, buff with slight pink cast having orange-brown, paint-like rinds on its sides. Very fine-grain, argillaceous (shaly) sandstone.

Location: A, Red Desert region of southwest Wyoming.

B, Badwater drainage; northeast Fremont County, Wyoming.

These artifacts are rarely found in private collections because their overall appearance is that of common sandstone cobbles. They do not evidence any shaping by man other than having their edges worn away by a rubbing action.

The worn surfaces are very smooth with a slight mirror shine. The contour of the worn surfaces are only slightly curved, indicating a soft material had been scraped. While this would account for the shine, a firm backing would have caused the slightly rounded surface.

In a rubbing action, the greatest wear would occur under the palm of the hand, rather than under the fingers. Patt's stone was held in the left hand, with the side displayed in left view toward the body. Jensen's was held in the right hand; first, it was turned one way (indicated by the narrow strip to the right), then turned and held by the other end. Again, the tool was held in the right hand, but for a longer period of use. This is indicated by the wider band of wear to the left.

This writer is not fully aware of all details of the tanning process; however, it is thought that these stones were used to work moisture out of the leather in order to keep it pliable. It is probable that oils had to be worked into the leather as well.

BEAUTIFUL AND OLD KNIVES No. 109
From the collection of:
Jess Bartlett
Casper, Wyoming

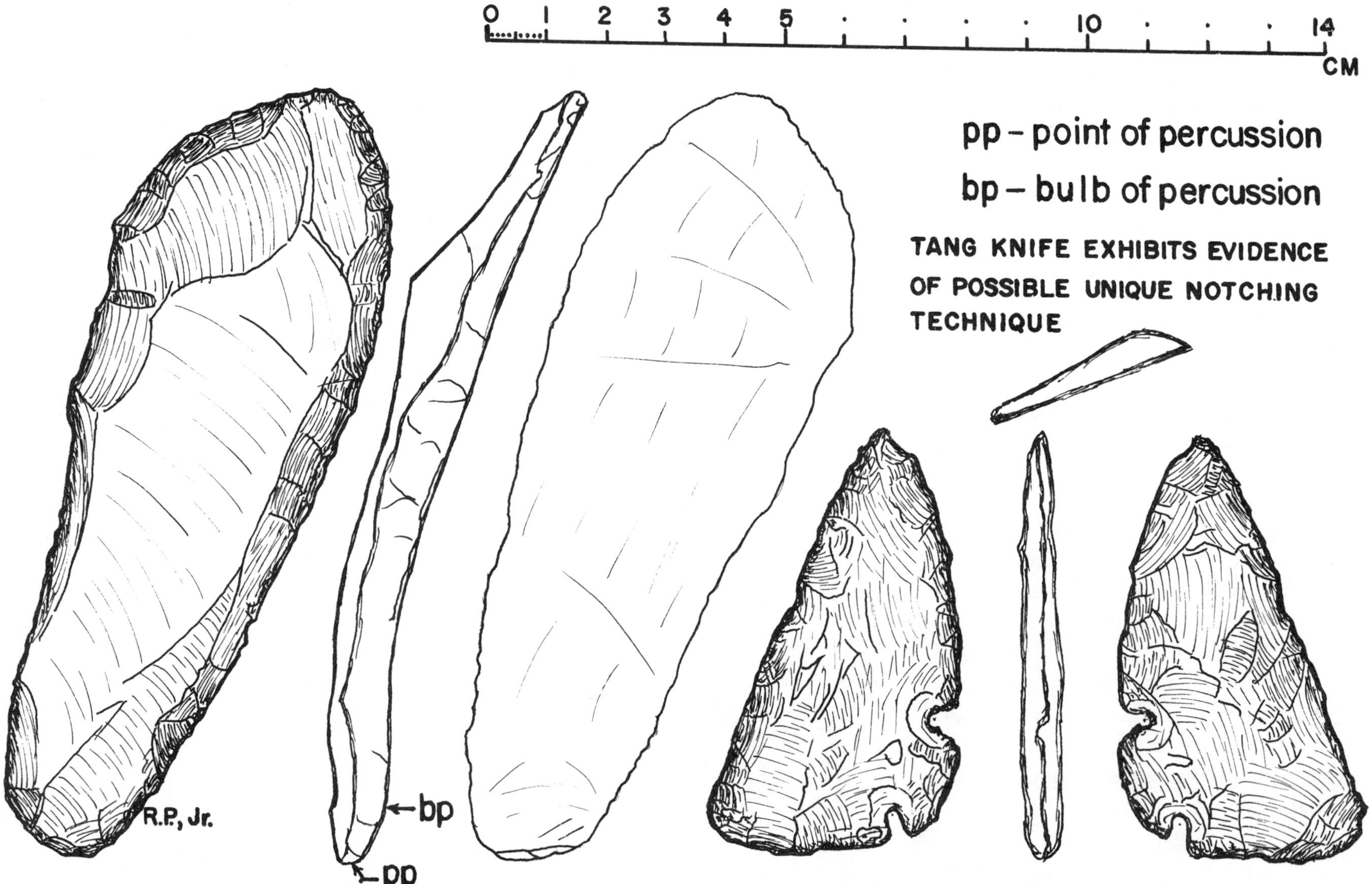

FLAKE KNIFE & SCRAPER

BACK-TANG KNIFE

BEAUTIFUL AND OLD KNIVES

Color & Material: Large knife, chocolate brown with light tan patina on concave surface only. Abundant light tan and brown oolites throughout the stone. Chert.

Tang knife, dark chocolate brown, having two, irregular, light brown inclusions and abundant light brown oolites throughout the stone. Chert from the same quarry as the large knife.

Location: Large, south central Uinta County, Wyoming

Tang, Wamsutter, eastern Sweetwater County, Wyoming.

It was a great pleasure visiting with Jess Bartlett and viewing his collection. The beautiful 42 pound metate evidencing many generations of careful and loving use, together with its accompanying mano, were fascinating to see. What a story they might tell! Unfortunately, their beauty could not be reproduced by hand drawings; hence a beautiful, curved knife-scraper was selected for publication.

After pencil sketches were made of the knife, it was apparent that there would be room for another small artifact. At that time Jess brought out the tang knife that he had found many years before. Thankfully, the author was permitted to take it home for further study because a remarkable notching technique was discovered.

The small dots (within the notches) indicate the approximate center lines of a drilling process, that was applied from both sides. It is thought that the drilling broke through, or came together, while crafting the upper notch. This was the reason for the small projection of stone remaining on the lower edge of this notch. The upper edge of this projection outlines the edge of the drilled hole.

The lower notch displays evidence confirming the use of this predrilled notching technique. The holes drilled for this notch did not come together to form a hole all the way through. Microscopic examination of the inner edge of this notch disclosed the remains of the thin lamina of stone. As this knife was being crafted, the usual technique of notching would have been applied after the drilling was completed. As the material was flaked away from the edge, this thin remaining lamina was chipped out last. It is this remaining portion of the lamina that is apparent under a microscope. There is no other way that the inner edge of the notch could display this configuration.

BEAUTIFUL AND OLD KNIVES No. 109
From the collection of:
Jess Bartlett
Casper, Wyoming

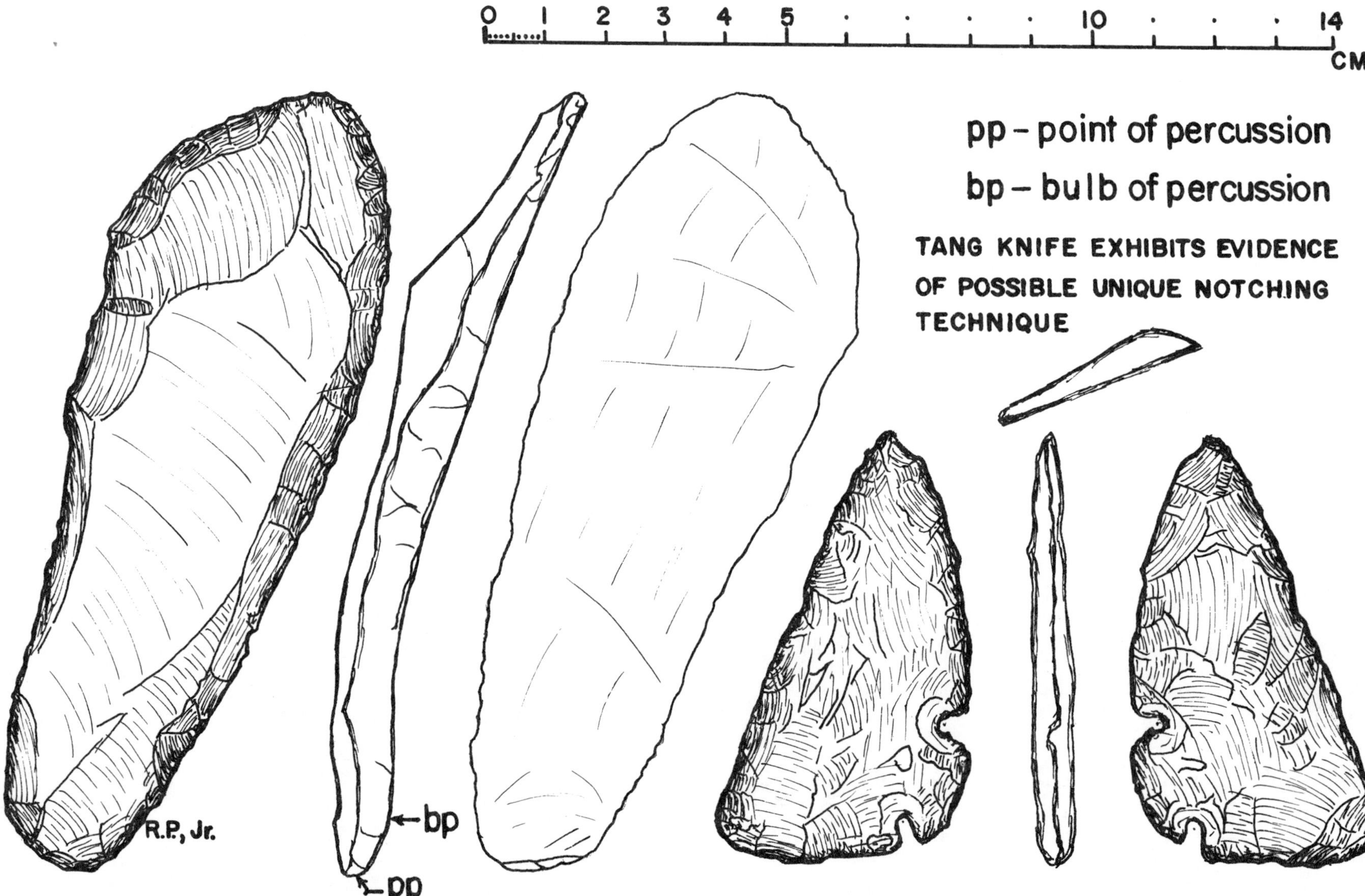

FLAKE KNIFE & SCRAPER

BACK-TANG KNIFE

Since this unique notching technique was discovered, close examination of tang knifes in other collections has turned up evidence of its use in the southeastern portion of Wyoming.

Two knives in the museum at Saratoga, Wyoming; Pete Todd's side tang knife (No. 7) in Riverton, Wyoming; and a beautiful knife from the collection of Milford Hansen of Cody, Wyoming; all display this technique having been used. All of these knives were found in this region of Wyoming.

This is thought to be an extremely rare notching technique. This is also the first publication of an artifact having been notched in this manner. Therefore, many have asked how this drilling process might have been accomplished, and why this notching technique was used.

The drilling process would be very much the same as that used for the drilling of gorgets, amulets, beads etc. A harder drill of chert, jade, or iron pyrite would have been necessary. After spinning the drill for a while: the drill could be lifted; a drop of water applied to sink the abrasive cuttings to the bottom of the indentation; and the drilling resumed. The process would be slow, but the holes could have been drilled in this manner.

It is very evident why this method of notching would be desired. Notches could be crafted more deeply into the knife blade, thereby providing a longer stem for the hafting of a handle. Using this technique would remove less material from the stem, leaving it much stronger.

Thank you, Jess, for making this discovery possible.

UNUSUAL POINTS No. 110
From the collection of:
Percy & Marian Scott
Casper, Wyoming

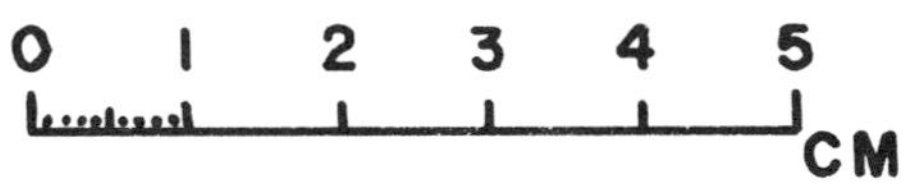

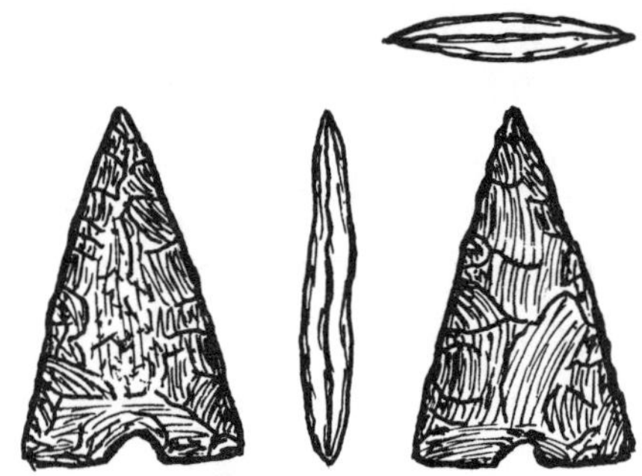

UNKNOWN

Possible GARZA or CARRIZO

SMALL

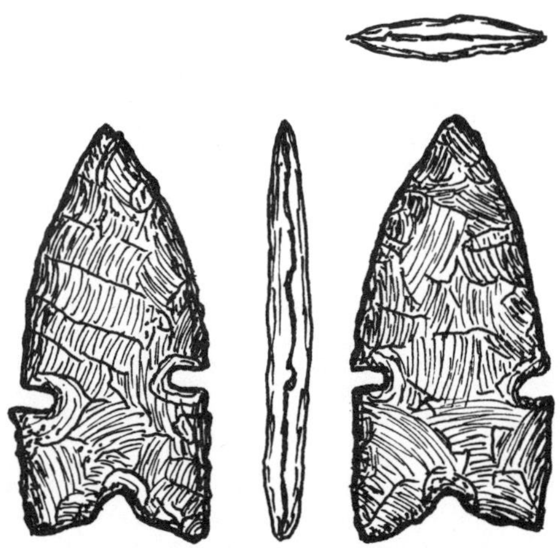

MALLORY /SAN RAPHAEL

Variant Base Notch

AND

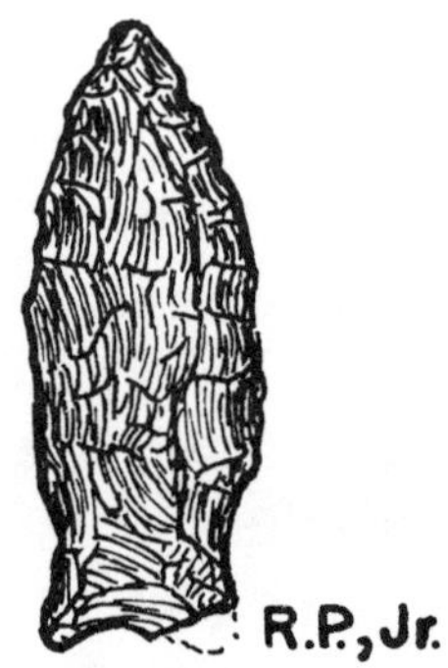

UNUSUAL

PRYOR STEMMED POINTS

UNUSUAL POINTS

Color & Material: Mallory/San Raphael, bone white chalcedony with tan, waxy patina.

Pryor Stemmed (both), red quartzite with pink cast.

Unknown, bone white chalcedony with slight, varnish-like patina.

Location: Mallory and Unknown, south central Natrona County, Wyoming.

Pryor Stemmed (both), unknown.

These projectile points were selected because they are variants of known types. In the case of one it was chosen because it was unknown.

The Mallory/San Raphael is thought to be from the early Archaic period, and one of the early, notched projectile points (side notching being the first). This particular Mallory/San Raphael has an unusual base notch in the center of a slightly concave base. The usual Mallory/San Raphael has a markedly concave base or a single, large, base notch.

The smaller Pryor Stemmed (three views) is most typical in configuration, with the exception that it is about one half the usual length. The larger (unusual) point has the typical beveled, right edges but appears to have been wider at one time. Could it have been a Paleo point, sharpened by flaking the right edges of both sides?

The unknown point probably has not been named. Two similar point types have been mentioned below the illustration. Are there others out there? If so please write to: The Wyoming Amateur Collector, P.O. Box 1665, Riverton, Wyoming 82501.

A COUNT OF COUP IN STONE No. 111
From the collection of:
Patrick Storin
Rawlins, Wyoming

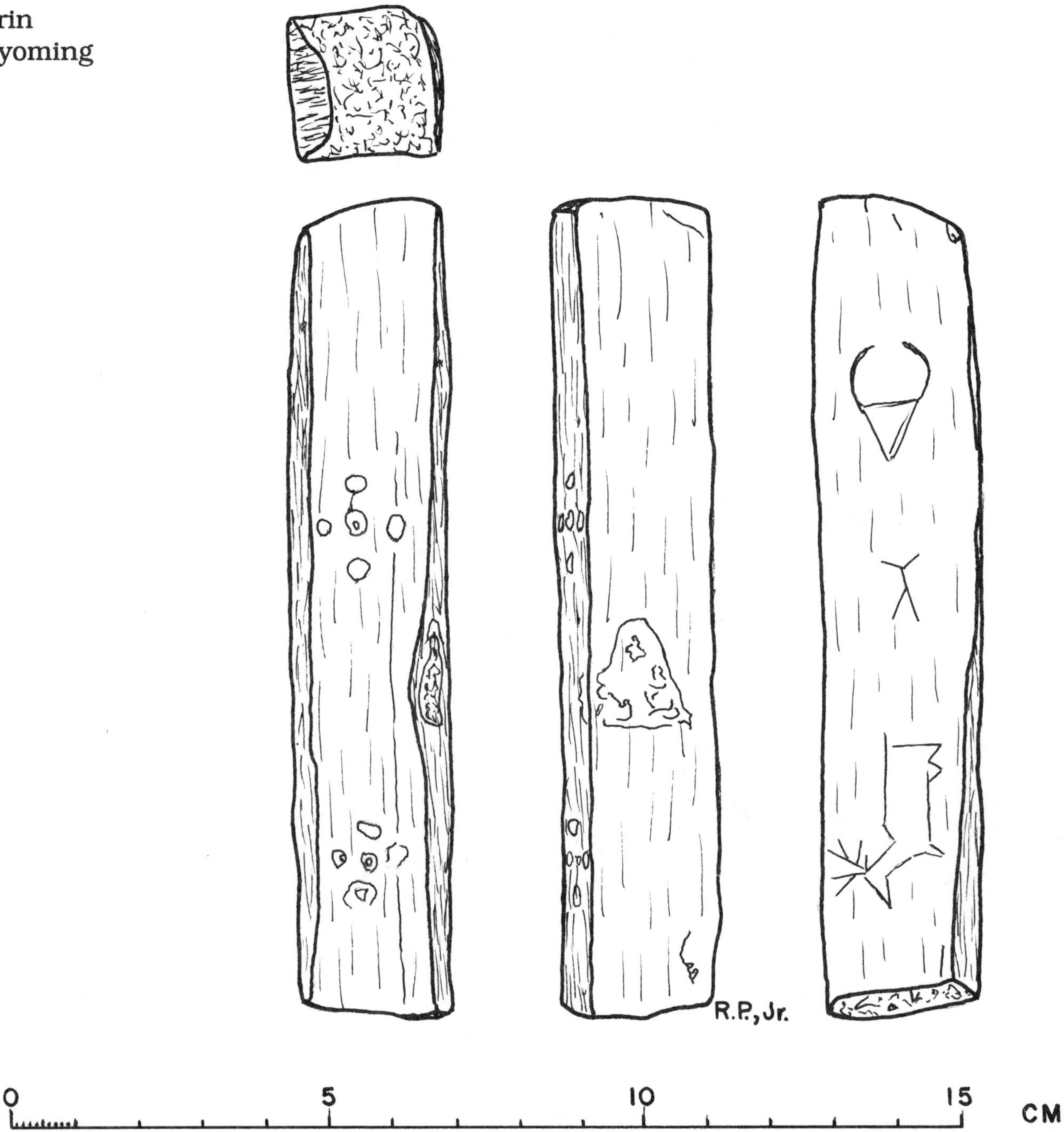

A COUNT OF COUP IN STONE

Color & Material: Dull, light to dark brown with green cast. Faintly laminated, siliceous sandstone. Slightly platy.

Location: Near Union Pass, northwest Fremont County, Wyoming. On Green River.

A good friend here in Riverton, Joe Downey, spoke of a friend having an artifact worth seeing. It led to an opportunity of meeting Patrick (Pat) Storin of Rawlins, Wyoming, and of holding a most interesting artifact. It will not be forgotten.

It is the nature of siliceous, sedimentary formations to fracture in perpendicular planes, so the author is quite sure that this stone was shaped by nature. The symbols carved into the opposite sides of it are the work of man.

It is evident that they were carved long ago, because the patina is uniform over each of the individual faces of the stone. Surprisingly, the two sets of five indentations (like the domino five) are not all man made. Most are drilled, but two are natural; three others are natural, but have been drilled also.

One must marvel that twenty, delicately scratched, straight lines so beautifully depict the elk. Pat was told that the other large, stylized figure was the tribal symbol for the Buffalo Clan. Consideration of where the artifact was found (high mountains), makes this hard to see. It is definitely buffalo though.

Several authorities have examined this artifact. Their opinions are so varied that one is free to use his imagination.

University of Utah, "Record of hunt on fork of Green River (the small symbol between elk & buffalo) during the tenth moon (this would be either September or October) of the year."

The Smithsonian Institute, "Your guess is as good as mine." (Pat said: "It was difficult getting in to see someone there, and the young man didn't even take his feet off his desk!")

Thomas Shakespeare (an Arapaho, now deceased, who was consultant to the Smithsonian), :"A personal medicine stone of a man much revered. Head of both Buffalo and Elk Clans of his tribe. Arms uplifted for guidance from the spirits. The five dot patterns indicate his tribe had contact with the Basketmakers when they moved southward through this area."

A COUNT OF COUP IN STONE No. 111
From the collection of:
Patrick Storin
Rawlins, Wyoming

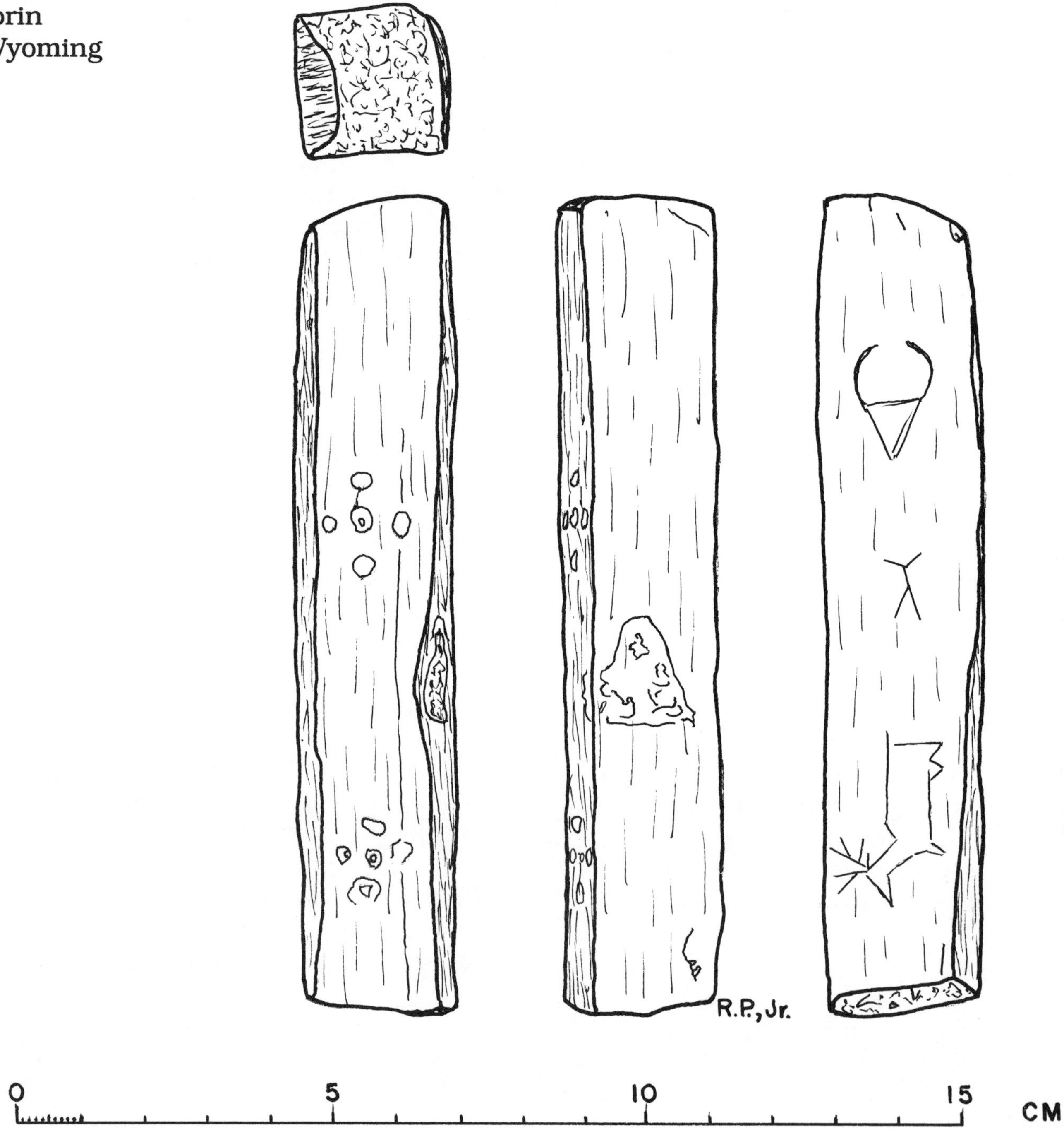

As the author was typing this copy, a young Indian man came to his desk and exchanged a few words and shared coffee and a smoke with the author. He was Wayland Shakespeare, the grandson of Thomas Shakespeare. The spirit of the young native American is being sorely tried, but will not be lost.

Author's note: Thomas Shakespeare's opinion of interpretation of this artifact is thought (by the author) to be the most accurate.

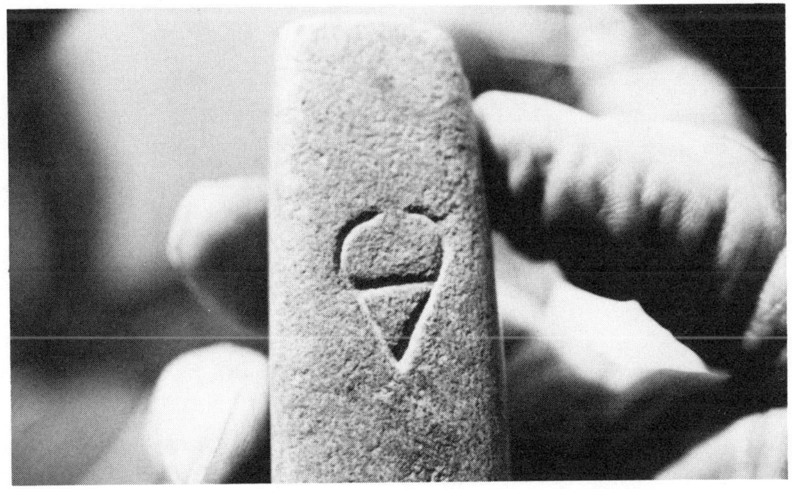

SALAMANDER EFFIGY No. 112
From the collection of:
Charles (Chuck) Rodabaugh
Rawlins, Wyoming

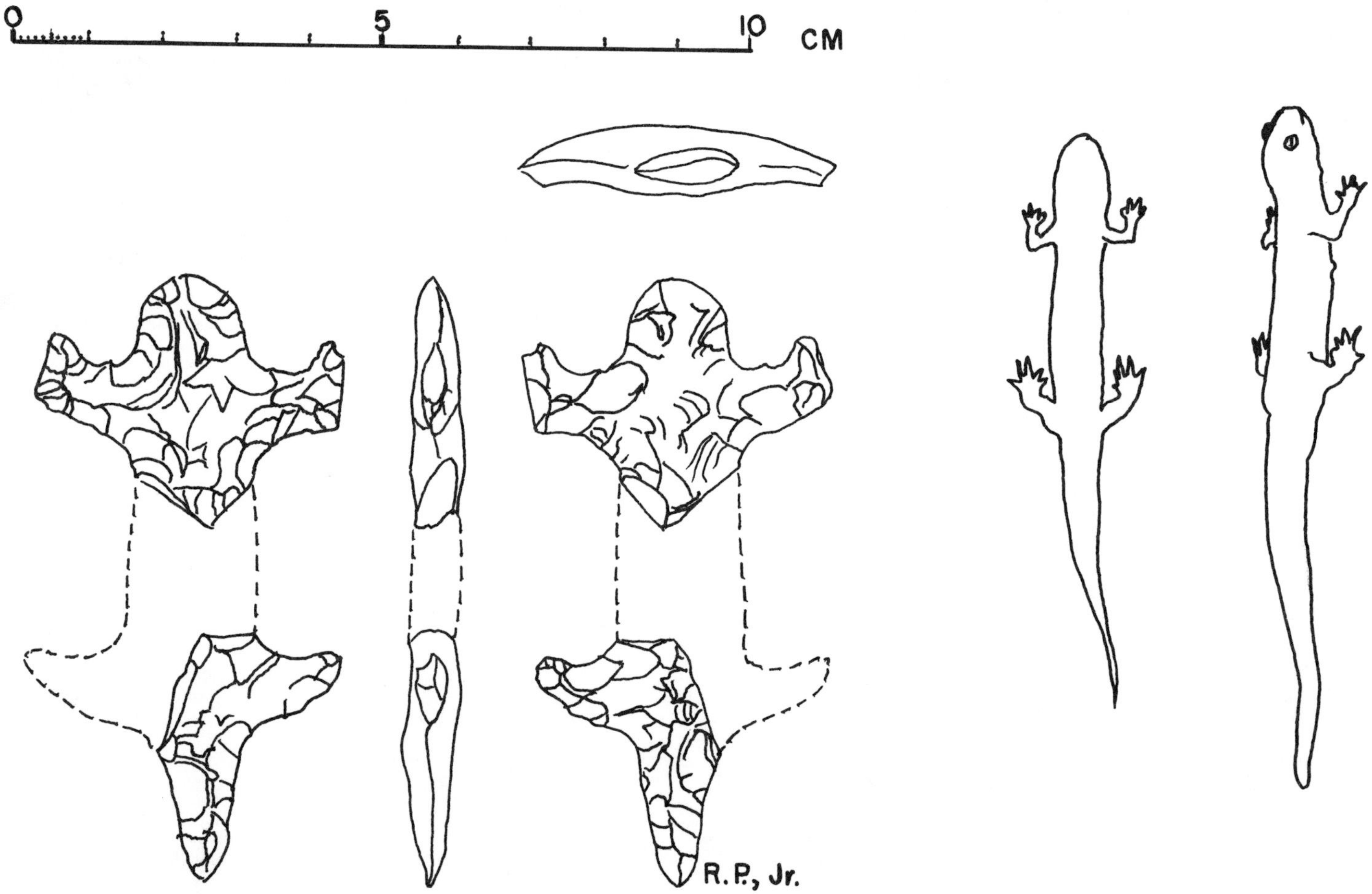

KOO HO' YEIT .... Arapahoe for Salamander
(kaw-ha-yate) or Water Dog

SALAMANDER EFFIGY

Color & Material: Light greyish black, slightly translucent. Obsidian from the Yellowstone quarry.

Location: South central Wyoming.

The Old One sat by himself, resting in the warmth of Greening Moon time. The time of the Hunger Moon had been most difficult for his people. It would be recorded as the Winter of Much Snow. There had been so much snow that the journey to the site of their summer camp had been a test for all.

Now, in the warmth of the first day at the new site, the young were being given endless commands by their mothers..."Move this there!"; "Take these to the stream and wash them all!"; "Clear all rocks from the center of the camp; bring stones for cooking, and the hearths as well!".

All of them, at one time or another had come to him asking..."Is there no end to these trivial demands of our mothers?" He answered simply..." Come, at first of darkness." He knew they were restless and could not wait to be out to their running games, to practice their hunting skills, and to bring in fresh meat of small game. He knew, too, they would come to him with darkness.

That evening, as the young sat about him, this effigy of Koo Ho' Yeit might well have been the one that passed from hand to hand. The Old One told a story of the hardships, trials, and tribulations that a waterdog, a tender animal so in need of water, had endured. "A Hawk had dropped him on the hill you will see to the south with the rising of the sun." The Old One told of the three days it had taken "Koo Ho' Yeit" to reach water..." at the stream where you, Darting Rabbit, washed clothes for your mother today."

Thank you Chuck, for making this rare find available. Many thanks to Pius Moss for recognizing the two fragments instantly, and telling how the Northern Arapahoe used the "water dog" to teach persistence and tenacity to their young. He also said that a similar effigy with a head thicker than it was wide, would be for the horned toad.

This pictograph appears on a protected sandstone bluff near the two caves from which artifacts Nos. 113-116 were taken in the Bridger Mountains in Hot Springs County, Wyoming.

INTRODUCTION TO NOS. 113-116

Author's note: This is my personal account of meeting Douglas K. Abbott, an avocational archaeologist who has made a significant contribution to the field:

Doug Abbott of Kirby, Wyoming, called one evening. He was at a restaurant in Riverton and had some bones he wanted me to see. I told him it would take about thirty minutes to get there. There was no way of knowing that I was just thirty minutes from one of the most profound moments of discovery in my life.

"I have been reading your column in the paper, and decided you should be the one to let the public know of these." He then began placing one fascinating artifact after the other in my hands. For a long span of time, I was able to utter only meaningless, fragmented words of wonder. I never did say very much that evening. I just listened.

If you have been to an early evening ball game, maybe you remember that when the floodlights first come on, they are hardly noticeable? Then when it gets darker, the floods become brilliant? My profound moment of discovery progressed in just that way---a single, dim bulb of awareness that grew slowly into majestic brilliance, three hours and ten cups of coffee later.

"Arch-a-facts", he called them. I started to correct him but could not. I was hanging on to every word he said: "...two caves.......yards apart......meadow.......more like rock shelters..." One of the caves (or rock shelters) was large, the other small and about thirty yards away. He had recorded which cave each of the artifacts had come from. Later, this was to prove most important. Never have I listened so intently, so speechlessly.

When I returned home that night, there was an awareness not only of the fantastic artifacts, but also of having been embraced by words. Words that could have come only from a brilliant mind. Later, when the entire story unfolded, there was no question of his brilliance.

Doug was a stock hand for the owner of the ranch on which the caves were located. Since graduating from high school, he had worked with cattle & horses; yet without formal training he was aware that the discovery of the caves was important. He went to the library where they suggested two books: one, a rather technical journal of Wyoming archaeological sites; the other, a report of the excavation of a rock shelter in northwestern Wyoming. Doug may mispronounce some of the technical words (there are many in the two books), but there is no question that he read and

This pictograph appears on a protected sandstone bluff near the two caves from which artifacts Nos. 113-116 were taken in the Bridger Mountains in Hot Springs County, Wyoming.

understood the meaning of each and every one of them.

For three years, Doug with the help of the owner's son, carefully sifted the sand in the caves. He was considerate of stratigraphy, did not disturb the entrances of the caves, and left halves of floors (front to back) totally undisturbed. He laid out grid squares, and recorded the recovery of each artifact. In total, Doug disturbed less than 15% of the floors of the caves.

The large cave is about 13 meters wide, and 6 meters deep. It is apparent, from the number of lithic and bone artifacts recovered from this cave, that it was the primary shelter. The small cave is thought to have been the tribal shaman's personal living quarters. It was approximately two meters wide, and three meters deep. The reason that this small cave was thought to have been occupied by the shaman, is that not a single, lithic projectile point or tool was recovered from it. Also, a greater number of the bone artifacts from this small cave would be considered stylized or effigies.

The lithic tools taken from the large cave made up the usual range of camp tools, such as pounders, awls, knives, dart points, and arrow points. There were about ten different types of Pelican Lake points, and a basal fragment (adequate for identification) of a St. Charles Dovetail.

All in all, this seems to the author to be a substantial contribution to North American archaeology, made more striking by the fact that it was recovered by someone without formal training.

The following three units show some of the bone tools found at this site.

AN ASSEMBLAGE OF BONE TOOLS No. 113
From the collection of:
Douglas K. Abbott
Kirby, Wyoming

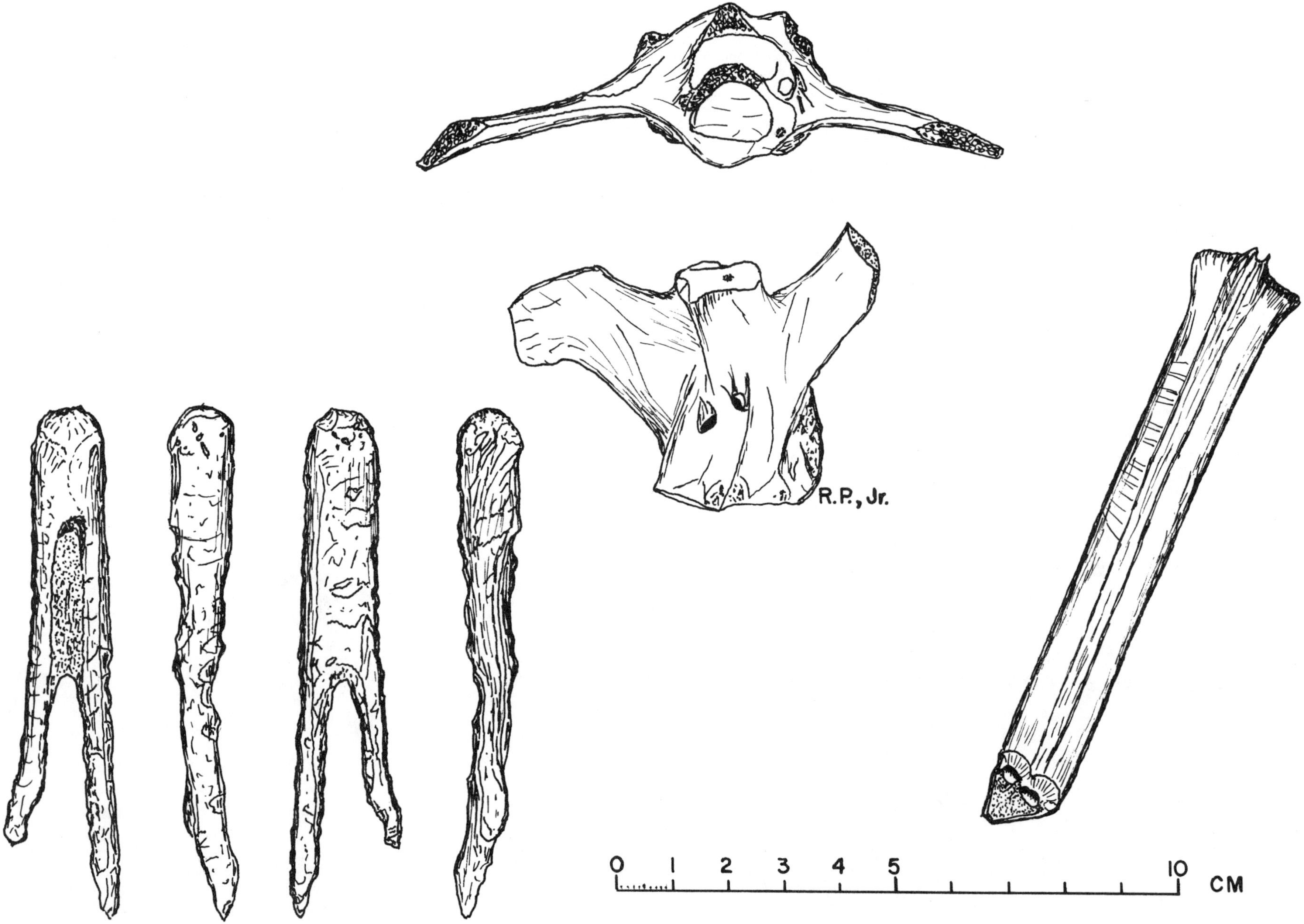

AN ASSEMBLAGE OF BONE TOOLS

Color & Material: Eagle effigy, literally bone white. The first or second caudel vertebra of buffalo (Bison bison).

Clothespin, predominately fire blackened with grey areas. Costal cartilage, species unknown.

Dibble, light tan, slightly darker on upper third of larger end. Oil-like patina that is heavier on darker end. Metacarpal of ungulate, species unknown.

Location: Bridger Mountains, southern Hot Springs County, Wyoming.

This eagle effigy was taken from the small shaman's cave. The ends of the lateral processes have been altered slightly, to give proper porportion to the wings. The most interesting feature is the eye. Under a microscope, it is possible to see the individual particles of charcoal within the cells of the bone and beneath the surface. The patina of the surface of the bone is continuous over the eye.

It is difficult to say whether or not the artifact called clothespin was shaped naturally. The groove up the surfaced displayed to the left does not look natural. The total surface of it has been blackened by fire.

The artifact to the right has been called a dibble (tool used to plant seed), because the larger end has staining from being held in the hand, while the smaller end has polishing from being shoved into the soil. It is hollow through its length.

BIG BEAR, LITTLE BEAR No. 114
From the collection of:
Douglas K. Abbott
Kirby, Wyoming

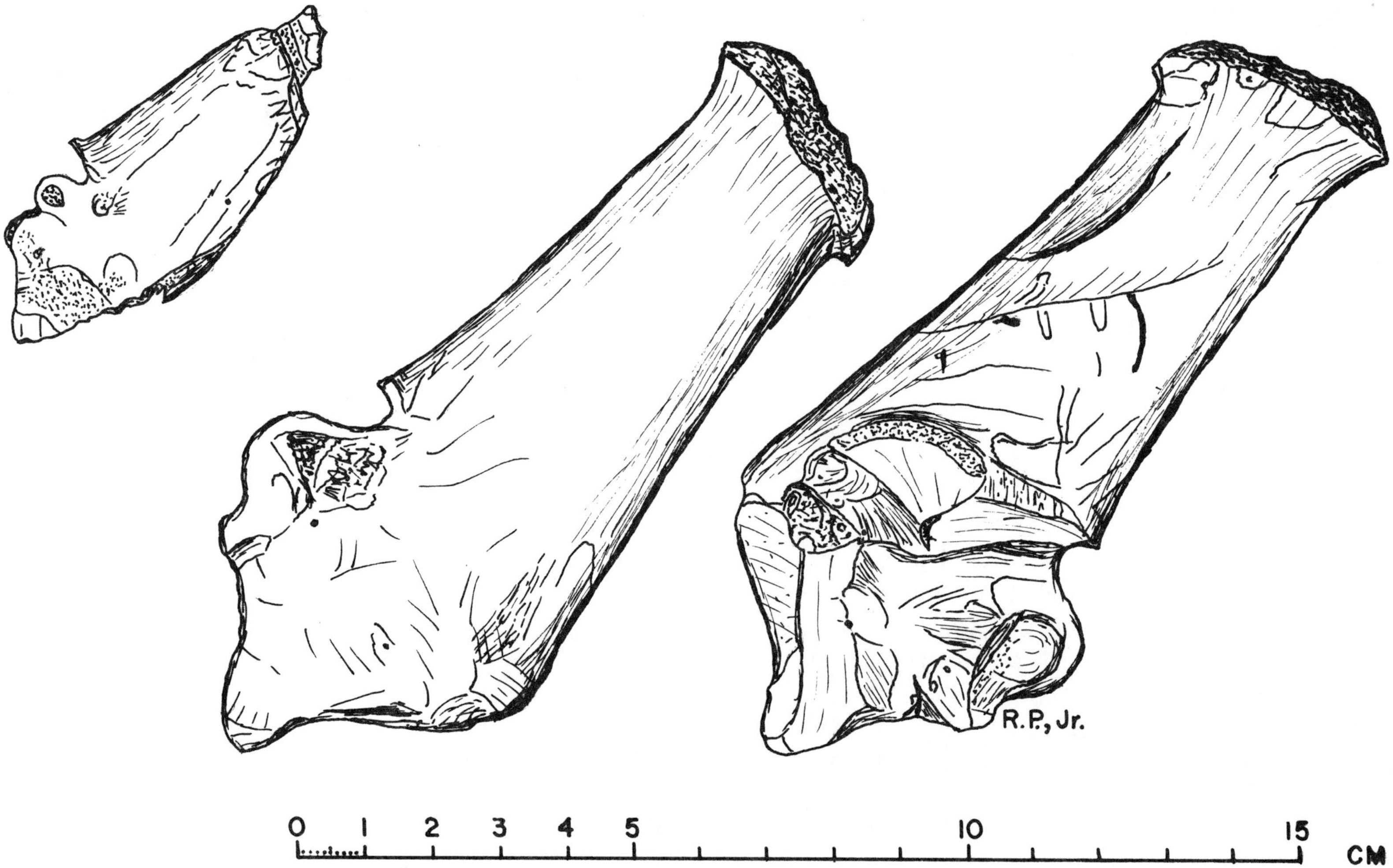

BIG BEAR, LITTLE BEAR

Color & Material: Big Bear, an older bone but not yet bone white.

Little Bear, light tan of younger bone. The right Tuber Calcis of probably elk, possibly bear.

Location: Bridger Mountains, southern Hot Springs County, Wyoming. Both from large cave.

The larger of these two bones is natural in contour with the exception of some gnawing by rodents. The smaller has been carved in such a manner as to represent a bear cub. The nose is the outer cortex of the bone. The ruff about the muzzle has been beautifully depicted by carving into the cancellous portion of the bone. The fur within the left ear has been depicted this same way.

The small mark that represents the eye was carved into the surface. It is not possible that a rodent could have selected and gnawed one single mark, at the exact spot for the eye. This artifact had to have been shaped by man.

The projection at the right end of the small bear is additional evidence of this bone being carved by man. Projections of this contour appear on two other bone effigies taken from these caves.

It is believed by this writer that this projection was for the attachment of a thong, so that this object could be worn about the neck. Pure conjecture places it about the neck of a young member of the "Bear Clan".

CLASSIC THUMB SCRAPER No. 115
From the collection of:
Douglas K. Abbott
Kirby, Wyoming

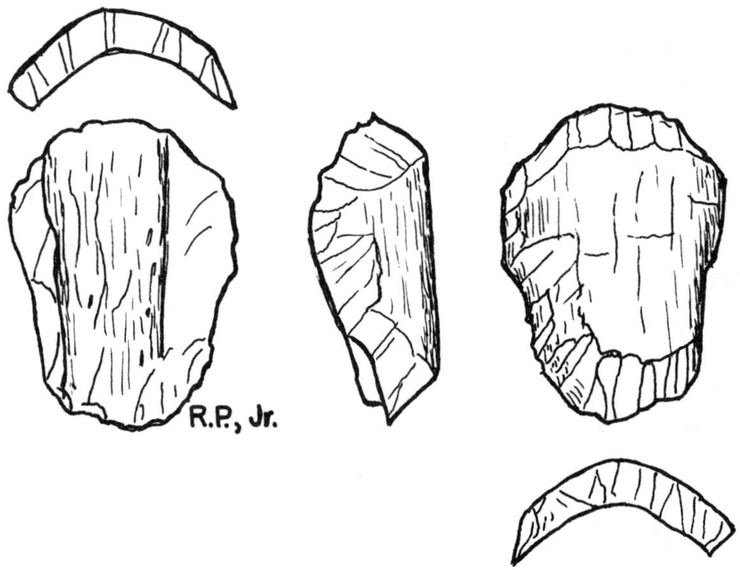

CLASSIC THUMB SCRAPER

Color & Material: Light tan with slight oil-like patina. Portion of a long bone. Species unknown.

Location: Bridger Mountains, southern Hot Springs County, Wyoming.

Many of the bones that Doug had removed from the two caves were taken to several professional people. All were of the same opinion. They were the products of the gnawing of rodents. If this is true, there needs to be more research conducted regarding two features of all of the bone fragments taken from the caves. The first is that in the course of their butchering process, man must have reduced the bones to the fragments that subsequently were gnawed by rodents. If this were the case, then similar bone fragments should be found in the assemblages of bones taken from other caves.

If these bones (called artifacts) are unique to these caves alone, then it follows that the inhabitants were aware of the manner in which rodents would gnaw on certain bone fragments. They could then expect to have the desired tool (or effigy) produced. The second feature that should be researched, is the carbon dating of bone fragments removed by Doug, to be compared with fragments subsequently removed by further professional excavation of the two caves. Surely, there will be fire pots found in additional excavations. The charcoal from these fire pots will accurately date many of these artifacts.

A BONE THONG CUTTER No. 116
From the collection of:
Douglas K. Abbott
Kirby, Wyoming

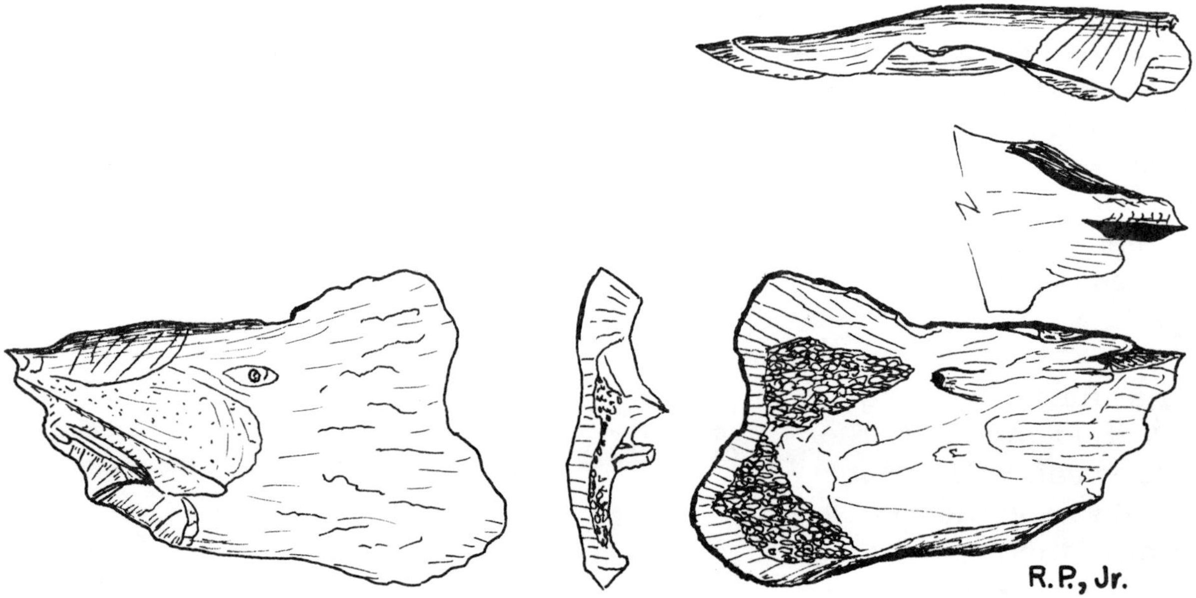

A BONE THONG CUTTER

Color & Material: Light tan, with oil-like patina that is slightly darker around the cutting blade, and in the center of the concave side of the tool. Believed to be a portion of the tibia of a large hoofed animal. Species unknown.

Location: This was one of the first artifacts that Doug put into my hands on the evening that we met. It has remained one of the more exciting ones as well. It is definitely a functional tool. The staining (the darker, oil-like patina) previously mentioned, occured only at the pressure points that would arise from its use as a thong cutter.

It is unfortunate that the angle from which the left side view was drawn has made the groove that forms that mouth appear straight. Actually, the contour of this surface required that this groove curve slightly in two different directions for this groove to appear straight from this one angle. It would not have been possible for a rodent (or rodents) to have gnawed this recurved groove; therefore, the representation of an animal's face must have been intended. This face utilized the foramen (the hole through which a blood vessel passed into the interior of the bone) as the eye.

The end view (between the two side views) has been rotated slightly, in order that the edge of the bone (the guide) and the sharpened projection (the cutting blade) would be displayed best. The additional, partial drawing (between the side and edge views) has been rotated slightly, so that the detail of the cutting blade could be displayed best.

This thong cutter would have been used on small hides. The overall size of the tool, coupled with the small blade, would not have permitted strips to be cut from the hide of any animal larger than a young doe.

First, a small nick would be cut in the edge of the hide. With this tool held in the left hand (cradled in the curve of the fingers with the blade up, and away from the wrist), the cutting blade would be placed in the notch. The thumb would be pressed against the surface of the hide to hold it against the blade, and the tool would be drawn along the left edge of the skin. This would cut a strip of the hide about three to four millimeters wide.

A BONE THONG CUTTER No. 116
From the collection of:
Douglas K. Abbott
Kirby, Wyoming

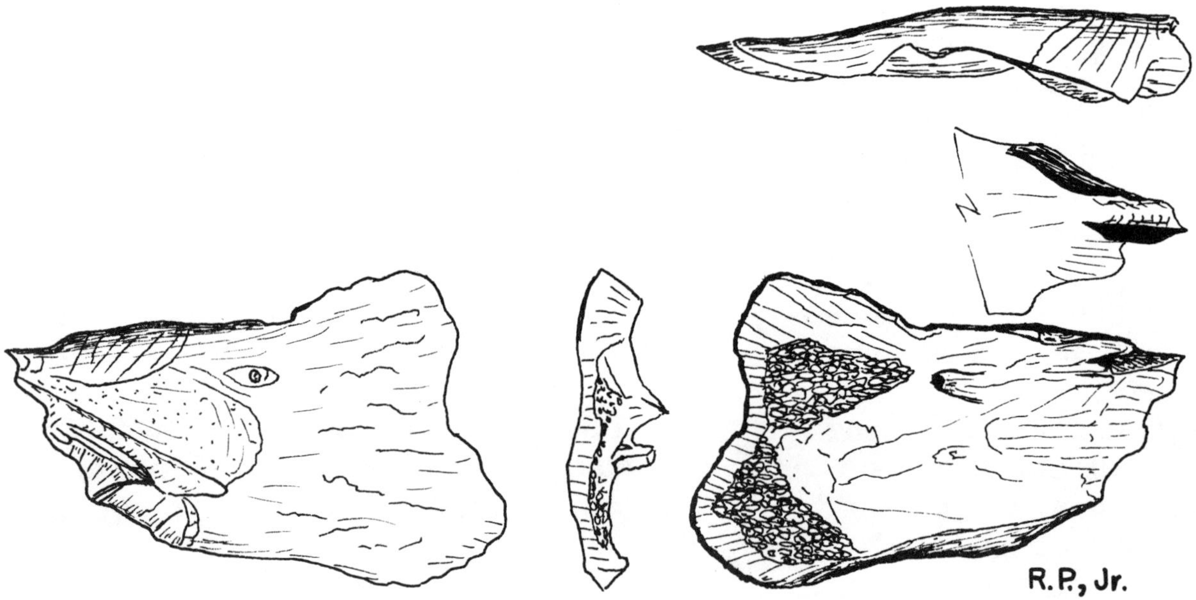

It is this writer's hope that sometime in the future, a student of anthropology, seeking a subject for the thesis of an advanced degree, will select the artifacts that Doug has removed from these two caves. Though it is this writer's understanding that the owner of the land on which the two caves are located has closed them until the son might conduct further professional excavations, the number of artifacts removed by Doug will provide an adequate base for comparative studies.

A POINT IN BONE No. 117
From the collection of:
Carey Powell
Riverton, Wyoming

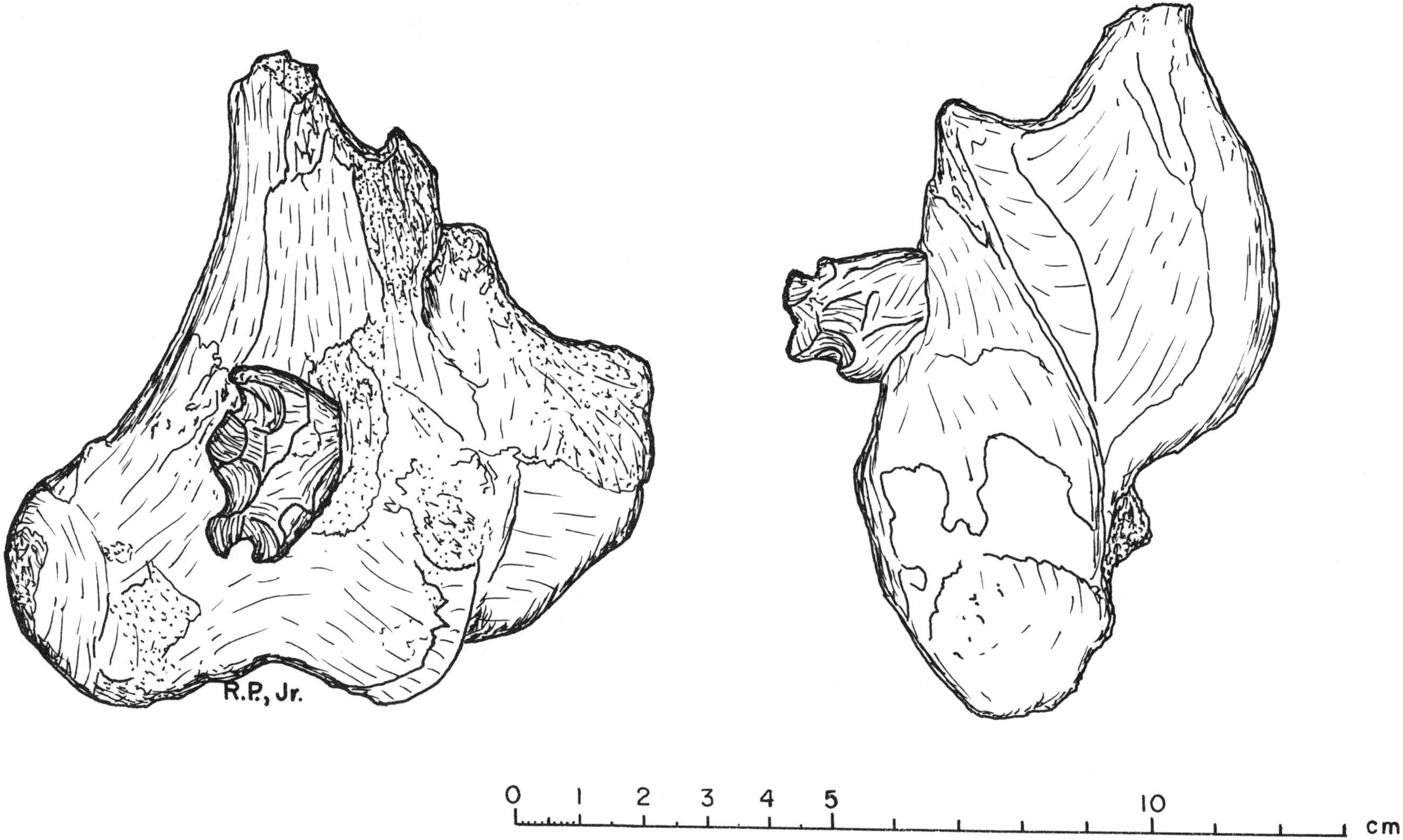

A POINT IN BONE

Color & Material: Projectile, light tan with slight grey cast to a moderate patina. Extremely fine-grain quartzite or orthoquartzite.

Bone-white to grey, desiccated distal portion of the right femur. Species-Buffalo (Bison bison).

Location: Believed to have been purchased from a small rock shop in Carey, Idaho in the late 1960s or early 1970s by Tony Zlatnik, who subsequently presented it, as a gift, to Carey Powell's grandfather. It has come to Carey from his grandfather's estate.

Holding this artifact in one's hands is truly the "once in a lifetime" experience. It certainly stimulated my imagination well into several nights.

Many thanks to Travis Bennett of Riverton, Wyoming, who located a similar bone taken from a three year old buffalo bull. In comparison, the bone of the artifact was about one third larger. Travis also suggested that the artifact be shown to A.J. White of White's Buffalo Sporting Goods in Shoshoni, Wyoming. There, it was possible to compare the artifact with various fragments of buffalo bones evidencing different amounts of deterioration.

While this artifact was examined under a microscope, one observation seemed to provide proof that this point had not been imbedded in an old buffalo bone in more recent times. Adjoining the surface of the point, bone cells had been distorted. These distorted cells were subsequently desiccated by the aging process of the bone. If the point had been driven into a bone already desiccated by age, the brittle cell walls would have been simply crushed. Some of the distorted cells also contained a very fine sediment that had invaded their desiccated cell structures. This would indicate a process virtually impossible to fake.

The point involved with this artifact has been identified as an Elko Eared point. A carbon 14 date of 1370 B.C. to 900 A.D. has been given for this point type by James F. O'Connell (1967). Distribution for this point type: Nevada, Idaho, southern Oregon, parts of eastern California.

Author's Postscript

The proposed approach to North American archaeology expressed here is that of the author's alone. It is expressed in hope of initiating a dialogue between avocational and professional archaeologists that will lead to opening public lands to the many, responsible, avocational archaeologists of this country. Their contribution to this fascinating science would be greatly enhanced.

Professional statements, i.e. "Archaeological sites are nonrenewable and should be protected." "Amateurs destroy archaeological evidence and should be barred from public lands.", were true and necessary at the time, in order to gain control of public lands and to protect sites from destruction by those seeking artifacts for monetary gain. These attitudes led to the passage of the Archaeological Resources Protection Act of 1967 which provided the necessary control. However, the total effect of this act essentially was to deny the responsible avocational archaeologist access to public lands, thereby markedly reducing his contribution to the science.

Installation of a gas transmission line in southwestern Wyoming has recently unearthed such extensive archaeological evidence of living floors dating 5,000 years B.P. that one must come to the conclusion that there are far more sites that can ever be excavated professionally.

I feel erosion is destroying valuable, and nonrenewable, archaeological sites that are on or near the surface of public lands at an extensive rate. In view of the insufficient numbers of professional archaeologists to survey these lands adequately, that opening of public lands to the avocational archaeologist, in the manner outlined on the following page, is the only way to salvage this evidence.

A NEW APPROACH TO NORTH AMERICAN ARCHAEOLOGY

- State archaeological societies (essentially avocational) to be granted blocks of excavation permits.

- Chapters of these societies to sponsor archaeology or anthropology clubs in high schools near their chapters.

- These clubs, under quidance of science teachers in the schools, to be granted excavation permits by sponsoring chapters.

- Excavations to be conducted in a manner sufficiently scientific to provide adequate recording, and reporting of excavations to sponsoring chapters, thus to state archaeologists.

- Artifacts recovered in these excavations to be curated with the schools hosting clubs conducting the excavations. These artifacts to be displayed in trophy cases in the entrance halls of the schools.

- Clubs conducting excavations to publish (copy machine letter) details of their excavations and to report, with detailed description and drawings, all artifacts recovered and curated by their club.

- Letters published by the clubs to be distributed to the office of the state archaeologist; the sponsoring chapter, and other clubs within the state.

- If an excavation site, conducted by a club, should be determined unique and archaeologically significant to warrant more professional excavation techniques, said site to be relinquished by the club involved.

- During professional excavation of the site, recovered artifacts are to be returned after a period of time not to exceed 12 months, to the club initiating the excavation, to be curated and displayed in the host school.

- Members of sponsoring chapters to be permitted to participate in excavations conducted by said clubs.

- Members of school clubs and members of society chapters to be permitted surface survey rights to all public lands. All artifacts recovered by these surveys (surface finds) to be reported in the manner aforementioned: club members by published letter; chapter members in a similar manner.

- Artifacts recovered in surface surveys to be curated: club members with the host school; chapter members in their private collections.

- At present, there is not adequate storage space within any state archaeologist's office. Display there would be impossible.

INDEX

PROJECTILE POINTS:

KNIVES:

HAND TOOLS:

EFFIGIES:

HOE OR CULTIVATOR:

UNUSUAL OR UNKNOWN:

INDEX OF ITEMS BY COLLECTORS